CREATING A VOLUNTEER-FRIENDLY CHURCH CULTURE

Marlene Wilson, Author and General Editor

Group's Volunteer Leadership Series™
Volume 1
Group's Church Volunteer Central™

Loveland, Colorado

Group's Volunteer Leadership Series™, Volume 1

Creating a Volunteer-Friendly Church Culture

Copyright © 2004 Group Publishing, Inc.

Visit our Web site: **www.grouppublishing.com**

Credits
Author: Marlene Wilson
Editor: Mikal Keefer
General Editor: Marlene Wilson
Chief Creative Officer: Joani Schultz
Art Director: Nathan Hindman
Cover Designer: Jeff Storm
Production Manager: Peggy Naylor

Produced with the assistance of The Livingstone Corporation (www.LivingstoneCorp.com). Project staff includes Chris Hudson, Ashley Taylor, Mary Horner Collins, Joel Bartlett, Cheryl Dunlop, Mary Larsen, and Rosalie Krusemark.

Library of Congress Cataloging-in-Publication Data

Wilson, Marlene.
Creating a volunteer-friendly church culture / Marlene Wilson.—1st American
        hardbound ed.
    p. cm. — (Group's volunteer leadership series ; v. 1)
    ISBN 0-7644-2745-8 (alk. paper)
    1. Voluntarism—Religious aspects—Christianity. 2. Christian leadership. I. Group
Publishing. II. Title. III. Series.
BR115.V64W55 2003
253'.7—dc22   2003022118

10 9 8 7 6 5 4 3 2 1   12 11 10 09 08 07 06 05 04

Printed in the United States of America.

Contents

Introduction

Does this picture remind you of your church?

Imagine walking into your church on a Sunday morning and seeing a beehive of activity . . .

- Classes hum along with smiling teachers ready to greet students.
- The music team is tuned up and ready to go.
- The coffee pots are filled and percolating.
- Visitors filter in through the doors because someone stopped by to visit newcomers in the community with fresh bread and invitations.

And it's all happening because at your church volunteers are in place and serving others. There's no scrambling around at the last minute—everything is right on schedule, right on time, right on target, and completely relaxed.

> "Imagine . . . everyone is a volunteer."

Imagine attending a church board meeting that's sharply focused, well-organized, and attended by people who can't think of anything else they'd rather be doing. People who are energized by the mission of the church and the purpose of the board.

And everyone around the table on that Thursday night is a volunteer.

Imagine walking down the hallway at church, glancing into offices where individuals and teams are busily pulling together a slideshow for next week's worship service . . . providing counseling for a man who's in emotional pain . . . planning a youth group retreat . . . and rehearsing a drama that will introduce a sermon later in the week.

And everyone—in each room—is a volunteer.

Does it seem like a dream to have so many volunteers so involved in important ministry? In some churches it is just a dream . . . but it doesn't need to stay a dream.

This Volunteer Leadership Series will help you turn your dreams of volunteer involvement into reality. There's nothing magical about the process you'll discover in this series. Many of the principles and procedures are straight out of the business world where they've worked for decades.

Some are from the nonprofit sector where they've worked equally well for just as long.

And some are from churches like yours that are a bit further along in the journey of creating a culture where volunteering is more than an obligation—it's a joy.

Throughout these books you'll discover a process that has taken me—and many, many colleagues—35 years to refine. It's tested and it works, and you'll see the results if you implement all of it in your church.

Maybe you're the pastor and you have a vision for a time when you're not the only one who's doing the work of ministry. You want to see volunteers join in the work of the church so you can have at least a little time with your family.

> "*See* volunteers join in the work of the church."

Maybe you're the Christian Education Director or Youth Director and you'd like to see enough volunteers signed up to cover the small group or outreach ministry you'd love to start. You have a vision for what your area of ministry could be, and you're tired of settling for less.

Or maybe you're a board member or other volunteer who knows the fulfillment of being involved and used by God in ministry. You want to invite others who are now filling pews to be filling volunteer roles instead.

No matter what your role in your church, imagine with me for a moment . . .

Imagine the power that would be unleashed if everyone offered to serve in an appropriate volunteer role. How much could your church accomplish? What might you do that you simply can't do now?

Imagine how the members of your church would grow if they were actively, intentionally serving God and growing in their faith. If everyone came together on Sunday not for a quick spiritual pick-me-up, but instead with exciting stories to share about how God is using them.

Imagine how your church would grow if you had the reputation of being the place where people don't just talk about their faith, but work together to make things happen in your community. What if church members were constantly forming groups to enthusiastically meet real needs of real people? How packed would your new members' class be? And how deep would you be growing in your faith?

If you have a vision for your church that includes any of the scenarios I've sketched above, you need a fully functioning, healthy volunteer ministry. It won't be enough to keep improving your church's programs, or to count on a remarkable pastor to draw new people to your worship services.

Excellent programs and a charismatic leader may help your church grow in attendance, but they won't help your church members grow deep in their faith or be satisfied with their spiritual growth. That takes involvement in ministry—which requires a volunteer program that's working.

> "You need a fully functioning, healthy volunteer ministry."

Don't believe me? I'll prove it, then.

In a *Leadership* journal article, Eric Swanson reported about a survey he gave his church to determine if there was a relationship between ministering to others and spiritual growth. Swanson asked the question, "To what extent has your ministry or service to others affected your spiritual growth?" and received a 92 percent "positive" response. When Swanson dug deeper and asked how service to others compared with other spiritual disciplines such as Bible study and prayer, 63 percent of respondents reported service to others was equally significant in their spiritual growth, and 24 percent of respondents said service to others was more significant than Bible study or prayer![1]

But how do you involve the membership of your church in significant service and ministry when many people don't express the slightest interest in getting involved? There are ways to encourage that change, and in this series we'll walk you through that process.

> "It's your vision . . . that sets the direction of your entire volunteer ministry."

It starts with building a firm foundation on solid biblical thinking about volunteers and volunteerism. There are several theologies you must embrace concerning how God has designed people and the church if you expect to see volunteerism grow in your congregation.

Later in this volume you'll do a quick assessment of how "volunteer-friendly" your church culture is and identify obstacles that might be blocking your progress.

Finally, you'll craft a vision for where you want to be.

This first volume is all about understanding what you believe as a church, where you're starting your journey, and where you want to go. It may feel as if you're not diving quickly enough into shaping up your volunteer program, and you may be tempted to skip over this "vision stuff."

Don't do it.

It's your vision for where you want to go that sets the direction of your entire volunteer ministry. This is the foundation on which you'll build your program. Skipping these key steps is like staking out a place to build a house on a beach and building your house on sand—and we all know how that turns out.

Are you ready to launch or expand your volunteer program? Ready for changes that will dramatically increase the number of people in your church who are enthusiastically serving?

Wonderful! Let's begin . . . with you and what you believe about volunteers.

1. Eric Swanson, "What You Get from Giving" sidebar in " 'Great to Good' Churches," *Leadership*, Spring 2003, Vol. XXIV, No. 2, 38.

ONE
The Biblical Foundation
for Volunteerism

What do you believe about volunteerism and volunteers? Here's a quick look at three theologies that are the foundation of volunteer leadership in the church.

I love the question *what if?*

When I ask *what if?* I can begin picturing what tomorrow might be like. Asking that question invites me to cooperate with God in imagining a vision for the future.

Your church will have a future—next week, next year, and beyond. Wouldn't it be best if your church had the future you prefer? One that's grounded in God's will for your congregation, that's spiritually healthy, and that's moving forward to do God's will in your community?

When it comes to involving volunteers in your church, there's no secret about what God wants to accomplish. It's all there in the Bible, and it is reflected in three interrelated theologies. Let's explore these together. As we go, think about your church and how you're living out these theologies.

The Priesthood of All Believers

True or False?—God intends for every member of your church to be active in ministry.

True! According to Scripture, we're all called to be active in the ministry of the church. God never intended for church to be a spectator sport. Just the opposite is what God has in mind, as we see in this passage:

> *But you are a chosen people, a royal priesthood, a holy nation, a people belonging to God, that you may declare the praises of him who called you out of darkness into his wonderful light. (1 Peter 2:9)*

That "royal priesthood" is for all Christians, not just professional clergy. Men and women—we're all part of the priesthood of all believers.

Age doesn't have anything to do with it, either. In the same way we're not expected to retire from service when we get to the age of 65, neither are we too young to be involved when we're in sixth grade. When you think of who's been called by God to be involved in ministry, include your entire membership.

When someone walks into your church, is it evident that you believe everyone has a place in ministry? Or is significant ministry done just by the paid staff or a handful of people? Maybe ministry is being done by just a few people because no one else will do it, but what's your preference? Does your church have an openness to lay people assuming ministry roles?

"Is it evident that you believe everyone has a place in ministry?"

Because if that's God's expectation—that lay people will have ministry opportunity—we'd better be providing those opportunities. Failing to do so only cripples the church.

I think there's ample evidence in Scripture that God is looking for us all to roll up our sleeves and get involved. When we made a commitment to God, he made a claim on our lives.

Paul wrote:

> *Do you not know that your body is a temple of the Holy Spirit, who is in you, whom you have received from God? You are not your own; you were bought at a price. (1 Corinthians 6:19-20a)*

In the book of Romans we read:

> *What then? Shall we sin because we are not under law but under grace? By no means! Don't you know that when you*

> *offer yourselves to someone to obey him as slaves, you are slaves to the one whom you obey—whether you are slaves to sin, which leads to death, or to obedience, which leads to righteousness? But thanks be to God that, though you used to be slaves to sin, you wholeheartedly obeyed the form of teaching to which you were entrusted. (Romans 6:15-17)*

Bought at a price.

Slaves.

Those words communicate that God owns us. He's paid for us. We're his. If he's got work to do, it's clear that we're all on his payroll. He wants to use us all.

Not everyone will preach, teach, or sing in the choir. But all Christians are supposed to be doing something that fits within their unique blend of abilities, skills, and passions. It's really not optional. Priesthood is all about *doing* something as well as *believing* something.

> "Priesthood is all about *doing* something as well as *believing* something."

What's the evidence in your church that you embrace the priesthood of all believers? Do church members see volunteers serving in significant and varied roles? Do they see every category of person involved in ministry of some sort?

If not, is your church willing to change?

By the way, here's the first place you should make changes: in the expectations of your leaders and lay membership.

When Jesus recruited his disciples, he called them to leave their businesses and families. It cost those fishermen something to follow Jesus. It often costs us little to follow Jesus, at least in the Western world. People expect to go to church and drop money in the offering plate, but that's about it.

So no wonder lay people look surprised when we explain they also need to serve in a ministry. It may be the first time they've heard they're required to do anything beyond showing up and writing a check.

We tell people all about the Savior Jesus. We teach about how Jesus saves people from their sins, loves them, and is preparing a place for them in heaven.

But we sometimes forget to mention much about the Lord Jesus.

The Lord Jesus calls everyone who follows him into the royal priesthood, where service and discipleship are more than theories—they're expectations. Joining a church isn't an invitation to retire; it's enlistment in an organization that's actively serving God. If you're going to expect people to volunteer in service, say so up front in your teaching and preaching.

- *Does* your church invite every member to be in appropriate ministry somehow?

- *Is* there a place for each person in your church to do ministry? Are you open to an influx of volunteers?

The Giftedness of Each Child of God

The Bible tells us that every believer can do ministry in some way. Each person has important work to do in the church regardless of gender, age, or education.

Here's what Paul wrote:

> *For we are God's workmanship, created in Christ Jesus to do good works, which God prepared in advance for us to do. (Ephesians 2:10)*

And again he wrote:

> *And in the church God has appointed first of all apostles, second prophets, third teachers, then workers of miracles, also those having gifts of healing, those able to help others, those with gifts of administration, and those speaking in different kinds of tongues. Are all apostles? Are all prophets? Are all teachers? Do all work miracles? Do all have gifts of healing? Do all speak in tongues? Do all interpret? But eagerly desire the greater gifts. And now I will show you the most excellent way. (1 Corinthians 12:28-31)*

Finally, consider this passage in Romans:

> *If it is serving, let him serve; if it is teaching, let him teach; if it is encouraging, let him encourage; if it is contributing to the needs of others, let him give generously; if it is leadership, let him govern diligently; if it is showing mercy, let him do it cheerfully. (Romans 12:7-8)*

Clearly, believers' God-given abilities, skills, and passions are to be used to build up the body of Christ and to glorify God. Those are the truths wrapped up in the theology of "the giftedness of each child of God."

> *"Our* job is to help people discover where to put those abilities, skills, and passions to use."

Our job is to help people discover where to put those abilities, skills, and passions to use. We need to do it for the health of the church and also for the spiritual health of individual believers.

But before you embark on that journey, you need to decide:

- *Do* you believe each person in your church has something valuable to contribute?

- *Are* you willing to help people who aren't sure what they can offer to discover ways to serve?

- *Will* your church make room for people to serve in ways that align with their abilities, skills, and passions?

The Whole Body of Christ

In the same way each believer has a God-given ability, skill, or passion to use in ministry, each believer has a particular function in the body of Christ. We all fit *somewhere,* but we don't all fit *everywhere.* There's a big difference.

The theology of "the whole body of Christ" acknowledges that each member of your church has something to offer, but it's a specific something. People aren't interchangeable; you can't just move them around on the organizational chart. Someone God has designed to be an empathic, caring people-helper isn't going to thrive in a volunteer role that's designed to enter data on a spreadsheet. If someone's a hand, he or she won't fit a role designed for a foot.

The programs in our churches are enhanced, changed, and expanded when we discover our church members' gifts and abilities. We get the right people in the right jobs, and everyone benefits.

Consider these passages . . .

> It was he who gave some to be apostles, some to be prophets, some to be evangelists, and some to be pastors and teachers, to prepare God's people for works of service, so that the body of Christ may be built up until we all reach unity in the faith and in the knowledge of the Son of God and become mature, attaining to the whole measure of the fullness of Christ. (Ephesians 4:11-13)

> Now the body is not made up of one part but of many. If the foot should say, "Because I am not a hand, I do not belong to the body," it would not for that reason cease to be part of the body. And if the ear should say, "Because I am not an eye, I do not belong to the body," it would not for that reason cease to be part of the body. If the whole body were an eye, where would the sense of hearing be? If the whole body were an ear, where would the sense of smell be? But in fact God has arranged the parts in the body, every one of them, just as he wanted them to be. If they were all one part, where would the body be? As it is, there are many parts, but one body.
> The eye cannot say to the hand, "I don't need you!" And the head cannot say to the feet, "I don't need you!" On the contrary, those parts of the body that seem to be weaker are indispensable, and the parts that we think are less honorable we treat with special honor. And the parts that are unpresentable are treated with special modesty, while our presentable parts need no special treatment. But God has combined the members of the body and has given greater honor to the parts that lacked it, so that there should be no division in the body, but that its parts should have equal concern for each other. If one part suffers, every part suffers with it; if one part is honored, every part rejoices with it. Now you are the body of Christ, and each one of you is a part of it." (1 Corinthians 12:14-27)

- *Are* you willing to encourage people to minister within the constraints of their unique abilities, talents, and passions? If not, how do you expect those volunteers to be successful and fulfilled?

- *Are* you willing to not do programs if you can't staff them appropriately?

Now let me ask a few *what-if* questions about your church—and mine.

What if we took seriously the implications of our theology when it comes to volunteerism in our churches?

What if we reflected biblical principles in our policies and procedures when it comes to recruiting and using volunteers in our own churches?

What if we learned from our brothers and sisters in Christ who have found ways to make volunteerism joyful—and we put their experience to good use in our churches?

I'll tell you what will happen in most churches when *what if* becomes reality: We'll see dramatic and profound changes.

That's because in most churches, volunteerism is suffering. Most of the work of the church is done by the hired staff or a small group of volunteers. The vast majority of church members sit and watch, or, at best, are peripherally involved. They certainly don't find any meaning in their service through the church.

Wouldn't it be wonderful if serving in and through the church became the norm instead of the exception? What if the days when you had to beg for volunteers faded into a distant memory because people were actively seeking to serve? Wouldn't that be a welcome change?

> "Not one volunteer program changed overnight."

The question is: How do we get from where we are to where we want to go?

This series will help you, but it's a journey and a process. There's no pixie dust you can sprinkle on your church directory and find that, suddenly, calls will pour in from willing volunteers. I've worked with many, many churches to improve their volunteer programs, and not one of them changed overnight.

But the churches that grew successful volunteer programs all had three things in common, and this is the place to briefly talk about them.

1. They approached the process prayerfully.

Sometimes the apathy in the pews toward doing the work of the church is a spiritual issue. It can't be fixed by doing a better job writing volunteer job descriptions. Nor can it be fixed by initiating a new process. It has to be fixed through what I call a "heart transplant," a renewing and refreshing of the heart.

Your church might just need a change of heart about serving God and serving the church. And that gets fixed through prayer and through sharing God's vision for what your church could be as God's representative in your community.

Will you commit to pray for your church? For your leaders, for your vision and mission, and for the members of your church who are willing volunteers—and those who aren't? They all need prayer.

In volume 2 we'll dig a little deeper into this facet of volunteer program development.

2. They embraced the entire process.

I can't stress this enough: *You must embrace the entire process we'll be describing.* If you pick and choose an idea here and a process there, you'll see improvement. It's all good stuff and it works. But you'll be sticking an adhesive bandage over a broken bone.

I expect you're already doing many things right. Were I to visit your church I'd find lots of things to praise. If you're like most people who are responsible for finding, recruiting, training, and maintaining volunteers, you have strong communication skills. You're already experiencing some success at the process I just described.

The problem is that the process I just mentioned—finding, recruiting, training, and maintaining volunteers—is missing several key components. You may be excellent at all those things; you've still skipped important steps. Until you have them all, your effectiveness and results will be compromised. Your success will be limited, and you'll have to work harder.

In this series, we'll give you those missing pieces. But please trust me when I say they're all important. You can't skip past any of them. There are no shortcuts in the process. We've already weeded out the fluff and extra steps.

What's left is a process for bringing volunteers on board that assures you—and the volunteers—that you'll have the right people in the right positions.

3. They built programs on a solid biblical foundation.

The three theologies we examined aren't new. We've all nodded in agreement as we've heard them preached and taught. But do we *believe* them? And if we *do* believe them, are the actions and attitudes expressed in our churches consistent with them?

Those three theologies are fundamental to your church's volunteer program. They reflect God's values when it comes to our doing kingdom work and how he has designed the church. When we let the values in these theologies slip, some terrible things can happen. Things that actually discourage volunteerism.

Consider this example of how a church leader chose to value a program over the people who were in his congregation . . .

The Little Drama Team That Couldn't

The pastor of a small church attended a conference hosted by a California megachurch. The pastor noticed how well drama was used in the megachurch's worship service, so he did a little investigating.

It turned out the drama ministry was comprised of a team of more than 50 people. They rehearsed regularly and performed two plays each year. They also sang musical numbers and performed skits each week that reinforced the sermon theme. They even had a sub-team of writers who did nothing but create original skits for the actors to perform.

The pastor couldn't wait to pull together a similar team back home. He just knew it would revolutionize his church's worship experiences.

So, two weeks after the pastor returned, he called a meeting for everyone interested in drama ministry. Two people showed up . . . and one was a junior high student who'd never been in a play.

The pastor made it a personal priority to get a team organized.

He made another announcement and did a bit of personal recruiting. That got his team up to five. Still not enough.

So the pastor called a few of the perpetual volunteers— people who always said yes when asked directly—and twisted their arms. Reluctantly, two of those people joined, too, giving the team a total of seven members. Not ideal, but for a church of one hundred, not bad. Not bad at all.

> "Most of the drama team was made up of the wrong people for the volunteer role."

It wasn't bad—it was worse than bad. The first skit was a disaster. Some of the team forgot lines. Others got stage fright and simply stood in place. The few people with an aptitude for drama couldn't pull the skit out of a tailspin. The effect was powerful—but not in the way the pastor wanted.

What went wrong? Plenty, but at heart it came down to this: *Most of the drama team was made up of the wrong people for the volunteer role.*

The pastor did respect the priesthood of all believers theology—everyone was invited to participate in this ministry. But the pastor didn't respect the unique giftings of church members or their function in the body of Christ.

TWO
Navigating the Rapids of Change

Launching or improving the volunteer leadership process in your church forces change. Here's how to deal with it.

I know that initiating change in a church can be a difficult process. It may feel that now isn't the time to go through the pain of changing the way you interact with volunteers; you'll just make a few adjustments to your current volunteer process and hope that works.

As gently as I can, let me suggest that won't work. If you want to experience real change, you're going to have to do more than fiddle with a few loose wires. You've got to dig in and rebuild the engine. You've got to commit to making true changes, and it's going to take time.

My question for you: If not now, when will you make the changes? After you again experience a volunteer drought? After another batch of volunteers grows discouraged and quits? After yet another staff member moans about how nobody seems to care at your church?

Now is the time to start making changes. Today.

I frequently present workshops and speeches on the theme of the changing world of volunteerism. Often I title these speeches "Suddenly It's Tomorrow." This is based on a lesson I learned from a five-year-old—the very best teacher when it comes to dealing with the timing of change.

I was at a board of directors meeting and we were on a coffee break, relaxing and chatting. A board member shared an experience his wife had just had as a kindergarten teacher. On the first day of school she asked, "Can anyone tell me what day it is?"

A bright-eyed little tyke raised her hand and declared, "It's tomorrow."

The kindergartner may not have had a firm grasp on the logistics of time, but she certainly understood the truth of time: It *is* tomorrow. Time is rushing by, and if we want things to be different in the future we've got to act now to create the tomorrow we're envisioning.

> "It *is* tomorrow... We've got to act now to create the tomorrow we're envisioning."

I expect you're feeling some urgency about changing how your church deals with volunteers. That's why you're reading this book. Honor that urgency—in most churches it's past time to initiate change. There's nothing to be gained by waiting longer to get started. Things won't get better by themselves, you know. Not without someone like you diving in and initiating change.

Tell me: If you had a friend who was experiencing a major health issue, would you suggest that she wait until things grew even worse before seeing a doctor? Of course not.

Would you suggest she live with the pain indefinitely because it might get better eventually? No—you'd urge her to get the help she needed right away.

Listen: If your church is experiencing pain in working with volunteers, it won't get better without intervention. You must act to initiate change, or you'll be stuck where you are today—forever. Is that what you want?

Let me suggest two more *what-ifs* for your consideration:

What if we took God seriously enough to act on the theology we declare—even though it means dramatically changing how we do ministry?

What if we honored the urgency we feel to see change happen and we actually started initiating that change?

It boggles my mind what the church could become!

Let me share with you the story of a church that has managed to implement the process we'll be sharing with you: the Community Church of Joy in Glendale, Arizona. You may know them as a megachurch that has more than 10,000 members. That's who they are today, but when the church's pastor, Walt Kallestad, went to the church in 1978 there were just 200 members.

When Walt arrived, he and the church leadership discerned that they were uniquely called to missions, to reaching out to the unchurched. That's a mission and vision that energized some members, but alienated others who wanted to maintain the status quo.

Once the vision was articulated, Walt saw some of the membership leave. It was a cost the church was willing to pay to get the entire church membership onto the same page and moving the same direction.

To grow 50-fold in 25 years requires a church to stay open to change. What works when a church is at a membership of 400 won't necessarily work when membership reaches 4,000.

> "Pastor Kallestad learned to change his language so he could connect with unchurched people."

One change that came up on Pastor Kallestad's radar screen was a need for language to be friendly to unchurched people. Much of the traditional church jargon was a mystery to someone not raised in the church.

The woman who is in charge of the women's ministry was once one of those unchurched visitors. She kept coming back, even though at times she was uncertain what certain words meant. So she started keeping a list, and when the opportunity arose she asked Pastor Kallestad to define the terms. Words like "evangelism" and "atonement" held no meaning for her, but she suspected they must be important—they were always coming up in sermons.

After having to explain the meaning of church words a few times, Pastor Kallestad learned to change his language so he could connect with unchurched people. Because that was the stated mission of Community Church of Joy, learning a new way to communicate was worth the effort.

Christian education courses were adapted so new members and visitors who had no Bible background at all could participate. When someone doesn't know if the book of Luke is in the Old Testament or New Testament, that changes how you approach teaching.

> "The work of ministry had to be passed to lay people, . . . or there would be chaos."

In time, it became apparent another change had to happen, too, and it concerned volunteers.

People with no church background—and there was an ever-increasing number of them involved in the congregation—were difficult to recruit as volunteers. They had no history of volunteering in the church. They had not grown up seeing their parents participate as volunteers. To these new members, attending a worship experience was like attending a play put on by a community theater: They were the audience. It never occurred to newly churched people that there was a role they could play in making things happen.

I received a call from Pastor Kallestad just before the church moved to a new campus. The congregation was already nearing 10,000 members, and church leadership expected they'd experience a new growth surge after the relocation.

Pastor Kallestad said, "We can't do it with our present structure." The work of ministry had to be passed to lay people more effectively than was happening, or there would be chaos.

Keep in mind the church was growing. Good things were happening. Lots of churches hungry to experience the same sort of growth were visiting, taking notes. And the church already had lots of volunteers involved. The church leadership could have sat back and rested on its laurels.

But instead they felt an urgency to move ahead. To be even more effective. To be sure that the three theologies they supported with words were also supported in action.

I'd like to share a letter I received from the Community Church of Joy staff after they put in place the process we'll discuss with you in this book series. I think what they've experienced will be an encouragement for you to see the process through.

We knew we needed to move to a new level of excellence in our volunteer ministry, but we weren't sure how to make that move. We knew the change would need to be monumental. . . . We enlisted Marlene to do three things:

1. Help us find a person to serve as our "Director of Volunteer Ministries."

2. Help us design a strategic plan for volunteer ministry at Joy.

3. Train our key leaders so that we could carry on the ministry.

All three of those goals have been accomplished. With Marlene's help, our Director of Volunteer Ministries, Joyce Pokorny, and a core team have developed the following teams:

The Connections Team—volunteers who meet with new members to assist individuals to serve and grow at Joy.

The Recognition/Retention Team—which implements an ongoing program for the recognition of volunteers, including an annual recognition event (a dinner with a guest speaker) and the commissioning of volunteers during a worship service.

The Ministry Liaison Team—which is comprised of volunteers who represent individual ministries, and who welcome new volunteers, train them, and follow up to make sure placement was a good fit.

The Training Team—which trains our staff in areas of recognition, empowerment, and recruitment/retention.

The Data Management Team—which provides support for all information received from volunteers regarding their gifts, talents, abilities, and passions.

The Special Events Teams—which implements special events such as the Celebration of Lights event and the Celebration of Easter event. Volunteers who join the special events teams will then be followed up for next steps of service. (This has been an awesome way to connect individuals to ministry!)

Through the coaching and mentoring of our Director of Volunteer Ministries, our Missions Ministry has increased volunteer involvement from 100 volunteers to more than 500 volunteers. Teams have been put in place for Feeding the Homeless, Habitat for Humanity, Acts of Kindness, and much more.

Our director shares, "There is no way I could have done this myself. I have learned to empower and release our volunteers for service."

Volunteers' lives have been changed, too. Once individuals have stepped up to volunteer and have served, they want to grow and know Jesus Christ through Bible studies, worship, and "going deeper."

As our key leaders have been trained, our church culture has begun to shift toward becoming better at equipping and releasing lay people into significant ministry.

Before Marlene helped us make the changes I've noted, we had about 80 people in volunteer ministry. Today more than 1,700 people serve at Joy, and through Joy in our community. We're so grateful to God for this breakthrough. Equipping our people has changed us, and is changing our community!

Gratefully,

Pastor Paul Sorensen
Executive Team, Community Church of Joy

Did you catch what Community Church of Joy did? Let me do a bit of highlighting . . .

1. They made a good thing better.

Remember, this was a church of more than 10,000 members. If you keep score by how many cars are in the parking lot, this church was already a clear winner. You'd think they'd just keep doing what they were already doing. It was working.

Except they didn't keep score by counting cars. That number mattered to them, of course, but so did this number: How many people are involved in ministry? Getting people out of the pews and into service helped the church hang onto the new members it was attracting, and it also helped those people grow spiritually.

How are you keeping score at your church? If it's just cars, the impact you're having on your membership is limited. If it's by how many people are involved in ministry, that's another issue altogether. Find out—it's a measurable number that's worth tracking.

2. They acted before they reached a crisis point.

The growth the church expected after the move to a new campus materialized—so it's a good thing they revised their approach to working with volunteers first.

Was it convenient to change their volunteer leadership approach while they were in the middle of planning a relocation? No—but it was important, because how volunteers were able to minister in and through the church was at least as significant a factor in meeting the needs of the unchurched as a new building.

3. They used sound management techniques to get organized.

Do the words "management techniques" bother you? Sometimes in the church world we want to stay as far away from business practices as possible.

Let me suggest this: Call the process you use to work with people anything you want. I prefer "management techniques" because those words describe the process of organizing positions and people fairly well. But it doesn't matter what you call the process—so long as you do it. The Community Church of Joy had some things organized—they didn't have people running around totally unsure what to do. But they couldn't tell how many volunteers they had or precisely what everyone was doing.

Like the Community Church of Joy, you must get organized

or you'll have volunteers uncertain what to do because they don't have volunteer role descriptions. They won't know who they're reporting to, or whether they've done a great job or a poor job. Projects will fail, people will be hurt, and the entire experience will be frustrating for everyone involved.

4. **They adopted a process for volunteer leadership that will carry them into the future—no matter how large they grow.**

You may be looking forward to seeing an attendance of 100. The idea of 10,000 people showing up is so far into the future you figure it will be your grandchildren who have to sort that out.

But why not put the process in place now that will encourage growth—and that will make sense when your church doubles or triples? It will only be more difficult to institute changes then.

> ### "What will happen if you *don't* change how you manage the volunteer process at your church?"

What's demanded of many congregations is this: change. And change is frightening in the best of circumstances. And when you're talking about changing church in some way—that's doubly frightening!

But think about it this way: What will happen if you *don't* change how you manage the volunteer process at your church? There are consequences either way, you know—if you act, and if you fail to act.

The unvarnished truth about change is this: It's difficult, often painful, and absolutely essential for the church to deal with if the church intends to remain healthy. Jesus never promised us insulation against change. God may be the same yesterday, today, and forever, but the church must be effective in communicating that unchanging love in quickly changing times. That takes flexibility and an ability to embrace change.

There have been times of stability throughout history, when the amount of change forced on people was minimal. That certainly doesn't describe life today! If life was a lazy, drifting river at one time, we're now hurtling down rapids and bouncing off rocks as we try to navigate quickly enough to stay afloat.

I learned a great deal about how to handle change from— quite literally—a whitewater rapids experience. Let me share what happened with you so I can draw some parallels as to how you can handle change in your church.

Eight Days, Seven Nights

Several years ago I went on an eight-day raft trip down the Grand Canyon. That's the same canyon people point to as an example of how rushing water is so powerful it can slice through rock, slowly carving a chasm more than a mile deep, and stretching as much as 18 miles from rim to rim. Any river that can do that sort of damage—even over an amazingly long time—is nothing to take lightly.

Normally, people like me consider the power of the Colorado River while staring down at it from a safe distance. From the rim of the canyon, the river looks almost picturesque. True, it's cascading down whitewater rapids, splashing a rainbow of spray high over boulders, but there's no danger . . . when you're standing on the rim.

But for eight days I left the safety of the rim and rafted on that whitewater.

The questions I faced about leaving my comfort zone and climbing into a raft are the same questions you have to answer about initiating or improving your volunteer leadership process. Both situations call for handling fast and furious change. And both situations make for one hectic but exhilarating ride.

The first thing you need to do is address your motivation.

To me, roughing it is staying at the Holiday Inn. I love the outdoors, but I'm no adventurer. Lying out under the stars by night and facing whitewater every day was a stretch—a big stretch. So why did I want to go at all?

The answer: My husband, Harvey, and another couple wanted to go, so I thought I'd go along. It was going to be a once-in-a-lifetime experience, and I wanted to share it with my Harvey. I knew there would be whitewater involved and that I was going to have to stretch beyond my comfort level to participate.

When you're looking at initiating change in any organization—the church included—you can assume you're heading into whitewater. What's your motivation? Are you committed enough to see it all through?

Decide where you want to sit as you hit the rapids.

When we found ourselves standing next to the river looking at the raft, I had to decide where to sit. It's not a casual question. When you sit at the front of a raft, you're the first one to make the acquaintance of any boulder you happen to hit, and you're the first person to dive down into the "holes" of swirling water that are everywhere on the river.

If you're in the back of the raft, you'll find yourself lifted high when the raft dives into a hole. And if you're in the middle, you may feel safer, but don't be fooled—you'll be thrown around as the raft rocks and slams down the river.

Harvey and I looked at each other and both nodded. We'd take the front. If we were going to do the trip, we were going to be in for the entire experience. We wanted to sit where we could see what was coming.

As you navigate change in your volunteer program, where are you sitting? Up front is where you get the most warning when something looms in front of you, and that seat gives you the best chance to respond.

Don't back into change. Embrace it and go for it.

Remember to take your sense of humor with you into the whitewater.

I assumed that I'd do lots of screaming and yelling, maybe even some crying. (I *told* you I wasn't an adventurer!) I probably did all of those, but mostly I laughed.

That's right: I laughed. With whitewater cascading all around me, with our inflated raft crashing over rocks, with whirlpools around every turn, I laughed.

When you deal with change, it's essential you bring along your sense of humor. Without the ability to laugh, you're dead in the water. And if you get the chance, surround yourself with other people who know how to laugh, too.

The other couple who rafted with us was the main reason I laughed so hard, so often. My friend Elaine is a five-foot Texas dynamo who's an international consultant in conflict management. She usually looks like she just stepped out of *Vogue* magazine.

Elaine forgot to look at the packing list until the night before leaving for the trip, so the only waterproof jacket she could find was an old, white plastic raincoat that had yellowed and cracked, and that was left from her college days. And her waterproof pants? Fishing waders she borrowed from her six-foot husband. The waders reached her shoulders.

So picture our first morning on the shore. There stood Elaine, looking distinctly *un*-Voguely in her cracked plastic jacket, oversize fishing waders, and a big, floppy hat.

All I could do was burst out laughing.

When we hit whitewater the first time we discovered that you take in *lots* of water on a raft. When we finally reached calm water and stood up to shake ourselves off, Elaine discovered her waders had filled with water. She literally had a geyser of water exploding up out of the waders, and that's a sight I will *never* forget.

Did she get angry? Blame herself or someone else for not having a spare set of waterproof pants on hand? No . . . she laughed.

Find an Elaine when you're heading for whitewater and bring her along. You'll need the humor of friends when you hit the whitewater of change.

Prepare to experience some pain.

With change comes discomfort—and sometimes outright growing pains. But when you step outside your comfort zone, things happen.

For me, the pain started on the third day of the rafting trip. I broke my shoulder. It wasn't an obvious break; we later discovered I had two hairline fractures. All I knew was it *hurt*—and I had a choice to make.

The fourth day of the trip was the last day a helicopter could come in and take me out. If I wanted to get to a hospital, I had to decide to go immediately. If I went further downriver, I was making the entire trip—no matter what.

I decided to stay.

It wasn't a foolhardy decision; it was a decision that the pain I was experiencing was going to be part of the experience. I could handle it—but I *was* forced to make some adjustments.

For instance, I couldn't sit in the front of the raft any longer. I had to move to the back. I couldn't experience the trip precisely as I'd expected, plunging headfirst into the water, but I was still making the trip. And from my new vantage point I saw the entire river differently.

I learned to do things differently, too. I can now dress myself inside a sleeping bag using just one arm. I can't imagine a time that skill will come in useful again, but I've got it. And even better, I know I can adapt. I can be flexible and versatile, and learn something new.

The process of energizing your volunteer process won't go exactly as you've planned, no matter how well you do your planning. Something—or *several* somethings—will happen to impact you. You'll need to learn new skills. You'll need to adapt. And you'll be stronger for the effort.

Stay flexible and versatile. Remember there's seldom one right way to do something. As my colleagues and I present a process for mobilizing volunteers in your church, keep in mind it's a framework. You'll have to adapt it. If you try something and it doesn't work, try something else. Don't get stuck. Don't become negative or obsessed with what fails. Move on.

Never settle for saying, "People are too busy to volunteer." Instead, ask, "How could people volunteer if we structured things differently?"

Decide what you'll focus on—and what you'll let go.

When big organizational change happens, I find a lot of people focus on the "ain't-it-awfuls?" and the "if-onlys," and people get stuck there. They can't let go of what once was or the comfort they once enjoyed.

When I got home from the rafting trip I had to get my shoulder fixed, and that process involved slings, therapy, and painful sessions. But when I think about the rafting trip, I can hardly remember the discomfort. What I recall is the beauty of the canyon, the roar of the water, and laughing until I cried. And I remember a wonderful week with Harvey. I wouldn't have missed it for the world.

One of the challenges for me, living in a changing, white-water world, is remaining an "optimistic pragmatist." By that I mean someone who sees the world realistically. I know there are difficulties that come with experiencing change. I know there are obstacles in the water in front of me. But I choose to remain optimistic as I face those things, confident in a God who's going to be there with me through all of it, come what may.

You get to choose what to focus on, you know. Maybe half of your volunteers deserted the ship when you instituted accountability. Well, what about the half who stayed and flourished, and the new people who were attracted to the volunteer program because it is well-organized now? Focus there.

You could think about the snide comments that came when you changed a process, or you could let those words go, forgiven by choice.

Realize not everyone can tolerate the same amount of change—or risk.

Change involves a certain amount of risk. Maybe nobody will *drown* if the music leader slips an old hymn in among the praise choruses your church has been using for the past few years, but there may be some negative comments. There's risk.

If you're going to initiate change, you need to find people who are willing to go out on the edge with you. Build teams involving those people.

Risk reminds me of another piece of my rafting story . . .

The only other experience I'd had with river rafting was when our son worked as a river guide for two years. Our family joined Rich for a two-day trip, and I'll never forget the first rapids we approached. Rich brought the raft to the shore, got out, and just stood there looking at the river.

I asked him, "What are you doing?" and he said, "I'm reading the river." "Well, why are you doing that?"

Rich said, "Every time we go down the river there are different currents and eddies, and I need to know where they are so we can get through safely."

I assumed Rich had to stop and look because he was a rookie. Experienced guides must certainly be able to handle it as they went, adjusting on the fly.

Only the very best guides lead trips down the Grand Canyon, and our guide frequently got out of the boat, climbed up cliffs, and scanned the river for several minutes before he returned and took us through the rapids.

Taking time to read the river is as important for sunburned old professional guides as it is for first-time rookies.

Guides know there are some principles that *don't* change: how water moves around rocks, what happens when oars are applied to the left side of the raft, how the boat moves through rapids. Those are the same—but the order in which they present themselves can change in the blink of an eye. And there can always be the first time something happens: a huge branch falls in just as the raft passes a cottonwood tree, or the seam on the raft splits.

When you enter the whitewater, change happens . . . sometimes at an alarming rate.

But we serve a God who is changeless in his love for us, and as we seek to involve his children in ministry we're cooperating with his purposes. The three theologies we've discussed are a firm foundation for instituting the process we're outlining. You stand on solid theological ground as change swirls around you.

I suggest that part of your leadership role is to climb up on the high, sturdy cliff of God's love and read the river for your people. You'll be guiding them through the rapids of change, and you want to bring them into places of service and joy safely.

THREE
The Need for Visionary Leadership

Why one person—like you—can make a huge difference.

What will be required of you to put in place a process for volunteer leadership that respects the three theologies we've already discussed? *And* that makes use of the techniques we've learned through years of experience?

Prayer, certainly—because initiating change always needs prayer.

It will take time, too. Don't expect everyone to immediately see the wisdom in the changes you're making. You may well encounter resistance from some of the volunteers and staff, for reasons we'll discuss later in volume 4.

Plan on effort being required. If you don't yet have descriptions of volunteer roles, they'll have to be written. If you don't have a top-notch training and orientation program, it needs to be created. This isn't an easy process, but the results you'll get will make any effort you invest worthwhile.

And you'll also need visionary leadership.

After all the reading, writing, and pondering about leadership I've done over the past 35 years, I believe the definition of leadership I like best comes from Presbyterian pastor and consultant, Mike Murray.

Mike says, "A leader is someone who dreams dreams and has visions, and can communicate those to others in such a way that they of their own free will say 'yes!'"

Here's why I love that definition . . .

Having dreams and visions is not about where you are, but where you want to be. Visionary leadership focuses less on the difficulties of today and more on where we'd be if we somehow got past our difficulties. It's a visionary way of seeing our situations. It's also a faithful way of seeing things.

It sounds easy, doesn't it? So why don't we do more of it in the church?

I think it's because we're so busy doing, surviving, and coping to spend time thinking about the future and where we're heading. When you've got a Sunday school to staff or a sermon to prepare, who has time to dream dreams—even at 2:00 A.M.?

One of our biggest challenges is to shift our basic paradigms about how we *do* leadership—not how we talk about it. And that takes vision.

One test of a good leader, rather than *How much have I done?* needs instead to be, *How many others have I involved?* This entails *not* doing all the work, but seeing that it's done and done well. This is an enormous shift for church leaders, but a shift that's absolutely crucial! To do it well requires the skills of sound volunteer leadership that we'll explore in detail in this series.

Let me suggest some more *what-ifs* you might want to ask:

> "A leader is someone who dreams dreams and has visions, and can communicate those to others in such a way that they of their own free will say 'yes!'"
>
> Mike Murray

What if your pastor's job description changed so the pastor was rewarded for involving others rather than simply getting things done?

What if you asked people to recommend ministry initiatives based on the abilities, skills, and passions they could bring to the table?

What if every leader in your church received training about how to delegate well? You'll learn the fundamentals in volume

3, but realize that it's likely your pastor has never received any training in that specific skill.

Why can I suggest that with some certainty? Because in a recent survey of pastors, Group's Center For Volunteer Solutions discovered that very few pastors had received formal training in working with volunteers . . . or in skills needed to work effectively with volunteers, like delegation.

That's right: It's possible to receive a post-graduate degree in ministry that does not include even one course in effectively working with volunteers. This in spite of the fact that pastors will spend their entire careers working in volunteer-based organizations.

> "One test of a good leader needs to be, *How many others have I involved?*"

By the way, if you're reading this book and you happen to have influence in a seminary or two, you have our permission to photocopy this page and send it to whoever you know at those seminaries. Ask why they're setting their graduates up for conflict and failure by not preparing graduates to master the necessary skills to work with volunteers effectively. This Volunteer Leadership Series would make an excellent textbook collection, and there are plenty of additional materials available to create some needed courses.

If we're serious about volunteer ministries thriving, let's prepare our leadership to value and embrace them.

And then there's the rest of Mike Murray's definition of leadership: the ability to "communicate those [dreams and visions] to others in such a way that they of their own free will say 'yes!'"

I love that. It wonderfully sums up the respect leaders need to have for volunteers.

There's no room for coercion when recruiting volunteers. There's no room for manipulation. There's always room for presenting a vision, dream, or mission and letting volunteers who are drawn to it respond with an enthusiastic "yes" that will drive their dedicated service.

> "The clearer the vision and the more enthusiastically committed to the vision the leaders are, the more likely it is people will catch the vision."

Here's what I've seen in my many years of working with volunteers: The clearer the vision and the more enthusiastically committed to the vision the leaders are, the more likely it is people will catch the vision. Volunteers have to see, feel, and experience the excitement, and clearly understand how they can help make the dream or vision happen.

When it comes to providing leadership in a volunteer setting, skills of strategy and advocacy are much more important than mere oratory. There are few places where talk is cheaper, or action more necessary.

Let me share a story that illustrates Mike's definition of leadership in action.

Mikey Weiss and 200 Flats of Raspberries

Mikey Weiss retired in 1987 after 40 years in the Los Angeles produce business. One day, Mikey visited his son's produce firm at the L.A. wholesale market just in time to see a forklift hoist 200 flats of raspberries into a dumpster. The fruit was unmarketable, but still edible.

Mikey, watching, had an "aha" moment, and a *what-if* question occurred to him.

Six hundred people were going hungry in a tent city just five miles away. Mikey thought, *What if I could find a way to get produce wholesalers to stop dumping their surplus and instead donate it to organizations that feed the hungry?* That was the day the Los Angeles Charitable Food Distribution Project was born.

Mikey pitched his idea to his produce colleagues, who caught his vision and agreed to help. An extensive volunteer network formed to collect and distribute produce from wholesalers in the area. After hearing about Mikey's efforts, two University of Southern California professors took Mikey's vision even further. They created a model framework of the L.A. project with the goal of helping other cities create similar programs. After all, if it was a good idea in L.A., why wouldn't it be a good idea in Detroit or Des Moines?

Their organization, From the Wholesaler to the Hungry (FWH), has advised and assisted over 38 communities across the country in developing perishable food recovery programs.

One person. One *what-if* moment. One vision. And because of a vision that was communicated clearly and in a way that others could choose to enthusiastically embrace with a "yes," thousands of people were fed.

I ask again, What are your *what-ifs*?

In these turbulent times you can't afford for your church's mission to be fuzzy or out of focus. If you want to inspire volunteers to get behind programs and projects, you'll need to share your vision in a clear, compelling fashion. And you've got to make room in that vision for the participation and ownership of church members.

> "You must make room in your vision for the participation and ownership of church members."

Hang onto that insight: You must make room in your vision for the participation and ownership of church members.

We have a picture of visionary leadership being like Moses coming down the mountainside, carrying tablets etched with the Word of God. Moses wasn't coming to negotiate or to invite commentary. He was there to announce that there was a new law, a new relationship with God. He was proclaiming a vision, and it was up to everyone to get behind it. Period.

But your vision of adding a second service probably doesn't come with that sort of clear-cut, God-given authority. If you want to enlist help making the vision come to pass, you're going to have to be more flexible than Moses was.

The nuts and bolts of turning a vision into a reality reside in the people who carefully craft, plan, and nurture the vision. People like you. People like your church leadership. People like your church membership. This is why I believe volunteer administration is important—I would say absolutely *vital*—in the world and in the church.

After 35 years of working, writing, and consulting in the field of volunteerism, I still fervently believe in volunteerism and the role of managing volunteers. Outstanding, ongoing volunteer participation doesn't just happen; it requires careful nurturing and direction. And it's worth the effort to build excellent volunteer participation.

Why? For many reasons . . .

- Because active participation in ministry often blocks the revolving door that's part of many churches.

In many congregations there are two key numbers that should be measured—but we keep track of just one of them.

The first number represents the number of people who have started attending the church in the past month. The second number represents the number of people who have *quit* attending the church in the past month.

We measure the first number, but often have no accurate idea about the second number. And while we know that people leave and go elsewhere, we don't really know why. There's no reliable mechanism in place to do "exit interviews" to reveal why people chose to leave. They simply disappeared through the revolving door that lets people in and lets people out.

Do this: See what impact getting involved in a ministry position has on the commitment—and longevity—of your membership. Check the numbers. I'm willing to bet that the group of people who have been plugged into appropriate volunteer roles and who are finding meaning in those service opportunities are far likelier to stay—and flourish.

- Because the world needs what the church offers and the good news we proclaim.

These are days that can be discouraging, because even though we know that in the end good will prevail, it certainly doesn't *feel* that way. Not when we see the crime statistics or drive through burned-out, boarded-up neighborhoods.

We can be despairing, believing things will never get better. Or, we can be motivated to reach out, asking God to use us in some small way. Volunteers choose to reach out. They choose hope.

And the world needs all the reaching out and hope it can get.

My friend and colleague Nancy Gaston told me about a woman who phoned her about participating as a volunteer in her church.

> Eileen phoned the Lay Ministry Director with a request. She was recovering from a bout of severe depression and anxiety and was hoping to re-enter the workforce. However, she wasn't sure she had the focus and stamina to work a full day. Was there a job she could do on her own schedule, gradually increasing the daily hours?

> There was. We assigned her the task of cleaning and reorganizing the supply room for the church school program. Coming in daily, she planned the work herself, checking occasionally to make sure her system was acceptable.

> At first she came and went without saying much, but as the daily hours increased, she shared coffee breaks and lunchtime with staff and volunteers—interacting with increasing ease. By the third week, she was working full days and soon completed the task. The supply room looked wonderful, transformed from disorderly piles to organized and brightly labeled shelves.

> We wrote her a letter of thanks and commendation to share with prospective employers, and Eileen started attending worship at the invitation of a volunteer she met over coffee. A month later, she called to say she had a full-time job as a warehouse manager.

> Eileen told us, "I never knew I could organize things like that until you gave me a chance to try it. I feel like a new person—a competent one."

Eileen needed what the church had to offer, and the way she plugged in and got involved was through volunteerism. Imagine the impact that church would have if it was intentional about including outside volunteers in community-based projects like cleaning a park or planting flowers along a public walkway.

We must build relational bridges if we intend to carry the gospel to people. Volunteerism is an excellent way to bring people together.

- Because as we capably manage volunteerism, we create opportunities for people to be at their best as they help others.

My husband's career was in corporate human resources, and I recall one time he turned to me and said, "You're so lucky to be working with volunteers. You get to be with people when they're at their best."

> "We must build relational bridges if we intend to carry the gospel to people."

He was right. People *are* at their best when they're so committed to a mission that they set aside their own agendas. When you're stacking sandbags next to a swollen river, standing ankle deep in mud and soaked from a cold, stinging rain, you've got lots of reasons to complain. You're wet and tired. The work is backbreaking. There's no hot coffee. But you and three dozen other Red Cross Disaster Team volunteers are saving a neighborhood, so nobody cares. Moments like that are when people are at their very best in service to others.

Those moments change the lives of people helped, but they change the lives of volunteers, too.

Consider what my friend Stephanie Adams had to say about a volunteer project in which she became involved . . .

Our church was doing a number of community outreach projects during the Christmas season. This particular project was at the Women In Crisis shelter. Our group went in to do some painting and cleaning of the shelter. So, the job itself wasn't that special: paint and wallpaper a bathroom. In everyday life that's no big deal.

What affected me was being in the shelter, a place of refuge for so many women who leave home with no possessions, no belongings, often just the clothes on their back. I glanced into rooms that mothers shared with their babies and children. These were women looking for safety and a new start.

After we'd finished for the day, I was relaxing at home when the full impact hit me. There I sat, in my beautiful home, the Christmas tree lit, safe and secure in the knowledge that I was warm and surrounded by love. Blessing and sadness both over-whelmed me.

Blessing, because I knew that God loved me and that every-thing that I have (and not just the material stuff) comes from him. Yet, at the same time, incredible sadness, because for a part of a day, I was in a place where warmth, love, and security didn't exist for many residents.

Volunteering has never been the same since. Now, whatever I do, it's a grateful response for all the blessings that God has bestowed on me.

- Because it creates new meaning and purpose in people's lives when they discover and use their God-given talents and abilities to make a difference.

A newly divorced woman once walked into the Volunteer Center I founded in Boulder, Colorado. She was new to the area, new to a life without her husband, and she wanted to volunteer at the center. Her realtor had suggested she get to know people by working at the center.

The woman told me she'd had a career as a secretary before getting married 25 years earlier. She said she'd enjoyed it, and I needed a volunteer secretary, so I put her to work.

By the end of her first day, it was clear 25 years away from a typewriter had taken their toll. Every letter she'd typed was filled with errors. I couldn't send out even one of them.

I circled the errors and called her in. "I think these typos slipped past you," I said, and she returned to her desk to retype the letters. Every one of them.

> "Something amazing happens when we receive time or services from volunteers: We feel worthy."

Here's what happened: She took a typing course and sharpened up those skills. Within a few years she became the supervisor for all the office volunteers. A few years later she was taking on even more responsibility.

Seven years after she walked into the Volunteer Center she left—to become the paid Director of the Big Sisters Program in Boulder. Her time with us turned out to be a seven-year internship that prepared her for a new profession at which she excelled.

- Because involvement in meaningful volunteer efforts can create hope for those who are experiencing life's difficulties.

One of my acquaintances was a volunteer in the Big Brother Program. "It was a life-changing experience for me," Lynn says, "but it had an amazing impact on Brian, my little brother. I couldn't believe what one morning per week did in his life. He and his mom met with social workers all the time, but nothing changed until a guy showed up to take him out for a pizza."

Of course. Think about it from Brian's perspective for a moment. This volunteer set aside Saturdays to spend time with Brian *by choice*. It wasn't the volunteer's job to take Brian fishing, or to talk about school as they kicked through a field looking for arrowheads. No wonder Brian felt special and he listened carefully when the volunteer talked.

Something amazing happens when we receive time or services from volunteers: We feel worthy. We know it's not part of that person's job to help us. It's a gift, and that makes a Saturday morning of time so much more precious. It's not *just* time—it's hope that things will get better.

Nancy Gaston has encountered how God has used volunteer positions to dramatically help the volunteers as well as the people the volunteer is serving.

When Nancy's church distributed a talents and interests survey, one person who responded was a woman named Kelli. Here's what Nancy says about what happened.

> None of us on the Lay Ministry Team knew Kelli—she was a member who seldom attended, wasn't involved, and didn't seem to socialize with other members. Kelli had marked "office support" on her questionnaire—the only item she expressed any interest in.
>
> So the office administrator invited Kelli to come for an interview. She came, but was so shy and withdrawn she didn't even make eye contact. A woman of about 70, Kelli was a recent widow who apparently seldom left her house. She agreed to come in for a half a day per week to do copying and collating.
>
> Gradually, Kelli warmed to the work as well as to the other volunteers and staff. She started to bring snacks to share, and started to show her sly sense of humor. After about six months, she was the person organizing groups to do mailings. She instructed the other volunteers assertively, and looked them in the eye. And after a year or so, she began "seeing" a neighbor who was a widower. They began to attend church together and even stayed for fellowship time—something Kelli had never done before.
>
> And her "gentleman friend" comes along to help in the office on occasion.

• Because when we work together, we create moments and pockets of real community and collaboration.

Visit a Habitat for Humanity worksite and you'll see something you don't often find in the world: a place where titles, roles, gender, color, and age don't matter. Not when everyone is working together for a mission everyone believes in.

You'll often find CEOs swinging hammers alongside teenagers. And when a piece of lumber is hauled past, there may be a successful businessman carrying one end and an economically-challenged single mother carrying the other end. Where else would such a diverse group of people come together to accomplish a task?

Volunteer programs can bring together people who would never get to know each other in any other way. Even in the church, we tend to cluster with our own friends, people who are like us and with whom we have a shared history. Community doesn't automatically happen just because we park in the same parking lot and sit through the same worship service.

But when there's a *what-if* that binds us together, barriers go down. Relationships form. Tasks are shared. Community is experienced.

What you do to encourage volunteerism is important, so it's worth doing well. It's more than simply organizing schedules—it's ministry to those who volunteer, to those whom the volunteers serve, and to the God who pours out talents, abilities, and passions to be used for him.

Let's not settle for "good enough" when it comes to volunteer leadership.

Let's give it our best.

FOUR
Determining If Your Church Culture Is Volunteer-Friendly

Take the temperature of your church to determine if it's volunteer-friendly or volunteer-toxic. Here's a test—and ideas for fixing what needs fixed. Also—the Core Values of Volunteer Leadership!

For more than a quarter century I've lived in a house that sits in the foothills of the Rockies, in the western part of Boulder, Colorado. It's no exaggeration to say that my backyard is in the mountains because my backyard *is* a mountain. I'm halfway up that mountain, so my front yard is a mountain, too.

When I was running a program at the University of Colorado I frequently hosted meetings at my house. Students learned fast that it was always smart to ask where someone lived in Boulder before jumping on a bike to pedal to that address.

If the address was near the University or in eastern Boulder, it was an easy ride on a bike. That part of town is flat.

But if the address was out *my* way, a student could expect a tough, uphill climb. More than once students showed up here looking as if they wished they'd asked a few more questions before heading over to see me.

The good news is that once a person has pedaled uphill this far to a meeting, it's all downhill on the way back!

I don't want to assume that I know exactly where you are as you begin your journey toward launching or improving your volunteer leadership program. Maybe you have a good system in place and it's pretty much easy pedaling for you to get where you need to go.

But maybe it's an uphill climb to get even one person to volunteer for a role at church. You're huffing and puffing and barely making any headway at all. *Anything* would be an improvement over what you're experiencing at your church.

As my colleagues and I write this series of resources to help you create a volunteer-friendly culture, we're aware there are a wide variety of churches in our reading audience. Each of you has your own unique situation, size, history, perspective, and role in the church. Some of you have a long experience working with volunteers, and some of you are new to the field. Some of you are confident, and some of you question God's wisdom in putting you anywhere near the responsibility of helping volunteers find the right fit as they seek to serve in the church.

But one thing you all have in common: *You are the experts where you are.* As we share tools and techniques with you, be open and flexible as you apply them. They must fit the reality of your unique situation to be useful.

For example, if you're a pastor or church leader who's looking for a system to revitalize your whole church's volunteer involvement and you need a centralized function to do it, you'll use the material one way. But if you're the Director of Children's Ministry, Youth Director, Music Minister, or you're concerned primarily with finding volunteers for just one program in your church, you'll use this material differently.

> "Grow toward centralizing the function of volunteer recruitment."

Both are legitimate uses of the volunteer insights and process you'll learn. But I would encourage you to *grow toward centralizing the function of volunteer recruitment*. That's where you'll find the most benefit from putting these tools to use, as Community Church of Joy discovered.

A "Volunteer Manager" or "Volunteer Coordinator" may be the *last* position you can imagine being funded by your church. That position is just now beginning to emerge as a staff function in churches and it's appearing—this is no sur-prise—first in churches with a large budget and large staff. But it *is* appearing, and I can foresee a day when the "Minister of Volunteer Involvement" is as typical a staff position as "Children's Ministry Director" is today.

Don't believe me? Wait until you see what putting in place a solid, sound process does for volunteer recruitment for your church. In a year see how plugging marginal members into service opportunities builds their commitment and retains them. Do a quick analysis of how many things you once paid to have done are being accomplished by volunteers. As ministry area leaders learn to delegate, see how they are more vibrant—and less burned out.

My prediction is this: In 20 years churches that have *not* centralized the function of volunteer leadership will be the exception. The benefits of doing so are just overwhelming and measurable.

But no matter how you intend to use this material, it's probable you'll run into some obstacles. By discussing them now—before you collide with them—you'll be better prepared to overcome them. It's like pausing to read the river.

It probably won't be terribly helpful to hear this, but you may encounter resistance to launching or expanding your volunteer program that has nothing to do with you. It's not personal. It's cultural.

There are attitudes and behaviors regarding volunteers that are toxic to a healthy volunteer program, and they may have taken root in your church culture decades ago. I've seen the following attitudes and behaviors again and again in churches. Place a check in the box next to any you've seen or experienced in your own church.

Toxic Attitudes and Behaviors

❑ **Committee chairpersons end up doing all the work on their committees.**

This can happen for a number of reasons. It may be that no one ever signed up to serve on the committee, so a single zealot took the project and ran with it. That happens, though it's seldom the best approach.

Another thing that happens is equally bad, if not worse. There *is* a committee, and it may even be comprised of volunteers who want to serve. But because the committee chairperson won't define what needs to be done, or isn't willing or able to share power through delegation, it turns into a one-person show.

For example, suppose Jenny Smith is the newly elected chairperson of the Christian Education Department. She has a new group of committee members sitting around the table in the church hall. It's their first meeting.

Jenny introduces herself and talks about why the project is important, provides information about what's been done in the past, and describes her vision for the future. She covers a remarkable amount of material, hands out printouts, and then closes with prayer.

It's not until the meeting is over that most of the committee members realize that the only person who did any talking was Jenny.

The second meeting comes up on the calendar, and once more the committee sits around a table. And once more they hear Jenny tell everyone what she's accomplished. And once again the members of the committee go home without really needing to be at the meeting. They contributed nothing. They were asked to do nothing.

There's no third meeting.

If you have people in places of power who don't know how to use volunteers, are you willing to provide training?

❑ **A handful of people (the Pillars) do all the work, while the majority of people (the Pewsitters) watch.**

Here's what often happens in churches . . .

The Pillars are those folks who show up for church each week, and who also can be counted on when it's time for the fall festival, the spring father-daughter dance, and the living nativity. They even take a week off work so they can help at vacation Bible school.

Because they *are* so involved, the Pillars have become buddies. And because they're buddies, they usually call each other when it's time to recruit for the next church program. Alisa calls Tricia and says, "Remember when I helped you out on mission weekend? Well, I need your help at the silent auction." They end up creating a club of sorts, one that isn't always open to new members.

Plus, the motivation to participate is often tinged with guilt. Tricia can't very well say no after Alisa housed two missionaries and also made authentic Russian food for the missionary banquet.

It may be that your church's Pillars aren't inclusive of new volunteers. Before you assume that Pewsitters refuse to get involved, find out how effectively Pewsitters are being invited to serve.

And also find out if the Pillars are making all the decisions about church projects and programs. If that's the case, it's no wonder the Pewsitters aren't excited about getting involved. They have no ownership.

❑ **Leaders are asked to cover several major jobs at once—and keep them far too long.**

There are churches that refuse to let someone be in charge of more than one ministry area. Why? Because each ministry area is worthy of having someone focus his or her best energies on it, and because when you stretch people too thin they tend to snap.

Are your leaders burned out? Have they passed the point where their passion sizzles into plain obligation? That didn't happen by accident, and the cause is often overcommitment.

One quick way to be assured you won't have this problem continue is to place a time limit on volunteer roles. Set a reasonable term for service and make it part of the volunteer ministry description. That way people know how long they're expected to serve,

> "Are your leaders burned out? Place a time limit on volunteer roles."

and how to pace themselves. Volunteers can leave the role when their term of service is over, or—if you're both in agreement—they can sign up for another term of service.

Some churches also set a limit on how many terms someone can serve in the same volunteer role. If you have a wonderful small group leader who's serving in an area of talent, skill, and passion, it may make little sense to remove that person simply because some calendar pages have flipped over. But if you have someone who's staked out the nursery as her private kingdom and refuses to make changes or to include others, you'll be glad you have a policy about terms of service.

❑ **Leaders require unrealistic time commitments that scare volunteers away.**

Accepting a volunteer role shouldn't be a life sentence. When we ask potential volunteers to take on open-ended responsibilities ("You'll only be in charge until we find someone else"), we're doing a poor job caring for our volunteers. They know what will happen when they say yes: We'll quit looking for a replacement. We've got them, so why should we continue searching?

There was a time that some volunteers practically lived at the church. These Pillars were the people who thrived on volunteering. But look around: You don't see many of those people around any longer. Because of the trends identified in volume 4, we can't create volunteer positions that are essentially part-time jobs. There must be "entry level" volunteer roles that are episodic or that require few hours.

Review your volunteer job descriptions: Are they so demanding that in a world of two-income families no one can fulfill them? Is either the duration or intensity of volunteer roles unreasonable?

Keep in mind that "unrealistic" is in the eye of the beholder when it comes to time commitments. A major trend in volunteerism is that volunteers prefer three-, six-, or one-month assignments rather than longer commitments. The shorter time commitments fit better into volunteers' busy lives.

❑ **There's no system for coaching volunteers.**

How long would you like to stay in a role where you're not sure you're doing well and there's no feedback? Or if a problem arises you don't know who to call for help? Not long. Yet that's what we do to many volunteers.

Is there a documented process by which you do evaluations of volunteers? If not, you're robbing them of the opportunity to get better in what they do. And that robs the people being served by your volunteers of the chance to be served by ever more excellent volunteers. Check out volume 6 of this Volunteer Leadership Series for more help in creating positive volunteer evaluations.

Plus, there's this: When your wonderful Children's Pastor leaves, will the program disappear with that person? If the pastor isn't developing a second line of leadership, everything ends when the pastor retires, goes to another church, or dies.

Some advice: If you have a program that's working well, *insist* that the leader of that program train others in the nuts and bolts of pulling the program off. You don't want to discover that nothing was ever written down the day after the founder of the program leaves.

❑ **Volunteers are more committed to a leader than to the church.**

Especially if you have a very engaging, inspirational leader, you can have a situation arise in which if the leader leaves, the volunteers leave, too. The volunteers aren't committed to the mission and vision of the church; they're committed to "Pastor Tom."

What draws your volunteers to serve? A relationship with your church's leadership is good—but is it all there is? What are your volunteers' relationship to the mission of the church?

❑ **Clergy and other leaders fail to delegate to volunteers because "It's quicker to do it myself," "I don't want to bother anyone," or "No one does it quite like I do it."**

What's insidious about this obstacle is that probably the staff member who dismisses volunteers as time-consuming is right: It *does* take time to direct volunteers. It *does* take time to bring someone up to speed on a task. It probably *is* quicker to do it yourself—if you want to do it yourself forever.

It's a variation on the old "Give a man a fish and you've fed him for a day; teach him to fish and he'll have food forever" proverb. A volunteer-centered version of that truism might be, "Teach a volunteer to prepare the bulletin inserts and it will take you four hours today. But next week you've got that four hours to go do something else."

Working with volunteers is an investment that will pay dividends—but not immediately. Are your staff and leaders willing to invest in volunteers?

And does your staff truly believe that volunteers *want* to be involved? That it's not a bother to volunteers to use their skills, talents, abilities, and passions in ministry? That it's fulfilling?

And is your staff willing to let loose of *how* a task might be accomplished so long as it's done on time and meets the goal? Frank may *not* design the newsletter quite the same way you would . . . but does it matter? Can you give him a bit of room for creativity and ownership as long as it's clear, accurate, and on time?

Any of these attitudes or behaviors can block your best efforts to involve more congregation members in volunteer ministry roles. Did you place a check in any of the boxes above? If so, you've identified a toxic attitude or behavior you'll need to address.

And I can tell you this: The more boxes you checked, the likelier your church is experiencing a lack of involvement by members and a decreasing membership. And why shouldn't people be drifting away? They're not church "members" in the full sense; they're church "attenders."

I've seen churches that actually *discourage* volunteerism in the congregation. Pastors in those churches would object to that assessment, I'm sure, but it's true. The policies and procedures in place were so toxic to a good volunteer experience that there's no way the majority of church members could participate in a meaningful way.

Every volunteer-toxic attitude or behavior is an obstacle standing between you and where you want to go. If you intend to reach a place where you have a volunteer-friendly church culture, you'll have to go over, under, or around those obstacles—and that takes time and energy you don't have to spare. Plus, getting around them won't solve your problem. What's required is to *remove* those obstacles so the way is clear.

Before tackling the most common obstacles you're likely to face, I'd like to describe the attitudes and actions that typify a *healthy* church volunteer environment. They're summarized in the document you'll find on page 54.

This set of "Core Values" came out of my sitting in a room for three days with volunteer leadership colleagues whom I treasure as friends. Between us, we had something approaching 250 years of volunteer leadership experience (just think: if we'd been able to put it all together, we could have recruited volunteers for the Boston Tea Party!).

> "I've seen churches that actually *discourage* volunteerism in the congregation."

We talked about which principles and "givens" are the foundation of an effective church volunteer program, and we combined those into one document.

The list of Core Values isn't complete—nothing involving volunteer leadership is ever truly the last word. But it's a solid start, and I suggest you copy the document and post it where you'll see it often (for a convenient, abbreviated version see page 111.) It's where you're headed. And if you can, as a church, embrace these principles, you'll find most of the obstacles you're encountering melt away. Couple these principles with the skills and techniques of sound volunteer leadership covered in this series and you'll get where you need to go.

Core Values of Volunteer Leadership

In light of our experience working with volunteers and our own experiences as volunteers, we hold these truths to be truly important—and hopefully self-evident:

Every volunteer experience in the church should encourage a healthy relationship with Jesus Christ.

If that's not a natural outcome of a volunteer experience, either the volunteer has been misplaced in a role or the role isn't one that belongs in the church.

We believe everyone in the body of Christ has something to give to the corporate body.

Volunteer leadership cooperates best with the discipleship and stewardship process by honoring the abilities, interests, and passions of volunteers. We'll take the time to thoroughly interview volunteers and see that they're placed appropriately.

Volunteers are respected as full partners in ministry.

That means we lead volunteers in the same ways we lead paid staff members. Expectations about time may differ, but the standards of behavior and excellence are the same.

Volunteers can be any age.

Adults, teenagers, children—there's room for everyone to volunteer in a meaningful role, doing meaningful ministry.

It's better to leave a volunteer position unfilled than to put the wrong person in the position.

We will place volunteers in accordance to their abilities, interests, and passions, not based on our need to get someone into the junior high boys class.

We provide the resources and training that volunteers need to be successful.

Volunteers can expect to receive careful screening, thorough interviews, accurate job descriptions, and exemplary training and evaluations.

It's okay for potential volunteers to say "no" to a request.

We view a "no" as an invitation to explore alternative opportunities for involvement, not a sign of a potential volunteer's spiritual immaturity.

Volunteer motivation and retention are outcomes of doing other things right.

Among those things are:

• Valuing relationships and celebrating them.

- Valuing experiential training for volunteers.

- Valuing applicable training for volunteers.

- Valuing learner-centered training for volunteers.

- Fostering an environment where there's no put-down humor or victims and where volunteers can count on a culture that's fair, forgiving, and fun.

Volunteer leadership happens best when there's a centralized volunteer leadership function.

Few churches have a designated person handling volunteer leadership. While that's the reality, it's not the ideal situation. We will provide resources to support the *function* of volunteer leadership, yet also encourage the emergence of the volunteer leader *role* in a church setting.

Episodic volunteering is legitimate.

Volunteering in a church setting doesn't have to be an "until death do us part" proposition. We recognize that volunteers may choose to volunteer in one role forever, or switch roles with some frequency. They may be available to volunteer at one stage of their lives and not at another. We'll honor any sort of appropriate volunteering they're prepared and willing to do while fulfilling the needs of the congregation.

We won't let volunteers burn out.

They're too valuable and precious to use up and toss away. We value volunteers serving well over a lifetime more than we value covering tasks.

The good of a local congregation supercedes the good of an individual volunteer.

The desire of a volunteer to serve in a specific area doesn't necessarily mean that's where the volunteer should serve. The corporate good of the congregation comes first in placing volunteers.

And we admit it: We can't motivate volunteers.

Though we can't motivate anyone, we *can* create environments where people experience motivation. Our goal is to "unlock" the innate motivation in individuals as we put in place those values, policies, and procedures that create "volunteer-friendly zones"—places where the culture is fair, fun, forgiving, and faithful. Where truth, trust, and clear expectations pave the way for communication success. Where direct communication is the norm and truth is spoken in love.

Obstacles to a Volunteer-Friendly Culture

The Core Values represent the attitudes and behaviors you want to see in your church. They summarize what a volunteer-friendly culture looks like at a practical level.

Now, what specific things might trip you up as you seek to build an effective volunteer program? Where are the obstacles?

No two churches face precisely the same obstacles. Each church—yours included—is in a unique situation. You may have the issue of having too few people to fill ministry roles. Another church has too many people for one area of ministry, while it's short of people in another area. A church of 50 members has a very different set of challenges than a church of 5,000 members.

You may have a budget that's too small, and another church might have—believe it or not—a budget that's too big. Either can derail a volunteer program.

Let me tell you about a church a colleague of mine visited in Ohio . . .

The Church with Too Much Money

The church building is a majestic stone structure, with steeples making it visible from the entire inner-city neighborhood. The once fashionable streets surrounding the church building have fallen into disrepair over the past 50 years, and what was once a wealthy community has become a needy community. Substantial homes have been divided into apartments and flats. And aside from a few convenience stores tucked into storefronts, merchants have long ago gone out of business or moved to a "safer" neighborhood.

But the church building is immaculate. Every brick has been scrubbed clean of gang graffiti, and an armed guard patrols the perimeter each night. The parking lot is freshly sealed, and not one pane of glass is broken or covered with wire.

It's as if the church property has been frozen in time. It may be a depressing, decaying new millennium outside the church fence, but inside it's 1951.

When my friend went into the building for a tour, he was greeted by an associate pastor who proudly showed him through the facility.

The sanctuary, which seated more than a thousand in carved wooden pews, smelled of fresh wood wax. The Christian education wing held more than a dozen classrooms, each with tiny tables and chairs in perfect rows. The nursery was spacious and newly carpeted.

All for a congregation of 32 people, with an average age of 67.

The associate pastor explained that on Sunday mornings the congregation enjoyed tremendous choral music—students from the nearby university's College of Music were under contract to sing and play. And another student was hired to sit in the nursery, on call to take care of any baby whose family came to visit.

No baby had been in the nursery for more than two years.

And the classrooms? Each week they were dusted and cleaned, but there was no Christian education program because there were no children—they'd graduated the last child out of the children's ministry department 15 years earlier.

What kept the doors open? An endowment funded by bequests in wills guaranteed that the building would always be kept in tip-top shape. The halls might echo when a visitor walked through on Sunday morning, but the halls were always perfectly waxed.

The church knew it was in trouble. It needed to attract visitors, preferably from the neighborhood, so my colleague was asked to make that happen. He'd be well-paid to put together community events that would bring people into the building, and hopefully into the church.

But because of their advanced age and busy schedule, none of the church staff or members of the congregation expected to be involved. My colleague could hire help as he saw fit from temp agencies, or through the university student union office.

My friend refused the assignment.

A huge budget had choked off volunteer involvement in this church because they could afford to pay others to do everything. In this case, too much money was a bad thing.

> "A huge budget had choked off volunteer involvement in this church because they could afford to pay others to do everything."

Assuming a bottomless budget isn't an obstacle in your way, what *are* the obstacles you're facing?

I've observed that obstacles tend to fall into one of three categories:

1. Staff members who resist volunteer involvement,

2. Volunteers who resist serving, and

3. Inadequate volunteer leadership.

Let's look at these one at a time, and how we can approach overcoming them.

Why Staff Members Resist Volunteer Involvement

- Leaders have had a poor experience with volunteers.

The volunteers were late. They didn't do what they were asked to do. They didn't follow the rules. They were more interested in talking with each other than in finishing the work. The list of what constitutes a "poor experience" goes on and on.

The obvious questions to ask would be what happened and whether it was specific to a particular volunteer or it was caused by the design of the role a volunteer was filling.

And what might keep the experience from being repeated?

Work through the issues with leaders and encourage them to approach future volunteer encounters with an open mind. If a leader simply won't work with volunteers, don't place volunteers with that leader. Let the success of the program in other ministry areas slowly change the leader's opinion of volunteers.

- Leaders fear they'll lose their positions.

There *is* something awkward about having a former administrative assistant from a successful business helping out a church secretary who isn't a stellar administrator. Sometimes volunteers do a job so well that people begin to joke that the leader being helped isn't really needed anymore. Everyone laughs—except the leader.

An insecure leader can create tremendous problems for volunteers, so discuss with leaders the benefits of using volunteers. The leader will be able to actually grow in his or her position because some tasks that formerly required attention will be handled by volunteers. Help the leader see the involvement of volunteers as an opportunity, not a threat. Assure leaders that volunteers will report *to* them, and aren't being brought in to replace them.

- Leaders fear the volunteers will make them look bad.

Perhaps it's fear that a retired principal who wants to help with the children's ministry will question decisions made by the children's pastor. Or that a board member who's helping with the ushering will tell the board that ushers really aren't needed, and the group should be disbanded.

Encourage these leaders to welcome input from volunteers, and to think of them as full partners in ministry. Encourage volunteers to be sensitive to the roles of their leaders, and to support those leaders.

- Leaders fear volunteers are unreliable.

This is a realistic fear—some volunteers *are* unreliable. Share with leaders the screening, training, and orientation you'll be doing with volunteers. Ask that the leader give volunteers a chance—and do your best to place reliable people in that leader's area.

- Leaders want to recruit their own volunteers.

This is the system at place in many churches—each ministry area is responsible for its own staffing. In many respects, the system works well. An area ministry leader has a good understanding of the sort of person who will fit and be successful.

In a centralized system of volunteer leadership, it's *still* the leader of a ministry area who does the final interview and determines if a volunteer will be placed in that area.

But there's a potential problem when each ministry does its own recruiting. Some leaders just aren't very good at recruiting, and they're perpetually short of volunteers when another ministry area is abundantly staffed. And if the children's pastor is recruiting just for only her ministry area, she may not know about positions in youth ministry or the choir. Her filter for who will make a "good volunteer" is someone who fits in the children's ministry area.

Unfortunately, this approach sabotages the overall volunteer program and builds resentments in areas where leaders aren't able to recruit effectively. Assure leaders that no volunteer will be placed in his or her area without that position being offered by the leader. No leader will be "stuck" with someone.

- Leaders don't want to bother with supervising volunteers or completing the necessary job descriptions.

Unfortunately, both responsibilities come with having volunteers involved. If a leader refuses, politely offer to help create the job descriptions and to provide training for the volunteers. If the leader still refuses, don't place volunteers with that leader. Let the success of the program in other ministry areas influence this leader. Encourage peers who are using volunteers successfully to share their stories with this leader.

- Leaders believe that using volunteers creates more work than it's worth, and they aren't rewarded for using volunteers.

Two issues are reflected here: the cost to leaders of supervising volunteers and the importance of volunteers being in ministry.

Discuss with leaders that it's *worth* paying a price to involve people in ministry. In the same way it's important to let children "help" at tasks until they master them, it's worth helping volunteers master tasks. Why? Because then the body of Christ has fully-functioning members who are serving others and glorifying God in service. Encouraging that is one of the primary responsibilities of leadership in the church. Working with volunteers needs to be seen as a primary part of the leaderships' responsibility and rewarded as such.

Do this to get a discussion going: Suggest that working with volunteers become a part of each staff member's job description for the reasons discussed above.

Staff objections to volunteer involvement fall into two general arguments: those borne out of experience and those fueled by fear.

If a staff member has truly had a negative volunteer experience, explore it in detail. Help the staff member determine how much of the problem was due to the volunteer, and how much was contributed by the staff member. What safeguards do you have in place—or *will* you have in place—to keep the same sort of situation from developing again? Sometimes just your continued involvement to monitor the staff member/volunteer role fit is enough to gain support.

But realize this: You can't *force* a volunteer on a staff member. If a specific staff member refuses to work with volunteers, that's a reality of your world. Work with the staff members who are willing to work with you, and encourage *them* to do the work you can't do: changing the hearts and minds of their peers.

Why Volunteers Resist Serving

Why do people refuse to become actively involved? Why do Pewsitters decide that a life of disengagement—which is boring and not consistent with their purpose in the church—is preferable to finding a place to serve? Again, the obstacles are numerous, but in my experience here are the most common obstacles you'll need to overcome:

• "There aren't any jobs I can do."

When your potential volunteers see programs being delivered with excellence, the potential volunteers tend to focus on their own limitations. They see outstanding musicians leading singing, top-notch teachers doing children's ministry, smiling ushers greeting everyone like long-lost friends—it's daunting.

Communicate to potential volunteers that there's training for any role they think suits them, and that you'll only place volunteers where they have God-given strengths.

- "I filled out one of those time and talent sheets and nobody called me."

All too often churches collect information about members and then promptly do . . . nothing. As you'll see in volume 4, the volunteer interview process tightens up that loop and removes the possibility of inaction.

What you don't want is to let a time and talent sheet officially reject people's gifts once a year. At a workshop I was leading, a lovely, silver-haired lady told me this sad story:

"My husband passed away, so I moved here about a year and a half ago to live with my daughter. One of the first things I did was join a church. When I joined, they asked me to fill out a form listing my interests and talents and how I'd be willing to serve. I wrote down a long list because I was very active in my old congregation and now had lots of time on my hands. I was also eager to feel like I belonged in my new church family. It's been a year and a half and nobody has ever called to ask me to do anything. It makes me very sad."

Filling out paperwork doesn't place potential volunteers in fulfilling positions. We do that. Whatever paperwork we use is just a tiny first step in the process.

- "I was so frustrated last time that I'll never volunteer again."

Here's a dirty little secret: Many of those "frozen chosen" Pewsitters *have* been volunteers in the past. They didn't quit because they got too busy, or too old, or too anything. People don't easily quit things they find personally rewarding.

They quit because they were in poorly defined roles, and they lacked the resources or authority to be successful. The problem wasn't with the volunteers—it was with the system in which they volunteered.

Again—a volunteer interview program eliminates most of the opportunity for frustration because before a position is offered to a volunteer, that position has a job description in place, as well as a structure that provides evaluation and support.

- "I hated my volunteer job."

Bad volunteer experiences happen to good people for a variety of reasons. Sometimes it's the fault of the volunteer—he or she isn't really committed, or isn't able to give the time and energy the role requires. If the volunteer misrepresented what he or she was willing or able to do, that's going to create tension and failure.

But sometimes the problem was that the volunteer was dumped on by a leader. By that I mean the task given wasn't really delegated, it was dumped.

The difference is this: If a leader thoughtfully thinks through how to share his or her work and hands off a task with the necessary resources and authority—that's delegation. If the task is something the leader *meant* to do but ran out of time and then in desperation handed it off—that's dumping.

Nobody likes to be dumped on . . . and few people will stick around to have it happen twice. When a volunteer has been delegated a task, that allows the volunteer to do ministry. But when a task has been dumped—that feels like anything *but* doing ministry.

And sometimes volunteers disliked the roles they were in because they were in the wrong role all along. The volunteer soldiered along either until the results were so poor the volunteer was asked to leave, or he or she was so miserable he or she quit.

The volunteer interview program offers the best opportunity to make a good fit for each volunteer, to get each person into the right job.

- "Nobody seemed to care about me—or my ideas."

Church leaders need to admit it: Sometimes we've made filling jobs the goal, not placing the right person in the right job. We're handed a list of sixteen slots to fill on the organizational chart, and that's our focus. As long as someone is willing to let us write down his name, that's good enough for us.

Then we're off to fill the next chart.

There's no training. No follow-up. No evaluation. Little communication.

Who wants to work in a place like that—especially since volunteers don't have to do it? Sooner or later, people leave, and they're not inclined to come back. We haven't communicated that we care about people.

And when it comes to caring about people's ideas, there are two things we should never, ever say: "We don't do it like that here," and "But this is the way we always do it here." Those are two of the most demotivating phrases we can utter.

The message with either phrase (and attitude) is that we don't need your ideas, that we're happy with the status quo.

Here's what I've found: Volunteers don't care whether you actually implement their ideas. They're happy when you do, of course, but it's not essential. What *is* essential is that you actually *hear* the volunteer's idea and communicate respect for the idea and the volunteer who suggests it.

• "I don't have time."

We'll deal more with this in the context of recruiting in volume 4, but let me quickly respond to this obstacle now.

We all have the same amount of time in a day, a week, and a year. The issue isn't a lack of time, but that the volunteer opportunity being presented isn't important enough to rate a time commitment. We all make time for what we value most.

Never be put off by the claim that there's "no time" for volunteering. There is. The true issue is something else.

• "I feel awkward talking about myself."

Under the best of circumstances, it's difficult for church members to tell us what they can do and what they can't do. It feels like bragging to point out one's strengths, and few people like to admit to weaknesses.

So potential volunteers wistfully wish they could be given a role that actually fits them—but it's never offered. And it's never offered because we don't know to offer it. Instead, we offer roles that volunteers either try and hate, or wisely refuse to take at all.

It's also hard for church members to tell us what they're *tired* of doing. That feels like giving up, or not being faithful. Here's a story that illustrates this point . . .

An acquaintance of mine joined a church and volunteered to help out in the Sunday school. She had a strong background working with junior-highers, so she was asked if she'd teach that age level. She agreed, and one Sunday morning she was walked up the stairs to where that class met.

Here's what she saw as she came through the door: a tired man reading aloud from the book of Judges. He'd been working his way through the Old Testament, reading it aloud, as his three students suffered along.

One student was busy scratching the varnish off the table with his fingernail. Judging from the almost total lack of varnish left, he'd been at it awhile.

The second student was gazing out a window.

The third student was sound asleep.

The new teacher was introduced, and the man leading the class looked up in surprise. He shook her hand, closed his Bible, and walked out the door without saying a word.

It wasn't until later that my acquaintance found out the man had asked three years earlier if he could be relieved of duty. He didn't want to teach junior-highers any longer; he wanted to transport elderly people to church from nursing homes. *That's* where his passion was.

And the boy who was sleeping? That was the man's son.

A final thing we fail to hear from volunteers: what they would like to learn. What skills they'd like to develop. What talents they want to explore. Those places are where their interests lie—but we never get to tap into that fountain of motivation and enthusiasm. Why? Because we don't directly ask.

Why Inadequate Volunteer Leadership Can Be an Obstacle

This last category of obstacles is all about us—the leadership and management issues *we* bring into the equation.

Nobody wants to rearrange deck chairs on a sinking ship. It's

Why Do You Call These People "Volunteers"?

Perhaps it's not appropriate to call someone who is supposed to serve (remember our three theologies: *everyone* is called into significant ministry) a "volunteer," but that's the term we've chosen to use.

Some churches use other words to describe people who fill roles in the church. "Minister" and "servant" are among terms that some churches feel more accurately describe a Christian's role, considering that all believers are instructed to make available their God-given abilities, skills, and passions for service in the body of Christ.

Our research has shown, though, that only the word "volunteer" was widely recognized by most people in a congregation. An announcement asking for "ministers" to participate in a service role may leave some lay people thinking that only those with seminary degrees need apply.

If you do choose to avoid the word "volunteer," consider simply referring to all people in volunteer roles as " unpaid staff." A Sunday school teacher would be a children's ministry unpaid staff member; a parking lot attendant would be a hospitality ministry unpaid staff member.

The word "staff" signals that every role is valuable, and invites volunteers to think of their work as meaningful and on a par with pastoral staff and other paid individuals. It respects their full significance in ministry, but again—it may create confusion in the minds of potential volunteers.

meaningless. When a ship is floundering, what people want most is to find a way off the ship. Everything else is busywork.

What's the reputation of your church when it comes to volunteers? Are you perceived as a sinking ship or a ship that's sailing along toward important places? When you run your mission up the center mast, do people salute?

When we ask volunteers to do things that aren't central to

the mission of our church, we're providing inadequate leadership. When we ask volunteers to sign up for roles without giving them the information they need, we're providing inadequate leadership. And when we put volunteers in roles that don't suit them, we shortchange volunteers. It's easy to commit each of those sins, and each sin helps sink our reputation.

The fact is, we can be our own worst enemies when it comes to working with volunteers. What we say, what we do—in spite of our best intentions, we can easily create systems that make getting and keeping volunteers difficult.

That's why I'm so excited that you're working through this series of books on volunteer leadership. You're clearly ready and willing to do your best to create a culture and structure where it's easy for people to embrace their God-given abilities, skills, and passions, and use those in ministry.

None of us will ever be a perfect volunteer leader any more than we'll ever be a perfect follower of Christ. There will always be room for improvement and growth.

But you're growing—and God will bless and multiply your growth.

Let's look at three obstacles we may be throwing in our own way . . .

- "I'll do it alone."

If you feel like a lonely voice crying in the wilderness, you're in trouble for two reasons. First, you're in the wilderness. You won't get much done there.

Second, nobody is listening to you. You're alone.

If you're the sole owner of the volunteer program in your church, the first thing you need to do isn't recruiting volunteers to fill the bell choir. The first thing you need to do is recruit people who'll share your vision and be your co-laborers.

You *cannot* run a volunteer program alone. It's too challenging and time-consuming. The work is never done. The phone calls never end. You must find some help. A team will provide you not just extra hands and feet, but also morale-building and fellowship.

If you're a person who thinks you've got to do it yourself to get it right, think again. Practice what you're preaching and recruit a team . . . even if you don't think you need one. *Especially* if you think you don't need one!

• "I'm relying on spiritual inventories."

Perhaps you've tried to determine where your congregation is concerning volunteer ministry by using a spiritual gifts inventory. I applaud you if using a gifts inventory, or a time/talent survey, has actually increased your membership's level of service and involvement.

Frankly, that's often not the case.

In many churches where inventories are administered, they don't result in the actual placement of people in meaningful ministries. Why? Because there's no system of volunteer leadership to connect people with volunteer roles. Too often church members are left frustrated as they think, *Now I know the name of my spiritual gift—but what do I do with it?*

If you want to use spiritual inventories and surveys, wonderful . . . but here are some shortcomings that tend to create issues:

They're based on self-reporting. People describe what they're like, and that often provides a skewed view of their skills and abilities. We often see ourselves as more or less gifted than we really are. Sometimes we don't have a realistic view of our own abilities at all.

One way to remove this shortcoming is for each person who completes an inventory to have three or four close friends complete the same inventory *about* that person. It greatly increases the amount of work involved, but you'll get a clearer view of the person. If Brian sees himself as a gifted administrator but his wife and two friends see just the opposite—that's good to know.

Churches don't act on information gathered. One church went to the expense and trouble of having every adult member complete a survey. The surveys were forwarded to the church office where they were carefully tabulated, collated, and filed away. When volunteer roles opened up in the church the leaders of those volunteer ministries skimmed through the surveys looking for a match.

The problem was that people who were interested in volunteering had already done so—and not necessarily within the church. The local Habitat for Humanity and Salvation Army offices received lots of volunteers after the survey was given. Why? Because after several months passed without hearing from the church leadership, potential volunteers assumed that they weren't needed at church—so they looked elsewhere.

If you've ever offered a personal gift to someone who unwrapped it, yawned, and tossed it aside, you know how it feels to fill out a time and talent sheet and have nothing happen as a result. It's a systematic rejection process.

Let me tell you about a friend I'll call Audrey Ferris. Her experience isn't uncommon.

Audrey was new to her church, St. Peter's, and didn't yet feel fully comfortable or accepted. It's not all the fault of the church—Audrey is a shy person who likes to be part of things, but doesn't always know how to go about joining in. So by temperament she was stuck a little on the outside, but wanting in.

Then, one day a letter came. The Stewardship Committee had sent out the annual form, and Audrey was in a quandary. Deciding how much money to give was no problem, but she agonized over the time and talent portion of the form. Did she have time to share? Yes . . . but she wasn't sure she had any talent.

But she wanted to give more than money—by signing up to serve in a ministry area she'd get involved, become part of the group. She'd be known and accepted.

Audrey lay awake for hours agonizing over what boxes to check. What if she tried something and failed? What if she checked the wrong box? What if she really didn't have any talents?

In the morning she reviewed the list again, and after prayer and nail-biting she checked two boxes: typing in the office and helping with kindergarten in Sunday school. She felt a small thrill of anticipation as she tucked the list in her Bible, and an even larger thrill when the next Sunday she laid her form on the altar.

Stewardship Sunday had come, and at last she'd stepped forward to volunteer.

She waited for the phone to ring. She waited . . . and waited . . .

She's waiting still, and two more Stewardship Sundays have come and gone. She no longer places an "X" in any of the boxes.

Even if you act on information given, we strongly urge you to do one-on-one interviews with church members. You'll discover a wealth of information that you won't find in any other way.

There's no personal interview to discover deeper information. Okay, so a potential volunteer is a talented professional musician. The volunteer has received tremendous ovations time and again. Music is a passion, a talent, and, as far as the potential volunteer is concerned, a curse. After 20 years of playing music non-stop, the person would rather do *anything* than play one more note.

A gift inventory might well indicate that this person would make a perfect worship leader, and were the volunteer's attitude different that's true. But the test won't reveal that the volunteer will take any other role before being condemned to do on Sunday what he does every other day.

Interviews reveal attitude, interest, and enthusiasm. You'll find out how to do effective interviews in volume 4. Don't skip this step—it's a powerful tool in placing volunteers where they'll thrive.

• "I'll get through this crisis, then start to do it right."

Think this and you'll just stay on the treadmill for another round.

Let's say someone hands you a list of "church jobs" to fill so programs can keep running. Maybe you've got a shopping list of three ushers, two committee heads, and a choir director. You fill those slots with willing people, but now you've got another five people who may be in the wrong roles. You haven't got the foggiest notion if they're going to thrive in their new jobs, or wither and die there.

There's no end to crises if you've got people in the wrong jobs. It's like being in the eye of a hurricane: You can walk outside to see how bad the damage is and what's still standing, but you know the second half of the storm is coming. There's always another crisis on the way.

Let me suggest this: If you haven't got time to do proper volunteer placement now, you'll never have time. That's because you're creating future disgruntled volunteers, unhappy volunteer managers, and an environment that's toxic for volunteerism.

Your intentions may be good—but your actions aren't. You're not following a key concept of volunteer leadership: *People are every bit as important as programs.* That sounds simple, but it has some huge implications, such as:

We won't sacrifice people so programs can continue. If there aren't enough volunteers to staff the nursery properly, we declare the nursery off-limits until we have sufficient volunteers in place. That may sound radical, but think of what will happen if you have two haggard volunteers caring for 23 infants. Not only is it unsafe, but you'll lose the two volunteers you have.

We won't think of "volunteers" as a unit, but as a collection of unique individuals. If you don't know the names of volunteers who serve in your ministry area, how will you help them feel welcome? How will you know how to thank them? How will you be able to help them grow in their service? May the words "Let's leave that to the volunteers" never again be spoken in your church. Rather, let us hear words like "That sounds like something Frank, Tim, and Lenora would do well."

Programs—even long-standing ones—may for a time be discontinued. If you think starting a church program is hard, try stopping one that's become a tradition. It will seem like you're pulling the life-support plug on a loved one. But if there aren't enough organ-playing volunteers who stand ready to maintain and play the pipe organ, maybe it's time to give it up, at least for a while.

In the following survey let me quickly summarize the attitudes and behaviors we've identified as contributing to a toxic environment for volunteerism:

Attitude and Behavior Survey

Check each box you think applies to our church as you experience it. Please check boxes on the basis of what we *actually* appear to believe and do, not what we *should* believe and do.

- ❑ Leaders don't truly believe that God has called each believer to do significant ministry.

- ❑ Leaders don't truly believe each believer has a God-given ability, skill, or passion to use in ministry.

- ❑ Leaders don't truly believe that each believer has a place where he or she fits into the body of Christ.

- ❑ Committee chairpersons end up doing almost all the work on their committees.

- ❑ A handful of people (the church Pillars) do most of the work while others (the Pewsitters) watch.

- ❑ Leaders are asked to cover several major jobs at once—and keep those jobs too long.

- ❑ Leaders require unrealistic time commitments that scare volunteers away.

- ❑ There's no organized system for coaching volunteers.

- ❑ Volunteers are more committed to a leader than to the church.

- ❑ Clergy and other leaders fail to delegate to volunteers.

- ❑ Leaders are hesitant to work with volunteers because of a poor experience in the past.

- ❑ Leaders fear they'll lose their positions.

- ❑ Leaders fear the volunteers will make them look bad.

- ❑ Leaders think volunteers are unreliable.

- ❑ Leaders want to pick their own volunteers.

- ❑ Leaders don't want to bother with supervising volunteers or completing the necessary job descriptions.

❑ Leaders believe that using volunteers creates more work than it's worth and that they aren't rewarded for using volunteers.

❑ Volunteers don't think there are jobs they can do adequately.

❑ The church doesn't follow up on spiritual gift inventories or time and talent sheets.

❑ Frustrating volunteer experiences aren't debriefed and resolved.

❑ Volunteers have been placed in inappropriate jobs.

❑ The church is perceived as unresponsive to volunteers' suggestions.

❑ Volunteers feel uncomfortable talking about themselves at our church.

❑ Ministry leaders prefer to accomplish tasks on their own.

❑ It's perceived as too big a challenge to change the existing system of volunteer placement—even if it's inadequate.

What are other attitudes and behaviors that affect volunteers and volunteerism in our church but aren't noted above? Jot them in below:

❑ _____

❑ _____

❑ _____

❑ _____

I am: a paid church staff member_____ a volunteer_____

Now glance at the boxes you and others have checked. Those are your prayer list. Ask God to work in the hearts of his people to change those attitudes and behaviors and to give you patience as you identify and deal with those attitudes and behaviors in others.

Also, pray that God uses you to help his people find appropriate places of service and experience joy in serving. You'll be cooperating with God's purposes as you assist in this ministry—may you find joy, too!

You know where you are—there are strengths in your church and weaknesses when it comes to volunteerism and the use of volunteers.

But where are you going? What's your destination?

May I suggest this? You want—you *need*—a Volunteer Leadership System built on solid biblical theology and solid volunteer leadership principles. Your next step is to catch a vision for a future that has that system in place.

FIVE
Defining Your Future

Use this 12-step process for getting you where you want to be: enjoying a healthy, vibrant volunteer program that places the right people in the right jobs, and serves everyone involved.

Okay, we've established that your church has some room for growth when it comes to encouraging volunteerism. That means you're just like every other church I've encountered in 35 years of consulting, including my own congregation. I've yet to see a church that doesn't have room for growth.

So what are you going to do about it?

Let me begin by saying this: *No matter what obstacles you face, they can be overcome.* Don't be discouraged. I didn't ask you to identify the challenges you face so they could stop you. I asked you to take a clear, realistic look at those challenges so you'll know how to proceed as you move forward.

In this chapter I'm going to outline a process that will be further developed as you read through this Volunteer Leadership Series. I'll briefly comment on the steps of the process so you can determine where you are at present and so you know what to do next.

But two cautions:

1. It's important you not skip steps. You may have to adapt some of the steps to fit your situation (remember: *you're* the expert in your situation!), but each step has a definite purpose. It's like baking a cake: You can skip an ingredient as you mix the batter and at first it won't show, but once you've cooked the cake it will be obvious from the results that something was missing. This process is your recipe for volunteer leadership success. Don't skip any ingredients!

2. It's important you take these steps in order. You can't jump right to placing volunteers (step #8) before you set objectives and goals (step #3). This is a linear process, and each step builds on those before it. Like the Core Values, I suggest you make a copy of this process (a summary is on page 89) so you can refer to it often. Hang it next to the Core Values list so you'll have a description of the culture you want to see created and the process by which you'll accomplish the following:

- You'll mobilize and energize more volunteers.

- You'll stop clergy and lay-leader burnout.

- You'll get the right people in the right jobs.

- You'll develop future leaders through effective delegation.

- You'll create a volunteer organization that's always being renewed and reinvented to stay current with trends that impact volunteerism in your community.

If that's the future you envision, let's get started!

The Volunteer Leadership System: 12 Steps

I've used the Volunteer Leadership System in hundreds of voluntary organizations and churches. It's a centralized volunteer leadership system that brings about a "heart transplant" in organizations. That is, once it's in place it engenders a culture that's open to volunteers, and it encourages volunteers to grow in their service.

I'll walk you through the steps in order.

Step 1: Establish a Vision

A vision answers the questions, "Where are we going?" and "Where does God want us to be in five years?"

It's determining what we'd like our future to look like. We can just limp along hoping everything will work out, but that's neither proactive or powerful. Volunteers don't rally around the call of "Well, let's hope things don't get any worse."

Here's the truth: Without vision the people perish . . . and without vision a local *church* perishes, too.

Not everyone is good at imagining the future and seeing where God is taking them. Not everyone is good at implementing things, either, or maintaining systems. Visioning requires a blend of skill, faith, and faithfulness to keep the vision grounded.

There often isn't anything terribly mystical about envisioning the future; it's doing some level-headed thinking about what truly is happening and what the implications are. Here's an example of how that can pay off for an organization . . .

My friend John was delighted to discover, on a long airplane flight, that he was seated next to the Chief Planner of McDonald's. Since at the time John was the director of Colorado University's Graduate School of Business Management, he couldn't believe his luck. What a great opportunity to uncover some top-notch business techniques! John asked if he could pump the Chief Planner for insights to share with students, and the man agreed.

"But," warned the Chief Planner, "I'm not sure you'll believe how we do it."

John insisted anyway, and he quickly pulled out a pen so he could take notes on how one of the world's fastest-growing international companies did planning that carried them into the future.

The Chief Planner revealed that at the top of the McDonald's corporate headquarters in Chicago there was a special planning room. In the room was a skylight, a waterbed, and nothing else.

"Every department manager is required to spend one hour per week up there alone," said the Chief Planner. "The manager has to be on the waterbed, looking out the skylight. As the head of planning, I'm required to spend one hour per *day* up there. It's in my job description."

The Chief Planner continued, saying it was when he was on that bed, staring out the skylight, that the implications of zero population growth really hit him. This conversation took place during the years when the U.S. birthrate had declined and grade schools were being closed almost daily.

At that time McDonald's entire ad campaign was Ronald McDonald selling burgers and fries, and it was aimed squarely at kids. "We've got an entire planning department," the Chief Planner admitted, "and the population statistics were around . . . but nobody had put those statistics together with our future."

It was at that moment, on that bed, that McDonald's breakfasts were born. An entire diversification aimed not at children, but at adults.

You've got statistics, too. You know what's happening in your church and in your community. But have you put those together? Have you invited God to help you apply your creativity to the future—to take what the statistics tell you and to determine how you'll navigate those realities? To read a statistic and then ask "so what?" and "what if?"

You need a vision for your church and your ministry. Begin with the church's vision, because the volunteer leadership vision must support that larger corporate vision.

In volume 2 we'll focus more on identifying and communicating a vision for your volunteer leadership program.

Step 2: Write Mission and Purpose Statements

Here's where you establish what business you're in—what problems you're trying to solve. If your mission is to present the Gospel to each person in your town, that's going to drive some of your decisions. It means you'll quickly fund an outreach in your community, but you might think twice about helping establish a seminary overseas.

If you're creating a mission or purpose statement for only your ministry area, you'll focus on how you can do children's ministry, youth ministry, or hospitality in such a way that you help the corporate church achieve its mission and purpose.

Start with your church's mission and purpose statements and be sure you support those. And if there aren't any corporate statements, encourage the church leadership to create them. The outline below will help them—or you—get started. So will the further discussion of mission statements found in volume 2.

What is God calling you to be in this time and this place? The answer today as you're a church of 100 may change when you're a church of 1,000. As your neighborhood becomes more urban, or suburban, your mission may change. What's important is that you're deliberate and prayerful about stating it clearly.

Step 3: Set Objectives and Goals

In volume 4 of this Volunteer Leadership Series there's a discussion of how to create goals for marketing your program. The elements of a goal are discussed in detail there, but here's a quick summary.

How to Create a Mission Statement

1. Get the right people involved. Anyone who has a stake in the outcome should be involved in the process.

2. State WHY you exist—your purpose and what you want to accomplish. Keep the statement simple, and be honest and direct. Flowery prose has no place; you're writing to inform, not inspire.

3. Define WHO you want to serve. Who's your audience? Who should be paying attention to you?

4. Outline HOW and WHERE you'll get it done. Are you delivering goods and services? working with a specific group of people or in a specific location? Say so.

5. Remember your mission statement isn't being carved in granite. It will change as your organization changes.

To be useful, a goal must be written clearly and simply, and it must be specific. What *exactly* do you want to accomplish? Until you're specific, you can't determine if you've met the goal.

Make goals attainable. It doesn't do anyone any good if your goal is so lofty that nobody believes it can be reached. Who wants to give their best efforts to stretch for a goal that won't be reached anyway?

Make goals measurable every way possible, too. By time, certainly—decide when something needs to happen and put a calendar date on it—and also by number. If you need to schedule 12 appointments each month to place 6 volunteers, then create a goal of scheduling 12 appointments each month.

It's human nature for some of us to shy away from goals. We don't want to be locked in or fail to meet the goals. In the same way some sales professionals find goals motivating, some people find that goals suck the joy out of a task. Besides, when we're talking about "church stuff," how do you set a goal? When you tell God you want to see ten new children join the Sunday school, isn't that stepping over a line?

Forgive me, but I don't see setting goals as telling God what to do or failing to live faithfully. Setting goals is about focusing your energy and putting on paper what you trust God will do to and through you. You already know the goals you set are in accordance with what you've determined God wants to do in your church because your goals have flowed out of your mission. Why *not* be specific about what you're trusting God to accomplish?

Step 4: Write an Action Plan

Action plans are where you determine what steps will get you to each goal. Here's where you put wheels under each goal so you can move it forward from intention to reality.

Because your goals are specific, you've got a visual picture of the desired outcome for each goal. You know how to measure whether the goal has been successfully accomplished. You know where the finish line is.

Now it's time to think through how to get there. For each goal, write down the actions you may need to take to accomplish that goal. Don't worry about getting actions in order at this point—just write them down. It's not uncommon to find that a fairly simple goal ("paint the sanctuary") actually requires dozens of steps, so allow plenty of time—and paper!

Once you've exhausted your list-writing, then circle those that seem necessary and non-negotiable. The circled items will be your Key Action Steps. If there's a step that, with

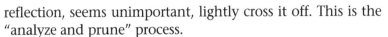

reflection, seems unimportant, lightly cross it off. This is the "analyze and prune" process.

Next, get organized. Place your circled Key Action Items in a logical sequence. What step has to happen first? second? Keep rearranging steps until you think you've got them in order. As you examine the list of Key Actions, are there any that could be simplified? that should be broken into several steps? that can be dropped altogether?

Get organized by estimating the amount of time each step will take and deciding who will be primarily responsible for each step. Accountability requires you to have each goal measurable in terms of time, budget, and people's performance, so keep those elements in place as you create an action plan.

It's wise to take your action plan even further by determining what resources you'll need to accomplish each step. By thinking it through on paper you may find that "painting the sanctuary" requires you to have scaffolding up for two solid weeks—which presents significant problems for Sunday worship services. That piece of information will help you schedule the project for the least-disruptive time. And it lets you know that you'd better have the pastoral staff's input, too!

Throughout this Volunteer Leadership Series you'll be encouraged to move from the theoretical to the practical—to applying what you discover here to your unique church situation. Only you (and your team, if you have one) can create action plans for your church, because only you know all the factors that impact your possible actions. A course of action that makes great sense at one church might create more problems than it solves at another church.

Step 5: Create Job Descriptions

This is how you define the work to be done. It's also where you decide if the work will be done by paid staff or volunteers.

Written job descriptions are essential for sound volunteer leadership. It's no different than at a paid position: Without a job description there's no way to know what each person should be doing.

If you want to see what life without job descriptions is like, attend a pick-up volleyball game being played at a church picnic. Everyone knows what's supposed to happen—his or her team is supposed to knock the ball over the net in three hits or fewer. The ball is supposed to stay inside the boundaries drawn on the grass. You hit the ball back and forth until someone scores a point, and then you start over by serving the ball back into play. Simple.

So why is actually playing the game so difficult?

The answer is usually that while everyone has a *general* idea what to do, nobody is exactly sure what his or her *specific* job is. Balls land between players who thought it was someone else's job to hit the ball back. Someone in the back row mows over two players in an attempt to spike the ball from the front row. And players rotate positions, but nobody's quite sure when that's supposed to happen.

Chaos reigns on the court . . . and chaos can reign in your church, too.

When the assistant choir director takes it upon herself to change the order of service while the choir director is out of town, is that okay? Does she really have the authority?

If the volunteer janitor finds a leaking pipe one Friday afternoon, who does he call? Who's been deputized to call for a plumber?

And when there are two office assistants, whose job is it to fold all the bulletin covers—the job *nobody* likes to do?

Job descriptions answer those questions, and more besides. They nail down what duties the volunteer job includes, who the volunteer reports to, and how long the job will last. Job descriptions provide all the information a potential volunteer needs to know to make an informed commitment.

And if you'll go to the trouble to place your volunteer job descriptions on your church web site, you'll let potential volunteers have access to information about opportunities with just a few keyboard clicks. New members can see what jobs are already available—which often prompts inquiries about those jobs or jobs that aren't there but could be.

You'll find everything you need to know about creating job descriptions in volume 3.

Step 6: Recruit Volunteers

This topic is explored in depth in volume 4 of this Volunteer Leadership Series, but here's a sneak preview definition of recruitment:

Recruitment is an invitation to come discuss a volunteer role. It doesn't mean the person responding will necessarily get the job.

For many churches, this is a revolutionary approach to filling volunteer roles. Not everyone who signs up for a job automatically gets it. Recruiting *includes* marketing, but marketing isn't the most important part of the process. It's how you communicate your message, but not everyone who responds necessarily qualifies to be a volunteer.

Don't worry—being more selective about who you place as volunteers and more particular about where you place people doesn't hurt your program. It *helps,* as you'll discover that volunteers are happier, stay longer in their roles, and happily give positive testimonies about their volunteer participation.

If recruitment has become a necessary evil, or the least favorite of your responsibilities at church, I hope you're ready for a fresh perspective on placing people in volunteer jobs. When done right, it's a *ministry* that can bring about enormous spiritual growth in the lives of volunteers.

Volunteering can be rewarding for many reasons, some of which are described in detail in volume 4. If recruitment has become a dreaded duty or an unwelcome, frustrating chore, prepare for a welcome change!

Step 7: Interview Potential Volunteers

You can't do a good job of placing people in volunteer jobs without knowing about them . . . and actually *knowing* them.

Perhaps you use surveys to collect information. That's fine, but it's incomplete. In volume 4 you'll discover the value of conducting face-to-face interviews with potential volunteers. And you'll learn how to develop and train a team of interviewers who'll do the job with excellence.

A quick word about this step in the process: It's where a tremendous amount of ministry can happen in the span of 25 or 30 minutes as potential volunteers are heard and encouraged. At church we're very good at transmitting information, and we're often excellent when it comes to providing inspiration. But there's less opportunity for people to be heard—honestly, deeply listened to—by another person.

By interviewing potential volunteers you'll provide that blessing. Plus, you'll be equipped to recommend the right volunteer roles to each potential volunteer.

Step 8: Place Volunteers

How will you ensure effective matches between volunteers and opportunities? The activities included in this step provide the critical link between the volunteer, his or her ministry supervisor, and the ministry area in which the volunteer will work.

Think of this as that last ten feet between the Space Station and one of the shuttles bringing astronauts to the Station. Everyone knows that the fittings on both vehicles will join together. There's no question that everyone is motivated for the "docking maneuvers" to go well. But no matter how far the astronauts have flown to get on board the Space Station, if they can't navigate that last ten feet and make contact, they're not getting aboard.

You'll learn what you need to do to make the connection to everyone's satisfaction: the volunteer, the volunteer's supervisor, and the people who are served by the volunteer.

Placement is more than just sending a potential volunteer down the hall to check in with the church secretary or singles pastor. You'll get a detailed list of the steps that make placement a win-win situation for everyone in volume 4.

Step 9: Train and Support Volunteers

Getting the right person in the right job is just part of what it takes to have a successful volunteer ministry. You're not successful until the volunteer has become successful, too, and that takes training and support.

How will your church orient volunteers so they have the information they need and they feel comfortable? How will you equip volunteers with the skills they need to be effective? How will you provide support if problems arise?

It's wise for you to be asking those questions, because it's certain your potential volunteers are asking them!

In volume 5 you'll discover how to provide orientation and training for information . . . skills . . . culture . . . and values. The vast majority of volunteers want to do an excellent job in their volunteer role; it's important we give them every chance to do so.

Step 10: Recognize Volunteers

How will you thank volunteers for what they do? How often? Will you affirm and thank volunteers individually, or by teams? Those are just some of the questions you'll ask—and answer—in volume 6 of this Volunteer Leadership Series.

And you'll consider more than how to create centerpieces for the annual Volunteer Appreciation Banquet. You'll think about how to provide appropriate "payoffs" for different types of volunteers as you identify what motivates them.

Step 11: Supervise Volunteers

In the same way you expect to supervise paid staff, you need to supervise volunteers. This is especially important because volunteers generally *want* to be supervised. They *want* to get better at what they're doing. They view their volunteer jobs as important and significant. They need to know you feel the same way.

You may find that supervision includes . . .

Coaching—as you work with volunteers to create and track their performance against goals, action plans, and time lines. If you want to be able to delegate to volunteers it's critical that you ensure volunteers are prepared to see the tasks and responsibilities through.

Serving as a liaison—as you help the volunteer understand the church's overall mission, goals, and policies. And, conversely, you help ministry leaders understand a volunteer's concerns.

Mentoring—as you help connect a volunteer with resources and experiences that will help the volunteer grow. Typically, it's the ministry leader to whom a volunteer reports that will fill this role, but there may be elements of mentoring in your relationships, too.

Your goal is to see that each volunteer is supervised appropriately. It's almost never appropriate for *you* to be doing direct supervision. That role will be filled by the ministry leader who directly supervises each volunteer—but you need to see that it happens.

Step 12: Evaluate Volunteers

Most people hate being evaluated. We associate it with tests we've failed or annual meetings with a boss who has a long list of our failures to review. And because we dislike *being* evaluated, we're hesitant to *do* evaluations.

Your goal is to see that each volunteer supervisor is able and willing to evaluate volunteers in his or her area—and is equipped to do helpful evaluations, *positive* evaluations.

Generally, your contribution to the cause is to ensure that there's a clear job description for each volunteer job and that performance standards are equally clear. And you must train into supervisors of volunteers the notion that performance reviews are an ongoing process, not a quarterly or annual matter. If an employee is willing to improve anytime throughout the year, why mention areas where improvement is needed just once every three months? Praise—and encouragement to grow—need to come far more often.

Make evaluations discussions rather than lectures and you'll find that volunteers actually *enjoy* them. And so will you.

There are two things you want to cover in a volunteer evaluation . . .

1. *What are the volunteer's "well-dones"?* These are the things that a volunteer is doing well and that you'd love to see continued.

2. *What are areas in which the volunteer could improve?* We all have them, and sometimes we don't see them until someone gently points them out. Begin with the assumption that the volunteer genuinely wishes to be excellent in his or her service, and help the volunteer plan how to achieve excellence.

You may discover, in the course of an evaluation, that the volunteer isn't actually doing what's in his or her job description. Maybe the person initially came on board to lay out the monthly newsletter, but now that's done on computer. So the volunteer has been running the folding and stuffing machine instead. If there's a need to adjust a job description, the evaluation is a great place to do it.

Also, ask what would help volunteers better fulfill their roles and what resources are needed. Invite volunteers' suggestions about what might help your church better fulfill its mission and goals. What ideas do volunteers have for improving how things get done?

Volunteers' suggestions are worth their weight in gold, because volunteers see and hear things that will never reach your eyes or ears. Plus, giving volunteers permission to make suggestions removes the "I'm just a volunteer" mentality that keeps some volunteers from fully engaging.

> "Volunteers' suggestions are worth their weight in gold because volunteers see and hear things that will never reach your eyes or ears."

When you've got a homemaker, a Christian educator, and a mechanical engineer all volunteering in the nursery, they're seeing that experience from three very distinct perspectives.

The homemaker will suggest ways to make the nursery a warmer, more nurturing environment.

The Christian educator will find ways to use music and interaction with the babies to do teaching.

And the mechanical engineer will figure out a way to isolate dirty diapers in an airtight container within ten seconds of the diapers being removed from the babies.

They're all helpful contributions! Be sure you ask for those ideas—and that you empower volunteers to implement good ideas they generate.

How are you doing with these 12 steps of volunteer leadership? A little self-assessment can be healthy, so pause and fill out the chart on page 89. Complete the form yourself, but first make photocopies of the chart. Give a copy to your pastor and other staff members (if there are any), and also to some of your volunteers. Then see how the answers provided by others compare to yours.

Also, chart how the answers of paid church staff compare to the answers of volunteers. Do your staff think volunteers have everything they need to be effective, but volunteers don't share that perception? If you find there's a discrepancy between how staff and volunteers perceive life, that's a great reason to go open up a dialogue with staff about why changes must be made in your current volunteer leadership process.

Volunteer Leadership Assessment Survey

	Not Done At All	Needs Improvement	Done	Done Well
Vision				
We have a clear idea where we're going, and that idea is shared by our entire church leadership.	❑	❑	❑	❑
Mission and Purpose				
We have a clearly articulated mission and purpose statement. We know what God wants us to be and do in this place, at this time.	❑	❑	❑	❑
Objectives and Goals				
We know specific things we wish to accomplish and why accomplishing those things will help us fulfill our mission and purpose.	❑	❑	❑	❑
Action Plan				
We know how we'll get things done, when, and who is responsible for results.	❑	❑	❑	❑
Job Descriptions				
We have written job descriptions for every volunteer role.	❑	❑	❑	❑
Recruitment				
We're inviting people to come discuss volunteer roles.	❑	❑	❑	❑
Interviews				
We have an established procedure (and trained interviewers) for conducting one-on-one interviews with potential volunteers.	❑	❑	❑	❑

	Not Done At All	Needs Improvement	Done	Done Well

Volunteer Placement

We have an established procedure for matching volunteers with specific volunteer opportunities.

☐ ☐ ☐ ☐

Training and Support

We have a volunteer orientation program in place and training programs that provide significant, needed information to volunteers.

☐ ☐ ☐ ☐

Volunteer Recognition

We have a planned, intentional calendar of group recognition events and/or a system for recognizing volunteers individually.

☐ ☐ ☐ ☐

Supervision

We have a system in place that provides each volunteer with competent supervision that helps volunteers develop and grow in their roles.

☐ ☐ ☐ ☐

Evaluation

Each volunteer is evaluated on a regular basis.

☐ ☐ ☐ ☐

SIX
How to Carry the Vision Forward

Two approaches for moving the Vision for Volunteerism forward—one for pastors, one for other church leaders.

What you do next to turn the future you'd like to see—where volunteerism is a natural and common part of your church's experience—depends on who you are. That is, the next step for a pastor is different from the next step for a Sunday school superintendent or youth leader.

Here are some suggestions for both groups . . .

If you're a pastor looking for a church-wide volunteer leadership system that will bring about transformational change:

• Pray about it.

Your very next step is to pray daily about the direction you believe God is calling you. Urge other church leaders to pray, too. *Is* instituting a church-wide volunteer leadership system God's direction for your church right now?

• Do your homework.

Have leaders and some of your existing volunteers (both active and inactive) fill out the Volunteer Leadership Assessment Survey (page 89) and Attitude and Behavior Survey (page 72). Summarize the data so you're ready to report what you discovered.

• Schedule a meeting with stakeholders.

Invite volunteers, church leaders, everyone who might be impacted by changes in the volunteer leadership system. The purpose of these meetings is not to condemn or create guilt, but to gain insight into where you are now and where you want to be as a congregation.

Begin your meeting(s) with devotions. Consider letting your devotions flow out of Scripture, perhaps these passages: Deuteronomy 1:9-15; 1 Corinthians 12:14-27; Ephesians 4:11-16; 1 Peter 4:9-11; or 1 Peter 5:1-3.

• Prayerfully do some dreaming about your *what-ifs*.

Ask God to give you a clear and exciting vision for where you can be, and the impact you can have in your community. Prayerfully ask God to give you a vision that lines up with his will for your church, your membership, and his plans for your neighborhood and town. Humbly seek to accomplish God's purposes.

If the vision that emerges is to have a volunteer-friendly culture throughout your church, then make it a priority to begin *now* . . . knowing it may take three to five years to accomplish such a church-wide change.

• Select a task force to take responsibility for implementation.

This topic will be covered in depth in volume 2, with step-by-step help to guide you through the process. You'll find photocopiable forms, as well as agendas for meetings. It's all there for you except for one thing—your willingness to turn over control of the process to someone else.

It may well be that you're not the right person to coordinate this effort. That's not a reflection on you personally; it's a recognition that as the pastor of your church you have other roles to fulfill. Plus, if the change is to be authentic throughout the church, having decisions made and implemented by lay people is essential.

The final outcome in a few years may not be precisely what you envisioned, or accomplished in quite the way you'd have done it, but it will be in place and powerful. Your church will have ownership of the process. And it will be successful and working.

Are you willing to trust your congregation to move ahead with something that's so important? After all, they're just volunteers.

By the way, if you're nodding in agreement with that last paragraph, please review the three theologies at the beginning of this volume. Your church members certainly *can* be trusted to do significant ministry! God wired them for it!

• Provide support and encouragement.

Your task force is going to hit some rough water along the way. It will be a wonderful contribution if you continually provide support for the project from the pulpit and in prayer.

If you're the leader of a ministry area and you're looking to transform just your corner of the church:

You'd like to change the entire congregation's view of volunteers and volunteerism, but that's beyond the scope of your abilities. Fine-tune the process in only your own ministry area and you'll see results in the lives of your volunteers and the lives they touch.

Here's how to move ahead implementing the volunteer leadership process in just the youth ministry area, or Christian education area, or wherever else you serve and lead.

• Begin with prayer.

Shifting how volunteers are brought on board and retained just *seems* like a small thing—it's huge! The impact will be felt church-wide even if you have nothing to do with another ministry area.

Volunteers will be treated differently in your piece of the organization. You'll do things for and with your volunteers that won't be part of every church volunteer's experience. You can expect to hear some questions about what you're doing and why. And you may discover that volunteers from other areas begin to migrate your direction.

And that will very quickly be noticed by other volunteer leaders.

How to Keep Anonymous Surveys Anonymous

You'll get more honest answers if survey responders trust that their responses will *truly* be kept anonymous— that you won't know who said what.

You can accomplish that by enlisting the help of a trusted person who is not closely associated with you. The pastor's secretary, for instance, or a trusted church layperson.

Along with the surveys include a note directing respondents to return their surveys to that trusted person, who will compile the information, re-key all written comments in a separate document, and then destroy all original surveys—without showing them to you.

Prayerfully ask God for both guidance and grace. Be sure your motivation is for the good of the volunteers you serve, not to "show the pastor how it's done" or to rustle a few volunteers away from other ministry areas.

Pray daily for guidance regarding which functions in the 12-step Volunteer Leadership System will offer the most help to your program. (It's often Volunteer Ministry Job Descriptions and Interviewing.) Confirm this with your present volunteers. Be realistic.

• Honestly fill out all the assessment tools in this chapter.

The Volunteer Leadership Assessment Survey (page 89) and Attitude and Behavior Survey (page 72) will give you huge insights—but not necessarily ones you enjoy. Ask some of your volunteers to anonymously fill out the surveys and compare their answers with your own. You may discover you don't understand life as volunteers in your church experience it.

• Prepare spiritually.

Do personal or team devotions that flow out of some of the passages listed on page 92. Let God speak to you about how he wants to use his church to impact the world. (Deuteronomy 1:9-15; 1 Corinthians 12:14-27; Ephesians 4:11-16; 1 Peter 4:9-11; or 1 Peter 5:1-3.)

• Watch for God's timing.

When you feel God's nudging, pursue one or two volunteer functions you want to add, or in which you want to improve volunteer participation. The resources you'll find in this series of books will help you.

• Keep moving ahead—but not alone.

Remember, one of our goals is that you not burn out. Getting volunteers to help you in significant ways is key to that goal. Volume 2 of this series will walk you through how to accomplish that task, and then to move on into gradually making the changes that will implement your vision for volunteerism.

SEVEN
Let the Countdown Begin

Before you get to the "how-to's" of the rest of this series, here's one last chance to make sure you're ready for blastoff.

Maybe I'm showing my age, but I remember the days when space launches weren't everyday occurrences.

Astronauts were national heroes in America, and when a lift-off was scheduled, every television channel (all three or four of them!) canceled all other programming to have cameras trained on the rocket standing on the launch pad.

Commentators breathlessly followed the ticking of the countdown clock, and it wasn't until the booster rockets started to rumble and a voice counted down 10 . . . 9 . . . 8 . . . 7 . . . all the way to 1 that we knew for sure the switch had been pulled and the launch was a "go."

Well, your volunteer program is on the launch pad. Maybe you've already got an organized program, so it's presumptuous for me to assume that you're starting from scratch. For you, this is more like that time in a space launch when the massive booster rockets break off and fall back to earth. You're firing up your secondary rockets that will push you up and out of the gravitational pull that's holding you back.

Either way—whether you're taking off from the ground or making mid-course corrections—there's a universe out there to explore.

- You've got your vision set; you know where you want to go. You've suited up and have everything you need to push into the launch.

- You've considered the three theologies that are the foundation of a biblical approach to volunteer leadership.

- You've decided it's worth dealing with the personal change that's going to be required.

- You have determined if your church is volunteer-friendly and have thought through how to deal with any issues that have arisen.

- You've defined your preferred future as you've worked through the 12-step process. You're ready to carry the volunteer program forward.

So what could possibly be left to do before you move into the final countdown and push the switch to "launch"?

Just this: a final check, just like they run in the space program. There on the launch pad, with the astronauts strapped in and ready to go, just before the final launch sequence, there's yet one final check to confirm that everything is in place and prepared.

If you're absolutely sure you're set, skip ahead to the next volume in this series. But if you'd like one last confirmation that you're ready for launch, read through the following pages.

Ten

You've switched your paradigm about volunteer leadership.

If you have any reservations about the three theologies I discussed in chapter 1, settle them now. It's time to stop looking at volunteers as the means to an end: completing tasks.

Instead, volunteers *are* the end. Getting them involved in ministry is worthwhile in itself. Even if they don't complete tasks the way you'd like, on the schedule you'd prefer, they're growing in discipleship because of their effort and commitment.

Switching paradigms is often a matter of looking at a situation ("I've got to get stuff done and I have to use volunteers") with new values in mind.

For example, one summer I took a few weeks off from a hectic travel schedule. My intent was to get off airplanes and out of hotels for a while and enjoy my lovely mountain home west of Boulder. I determined that one thing I wanted to do to enhance my vacation at home was plant my rock garden with all kinds of lovely flowers.

The difficulty was that each year I'd planted flowers, deer came and ate them.

I went to the best mountain nursery in town and asked for the most deer resistant plants they had. One of the nursery workers designed a garden for me, then helped me plant the most spectacular garden I'd ever had. I also followed their expert advice on how to keep the deer away. This included adding blood meal to the soil, spraying the plants with Repel, and sprinkling everything with cayenne pepper.

For several days I sat on my deck, read, and looked down on my beautiful garden. Then I began to notice there were fewer and fewer flowers. I was mystified. I hadn't seen any herd of deer in my yard, but the flowers were steadily disappearing.

Then, one morning as I sat on the deck, I heard a funny wheezing, coughing sound. I looked down at my garden, and there was a deer chomping away at my flowers. Apparently she had asthma and couldn't smell a thing!

I began to wage a battle to save my flowers. I rushed out to the deck earlier and earlier each morning. I hated to leave my house for fear the asthmatic deer would again invade my flower garden and turn it into a salad buffet.

And all the time I was defending the garden I was missing the point that my vacation was being ruined. There wasn't any relaxing going on—not for me or the deer.

I finally realized I needed to change my paradigm. So, I went from thinking "flowers are beautiful" to "deer are beautiful." Then I relaxed, read, and watched my doe eat contentedly through my summer break.

That's when I became convinced of the power of paradigms!

Any paradigm shifting you feel convicted to do before we jump into the practical, how-to suggestions you'll find in volume 2?

Now is the time.

The countdown has begun.

Nine . . .

You're ready to treat volunteers as full partners in ministry.

And not just you—everyone in leadership who will impact your volunteer program. You recognize that you're not "recruiting helpers" or "filling positions"; you're inviting members of the body of Christ to participate fully in service.

That may mean you need to teach some church leaders to delegate. You may have to renegotiate expectations on how tasks are accomplished. And you'll *definitely* need to see to it that volunteers receive the same respect that paid staff receive.

Part of what will fuel this change is a willingness of paid staff to incorporate in their definition of "success" the answer to this question: "How many people did we involve in the process?" We need to understand that encouraging a significant contribution from several people is often better than accomplishing the same task through the zealous efforts of one person. It's not more efficient. It's not necessarily cheaper. But it accomplishes more.

And consider how you define the words "ministry" and "service." Does it *have* to happen within your church building, or within your church's family of believers? What about a church member who serves through a community agency, or simply spends two evenings per week with a shut-in neighbor? Is that Christian ministry, too?

The answer varies from denomination to denomination and congregation to congregation. I've personally been made to feel like a deserter at times, especially when a ministry in the community has been my primary focus. Some people didn't view that as "real church work." They still don't.

But today's church members seek validation for their ministry not only in church, but in the community, and also through their vocations and occupations.

After all, that's what being "in the world but not of it" is all about.

Eight

You're ready to help people discover their abilities, skills, and passions for ministry.

My friend Nancy Gaston shared this account with me from her work with volunteers at church:

"I conducted an interview with a woman who wasn't sure what she wanted to do. She was a retired home economics teacher but didn't care to teach.

"In the course of the interview she mentioned the church library—what a good collection of books we had, but how it seemed disorganized. Further questions revealed she knew little about organizing libraries but had always been fascinated by the process.

"With some instruction from a librarian and some printed materials, she learned to catalog and process all the new books and to supervise volunteers who kept the library organized and attractive.

"She agreed to 'try it for a year' and is still at it five years later—and loving the job."

Note that the job at which the retired home economics teacher excelled wasn't teaching Sunday school. It wasn't cooking for the church dinners. The job didn't actually *exist* until the woman identified it herself. It was her passion that recommended her for the position.

You're ready to help people discover their abilities, skills, and passions for ministry when you're ready to let *volunteers* lead you toward placement rather than letting open *positions* dictate what you'll recommend.

Still on the launch pad? Good—let's continue the count-down . . .

Seven . . .
You're ready to deal with organizational change.

I firmly believe the best possible way to do volunteer recruitment is through a centrally organized function: by establishing a Volunteer Director who interviews across the entire church and refers volunteers to various ministries.

But that may not be where you are. You may have neither the resources, time, or influence to make that happen. You may be the person who's struggling to get enough greeters at the doors each Sunday. What happens in the youth department may be the furthest thing from your mind.

Listen—as you institute changes you're launching your church on a journey. You've determined where you are, and you have a vision for where you want to be, so you've got a destination mapped out. All that's left to decide is how you want to go about getting there.

I once was giving a speech to a national conference of Methodist educators. Their theme was "The Christian Journey," and as part of my preparation I looked for a good definition of the word "journey." I discovered there were three general understandings of the word:

"Moving, progressing, trek, and pilgrimage" summarize the first understanding of "journey." This is a purposeful journey where you're making progress.

"Wandering, roaming, rambling, and drifting" summarize the second understanding. This is a journey that's somehow strayed off course. These journeyers are making progress . . . but they may not know where they're headed.

"Creeping, crawling, pussyfooting, or groveling" summarize the third understanding. This timid journeyer is barely making any progress at all—and may not *want* to make much.

I realized with amazement that I know people—and churches—who represent all three kinds of journeys. But what a difference how they take a journey makes in the destination they reach, and the fun and excitement they have getting there!

If you're beginning a journey of change, determine now what sort of a journey you want it to be. Do you want to move boldly and purposefully? ramble along? or plod along?

Wherever you are in your ministry of connecting volunteers with appropriate service opportunities, taking the next step will cause some disruption. Have you prepared spiritually? Are you praying? Did you skip over the suggestions that you do devotions on selected passages (see pages 92 and 94)? If you haven't meditated on those passages, do so before you go further. Let God's Word guide and sustain you through the rapids of change you'll likely encounter.

Six
You're ready to be changed—personally.

In the Old Testament, God's message to the patriarch Abraham was, "You are blessed to be a blessing." For me, this statement sums up the rightful relationship between receiving and giving, and between beliefs and action.

I believe that each of us has been given unique abilities, skills, and passions. The true joy of these gifts is only realized when we share them with others. Hoarding or ignoring them brings nothing to anyone, including ourselves.

Once in a while we experience truly life-changing events. What's strange about these events is that on the surface they often appear to be ordinary, even mundane occurrences. Nothing amazing, nothing spectacular, nothing that makes a journal entrance.

Yet, when those moments come we somehow know that our life will never again be the same.

One of those events happened to me while I was reading an article in a denominational magazine. At the time it seemed I was just reading another couple of magazine columns, but my response to that article catapulted me out of my safe, comfortable church pew and into a hurting world.

The article was entitled "So You Ask Me What Is Poverty?" In it a woman who had lived in poverty all her life graphically described how being poor felt, tasted, and smelled—and how hopeless she felt as she watched her children become trapped in the same web of despair.

It has been more than three decades, but I remember that long-lost article ended with these words: "I did not come from another time. I did not come from another place. I am here, now . . . and there are others like me all around you."

Something in that woman's story spoke to my deepest being and made the command to be "doers of the word and not hearers only" come alive for me. I fell to my knees and prayed the only prayer possible, "I'm available, Lord. Show me what you would have me do."

Since that day, more than 35 years ago, I've been on an incredible journey of discovery. The Lord has led me, sometimes gently and sometimes by the scruff of the neck, to people and places in this world that are hurting. This journey began as I served as one of the volunteer founders and then executive director of an agency designed to match volunteers with the needs and resources of my community. We handled hundred of calls for help and found agencies, churches, or individual volunteers who provided what was needed. We also served as the connector between volunteers and more than 90 health, youth, senior, and welfare agencies. What an education—to finally learn about need in the specific versus thinking of it in the abstract.

My life was changed when I told God that I was available. Your life will change, too.

My life was changed when I became willing to serve people who want to do ministry in and through the church. Your life will change too.

Are you ready for a life change?

Good . . . because we're just about ready to blast off.

Five

You're serious about getting every volunteer trained.

Adequate training takes more than lectures. There's mentoring involved, and time for people to grow into their responsibilities. There's direction and encouragement.

And there's a decision made by your church's leadership that adequate training is a priority worthy of funding and focus.

One of my favorite stories about training involves a teenage boy who was preparing to teach Sunday school for the first time. He was assigned to the four- and five-year-olds, and he took his new volunteer job seriously.

It was Wednesday night and already he was sitting at the kitchen table studying the lesson, highlighting sections, and writing notes in the margins of his lesson guide.

His mother came into the room and saw him concentrating fiercely, so she asked him what he was planning to teach.

"Well," he answered, "the lesson plan says to show the kids that each person is an individual with different potential and abilities; that each person is valuable for their particular capabilities. . . and that there is value in differences as well as conformity."

His mother was deeply impressed until her son then added with a sigh, "And if that doesn't work, I guess we'll make clay bunnies."

That young man knew *what* to do . . . but no idea how to actually *do* it. He wasn't trained to accomplish the job that had been delegated to him.

You're ready to do training, right? No clay bunnies for *your* children!

The countdown is even closer now . . . prepare for blastoff.

Four

You're determined to do systematic, careful interviewing and placement.

There are shortcuts in every system, but when it comes to volunteer recruitment and placement, shortcuts are also shortchanges.

Skip interviewing and you shortchange every volunteer of the opportunity to be known and affirmed. You remove any way to collect the very information you most need to guide volunteers to the most appropriate places of service. And, if the truth be known, you remove one part of your job that's a lot of fun.

I'm guessing you're a "people person," someone who enjoys working with people more than working with things or manipulating data. That certainly describes most of the volunteer managers I've known through the years, though they're also able to create budgets and track people. But if left to their own devices, they'd rather spend time getting to know people and helping people.

Interviewing is where that begins. It's a valuable tool and great fun.

And if you place volunteers too quickly, or without their full involvement, you shortchange the volunteers and the people they'll be serving.

Trust me: You can do a poor job thanking volunteers and giving them the recognition they deserve, and many of those kind-hearted people will stick with you anyway. They'll hang in there because they find the job they're doing so rewarding.

But if you get a volunteer in the wrong job, you're doomed. The volunteer is doomed. It will be an unrewarding experience, and the volunteer won't find a good enough reason to stick.

Build a good system. Follow it. Don't settle for shortcuts.

Settle back in your seat. You're about ready for liftoff.

Three . . .

You've decided it's worth the effort to see it through.

When you picked up this series you may have thought it held the silver bullet that would fix everything in your church with one simple action.

Unfortunately, that's not the case. If it were, you'd have undoubtedly done it yourself. My colleagues and I have absolute confidence that you're the right person in your church to do volunteer leadership. You care enough to launch the rocket or fine-tune your orbit. You want what's best for your volunteers and your congregation.

But you now know it won't be a quick, easy fix. There are systems to put in place, biases to weed out, and good habits to form. And it's not just for you—you need to have your entire leadership buy into the changes that are coming.

Is it worth it? Yes—for at least three reasons:

It's worth it for your volunteers. You'll mobilize volunteers and give believers a chance to plug into appropriate ministries. They'll grow, blossoming as they do what God designed them to do.

It's worth it for your community. We live in a hurting and unchurched world. We must learn to be the scattered church, reaching out to the communities in which we live. That reaching out begins within our communities of faith, but it stretches out beyond, too. You'll help your church's ministry move beyond the walls of the church, and believe me—those people need you.

It's worth it for your church. Do you know what the major difference is between the Red Sea—a life-giving body of water that teems with fish—and the Dead Sea, which kills fish almost instantly?

They're both seas. They both have streams feeding into them.

It's that the Dead Sea has no way for water to flow *out* of it. The salt and other minerals that are washed into the Dead Sea accumulate there and build in intensity. The Red Sea is fed by streams and also empties into others—and that gives the Red Sea life.

If your congregation is focused only on what happens within your walls, you're the Dead Sea. If you're pouring out the sparkling, God-inspired life you have into others, you're the Red Sea.

Share the life you've been given.

Do you feel the booster rockets rumbling beneath you?

Two . . .
You're determined to create a volunteer-friendly culture in your church.

It won't be quick. It may not be pretty. But it *is* achievable.

My experience says that authentic change may well take three to five years. You'll see dramatic improvements in your recruitment efforts as soon as you start using the 12-step volunteer leadership process my colleagues and I will share with you in this series of books.

But until your church's very culture changes, you're sticking little plastic bandages on deep, deep cancers. The temporary fixes are good, but they won't last unless your church leadership believes the three theologies I've outlined. Unless your congregation comes to understand that using their God-given abilities, skills, and passions for service isn't optional. Unless you're willing to embrace changes that will allow leadership to delegate thoroughly, volunteers to respond faithfully, and people to serve joyfully.

Are you ready? You're looking to create a place where what happened at a church I know can happen frequently at your church.

A retired woman had been an accountant for many years, and after retirement she didn't slow down a bit. She became deeply involved in community and church volunteering.

She said, "Now that I'm retired, I can give all my time to service and church-related projects . . . I don't give of myself because I 'should.' I don't like the word 'should' because that makes me feel I have to do something, and takes the joy out of it for me. I'm just selfishly doing what makes me happy."

Wouldn't you like to have a culture where people looked forward to getting involved as volunteers—because it made them happy?

The thunder you hear is the power of the rockets building thrust beneath you. You're nearly on your way to a grand adventure . . .

ONE
You have a clear vision—and God's permission to get started.

Have you determined that God wants you to improve how volunteer leadership is done in your congregation? Do you know where you're headed?

If so, Godspeed. We're here to help.

Let nothing stop you.

God bless you.

Liftoff.

Core Values of Volunteer Leadership

- Every volunteer experience in the church should encourage a healthy relationship with Jesus Christ.

- We believe everyone in the body of Christ has something to give to the corporate body.

- Volunteers are respected as full partners in ministry.

- Volunteers can be any age.

- It's better to leave a volunteer position unfilled than to put the wrong person in the position.

- We provide the resources and training that volunteers need to be successful.

- It's okay for potential volunteers to say "no" to a request.

- Volunteer motivation and retention are outcomes of doing other things right.

- Volunteer leadership happens best when there's a centralized volunteer leadership function.

- Episodic volunteering is legitimate.

- We won't let volunteers burn out.

- The good of a local congregation supercedes the good of an individual volunteer.

- And we admit it: We can't motivate volunteers.

HOW TO ENERGIZE YOUR VOLUNTEER MINISTRY

Susan A. Waechter and Deborah L. Kocsis

Marlene Wilson, General Editor

Group's Volunteer Leadership Series™
Volume 2
Group's Church Volunteer Central™

Loveland, Colorado

Group's Volunteer Leadership Series™, Volume 2

How to Energize Your Volunteer Ministry

Visit our Web site: **www.grouppublishing.com**

Credits
Authors: Susan A Waechter and Deborah L. Kocsis
Editor: Mikal Keefer
General Editor: Marlene Wilson
Chief Creative Officer: Joani Schultz
Art Director: Nathan Hindman
Cover Designer: Jeff Storm
Production Manager: Peggy Naylor

Unless otherwise noted, Scripture taken from the HOLY BIBLE, NEW INTERNATIONAL VERSION®. Copyright © 1973, 1978, 1984 by International Bible Society. Used by permission of Zondervan Publishing House. All rights reserved.

Produced with the assistance of The Livingstone Corporation (www.LivingstoneCorp.com). Project staff includes Chris Hudson, Ashley Taylor, Mary Horner Collins, Joel Bartlett, Cheryl Dunlop, Mary Larsen, and Rosalie Krusemark.

Library of Congress Cataloging-in-Publication Data

Waechter, Susan A.
How to energize your volunteer ministry / by Susan A. Waechter and
      Deborah L. Kocsis ; Marlene Wilson, general editor.—1st American
      hardbound ed.
     p. cm. — (Group's volunteer leadership series ; v. 2)
     Includes bibliographical references.
     ISBN 0-7644-2746-6 (alk. paper)
     1. Voluntarism—Religious aspects—Christianity. 2. Christian
leadership. 3. Church work. I. Kocsis, Deborah L. II. Wilson, Marlene. III. Title. IV. Series.
BR115.V64W34 2003
253'.7—dc22   2003022119

10 9 8 7 6 5 4 3 2 1   12 11 10 09 08 07 06 05 04

Printed in the United States of America.

Contents

Contents

7. The Leadership-Energized Volunteer Ministry

A task force can take you just so far. It's time to put someone in charge . . . someone who'll keep the volunteer ministry energized and on task.

Meeting with Leaders to Create a Volunteer Ministry

Sample Volunteer Ministry Vision and Mission Statements

Creating Vision and Mission Statements

Volunteer Ministry Manager Sample Job Descriptions

Introduction

How to build an energized volunteer ministry that thrives . . . even after you're gone.

You're determined to move ahead with your vision for a volunteer program that supports and empowers your church's ministries . . . good!

You want to involve church members in appropriate volunteer roles that make use of their unique abilities, skills, and passions . . . even better!

You've got a vision that's compelling. A desire to see change happen. A commitment to see that change through . . . outstanding!

So . . . *now* what?

The remainder of this Volunteer Leadership Series is packed with step-by-step help implementing the management process Marlene shared in volume 1. You'll get lots of practical assistance putting in place the practices that will ensure you create an effective volunteer ministry.

But before we dive into the details, let's pause, take a deep breath, and talk about how you can build a volunteer ministry that's *energized*—that's going to thrive long term.

An energized ministry is one that isn't dependent on you to survive.

You may be the visionary who launches the ministry, or who helps it move to the next level, but in time it won't need you to survive. It's a bit like raising a child—in time you want that child to be self-sufficient. Energized, thriving programs are the same way. You're a steward of the program, not the owner; it belongs to God.

An energized ministry is one that finds its own pace and place.

By that we mean your volunteer ministry will probably change as time goes on. That's okay, because it's adapting to meet the needs of the church as *it* changes.

Twenty years ago, few churches had the need for someone to run the sound board or media desk; today volunteers have those roles. And in 1975 if you'd asked someone to handle the information technology needs of your church, you'd have been met with a blank stare. Now any 14-year-old nods sagely and asks what sort of computer equipment is in the church office.

For a ministry to thrive, it must have built into it the ability to adapt and change to meet not just the *current* needs of your church, but the church's *future* needs.

And to thrive, your volunteer ministry needs to have a place at the table when church leaders are determining budgets and priorities. Thriving ministries aren't afterthoughts or stepchildren; they're regarded as highly as other church programs.

An energized ministry is powerful.

Not powerful in the "I can rule the world" sense of the word, but in the kingdom sense of the word. Energized, thriving programs serve others. They praise God. They cooperate with God's purposes.

Energized ministries are also powerful because they're fueled by something. They roll on and on, adapting and changing as needed because somehow their tanks are being filled by enthusiasm, funding, and purpose.

Now is the time to make sure your ministry is adequately energized. A thriving volunteer ministry must be powered in four ways:

- It must be powered by people—including both church leaders and the congregation as a whole,

- It must be powered by vision,

- It must be powered by mission, and

- It must be powered by prayer.

In this volume we'll tell you how to design your ministry so you're energized and sustained by all four power sources.

Building a volunteer ministry is a great thing. Volunteers grow in their Christian faith, and through those volunteers other lives are touched. The mission of your church is supported. Your efforts in creating or improving your volunteer ministry will return fruit a hundredfold.

But when you build an *energized* volunteer ministry that thrives—one that keeps giving and growing long after your involvement with it ends—that's an effort that returns fruit a *thousand*fold.

If you're going to create, rejuvenate, or tweak your volunteer ministry, why not do it right? Why not create an energized, thriving ministry that's built to last?

You can do it—and we'll help. In this volume not only will you discover how to stay connected to energizing power, but we'll help you form a task force to help shoulder the leadership load. Then we'll show you how to transition from that task force to a volunteer director.

You'll also get a quick tutorial on how to ease your church through the changes that building an energized ministry creates. You'll learn to *gain permission* for making changes and keep your progress on track.

Energizing power. Solid leadership structure. Helping others embrace change. They're all essential ingredients in an energized, thriving volunteer ministry.

ONE
The People-Energized Volunteer Ministry

An energized volunteer ministry is powered by people—both the church leadership and church membership. Here's how to involve people you need in a task force that gets things done.

Some evening after everyone else has left the building, walk through the facility where your church meets. Perhaps you have your own building; maybe you rent or borrow a space. It doesn't matter—just go when the lights are dim and the rooms are quiet.

What do you see?

You see tables and chairs. Books and curriculum. Scuffed tiles and empty nursery cribs. Stuff. You see stuff. Lots of stuff.

But what you *don't* see is the church.

The "church"—the bride of Christ—is made up of people. *We're* the church, not the stuff we use to make programs happen. Nothing you see or touch or taste as you make your tour of the empty facility is designed to last for eternity (though the

> "People are the point, so involve them!"

janitor might disagree about the dried gum shoved up under the tables). Only people are made to last forever.

And at church, without people nothing happens.

In your volunteer ministry, without people nothing happens.

People are the point, so involve them!

We'd like to suggest that you be intentional about involving several groups of people as you launch or revitalize your volunteer ministry.

The first group is church leaders. These are people who, quite simply, have influence. Others tend to follow these people whether or not the leaders have formal leadership positions. Their opinions are sought in decision-making and problem-solving.

The second group is the church membership. These are people who have a stake in your congregation and identify with the church and its ministries. As Marlene Wilson discussed in the first volume of this Volunteer Leadership Series, they have gifts to give and ministries to provide—but they may not know how or where. The vast majority of your volunteers will come from this group of people.

First, let's take a look at how involving church leaders can energize your volunteer ministry.

When Church Leaders Get Involved, the Program Is Energized

A leadership-powered volunteer ministry happens when most, if not all, of these identified leaders are making decisions that support the volunteer ministry.

What does it look like when the leaders in your church plug into your volunteer ministry and provide power and support? It looks like this . . .

- There's encouragement for the ministry—both privately in conversations, and publicly from the pulpit and in church-wide written communications.

- Resources flow to the ministry. Because the value of the ministry is understood and appreciated, needed resources (an office, supplies, time with the pastor) are available.

- There's personal involvement from leaders. When there's an appreciation banquet for volunteers, church leaders attend. When volunteers are asked to stand and be recognized in the church service, church leaders lead the applause. And when the ministry needs help, church leaders step up to personally respond.

Having church leaders actively involved is important because, by definition, where leaders go, others follow. Your church's leaders define the congregation's priorities not only by what they say, but by what they do. Where do they devote their time and attention? What church ministries get their undivided attention? What ministries get enthusiastic mentions on Sunday morning?

> "Your church's leaders define the congregation's priorities."

If the volunteer ministry is among those favored ministries, the congregation will begin to think of it the same way.

As you develop volunteer ministry, keep in mind you need the full understanding and support of church leadership. You need it in part because the volunteer ministry is unique—it doesn't reside in just one ministry area of the church. It's not the exclusive property of the children's ministry or the administrative area. It intersects with all ministries within your church, because when there's a ministry there are usually volunteers. The person leading your volunteer ministry needs access to *all* ministry leaders within your church.

When there's a program or ministry in the church that isn't powered by leadership, there's often a poor outcome. Consider the following true story . . .

A Story without a Happy Ending

This story begins with a group of nine committed volunteers who wanted to bring a midweek children's program to their church. The program already existed in other churches, so the volunteers took vacation time from their jobs to go receive training in how to organize and run the program.

The volunteer team met almost weekly for months to get the program up and running, and one of the pastors was committed enough to travel with them to receive training.

It looked like all systems were go, and everything was running along like clockwork. The team recruited more than 35 volunteers to be part of the midweek ministry, from working in the kitchen to providing meals for the children and volunteers, to teaching a Bible study curriculum.

The first few months of the ministry went well. Both the leaders and children were having fun. Attendance stayed high and enthusiastic . . . until something changed.

The church leaders who had been so involved and excited about the program quit participating. The church staff had other programs to run, and before long the midweek program fell off their radar screen. Even the pastor who'd been trained to help run the program faded away.

Soon the volunteers noticed that paid staff wasn't participating, and the volunteers started to feel ignored. When the program's second semester was launched, enrollment of children dipped, and it became increasingly difficult to recruit and retain adult volunteers. Church leaders were actively soliciting volunteers for *other* programs, since the midweek effort was established.

Within the year a very painful decision was made to abandon the midweek program. The dedication of many volunteers was essentially negated, and to this day some of those volunteers have not become fully involved in other work of the church.

Was the decision to cancel the program a good one? a bad one? We don't know—but we *do* know one reason the program faltered was that key leaders pulled out, resulting in volunteers losing focus and energy.

The senior pastor can't be personally involved in every church program. That's not practical. But for church ministries to be connected and powered by leadership, *some* leader needs to be in the loop.

We also know of ministries where senior leadership participated for a time and then left—*but that was part of the plan.*

Everyone knew that the pastor wouldn't stay on the worship committee long-term; the pastor's role was understood to be temporary, so when he left it was with the blessings of everyone involved. He'd made his contribution during the vision and mission stages of the committee formation; now he was done. No one felt abandoned.

Had the team putting together the midweek program asked some hard questions (listed below), expectations would have been realistic and the level of commitment from leadership understood from the beginning.

And the program may well have survived the leadership crisis it experienced.

Without the support of church leaders, volunteers feel unsupported and unrecognized for their efforts and contribution. When leaders aren't actively demonstrating support, the congregation tends to have a lukewarm commitment to a church ministry. For better or worse, church members take their cues from church leaders.

So you want the volunteer ministry to be energized by people in leadership. You *need* to have the volunteer ministry energized by people in leadership. How do you make that happen?

> "For better or worse, church members take their cues from church leaders."

How to Create a Leadership-Energized Volunteer Ministry

There are two steps in gaining leadership energy for your program: Engage church leaders from the beginning, and keep leaders in the information loop at all times.

Engage leaders from the beginning.

Meet with church staff to determine their level of interest and commitment to a volunteer ministry. In the meeting, discuss the leaders' vision for the volunteer program and how they see the program impacting the church's mission. Share information freely, and allow time for dialogue. This meeting is a great time to determine who on the staff will serve as an "invested individual" and participate in the vision statement and mission statement meetings (more about those later in the next two chapters).

You can expect to hear that a volunteer ministry is important. Those words will be comforting, but what also counts is how church leaders will become involved and stay involved as the ministry develops. It's fair to ask some hard, probing questions:

- How do you think God intends for our church members to be engaged in service to one another and the community?

- How do you think our congregation will benefit from a more organized volunteer ministry? (Describe what a "more organized volunteer ministry" would look like.)

- What specific things can we improve when it comes to getting our members more involved in the work of the church?

- How would being more involved in a volunteer ministry benefit the members of our church?

- How much time will you commit to getting this effort started, and then to providing ongoing support?

"Don't be hesitant to directly ask for support."

- Where do you see the volunteer ministry residing in the organization? Who will be responsible for it?

- What resources will the church devote to the ministry (for example, financial support, people, space, equipment)?

As you discuss the leaders' commitment to the volunteer ministry, don't be hesitant to directly ask for support. Be prepared to define "support" so leaders know precisely what you're asking. Here are some possible questions that get at specific ways to provide support.

- Will you frequently refer to the volunteer ministry in meetings and from the pulpit?

- Will you describe the impact of the volunteer ministry on how our church is accomplishing the church's mission?

- Will you tell people you expect them to be involved in service through the volunteer ministry?

- Will you attend some or all of the meetings for the volunteer ministry? If not, what church leader will?

- Will you periodically write articles for the church newsletter about the volunteer ministry and what it's accomplishing?

These sort of actions set an example for the rest of the congregation and also cement your relationship with church leadership. They energize the ministry!

And here's some practical help: If you want to meet with your church leadership to present the volunteer ministry, consider adapting and using the leadership meeting outline on page 84.

Keep leadership in the information loop.

When we're thinking and praying about something, it naturally takes a place of priority in our lives. We identify with it.

That's one reason you want to keep church leaders in the information loop—so they'll have the volunteer ministry top of mind. They'll remember to pray for you and the ministry. They'll be inclined to send possible volunteers to you. They'll think of the ministry as a solution to challenges that arise in church programming.

But delivering information—reports, briefings, and statistics—isn't the only way to keep in touch with your church leaders. Consider these practical approaches for closing the distance between your leadership and the volunteer ministry:

- Create a recognizable logo for the volunteer ministry and use it often. It will remind leaders that you're out there and available.

- Create bookmarks for leaders to use in their daily devotional materials.

- Send simple, quick-read e-mails with messages about the volunteer ministry. Make the messages encouraging and upbeat.

- Create a button for people involved in the ministry to wear on their lapels.

- Insert a page of accomplishments or outcomes from the volunteer ministry in the church newsletter.

- Send birthday cards celebrating the milestones in the volunteer ministry to the leaders to share successes of the ministry. (for example: "Happy Birthday to our volunteer ministry! We're officially one year old!")

> "Be intentional about bringing the volunteer ministry to the attention of your church leaders."

- Highlight leaders in the church newsletter and talk about their connection to the volunteer ministry.

- Include a celebration during National Volunteer Week. (In the United States, it's usually in April.)

- Give a volunteer ministry statistic during each leadership meeting.

- Include key leaders on the initial task force (find out how to create a task force on page 19).

Be intentional about bringing the volunteer ministry to

the attention of your church leaders. You aren't bragging when you tell of the success volunteers are having in doing effective ministry. You aren't lacking humility if you draw attention to what God is doing in the volunteer ministry. Rather, you're celebrating a ministry that will bless both your volunteers and the church leaders who rely on those volunteers.

Consider this passage, where the Bible writer shares his joy at hearing how a friend is being faithful in his ministry and message . . .

> *It gave me great joy to have some brothers come and tell about your faithfulness to the truth and how you continue to walk in the truth. I have no greater joy than to hear that my children are walking in the truth. (3 John 3:3-4)*

Your pastor feels the same way. Brighten your pastor's day with a good report about what's happening in the volunteer ministry.

When Church Members Get Involved, the Program Is Energized

We like to think of creating a membership-energized volunteer ministry as creating a groundswell.

A groundswell is actually a wave in the ocean—a powerful wave in the open sea, the result of an earthquake, a storm, or another event far away. The wave can travel thousands of miles, and while they're sometimes hard to notice on the open sea, they hit the shore with surprising force.

Perhaps that's why the term "groundswell" has come to mean unexpected support that builds for a cause or political candidate. At first you may not even notice the momentum building, but then it's there, and it's powerful.

You want your volunteer ministry to have a "groundswell" feel to it. That is, it needs to have an exciting, excellent reputation that draws people to it. It needs to build power as it travels along. You want people to be *clamoring* to join as volunteers, and for the energy to grow as it radiates throughout the congregation.

A groundswell of support is spread over a large number of

people. It doesn't depend on one person climbing up on a soapbox and expounding the virtues of the volunteer ministry.

Groundswells can't be manufactured. They come about because something happens—an event, a success, a testimonial—that generates a response in people.

You can't *make* it happen . . . but you can *encourage* it.

And a great place to begin encouraging support is by creating a volunteer ministry task force that will in time energetically help spread the word about the ministry.

In the same way the senior pastor can't participate in every church ministry and planning meeting, neither can every church member get involved on your task force. In fact, you don't *want* every church member serving on the task force. The group would be too large and unwieldy. Nothing would ever be decided.

> **"You're looking for people who will be the hands and hearts of the volunteer ministry."**

You're looking for a small group of people who'll infuse the ministry with the people-power that flows from the members of your congregation. You're looking for people who will be the hands and hearts of the volunteer ministry. You're looking for people who'll help you enjoy the benefits of synergy.

Synergy: 1 + 1 = 3

We often use the word "synergy" to describe what happens when people work together and a groundswell forms. Synergy is an equation that lets you add one plus one and get a total of three. Odd math, but it represents what happens when people join forces to work together on a task force or other project. Properly focused, their output is greater than the sum of the individuals working independently.

It's not a new concept. God describes synergy this way: "For where two or three come together in my name, there am I with them" (Matthew 18:20). One plus one equals three.

God calls us to pray and do his work, and he powers our efforts. That's the same power that in turn can support and sustain your volunteer program. It's what lets your volunteer program thrive.

Want to get people involved? Start by forming a task force.

> "Want to get people involved? Start by forming a task force."

Creating a Volunteer Ministry Task Force

A task force is a small team given responsibility for a short-term assignment with specific goals. The group isn't intended to stay together forever. It gathers around a specific task and then disbands when the task has been completed.

And that means you've got to be *very* clear about the specific task you're asking people to accomplish. What exactly do you want people to do?

We'd like to suggest that you form a task force around actually launching your volunteer ministry, not around just the fact-finding portion of the process. In many churches—especially churches of 500 members or fewer—it's most effective when the task force members actually take on key responsibilities such as creating job descriptions for volunteer positions and doing interviewing.

As far as recruiting task force members, you've talked with church leaders who may serve on your task force. You know people who are already volunteers serving in the church. These people are possible task force members. But you'll have to ask them.

You're asking for a commitment to work with you as you establish a volunteer ministry, or as you take your existing ministry through some significant changes. You want people to help you pray for God to work his will in and through the program. To help you design the steps necessary for achieving new outcomes for the program. To help you evaluate the progress along the way.

Your task force will get the new or revitalized volunteer

ministry up and running and then, when the time is right, transition into a different role—providing support and advice to the person selected to be the Director of the Volunteer Ministry.

Keep in mind that whoever is serving as the director does *not* want to be in the role as a "lone ranger." The director needs support and help! The task force will need to shift to a new focus, but there will always be a need for the involvement of good people who are committed to the ministry and its success.

> **"Selecting the right people for the task force is important."**

Clearly, selecting the right people for the task force is important. In the next few pages we'll give you some advice about how to make sure you're pulling together the right team.

The following chart will help you think through a list of "invested individuals" who should be part of your task force. Your life will be easier if you keep the list short, but remember: If you expect your pastor to support the vision statement later, you'd best get your pastor on the task force early on.

There's simply no better way to energize your volunteer ministry with people-power than to carefully create a task force. Here are three things to keep in mind as you think about your task force.

1. Don't think you can make it without a task force.

It's tempting to just push on ahead without a task force, but you won't last long if you make that mistake.

The job of creating or changing the volunteer ministry, even in a small church, is just too big. Plus, when you involve people in the creation of a ministry they're more likely to go to great lengths to see it survive and thrive.

The people on your task force will protect and promote the volunteer ministry in your church and community. They'll make sure the ministry is supported, organized, improved, and sustained. They'll provide the prayer, commitment, and

"Invested Individuals"
Analysis Chart for Creating a Vision Statement

Who are "Invested Individuals" in the volunteer ministry? (could be individuals or groups)	What is their stake in the volunteer ministry? (e.g., they control the resources)	How can we get them to support and participate in the volunteer ministry?
_____	_____	_____
_____	_____	_____
_____	_____	_____
_____	_____	_____
_____	_____	_____
_____	_____	_____
_____	_____	_____
_____	_____	_____
_____	_____	_____

effort that makes your program thrive. They'll energize your ministry!

Remember: You're not in a sprint. You're in a marathon. You can't do it all alone or run the race without help.

2. Charter your task force.

Chartering is the process of becoming crystal clear as to what the task force exists to accomplish. It identifies the commitment needed and the outcomes

> "Remember: You're not in a sprint. You're in a marathon."

desired—what you intend to accomplish. Any group that intends to collectively work toward a desired outcome can benefit from the process, and an effective task force requires it.

The best charters emerge from discussions, and the following questions will lead your potential task force members to a thorough understanding of what's going to be required of the task force.

- Who is responsible for our task force's outcomes (for example, the elders, board, pastor)? How will we interact with that person?

- How will our task force be known in the church? What's our name?

- What's the mission of our task force? (Note: It will be different from the mission of the volunteer ministry.) What's our mission statement? Why do we exist?

- How will we know when we've succeeded and our work is complete? What's our vision for our preferred future? What outcomes do we desire to see?

- What authority does our task force have? What can we do on our own, and for what must we seek approval?

- Who on our task force will call meetings, communicate with the rest of the church, and perform other duties? What duties need to be accomplished?

- How long does our task force expect to exist?

- How will decisions be made on our task force (for example, by consensus, majority vote, or other)?

- How will we conduct our task force interactions? What are the ground rules for our meetings?

- To whom must our task force report about progress? How will we do that?

- How will we measure progress on our task force?

- How will we obtain feedback on our effort, and what will we do with that feedback?

- How will we celebrate our successes as a task force?

- With whom should we communicate and send meeting notes (absent task force members, church ministry area leaders, among others)?

Once you've talked through your shared understanding of the answers, ask each potential member to decide if he or she wants to sign on to work toward those goals.

Be clear you want people to make an *informed* decision about serving on the task force. If, at the end of the meeting, someone chooses not to join, bless him and bid him farewell.

Ask the remainder of the people to finish the charter process with you.

If you're thinking this might take some time, you're right. Plan on a two and one-half hour meeting. But it's time well spent, as this first task force meeting begins the work of creating the volunteer ministry or taking your existing ministry to the next level.

In the long run, it saves time to discuss these issues and to get agreements at the *front* end of your time together. If you wait until later, groups of people working together may become confused and experience conflict.

> "Get agreements at the *front* end of your time together."

We call this "going slow to go fast": going slow in the beginning of the process to go faster during implementation. Trust us: It's better to move slowly at the start so you don't speed along only to hit a wall later.

Sum up your answers to the discussion questions noted above. They'll become your charter. As soon as practically possible, put the summary in front of people and ask them to sign it—formalizing the process.

See page 87 for a sample completed charter document.

3. When the time comes, transition the task force.

Once the task force has completed its initial work, don't let the task force members wander off into the sunset. Instead, pause to celebrate! Throw a party! Make the transition a time of fun and joy as you thank people for a job well done.

> **"Don't let task force members wander off into the sunset."**

Provide a time for refreshments and swapping stories, for task force members to affirm each other. And, if you've already identified the person who will be directing the volunteer ministry, let that person soak up the history of the task force.

Be sure every member of the task force feels valued and appreciated. These are people who've energized your program—they deserve heartfelt thanks. They've provided leadership and accountability as your church started on the road to experiencing significant change.

And hold this thought in mind: The Director of the Volunteer Ministry needs an advisory committee or a board. The members of your task force are people you may want to ask to serve in that capacity. They've demonstrated they're committed to the success of the ministry, they're willing to work, and they've likely formed relationships with each other.

Energize your volunteer ministry by making room for people not just as "workers," but as leaders. Let your task force pull together those people God has gifted to help shape and reshape the ministry.

There's energizing power in a ministry built to thrive—and to thrive it must be more than just *your* ministry.

TWO
The Vision-Energized Volunteer Ministry

An energized volunteer ministry has a vision that inspires, defines the program, and attracts volunteers. Here's how to write a vision statement that makes your ministry magnetic.

The speech was delivered in front of 250,000 people on the Mall in Washington, D.C., on August 28, 1963. It may be the most influential speech ever delivered in America's capital.

Martin Luther King, Junior, stepped to a podium placed at the foot of the Lincoln Memorial, and in the cadence of a Baptist preacher launched into an address that will forever be known as the "I Have a Dream" speech.

Great oratory? Yes. Powerful imagery? Yes. But it was more. It was a *vision* held up for the world to see.

In 1963, there was no guarantee the American Civil Rights Movement would succeed. Some scholars and authors point out that the movement was essentially stalled when King walked to the podium in 1963. The March on Washington for Jobs and Freedom had proven successful, but what was the next step? Where was the movement to go?

Then King delivered his speech.

What King accomplished was to rise above the current challenges and paint a vision of the future—a future where equality was a given, where the benefits of freedom would be enjoyed by all regardless of color.

That vision energized the Civil Rights Movement.

Visions—expressed in passionate rhetoric or in simple vision statements—have enormous power to prompt action and commitment, and not just in 1963. And not just in social movements. A powerful vision can energize people in your church today.

The Vision Statement

If you want to benefit from the power of a vision, you've got to communicate that vision clearly and specifically. The way that's most often accomplished is with a vision statement.

A vision statement provides definition and direction for your volunteer ministry. It answers the question, "What would our future look like if we were completely successful in accomplishing what we want to do?" Your vision statement describes your preferred future—the way you'd shape the future if it were completely up to you and your task force.

> "A powerful vision can energize people in your church today."

In Rev. King's case, the preferred future he wanted to attain was living in a society where color mattered less than character. The image he held up was one of America not as it was in August of 1963, but as it could become.

Your description of a preferred future needs to be just as clear and specific. Is it a church where every person participates in ministry? a church where everyone serves in an appropriate position? Is it a church where some of the members are serving in community efforts as well as within the church?

Your vision statement becomes a magnet that attracts people who want to help you achieve the vision you've articulated. It's your declaration of purpose and intent, the summary statement when people want to know what you're trying to accomplish.

For many people, the idea of crafting a vision statement is daunting. They fear it's difficult and complex, and that they'll be stuck for days moving around words on a page until every nuance is perfect.

We've helped dozens of organizations develop vision statements, and we can tell you from experience: The process is about as complicated as you decide to make it.

It's *important*—that's true.

It's *essential*—that's true, too.

It's *challenging*—no question about it.

But it doesn't have to be *complicated*.

We'll walk you though the process in the steps that follow. And please—*don't skip creating a vision statement.* It's the only way you can plug into the energizing power a vision statement provides and enjoy the benefits that come with it.

Here are some thoughts and suggestions about creating both a vision-powered program and a vision statement. This section will walk you through the process gradually. If you'd like a "cut to the chase" set of instructions, see the Steps for Creating a Mission Statement Worksheet on page 97.

1. Involve others in shaping the vision statement.

If you want to tap into the true power of a vision statement, get others involved from the very start. That's where your task force comes in.

When we do strategic planning with organizations, we talk about "gaining *shared* vision" in the organization. A shared vision is one that most people in the organization understand, talk about, and move toward together.

In a church with a shared vision, you'll hear people talking about that vision in meetings, planning sessions, and even the hallways. The vision is consistently communicated to everyone. And someone intentionally does things that keep that vision in front of church leadership.

> "Don't try to write a vision statement as a complete task force."

To create a shared vision for your volunteer ministry, include your task force in the process of brainstorming a vision statement.

But when the time comes to actually *write* the statement, don't try to do it as a complete task force. Instead, ask several people to draft a vision statement based on what they've heard the group say, and bring that first draft back to the task force. Then, as a group, you can revise it until you've reached agreement.

2. Do some dreaming.

The most powerful vision statements usually begin with dreaming. That is, you dream about your world as it *might* be rather than the world as it *is* or how it has been in the past.

You think about *your* preferred future—the way things would look in five years if your volunteer program accomplished everything God has in mind for it. What would that world look like? It's important that you and your task force zero in on some specifics, because the next step in the process is to actually describe that future you've imagined.

3. Describe your future.

You've dreamed about what your church and your program would look like if you were totally successful . . . now put that picture into words. Remember: Your vision statement answers the question, "What do we want to look like in five years?" You're not concerned at this point about why it's important to do it, or what the first ten steps of the journey are. Focus on where you want to be.

Maybe your current reality is that 20 percent of your church membership is active as volunteers, but 80 percent of the membership just sits. In your ideal future, 100 percent of the membership would be active as volunteers.

You might describe that preferred future in a statement like. . .

> The volunteer ministry helps First Christian Church involve every member in significant, appropriate ministry.

Notice that in just a few words the statement describes what the church will look like in five years . . .

- Every member of First Christian will be doing significant ministry.

- Church members will be using their abilities, skills, and passions for ministry.

For several more examples of volunteer ministries' mission statements, see page 95.

If this business of "visualizing a future" feels a bit mystical for you, don't misunderstand. Your visualizing the future won't necessarily make it happen. This isn't a New Age approach to creating a ministry!

Rather, you're faithfully describing what life would be like if God had already accomplished what he has in mind for your volunteer ministry. The power isn't in the mental image you conjure up. The power is in letting God infuse your thinking with *his* vision for what he wants to accomplish, then as a task force listening to God through prayer and stating that future clearly.

And, taking it a step further, it's agreeing as a task force that you want to *do* what God directs you to do in the volunteer ministry.

Remember that one source of power for your ministry is prayer. See chapter 4 to see how prayer must infuse every facet of your volunteer ministry if you truly want a thriving, energized ministry—and that includes creating a vision statement.

Do some informed dreaming, too. That is, make sure you thoroughly understand the current context of your church. Who's in it? Who are you reaching? What's your history? What are your current shared values?

Also, look at your environment. Is your community changing demographically? by income? by political party?

> "Do some informed dreaming, too."

What do those trends tell you about what it will take for you to be relevant in three or five years?

Then consider how your volunteer ministry might look in five years. Who will you be serving in the church and community? What are the volunteer opportunities you'll offer? What paid and unpaid staff will you support?

With so many variables, it's unlikely that even with God's guidance you'll have an exact idea of what the future holds for your volunteer ministry. But as you dream alongside your task force members you'll sense a general direction, and you'll find that a vision for your shared future begins to form.

4. Be brief.

Notice that the sample vision statement on page 28 is brief. A vision statement is no place to use vague or flowery language; it's a place to be brief, compelling, and hopefully inspiring.

Keep your vision statement to no more than a paragraph, and if possible just one sentence. The most powerful vision statements . . .

- focus on a better future,

- encourage hopes and dreams,

- appeal to commonly shared values,

- state positive outcomes, and

- emphasize the strength of the volunteer ministry as a team.

When you've got your direction set and you've touched all those bases—all within a very short paragraph, of course— you're ready to communicate the statement to the world.

5. Communicate, communicate, communicate.

If you communicate the vision statement frequently, it can truly become the working premise for the volunteer ministry. You'll need time and persistence, and though you've communicated the vision statement so often you're tired of hearing it, communicate it again. And again.

There's power in repetition.

6. Build on the vision statement.

The shared vision becomes the basis for planning. Once you've clearly described the future, it's time to think about what actions are required to reach that desired future.

Having a shared vision is useful to your ministry—and to you—in so many ways.

- It provides you the opportunity to speak enthusiastically about what has happened within the volunteer ministry. Since the vision is endorsed by leadership (they're on your task force, remember), you won't be perceived as being overly enthusiastic.

- It clearly communicates to everyone what's expected, especially when volunteers are working independently.

- It brings clarity to planning and to implementing daily activities.

- It can be used in problem-solving and selecting opportunities for improvement.

- It prompts activity. We tend to move toward whatever we think most about. If we're thinking about the vision statement and the future it describes, we'll start to see more opportunities to act in ways that make it real. If many people are doing the same thing, we'll see synergy and teamwork develop naturally.

Think Outside the Box

There's a lot of wisdom in having a carefully worded vision statement that neatly summarizes how you see the future. But there are organizations that depict their ideal futures graphically, or through an art medium.

Either way works—so long as others can grasp and sign onto the vision. The precise form the vision statement takes is less important than the fact it's shared and regularly communicated.

If the smoking cessation support group has as its vision statement a photo of a broken cigarette and a crumpled carton of smokes, that's a shared vision for the future that everyone in the group understands. There's no need for words.

We think a written vision statement is something you'll eventually need even if you have a strong visual image. But if

you can somehow enhance your vision statement with graphics, a logo, a piece of music, or otherwise—go for it.

About the only way your vision statement should never be presented is as words carved into granite. That's because your vision statement is subject to change; getting too attached to a certain wording or presentation of the vision is dangerous.

> "Your vision statement is subject to change."

God may update or change it at any time. As the future for which you prepare becomes reality, there's still another future out ahead of you—one in which you want to be effective and faithful.

THREE
The Mission-Energized Volunteer Ministry

An energized volunteer ministry has a sense of mission that provides purpose and power. We'll walk you through creating a mission statement that keeps you on track and making progress.

It's amazing how many churches (and ministries within churches) aren't clear about their mission. There's no concise mission statement or, if there is, the volunteers and staff members have no clue what it is. They certainly can't recite it or explain it to others.

After creating a vision statement for your volunteer ministry, your task force's next step is to craft a mission statement—a statement that will help volunteers know why your volunteer ministry exists.

Your mission statement is like the foundation of a house. It's the solid base on which you'll build goals and objectives. It provides guidance about where to place volunteers and how to use your limited resources.

> "Your mission statement is like the foundation of a house."

A mission statement answers the question, "Why do we exist?" If a newspaper reporter stuck a microphone in your face and asked that question, your mission statement should serve as an answer. It defines who you are, what you're called to do, and who you're called to serve. If you know that, you're ready to answer the question, "Why do we exist?"

Some people in your church might view the volunteer ministry as a way to fill "helper" slots or as a method for getting more people involved. Your volunteer ministry can accomplish both those outcomes, but they're not at the heart of your mission.

You're wanting to implement the three theologies Marlene discussed in volume 1, and that means you'll do more than recruit "helpers." You'll connect church members with significant ministry opportunities that flow out of their individual, God-given abilities, skills, and passions.

The question is: Why do you do it?

Ready to guide your task force toward crafting a mission statement? Let's get started . . .

The Mission Statement

A mission statement is *not* the same as a vision statement, though the terms are often confused.

A *vision* statement describes your preferred future. It's about definition and direction—what you want to accomplish, and what success looks like. It's out on the horizon.

A *mission* statement is about why you're in business at all. It describes your purpose for doing what you do.

For example, your *vision* may be for your church to be a place where 100 percent of the membership is joyfully involved in volunteer ministry, with each person serving in an area of ability, skill, and passion. That's your preferred future. You'd know you're successful if you asked the question, "Who here is volunteering?" and every church member enthusiastically raised a hand.

But your volunteer ministry's *mission* is to connect church members with appropriate ministry opportunities.

Does your mission as described assure you that you'll reach the future you envision where every church member is volunteering? No.

Will accomplishing your mission move you that direction? You bet.

That's why you need a clear mission statement that nails your purpose clearly and concisely.

Why Bother with a Mission Statement?

What difference does a mission statement make for your volunteer ministry besides giving you something to print on your letterhead? Why should your task force go through the pain of creating a mission statement?

We'll share some of the benefits a mission statement brings to your ministry below, but let us highlight one outcome that would probably be a good enough reason all by itself: *Mission is a powerful motivating factor.*

Having a compelling mission, powerfully communicated, motivates potential and current volunteers when they realize they're a part of something bigger than themselves. Having a mission statement matters!

> "Having a mission statement matters!"

And before we move on, this caution: It's important you develop a mission statement *no matter how large or small your church.* Whether you're in a church of dozens or thousands, and whether your volunteer ministry is churchwide or designed to serve just one ministry area, it's worth creating a mission statement.

So . . . what will a mission statement do for you?

- **It provides information people need to feel comfortable.** Your mission statement answers the "why" question many people want answered before making a commitment. After all, nobody wants to sign up to do something insignificant or without purpose. Potential volunteers want to know that their volunteer hours will be well-spent.

- **It communicates philosophy and values.** When your ministry clearly states why it exists, it takes a position on what you believe. When you let people know you exist to place volunteers in significant ministry roles, you tell others what you think of volunteers (they can do important things) and what you think about ministry (it's accessible to volunteers, not just paid clergy).

• **It helps you set priorities.** Once you know your purpose you're able to develop a more complete understanding of what's important to do first, second, . . . or not at all.

• **It motivates existing volunteers.** In the long term, a clear mission statement keeps volunteers plugged in and plugging away. Volunteers are able to understand why their hard work matters and makes a difference.

• **It helps with conflict resolution.** An agreement on mission allows for effective conflict resolution. The likelihood of effectively resolving conflict is increased, because the focus is on fulfilling the mission, not on who's right or wrong.

• **It keeps people focused on the common good.** Your volunteer ministry exists to serve—to serve God, the church, your volunteers, and the people whose lives your volunteers touch. That's a lot of constituencies, and each may have a slightly different agenda. Your mission statement helps everyone focus past his or her own interests to the big picture.

> "You can't do everything or respond to every need in the congregation."

• **It helps your ministry stay focused.** You can't do everything or respond to every need in the congregation. If God has called you to do a volunteer ministry, do it with excellence. That requires focus. It's easy to drift away from your purpose when good ideas or available resources come along.

Having a mission statement served one group well in their decision-making process. A large Presbyterian women's group worked diligently during a retreat to create a shared mission statement. The shared statement they produced was:

> God empowers the women of [Church], united by the Holy Spirit, to serve Jesus Christ in our homes, church, community, and world. Celebrating our diversity, we model the compassion of Christ through support, nurture, and presence. Undergirded by prayer, we offer study, fellowship, and service to the glory of God.

Three months later, the Senior Pastor approached the group requesting they take on a new project he had in mind. The project was a great idea, and it would be useful to the church. The pastor decided the women's group might be the right group to adopt the project.

The members of the women's group spent about one minute reviewing their mission statement and quickly decided that the project wasn't in alignment with it. They politely informed the pastor of this. Although he was surprised, he was impressed with their focus. This story ended happily when another group within the church embraced the project because it fit that group's mission.

The reason to have a mission statement isn't so you can justify saying "no" to your pastor. Rather, it's so you can joyfully say yes to those things God has gifted and called you to do.

And—just like with a vision statement—your volunteer program's mission statement must fall under the umbrella of your *church's* mission statement. Your job isn't to strike off in totally new directions; it's to support the larger mission of your church.

How to Create a Mission Statement

Here's how to create a mission statement that energizes your task force, your church leadership, and your church membership. *And* that energizes your volunteer ministry!

1. Get the right people involved in creating the mission statement.

As with your vision statement, you want a shared understanding of the mission.

Plan for a meeting of invested individuals that includes time for discussion, debate, and—eventually, we promise—agreement. The process may feel long and tedious, but the dialogue is valuable. It reveals expectations and perceptions that will emerge eventually, so you might as well hear them early.

Use a process similar to the one you used to lead your task force through creating a vision statement. Decide who *must* be present at the meeting, who'd be nice to involve but isn't required, and who to not have attend.

Answering the three questions below will help you determine who's on your "must attend" list. Try to include people who can adequately represent others. You don't need every church leader involved, nor every member. Whenever possible have individuals represent groups of people.

> "We suggest that you narrow the number of participants at your meeting to fewer than ten."

• *Who are "invested individuals" when it comes to the mission of the volunteer ministry?* (This list could include individuals or groups, and it's likely you'll have some overlap with the people who were invested in the vision statement.)

One challenge you'll face when generating your list is that practically *everyone* in your church is an "invested" person! Church leadership cares about the volunteer ministry, and each church member is a possible participant. The list gets too long, too fast.

We suggest that you narrow the number of participants at your meeting to fewer than ten. It takes tremendous skills as a facilitator to keep a meeting with more participants than that on task.

If your task force is representative of the people you need, by all means just ask your task force to tackle the mission statement.

- *What is their investment in the volunteer ministry?* (for example, they hold the resources)

People can be invested for a variety of reasons and to different extents. You want to have several viewpoints represented as you create the mission statement. The following questions will help you determine the investment of the people or groups you've identified who have a stake in the mission statement:

How much does this individual or group know about the volunteer program?

To what extent is this individual or group impacted by the volunteer program?

What will the role of this person or group be in the volunteer program?

- *Should they be a part of the meeting to agree on a mission or just kept informed of its outcomes?*

You'll have to be politically sensitive and communicate carefully, but remember that not everyone in the church can possibly be included—nor does everyone *want* to be included.

Use these questions to help you determine the appropriate level of involvement for each of your invested individuals:

Why would this individual or group want to attend?

How will the participation of this individual or group help reach the desired outcome of our clarifying our purpose and focus?

Whose viewpoints are essential for effective, sound decision-making?

A practical note: You will never, *ever* find a time that all "invested individuals" can come together to discuss the mission. You'll have to strike a balance: The greater the participation in creating the mission statement, the higher the commitment and support your volunteer ministry will enjoy.

But if you wait until everyone can be in attendance, you may never have a discussion at all. That's why you've got "must have" and "nice, but not necessary" lists. When you can get all your "must haves" available, hold the meeting.

We've provided a sample meeting agenda and facilitator script on pages 98-106. Adapt it and other meeting scripts we provide as you wish; it's simply an example of something we've used with success in a variety of settings.

> **"Don't rush through the crafting of something so critical as a vision or mission statement."**

An assumption built into the material provided is that you'll create both the vision statement and mission statement at the same meeting. In a perfect world, that's possible—and desirable. But very often these become two different meetings, so don't feel discouraged if that's what happens to you.

Adapt the material as needed, but be sure you cover all the material somehow. It's essential that you don't rush through the crafting of something so critical as a vision or mission statement.

2. **Make sure your mission statement lines up with your vision statement.**

Your mission statement must provide the "Why?" to your vision statement's "What?". If you can't look at your mission statement and see how it connects with your vision, you're off the mark. You either need to revise your mission statement or rethink your vision.

Ask yourself and the people gathered around the table with you: "If we're really good at existing for this reason (your mission statement), will it help us create that future (the vision statement)?"

Don't settle for a mission statement that elicits anything short of an enthusiastic "yes!"

3. Be brief. And clear.

Long, complex sentences that leave everyone scratching their head have no place in a mission statement. You want clarity, and one way to achieve that is to be brief. Ideally, your mission statement will accomplish each of the following:

- *Educate others about the reason for your volunteer ministry,*

- *Keep everyone focused on what the ministry exists to accomplish,*

- *Prioritize where you should and shouldn't invest time and energy, and*

- *Quickly explain why you can serve the church and volunteers.*

These benefits won't emerge unless you're very brief.

Your mission statement will have power to engage and motivate people in direct proportion to its brevity, clarity, and passion. Eloquence may be poetic, but it won't capture anyone's heart or command his or her attention. Force yourself to be brief.

> "These benefits won't emerge unless you're very brief."

Be especially careful of including language that everyone seems to understand, but which isn't clear without an explanation. Remember: It may be that in two years none of the people sitting at your meeting will still be involved in the volunteer ministry. If your mission statement requires someone to interpret it, the people who inherit the mission statement will be lost.

A mission statement that says "We help people do ministry" is so vague it might include organizing bake sales to send students to seminary or providing rides to kids who want to go to church camp. Everyone knows that what's *intended* is to provide a volunteer ministry—but that's not what you said.

"We'll help church members discover how and where to use their abilities, skills, and passions in volunteer ministry roles" is flexible, but clear. It's a mission statement that provides guidance.

Here are three examples of mission statements that do a good job of being brief and clear:

> "In order that all may experience and appreciate their God-given gifts and grow in their faith, we will empower, equip, and mobilize God's followers to share his love in service for the greater community."

> "The purpose of the volunteer ministries program is to both extend and deepen the life of this congregation, and to more fully put into action our belief in the priesthood of all believers. Our goal is to enable each person in the congregation to . . .
>
> • Discover and use his or her unique gifts as a child of God and
>
> • Grow as a caring person, sharing time and skills with other members, with this church, and with the community."

> "The volunteer ministries program in this church will enrich the church's mission through voluntary service by providing more members with opportunities to serve as volunteers in the congregation and the community, and by improving and coordinating our systems of recruiting, training, supporting, and affirming our members and volunteers."

If you'd like to see more mission statements, see the list of sample mission statements on page 95.

4. Keep the mission—and mission statement—alive.

A mission statement hanging on the wall accomplishes nothing. Mission statements are *action-oriented* statements; if they're not being used to direct action they lose their reason for existing.

Here are three practical ways to keep your mission statement in front of people and working for you.

- If possible, print your mission statement on documents used in the church—brochures, newsletters, and bulletins. You'll let the church membership know there's a ministry that will help them find ways to volunteer in the church.

- Make sure the mission statement is regularly communicated to and through the church leaders and ministry areas you serve. Your mission statement will help people understand the larger purpose of your ministry and keep people from mistakenly assuming you're just a glorified recruiter.

> "A mission statement hanging on the wall accomplishes nothing."

- Begin all volunteer ministry meetings by reading the mission aloud and spending five minutes discussing key words or sharing stories about how the ministry is fulfilling its mission.

For example, one church's mission statement says, "We extend the healing ministry of Christ to those in need, so that we may deepen our relationship with God, self, and others."

You might begin the discussion by asking which word has special meaning to people, given what they're currently experiencing as a volunteer. One person might answer, "The word 'healing' is significant for me because I'm visiting church members who are homebound." Another person might say, "The word 'deepen' is important to me because I'm reading Scripture more often than I've done before."

5. Keep the mission—and mission statement—relevant.

Once a year, formally revisit the mission statement with invested individuals. *Do this even if you don't think anything has changed.* Why? Because . . .

- *You'll discover things you didn't know.* Perhaps there's a new area of ministry being developed and nobody has thought to tell you. You'll get information to start creating appropriate volunteer roles to support that area before the last possible moment. You'll also have the opportunity to get feedback about how you and the volunteer ministry are doing.

• *You can tell new invested individuals your story.* In the context of the meeting you can summarize the dialogue that happened when your task force created the mission statement. This is your oral history and your chance to make everyone an "insider" who has a complete understanding of the volunteer ministry's journey.

It's helpful to refer to notes taken during the initial dialogue—and ask that notes be taken of the annual meetings, too. Don't rely on people's memories—including your own!

• *You'll help invested individuals feel ownership of the mission statement.* Even if it doesn't change, the opportunity is there for people in the room to suggest changes . . . and that means the final mission statement has their seal of approval. They've ratified it. It's theirs.

Most mission statements don't change often. Only when

> "Most mission statements don't change often."

the people you're serving in the volunteer ministry or what you're providing through the ministry changes will you revise the mission statement. But checking every year guarantees you'll stay relevant . . . and there's no power in a mission statement that's out of touch with reality.

Remember: Mission statements help you shape goals and objectives that will move you closer to your preferred future. Once your mission statement is in place you're ready to work with your task force to develop goals and objectives.

Or, at least, *almost* ready . . .

But before you get busy writing goals and objectives, there's one more place for you to find power to sustain your volunteer ministry. It's in prayer—and it's the single most important energizing source of all.

FOUR
The Prayer-Energized Volunteer Ministry

An energized volunteer ministry is powered by prayer, both personal and corporate. Here's how to plug your ministry into this power source.

Have you ever run out of gas? Been driving down the highway and suddenly the engine of your car started to skip and cough, and then you could hear nothing but the wind whistling past?

Running out of gas turns any cross-country drive into a hike to the closest gas station. Because no matter how powerful your car's engine, no matter how important you or your trip are, if you run out of fuel you're going nowhere. You're stopped cold.

There's no question about how important your volunteer ministry is—it has the ability to literally revolutionize your church. If over the course of the next few years the number of people in your church who volunteer doubled, imagine the impact. *That's* significant.

And there's no question about how important this trip you're making is. It's vital. You're establishing or improving a

"You need prayer."

ministry that will help people enter into ministry and service. That's *amazingly* significant.

So don't risk running out of gas.

Even being energized by people, vision, and mission isn't enough to sustain you for the journey. You need something more.

You need prayer.

You've Got Something to Pray About

When Jesus called his disciples, he ushered them into a life of service and obedience. He expected them to follow where he led. They entered into lives of ministry.

Plus, they were expected to bring others along with them. Not only did *they* have to get on board with Jesus' vision; they were told to recruit additional volunteers, too.

The body of Christ—the church—is a service organization. Ministry is in the church's very DNA. For a Christian to be involved in service is the natural state of things—it's how we were created to live.

Consider this observation from Dennis Campbell . . .

> The call to ministry is a basic idea in the life of the church. The Greek word from the New Testament is diakonia. Its meaning is service. To be a member of the community of those who follow Jesus is to be part of a community committed to service.[1]

If your church is like most, it *needs* an energized, thriving volunteer ministry! The ministry helps engage church members in significant service, which means you'll help your church *be* the church. It's a high calling to prayerfully, intentionally connect people with volunteer opportunities.

So understand this: *You're in ministry.* Whether you're paid staff or unpaid staff, you're in ministry. Whether you place fifty volunteers this year or just one, *you're in ministry.*

And like any person in ministry, *you need prayer!* You've got things to pray about—both for yourself and your role in this ministry and for the volunteer ministry. To create and sustain a volunteer ministry in your church, you want God's guidance. You *need* God's guidance.

It's tempting to think of the volunteer ministry as secondary to *real* ministry. After all, you don't decide if the church will launch a new building campaign, call on the sick, or do counseling with discouraged people. But you may well be called on to create job descriptions for the volunteers who do those things and to interview those people. Those front-line ministry positions may never be filled without your active involvement.

That makes your volunteer ministry not just a behind-the-scenes administrative function. It's a front-line ministry.

So let us say it again: *You need the power of prayer.* You need God's guidance. You need the discernment that comes with prayer.

But you already pray, right? What Christian doesn't?

What we're suggesting isn't that you casually pray about the volunteer ministry, but that you intentionally create a ministry that's *energized and powered* by prayer.

You Can Design a Prayer-Energized Volunteer Ministry

A *prayer-energized* ministry is one where prayer comes first. It's not just something we do after we've gotten ourselves into a pickle! It *precedes* our actions and opens our hearts to hearing God tell us what ministry is needed and how we can fulfill that ministry.

Prayer helps ensure that our volunteer ministry comes out of God's agenda for our congregation and not our own agendas. Ministries based on our own agendas are dependent solely on our presence and commitment. As soon as we become discouraged, move away, or get stressed, the ministry falters. That's not the sort of ministry that will thrive.

Ground your volunteer ministry in prayer and you'll reap short- and long-term benefits. And since the work of your volunteer ministry is the work of the Lord, why not let God run it?

Here are some suggestions about how to design a prayer-energized ministry.

"Here are some suggestions about how to design a prayer-energized ministry."

1. Begin by valuing prayer.

How important is prayer to you? to members of your team? to your church? We don't mean to be insulting by asking, but those are important questions. It's not necessarily true that every church places a high value on intercessory prayer—asking for God to enter into situations to make his will known and to affect outcomes and people.

The issues that accompany launching or revitalizing a volunteer ministry can be a tremendous catalyst for prayer. A vital prayer life will be a lifeline for your faith through what's coming in the months ahead.

Recognize this: Not everyone in your church will feel the need to join you in prayer for the volunteer ministry. Probably not everyone in your church prays regularly. Some people pray infrequently at best.

We point out those obvious truths because for your ministry to be successfully energized by prayer it *doesn't* require that every person in your church pray and fast for the ministry. That would be great—but it's not essential. What *is* essential is that you and a group of people who are drawn to the ministry agree to pray for God's guidance and direction and that you listen to God's voice.

And don't be mistaken: This isn't just a matter of tradition or habit. Prayer is an energizing force that can create enormous changes in and through your team.

Consider what we read in the book of James . . .

> *Is any one of you in trouble? He should pray. Is anyone happy? Let him sing songs of praise. Is any one of you sick? He should call the elders of the church to pray over him and anoint him with oil in the name of the Lord. And the prayer offered in faith will make the sick person well; the Lord will raise him up. If he has sinned, he will be forgiven. Therefore confess your sins to each other and pray for each other so that you may be healed. The prayer of a righteous man is powerful and effective. (James 5:13-16)*

From the very beginning, when you're creating a vision for your volunteer ministry, there's a central place for prayer. There's nothing more important than making sure your vision reflects what God wants to do with your ministry, that you're in harmony with God's vision. That involves asking God what he wants to do with and through you, and it mandates listening for an answer.

> Prayer is the act by which the community of faith surrenders itself, puts aside all other concerns, and comes before God Himself.[2]

2. Be disciplined in praying for your volunteer ministry yourself.

You're a key person God is using to launch or improve your volunteer ministry, so be available to God. Schedule daily time for prayer the same way you'd schedule time for anything else that's important to accomplish.

Countless books and resources are designed to help you improve your prayer life and deepen your understanding of prayer's power. Explore using one or more of those resources, or simply do this: Every day, come before God and say, "Here I am, your person in my world. I'm available for your use today. What do you have to teach me? How do you want to use me?"

You'll be amazed at how God answers those prayers.

> *"For I know the plans I have for you," declares the Lord, "plans to prosper you and not to harm you, plans to give you hope and a future." (Jeremiah 29:11)*

3. Pray corporately.

Ask the leaders of ministry areas to pray for the volunteer ministry at each staff meeting, and contact whatever prayer chain or intercessory prayer ministry exists in your church. Not only will there be regular, disciplined prayer for the volunteer ministry, but volunteers who already work with you will know someone is praying for them.

And there's another benefit: You can be certain the direction you understand from God for your volunteer ministry is *collectively* discerned. We once heard Sam Leonard, from the Alban Institute, say it well:

> Hearing the will of God individually that is not tested in community can lead to madness . . . This is personalized theology— "the blood of Christ for me"—not for us. Volunteer work needs two "yes"es: called by God and called by the church.[3]

When you understand that it's God's will that you move the volunteer ministry a particular direction, you can test your discernment with others. Share with them what you've prayed and how you heard God speaking to you. Corporate prayer helps you know you're faithfully following God's lead.

Identify a team of people who will become prayer partners for the volunteer ministry. Seek out individuals with enthusiasm for the volunteer ministry, others with deep spiritual discipline, and still others who have some experience (successfully and unsuccessfully) in trying to organize volunteers in the church.

> "Identify a team of people who will become prayer partners for the volunteer ministry."

Create a discipline or process for the individual and corporate prayer effort. Choose specific times, places, and methods for keeping partners in prayer. Prayer partners can meet for prayer time or make a covenant to pray at a certain time of each day.

Recognize and affirm that people pray in different ways, and this is not only acceptable, but valuable. Suggest that people may want to regularly ask God to help them notice with new eyes the gifts and resources of the church and the needs of the local community and world. Some may want to keep a short journal of these new insights. If a particular phrase or section of Scripture stands out as relevant to God's call to the church, encourage them to make a note of the passage and their new understanding so they can share that later with others.

Let everyone involved in praying for the volunteer ministry know that the goal of this prayer process is to develop an openness to God's leading of the ministry, so it can function the way God intends.

You want to join the psalmist in declaring . . .

> *I am your servant; give me discernment that I may understand your statutes. (Psalm 119:125)*

Share the results of your individual prayer experiences with each other. This will provide the opportunity for the testing of discernment from prayer, and you'll achieve both yeses: called by God and by the church.

Keep people praying for the volunteer ministry by keeping information regarding the volunteer ministry in front of them. Send out daily or weekly messages about the program to focus prayers on pressing issues. Be creative in all the ways you can put those reminders in place: e-mail, cards or postcards, and telephone calls all can work. Create bookmarks, lapel buttons, or stickers your church members might use. We've even seen colorful and creative refrigerator magnets used to keep the volunteer ministry in front of people.

4. Pray specifically.

It's helpful to give people something specific to pray about. Following are some topics you can share to prompt collective prayer. Ask prayer partners to pray for . . .

- God's vision for the work of volunteers in your congregation.

- Church leaders to accurately identify the needs in your church, community, and world that could be met by volunteers in your congregation.

- Your congregation's commitment to ministry and service.

- Your staff's ability to support the volunteer ministry.

- The wisdom of individuals who are helping build and lead the volunteer ministry.

- The guidance of the Holy Spirit in the volunteer ministry.

- A fair distribution of work among your church's membership so the 80/20 rule does *not* prevail (20 percent of the volunteers doing 80 percent of the work).

- Increasing support of the volunteer ministry by the congregation.

- An ongoing renewal of volunteers.

- New connections to form with marginal members who could benefit spiritually from serving as volunteers.

> *Again, I tell you that if two of you on earth agree about anything you ask for, it will be done for you by my Father in heaven. For where two or three come together in my name, there am I with them. (Matthew 18:19-20)*

"Here are some practical ways to keep your ministry energized by prayer."

5. Keep praying.

An ongoing dialogue with God about your volunteer ministry invites God to continue providing energy, wisdom, and compassion. You'll need all three!

Here are some practical ways to keep your ministry energized by prayer . . .

- Ask existing small groups within your church to adopt you as an ongoing prayer concern. Keep them in the loop about issues for which you'd like prayer.

- In the church newsletter or bulletin share some meaningful outcomes of the ministry (for example, the growth a volunteer experienced in doing a new activity).

- Include the volunteer ministry as a prayer concern during worship services.

- Include prayer requests in your church newsletter. This will also serve as a way to inform the congregation of what is happening in the ministry. It may even end up serving as a recruitment tool.

- Begin all volunteer ministry meetings with prayer.

- Personally take time daily to pray about the volunteer program.

> Prayer and action . . . can never be seen as contradictory or mutually exclusive. Prayer without action grows into powerless pietism, and action without prayer degenerates into questionable manipulation.[4]

It's important you stay in prayer and that you're confident you're hearing God about your church's volunteer ministry, especially if you're just beginning a ministry. This is actually hard to do, because it's a natural human tendency to jump in and begin working on tasks as soon as a critical level of enthusiasm is reached. There may be other people in your church who are urging you to move ahead.

But prayer *precedes* action. Pray often, individually and collectively sharing the insights God has provided to direct you in service. Then act, create, and continue to pray for your volunteer ministry. Have the patience to wait for God's guidance, and submit to God's will no matter how much you think you know, or how certain you are that your way is the best way.

Pray as if your volunteer ministry depended on it.

In many ways, it does.

1. Dennis Campbell, quoted by Reuben P. Job and Norman Shawchuck, *A Guide to Prayer for All God's People* (Nashville: Upper Room Books, 1990) p.33.

2. Charles Colson, *The Body: Being Light in the Darkness* (Dallas: Word Publishing, 1992), 136.

3. Sam Leonard, The Alban Institute, from a workshop given March 4-6, 2002.

4. Donald P. McNeill, Douglas A. Morrison, and Henri J. M. Nouwen, quoted by Reuben P. Job and Norman Shawchuck, *A Guide to Prayer for All God's People* (Nashville: Upper Room Books, 1990), p.112.

FIVE
The Goal- and Objective-
Energized Volunteer Ministry

You're charged up and ready to move toward your vision. Here's how to take the next steps by creating goals and objectives.

You're energized—by people, vision, mission, and prayer—and now it's time to put some wheels under your mission statement.

That happens when your task force develops goals and objectives . . . and it's time to do that.

You might typically use different terminology, but let's look at one definition:

Goal—This is the end you're aiming for. It's where you want to go. Goals are short-term actions by which you'll accomplish your mission. Or you might simply ask yourself, "What are we *doing* about our mission this year?" A goal is a broad statement that defines the "why" of your ministry.

The first draft of goals are almost always vague and hard to measure. For example, your church might set a goal of "sharing faith in our neighborhood and community." Good intention, but how will you know when you've reached the goal? When everyone has been handed a brochure about the church? When everyone has made a faith commitment to Christ?

When goals get specific, they become useful. A goal that has been sharpened and honed is sometimes called an objective. We think of it as simply a *good* goal—but let's use the term "objective" as you work with your task force. When a goal meets all the criteria I describe below, announce it has been promoted to "objective"; your task force will have something to celebrate!

Here's how we'll define "objective": An objective is a goal that has become a definite, measurable target. An objective includes standards of performance and achievement both for your area of ministry and for the people involved.

> "When goals get specific, they become useful."

For example, the church with the goal of sharing their faith in their community can make their vague goal an objective by asking and answering questions such as:

- How exactly will we share our faith?

- What outreach events will we hold that are geared toward our community?

- When will we hold these outreach events?

- How many such events will we hold this year?

- Exactly who do we want to reach—what neighborhood, what age range of individuals, what ethnic group?

If you've ever driven through tall mountains, you know about switchbacks—roads that turn back on themselves as they zigzag up the face of a mountain. Because the roads climb the mountain gradually, cars can make the trip.

The *goal* of a driver is simply to reach the top of the peak. The switchbacks are like *objectives*—short, manageable, measurable steps to help drivers reach their goal.

When it comes to volunteers, many churches forget the switchbacks and just try to drive right up the sheer mountainside. No wonder so many volunteers burn out quickly!

How to Turn a Goal into an Objective

I'd like to suggest five yardsticks against which you can measure goals and objectives. If a goal measures up in all five areas, it's an objective. Promote it, celebrate it, and use it. But if the goal comes up short in any of these five areas, run it through your task force again to shape it up.

And be brutal: Promote no goal before it's ready! If people are fuzzy when they're *talking* about a goal, wait until they try to *act* on it. That's when things break down in a *big* way!

Yardstick #1: Is the goal specific?

How many? By when? At what cost? How will you know when you're done? Those are all things you need to know before you can delegate a goal to someone.

Some people become concerned that if you're too specific about goals (or any other part of your planning), you're not trusting God to lead your ministry. I don't think that's the case. By all means, ask God if it's his will for you to add four volunteer Sunday school teachers by next July, or if it's his will that you recruit an additional twelve male voices into the choir before you start Christmas program rehearsals. If you sense that the answer is "yes," then move ahead with the goal you've prayed about.

On the other hand, if you're not clear about your goal, how can God respond clearly? If you're praying, "Lord, please help me know if you want us to make the nursery safer and more efficient," I can tell you right now the answer to that prayer is yes. God loves children. God cares about children. Of *course* he'll want you to do the best possible job in the nursery.

But if you meant, "Help me know if you want us to add Mary and Jack to our nursery staff," that's an entirely different question.

And being specific is helpful in more ways than simply guiding your prayer life. It also lets you know when you've completed what you set out to do.

If you only say, "We need more volunteers to staff the nursery," are you successful if you recruit just one? If you don't say "We need to recruit those volunteers by April 1 of next year," then do the people charged with accomplishing that task have forever to get it done? You'll quickly learn that while specific seems scary (remember, someone might hold you accountable), it's actually a key element to reaching your objectives.

Yardstick #2: Is the goal measurable?

If you're specific—stating how much and by when—you've got good measurements in place. A goal is measurable if it includes clear wording about budget, growth, time, and achievement—all the specifics that might impact the goal.

> "A goal is measurable if it includes clear wording about budget, growth, time, and achievement."

Don't be quick to slap those measurements onto goals, though. If you want to achieve a goal by June 1, have a good reason for selecting that date. If you want to define "success" as hitting 100 percent participation in the church work day, is it a reasonable goal? Before you formalize the numbers and dates associated with your goals, consider yardstick measurement 3 below.

Yardstick #3: Is the goal challenging but achievable?

Set realistic goals. You want to help people stretch, but not be stretched so far they snap. Being handed an unachievable goal can be demoralizing and defeating. If the numbers are too big or the time too short, your volunteers may feel like huge failures—*even when they've done great work.*

Although you want to challenge your volunteers, you also want to be realistic when determining what you'll accomplish. For example, maybe you've been involved in a fundraiser for a new church building. Your stated goal was to raise $1,500,000 in two years. At the end of two years you'd raised $1,350,000. Did you succeed or fail?

You didn't reach the goal, so maybe the correct answer is that you failed.

But do you want your team of fundraisers—people who managed to raise $1,350,000 in two years—to go home feeling like failures? If you'd set your goal at $1,300,000, they'd be celebrating enormous success and be ready to sign on for whatever committee work needed to be done next.

Be realistic about defining success when you put numbers to it. Be realistic—but achievable.

And here's where goals *really* become objectives . . .

Yardstick #4: Is the goal delegated to someone?

If nobody is responsible to accomplish the goal (or each piece of it), it's likely the goal won't be met.

It's not just that people won't jump in and help—for the most part, they will. Especially people who've already joined your task force. It's that nobody knows if they're allowed to act on the goal. Will they be stepping on others' toes? Will they discover there's something they didn't know—like that the entire goal had been cancelled last month? And do they have the authority to accomplish the goal? Nobody likes to jump in and do something, only to discover he's wasted his time, or she's wasted resources and actually sabotaged a project.

Goals must be connected to real people, who have real authority to act.

Yardstick #5: Does the goal help you fulfill your mission statement?

You may create a wonderful goal that measures up to all four of the previous yardsticks. The goal may generate energy and excitement among members of your task force. But if the goal doesn't help you fulfill your mission, it's distracting you from being who God has called you to be at this time and doing what God has called you to do at this time. You need to set aside the goal and work on goals that *do* help you fulfill your mission.

The Hard Work of Writing Goals and Objectives

Many ministry leaders don't like to write goals and objectives. They think, You can't measure what we do in ministry; we do good stuff and you can't put numbers on it.

That sort of thinking leaves goals in some sort of ephemeral world. As long as leaders don't measure what they do, they feel good about it because at least they're accomplishing something—even if they aren't sure how much.

Or they fear that the moment they go public with goals they'll be held accountable by the board or the pastor.

But if you're going to accomplish something, you need to be bold about goals and objectives. If you state, "We need more volunteers for our program," that's not really an objective, because it's not measurable or specific. Instead, it's more of a wish. And it's a statement that no one can really hold you accountable for. If you recruit just two more volunteers who happen to wander in, you'll reach your "objective" without doing much of anything.

> "Be willing to be held accountable."

Be willing to be held accountable. Think through:

- Who is going to recruit new volunteers?

- How many additional volunteers do we need?

- When do we need these volunteers in place?

- How will we use them when we get them?

Getting important things done requires that we be willing to step up and take responsibility—in part by setting goals and objectives.

Maybe you can't accomplish everything right now—or ever. That's why you need to concentrate on goals you can achieve within a set time period. During this process, you also decide what you're *not* going to do.

As you set goals for your ministry, you'll quickly realize that there may be too much for you to reasonably accomplish in the amount of time you have available, or with the staff you have on board. You have to pick and choose which goals will give you the best return on your investment of resources (for example, time, staff, energy, budget). You have to decide what goals to not address because you simply can't do them for now.

How Your Task Force Will Operate

Once you've established some goals and objectives, it's time to decide who's going to take responsibility for them. Unless you want to see all the heads in the room turn and look at you (not a good sign), lead a discussion about how your task force is going to operate. That is, will the members of the group do everything, do some things, or simply give sage advice?

Here are some options to consider:

1. *Your task force members could divide up the major tasks and ask other church members to help them.* Each individual would take responsibility for a different aspect of the work (such as designing job descriptions, identifying potential volunteers, and training). This makes the task force a working group rather than just a policy group. This is often a good option for smaller or newer congregations.

2. *Your task force might decide it wants to determine program and policy decisions, but use existing church committees or ministries to implement the program.* For example, the church nominating committee might prepare volunteer job descriptions and the church board might write the mission statement. Instead of doing the work, the task force will see that it's done effectively. This isn't good news for the person who ends up having to do the actual work of the volunteer ministry.

"Pick and choose which goals will give you the best return on your investment."

3. *Your task force might decide to focus on the area of greatest need and do nothing else for six months or a year.* For example, if no job descriptions exist for volunteers, the task force may want to spend several months just designing job descriptions.

4. *Or, your task force might decide it needs to find a director for the volunteer ministry.* This person—whether volunteer or paid—is charged with staffing the program and will organize and administer the details of the ministry. The director is accountable to the task force but might report directly to the

Senior Pastor. The task force can then devote its time to guiding, advising, supporting, and promoting the volunteer program among members of the church.

Note: One of the first things the newly-designated Director of the Volunteer Ministry should do is to find and involve a group of volunteers who will provide active support and help—essentially to function as a task force. If you can recruit a task force that will function in a hands-on fashion it will make that step unnecessary.

> "Have you made a decision yet about how your task force will function?"

Have you made a decision yet about how your task force will function? If not, make this your top priority, and be sure to create an objective that deals with it!

SIX
The Change-Energized Volunteer Ministry

You're about to create some major changes in your church—and that can energize everyone involved. Or not. Here's how to gain permission to move ahead so your ministry thrives.

Some people love change. They're energized by it, and they love the thrill of the unexpected.

Unfortunately, they're in the minority. Most people hate change—at least change initiated by someone else. Unless most people see the need for change, they'll tend to resist it.

If you're going to create a thriving volunteer ministry, you need to gain permission for the changes you'll cause. Launching or revitalizing a volunteer ministry may change the way volunteers do their current jobs. It will change lines of communication. It will change what's expected of people. It might even change the staff configuration.

The good news is that with some planning and forethought you can nudge people toward deciding the discomfort they feel is a "growing pain," not another kind of pain.

If you don't do enough planning . . . well, you may experience what I (Sue) experienced . . .

The World's Most Expensive Paperweights

I was the volunteer administrator in a hospital a number of years ago, and we had the opportunity to computerize the reception area so we could retrieve patient information from the hospital's computer system.

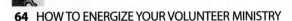

The volunteers assigned to the reception area were skeptical about using these machines when the old index card files they'd always used were still functional (and familiar!). In the volunteers' minds, nothing about the way they were doing their work was broken.

So I provided all the reasons we should install computers. It would be so much more state-of-the-art to have computers instead of card files. Information would be more accurate and timely. It would be easier to update information. It would look more professional. The benefits were obvious, at least to me.

"What had gone wrong?"

I spent weeks selling the idea to the volunteers. They all attended the computer training that I'd arranged for them, and together we awaited the day the computers were installed.

Once the boxes were unpacked I set up the computers and got them ready for the next day's volunteers. I could hardly wait. When I arrived at work the next morning I rushed down to the lobby, and there, to my amazement, were two volunteers with the card files at their fingertips—and two computers pushed to the side. My computers had become the world's most expensive paperweights.

What had gone wrong?

Getting computerized was the culmination of *my* dream, not theirs. I'd sold the idea based on benefits I perceived, but I hadn't identified any benefits *they'd* perceive. All they saw was the need to master a complicated system they hadn't requested, didn't want, and could live without.

Ouch.

I slowed down and started over, spending time helping them discover benefits from their perspective. I allowed them to gradually get more familiar and comfortable with the computers. Eventually, the volunteers came around and the computers earned a spot on our reception desk.

Was installing computers the right thing for the hospital, and did it meet the needs of the hospital clients? Absolutely. Had I effectively managed the change in the volunteers' eyes?

Absolutely not. I didn't consider the losses they would experience—no matter how positive and small the changes seemed to me.

Sometimes changes made in church strike people the same way my changes struck the hospital volunteers. The changes are thrust on people without sufficient time for ending the "way we've always done it" and integrating the new way. People naturally prefer what's familiar, and change represents the unknown.

And your speeches about the benefits from your perspective will fall on deaf ears. Until people discover for *themselves* that making the change is worthwhile, you won't gain permission to lead the charge into bringing about change.

We've observed over the years that congregations seldom respond warmly when someone messes with the "things of faith."

We remember an interim pastor who used a different rhythm when reciting the Lord's Prayer. It so annoyed some of the church members that they griped about it for weeks. The pastor had used the same words. The exact same content. But varying the rhythm was enough to set off a month-long conversation during coffee-hour.

How you go about gaining permission to lead change can make or break your volunteer ministry.

How to Gain Permission to Make Changes in Your Church

There are several ways you can help members in the church deal with change and reassure them that it's positive to embrace the change you're proposing.

Most approaches involve face-to-face conversations where you can establish that you're capable of leading the change, establish that you have no ulterior motives, and explain the change clearly. It's also important that you allow enough time for people to discover the good things that will come about as a result of the change and to let go of the past.

Consider these practical suggestions.

Help people articulate why things must change.

Del Poling, a consultant who helps churches deal with conflict and change, shared a truly wonderful question with us recently. When Del engages in discussions with a church about change he begins the process with these questions:

Who are we? And . . .

> "Why can't we stay where we are?"

Where are we now?

After the group discusses who they are, what their ministries include, and what their strengths and weaknesses are, he asks them to answer this third question—the wonderful one I mentioned earlier:

Why can't we stay where we are?

What a profound question! It's all well and good for us to describe what we want the future of our congregation to look like. We need to do that. But until we feel the pain of staying in our present situation, we won't be motivated to push ahead into that new, unfamiliar future. As people answer the question they take on the role of change-agents, suggesting why things should change. They begin to get energized about making a shift, rather than resenting it.

Del told us about a church that asked him to facilitate strategic planning with the church elders. Del knew the church building included a gorgeous parlor, an attractive sanctuary, a welcoming fellowship hall, and a deplorable, run-down Christian education area.

Del asked the person arranging the first meeting to hold it in the Christian education area. When the meeting was scheduled to begin it was raining, and the meeting attendees sat in an uncomfortable, cramped room where the windows were leaking and wind blew through.

Finally, one leader said, "We can't stay in here any longer!"

That moment presented a memorable opportunity for the group to realize they couldn't stay where they were in how they offered Christian education, either.

This experience was a compelling illustration of what needed to change in that church. Until the leaders experienced the pain of the present, they were not motivated to move into the future.

Some additional questions to ask in regards to your volunteer ministry are:

- What happens now when church members try to serve as volunteers?

- What pain happens in their experience?

- If we keep things exactly as they are, what will be the consequences?

- In what ways are we failing to live up to our commitment to be disciples of Christ?

- What do we need to leave behind if we want to become better disciples of Christ?

Facilitate a dialogue about the coming change.

Remember—for your volunteer ministry to thrive you've got to help others discover for themselves the benefits of making the changes you know are coming. Your lectures won't do the trick. You've got to get people engaged in dialogue.

Use the same techniques and skills you used to plug church leadership into your ministry. Start by determining who should be involved in the dialogue, who are the invested individuals. Include key decision-makers who have the power to be a barrier to the volunteer ministry either through direct action or by passively not supporting the ministry.

Also include anyone who's expressed an interest in the program, and anyone who's expected to carry out program functions. And most *definitely* include people who control resources the program needs such as money, office space, or equipment. They can starve you out if they don't support the volunteer ministry.

Another person to bring on board is the person who'll direct the ministry, if that person has been identified.

And be sure to include those folks we call the "Reed People." These people have the power or position to hinder your program. If you fail to include them in the dialogue, they'll hang in the reeds and wait for an opportunity to shoot you out of the water.

Get these people together for a discussion. Use the dialogue about change agenda on page 92 to help direct the meeting.

Help people manage the transitions of change.

In his book *Managing Transitions*, William Bridges describes the stages of change. He writes that it isn't changes that are difficult, it's transitions. "*Change* is not the same as transition. Change is situational: the new site, the new boss, the new team roles, the new policy. *Transition* is the psychological process people go through to come to terms with the new situation. Change is external, transition is internal."[1]

> "And be sure to include those folks we call the 'Reed People.'"

How true! But the good news is that there are three steps you can help people go through that will enable them to transition through change.

Say goodbye to the old way.

In your case, it's the way your church has always recruited volunteers and how you've always worked together.

You can help people say goodbye by . . .

Identifying who's losing what. Talk with people to find out what will be hard to let go of. It might be power or a position. It may be that they worked for years with their best friends and now they won't be on the same volunteer teams. They might be required to work in a new place that's more in line with their abilities, skills, and passions. They might even be asked to give up their favorite job!

Validating those losses for individuals. Listen as people talk about the loss they're experiencing, and fully accept that it's painful no matter how small the loss may seem to you.

Allow people to grieve openly. Give people permission to talk openly about their sadness or even anger.

Continue to give people information. In the absence of information, people tend to assume the worst. The more information you can share about what's happening with the volunteer program, the better.

Make the goodbye final. If necessary, tell people the old way will no longer work. I had to finally remove the card files from the reception desk in the hospital so that they were no longer available to use.

Celebrate the past with respect. Talk about the way things were done with respect. Don't invalidate the past.

Transition toward the new way.

This is the period of time when new things are being introduced and people are still unsure of what's expected. They also wonder what things will look like when everything is in place.

Pray for people to not find the transition too confusing or uncomfortable. It's aggravating to have to deal with change on someone else's schedule, especially when you don't see the need. Ask God to guard the hearts of your volunteers from bitterness or disappointment. Even better—ask God to energize your volunteers for change!

"Ask God to energize your volunteers for change!"

Acknowledge that it may be a difficult time. Some people will accept the new approach to volunteer ministry quicker than others. Some people may never accept it. Let people know you understand it may be hard to make the changes.

Redefine this period. The change being experienced isn't watching a ship go down. It's taking a last voyage on one ship and then boarding another—a ship heading toward an exciting destination.

Be clear about processes and procedures. Be specific about how you expect people to do things at this time, even if the processes are temporary.

Keep talking. Create a small team to help facilitate dialogue through the transition, expressing feelings and concerns back to leadership.

Begin the new way.

This is the exciting, energizing initiation of the new way of doing things and working together.

Pray for everyone to see God's vision for the volunteer program at your church, and pray that everyone remains faithful to that vision. The changes you're making aren't random or thoughtless; they're designed to help you more faithfully fulfill God's vision for your program. They're important.

Communicate the big picture and why the volunteer ministry is changing. Do this through newsletters, in meetings, and from the pulpit. Don't rely on one communication channel to reach everyone.

Paint the picture of how it will be when the change is completely integrated into day-to-day life. You can begin to create familiarity with the vision of how things could be.

Ask people what they need during this time. Especially if you see them struggling with new ways of doing things, ask people what information or resources they lack. Be gentle and kind.

Celebrate and give praise to God for the success of the change.

And here's one last practical idea for encouraging the change process. In a staff meeting or other appropriate gathering, ask people to decide for themselves whether they're just beginning to deal with the change or have already moved through the transition completely.

Ask people to stand somewhere along an imaginary line in the room, with "just beginning to accept and deal with the change" at one wall, and "fully accept the change" at the other wall. Tell people to stand at one extreme or the other, or anywhere in between—whatever spot represents where they are emotionally.

This technique provides an opportunity for people to discuss what barriers or struggles they're experiencing. It also allows people who are further along with the change to provide encouragement to those who are struggling.

1. William Bridges, *Managing Transitions—Making the Most of Change* (Reading, Mass.: Addison-Wesley Publishing, 1991), p.3.

SEVEN

The Leadership-Energized Volunteer Ministry

A task force can take you just so far. It's time to put someone in charge . . . someone who'll keep the volunteer ministry energized and on task.

It's great to have a task force create a vision statement, mission statement, goals, and objectives. Having representatives from each of the volunteer ministry's constituent groups guarantees that you'll design documents that have widespread support and wisdom.

But you *don't* want to have a committee making day-to-day decisions as you implement those goals and objectives. That's a cumbersome process that will slow down decision-making dramatically.

It's not that you never want to reconvene your task force. You may well need one often as the ministry develops and grows. And many of these people may serve as an ongoing board of advisors, if you structure your ministry to include a board. (Hint: Reasons that's wise will be discussed later!)

But for daily decisions? It's important you find a Volunteer Manager to run the show.

> "It's important you find a Volunteer Manager to run the show."

What Do You Call Your Leader?

There are several common titles in use for the person who directs and manages the volunteer recruitment and placement process in a church. *Volunteer Manager* is one common title, as is *Director of Volunteers.* Some churches communicate the importance of the role by referring to this person as the *Pastor of Congregational Involvement* or another title that prominently includes "pastor."

Pick whatever title works for your church and communicates the role clearly, but be aware that first impressions count. There's some wisdom in using the term "Pastor" or "Minister" in the title if you want to notify the church that the volunteer ministry is worthy of respect and attention.

However, for ease, we'll refer to the role as Volunteer Manager for the duration of this volume.

Take Me to Your Leader

The Volunteer Manager may be paid staff or unpaid staff. It may be a full-time or part-time position. In some cases, the position is staffed by several people who have a "job-share" situation.

But however the role is staffed, the basic responsibilities of the Volunteer Manager remain the same: to identify the ministries that can benefit from volunteer involvement, to recruit volunteers, to promote the volunteer ministry, to interview volunteers, to screen volunteers, to place volunteers in positions, to orient and train volunteers, to ensure supervision for volunteers (defining who volunteers are accountable to), and to evaluate and ensure recognition of volunteers.

That's a *lot* to get accomplished! Small wonder the Volunteer Manager needs a group of people who'll help!

When you're putting a Volunteer Manager in place, you need a job description that captures the essential information. *Even if you're the Volunteer Manager yourself, you need a job description!* It's one way your Volunteer Manager can stay focused, do what's most important, and be evaluated.

Here's a template for creating a job description for this role:

Title: Volunteer Manager

Position Summary: a paragraph describing the duties and responsibilities of the position

The Strategic Fit: how the volunteer ministry fits into and supports the overall strategy of the church

Key Job Responsibilities: a list of the most common and important job responsibilities (for example, interview all potential volunteers for positions)

Benefits: a list of not only paid benefits, if this is a paid position, but also the more intangible benefits such as the opportunity for growth in human relations skills. Keep in mind that the benefits need to be from the Volunteer Manager's perspective!

Qualifications: a list of non-negotiable requirements for the position (for example, is a Christian, has a bachelor's degree) and the qualifications that "would be nice" to have (for example, previous experience as a Volunteer Manager)

Supervision: Who is this person(s) responsible to, and who are they responsible for? With whom is the Volunteer Manager expected to effectively interact?

Want to see several sample job descriptions for a Volunteer Manager? See pages 109-112 for two that are currently being used in churches.

Be strategic in selecting a person to lead the volunteer ministry. This individual will play a key role in energizing the volunteers and communicating the vision of the program. A strong leader may not keep a floundering program afloat, but a poor leader will certainly sink it.

> "A strong leader may not keep a floundering program afloat, but a poor leader will certainly sink it."

Create the job description before selecting someone to fill the role. It's tempting, if you have someone in mind for the job, to design a job description that reflects the skills and experience of that person instead of the position.

Also, take care that the position as described will be respected and understood by your congregation and staff. Here's a story where that didn't happen. Don't let it become your story.

In one church, the Volunteer Ministry Manager was recruited (as an unpaid position), given a desk and enough money to create a database, and encouraged to go "do good things." The manager, a member of the church, was nominally introduced to the congregation, but it was never made clear what the vision of the ministry was, nor did the congregation truly understand what this person could and would be doing in the position.

Within a short time, the manager was highly frustrated. Her position had turned into a glorified telephone recruiter for other programs within the church. She was spending her days recruiting individuals to cook for funerals, staff the nursery, and stock the food pantry. This was *not* her vision or what she'd expected!

After a long year, she finally resigned and her resignation went virtually unnoticed. No one has stepped forward to assume the position since.

If this church *does* find another person for the position, it will have to undo the bad feelings and misunderstandings around the volunteer ministry.

What Are You Looking for in a Volunteer Manager?

Once the position is clearly and explicitly defined, think about who can best do the job. The first person to consider is a champion of the volunteer ministry. Since you're reading this book, this might be you!

Look to see who's served on the task force from the beginning. See who's focused solely on the volunteer ministry. The role will be demanding, so if the person is also singing in the choir, helping in VBS, and organizing the annual rummage sale, you're looking at someone who's too busy.

Here are some general characteristics that are good to see in your Volunteer Manager.

The Volunteer Manager is typically . . .

- Able to see potential in anyone and everyone,

- Able to perceive gifts, abilities, skills, and passions,

- A good listener,

- Assertive without being aggressive,

- A good delegator,

- Approachable,

- Comfortable interviewing people,

- A skilled manager,

- Capable of maintaining a computer database (or willing to learn how!),

- Someone who knows the congregation, and

- Someone whose enthusiasm and positive regard will *energize* the ministry!

Notice that last characteristic: enthusiasm that will energize the ministry. That's not an afterthought; it's an essential to keep the ministry on track.

Our friend and colleague, Marlene Wilson, describes herself as an "informed optimist." That means she understands that leaders and volunteers can be petty, caustic, and negative. She knows that sometimes people operate out of less-than-ideal motives. But so what? It's still her job when she's managing volunteers to draw out the best in people. To provide encouragement and vision. To keep everyone on the same page.

We think that's a good place for a Volunteer Manager to spend time: informed optimism. But not everyone is wired that way.

Being a solid manager is great—but not enough.

Being a good salesperson is great—but not enough.

You need someone who's engaging and a leader. And someone who is determined to be an informed optimist. It's that blend of positive realism that will energize your ministry from top to bottom, stem to stern.

So when you find the right person, how do you bring him or her on board? As a paid staff member or an unpaid volunteer staff member?

> "It's that blend of positive realism that will energize your ministry from top to bottom, stem to stern."

Should You Pay a Volunteer Manager—or Not?

The short answer is: It depends.

Does your congregation have the resources to pay someone to fill this role? If so, you'll have more access to that person. Your Volunteer Manager won't be fitting in the tasks and responsibilities around a money-making job.

But there's no guarantee that just because you pay someone, that will make the person perform better or that the person will be more reliable or stay in the role longer.

Still—we live in a society that tends to believe we get what we pay for. That is, if it's a paid position, the manager will be perceived as having more power and "pull" than if it's an unpaid position.

So what's the right answer? Again: It depends.

If you, as a church, feel that having a well-organized volunteer ministry is of sufficient value to invest time, energy, space, and prayer into the effort—it's not a stretch to think it's valuable enough to be worth some money, too.

Here are some relevant questions to ask—and answer—as you consider whether to create a paid staff position:

- What role in achieving your vision will the volunteer ministry have? How important will it be, given that role, to have someone in that position seen as an equal to other professionals and leaders of ministries?

- Do you have the resources to fund the position? If not, can you raise funds for that position? Are you *willing* to raise the funds?

- Do you have individuals with the skills and experience necessary to carry out the position? Will one of them be willing to accept the role as an unpaid staff member?

Some *irrelevant* questions to *not* ask are:

- Will the person be more committed if we do/don't pay him or her?

- Will the person stay with the position longer if we pay him or her?

- Can we still expect a high level of performance from this person if he or she fills the position as an unpaid volunteer staff member?

You don't ask those questions for several reasons:

1. *Money doesn't buy commitment; it buys availability.* Paid staff aren't more committed than unpaid volunteers, but they're probably more available. You insult the integrity of volunteers to imply they can be bought. The best ones can't.

> "You insult the integrity of volunteers to imply they can be bought."

2. *Nobody can guarantee longevity.* If you pay a Volunteer Manager, she may move. If you pay her, she may quit. Ditto if you don't pay her.

The simple fact is that paychecks don't guarantee longevity—unless someone needs a paycheck and is stepping into the role until a full-time job can be found. In that case alone longevity is likely to be enhanced . . . but not necessarily.

3. *It's a foundational principle that we don't lower standards for volunteers.* If you'd expect a paid staffer to hit a level of excellence, expect an unpaid staff member to hit the same mark.

A colleague discovered that her pastor was growing ever more uncomfortable with her because she was serving in a full-time, unpaid position as a church Volunteer Manager. He was wondering if he could truly hold her accountable without having a paycheck as leverage. That situation is less about paychecks than the pastor's belief that only money can be a motivator and only paid ministry truly counts.

Your church can pay someone—or not. It's up to you. There are pluses and minuses on both sides of the equation, depending on what resources your church has available.

Some churches begin the Volunteer Ministry Manager role as an unpaid position, and eventually they come to value it so highly that it becomes a paid role. Other churches successfully maintain the position as an unpaid staff position.

But either way—it's a staff position. It must have the power and prestige that comes with a true staff position so the person serving as Volunteer Manager can function effectively.

> "But either way— it's a staff position."

Make the "paid/unpaid" decision through prayer and discussion, and share with your congregation how that decision was made, and why. And remember: It doesn't pay to cut corners. If you're trying to cut corners by not paying someone, where else are you cutting corners? Will you provide the funds, support, and involvement the volunteer ministry needs to be viable?

Two Ways to Support Your Volunteer Manager

First, ensure that the Volunteer Manager is directly responsible to the senior pastor or an associate pastor.

Whether the person responsible for leading your volunteer ministry is an unpaid volunteer or a paid staff member, the Director of Volunteer Ministries should be considered *at the same level as any other ministry director in your church.*

In other words, the Volunteer Ministry Director is just as important as your Music and Worship Director, your Youth Director, or your Director of Christian Education. Your

Volunteer Director needs to be on the same routing slips as other leaders, and sit in the same staff planning sessions.

The volunteer ministry exists to support every other area of ministry by finding volunteers to fill key positions. Volunteer ministry directors need to know what's going on, which ministry areas are expanding or shrinking, and what upcoming needs might be.

A second way to ensure support and nurture for your Volunteer Manager is to establish an advisory team or board. This team will provide continuous feedback and input to the ministry. As already mentioned, it can be comprised of . . .

- Representatives from the original task force,

- Program or ministry leaders from within the church,

- Other church staff members, and

- Active volunteers in the church.

Just like your original task force, the advisory team will be chartered and given job descriptions. Approach chartering an advisory team the same way you approached chartering a task force.

This team can meet periodically to give input, assess the volunteer ministry, and continue to uplift the ministry in prayer. In addition, this team can serve as ambassadors for the volunteer ministry throughout the church and into the community.

A well-chosen task force is worth its weight in gold. Work with your Volunteer Manager to create one. The right blend of people will energize your energizer, and keep him or her mindful of all the good that's being accomplished through the volunteer ministry.

In ministry, like life, little happens without energy. But energy isn't a bottomless well; without help your reserve of enthusiasm and energy will eventually be used up.

That's why you need for your ministry to be energized by more than you. You can do—and *are* doing—tremendous things. But you can't do *everything,* so you need to plug your-self and the volunteer ministry into the life-giving energy of . . .

People—both the church leadership and church membership

Vision—one that inspires, defines the program, and attracts volunteers

Mission—that provides clear purpose

Prayer—personal and corporate time with God that refreshes your heart and renews your perspective, humor, and perseverance

The energy sizzling from these sources will empower your goals, invigorate your task force, and fortify your spirit as you continue to charge full speed ahead toward the future God has in mind for your church and your ministry.

Ready to keep going? Next you'll take practical steps to turn your vision and mission into reality!

Meeting with Leaders to Create a Volunteer Ministry

Leadership Meeting Agenda
(est. duration of meeting: 2.5 hours)

Purpose of the Meeting

To provide an overview of what a volunteer ministry is, and what it does.

To hear and understand the leadership's vision for the volunteer ministry.

To identify any barriers or concerns the leadership might perceive exist.

Desired Outcomes of the Meeting

The leadership understands the big picture of volunteer ministry.

The leaders understand their roles and what is expected of them.

Any barriers and concerns are shared.

Meeting Topic	Desired Outcome	Time
Meeting Opening: Pray, read Scripture, and review the agenda	Everyone understands why we're here	10 min.
Overview of volunteer ministry	Everyone understands the concept of volunteer ministry	15 min.
Leaders share their vision for the volunteer ministry for our church	Everyone understands the various visions from all perspectives	15 min.
Leaders discuss their roles in relation to the volunteer ministry	Agreement on each leader's roles	30 min.

Leaders identify and discuss any barriers and concerns they have regarding implementing the volunteer ministry	Barriers and concerns are listed and actions defined to address them, if possible	45 min.
Meeting closure: Next steps for the volunteer ministry, end with prayer	Everyone understands the next steps for the volunteer ministry	15 min.

Facilitator Outline for the Leadership Meeting

1. Meeting Opening
Your **purpose** is to . . .

- Focus on God's intent for the volunteer ministry.

- See that people understand the purpose and desired outcomes of the meeting.

The desired **outcomes** are:

- Everyone will seek God's will on proceeding with the volunteer ministry.

- Everyone will understand the purpose and desired outcomes of the meeting.

Open this meeting with prayer asking for God's guidance. Read Romans 12:3-8 aloud, then briefly explain how a volunteer ministry will help this process happen. Read through the desired outcomes of the meeting, and then read through the agenda topics, giving an outline of how the meeting will proceed.

2. Overview of Volunteer Ministry
Your **purpose** is to . . .

- Paint a picture of an effective church volunteer ministry.

- Identify essential components of an effective volunteer ministry.

The desired **outcomes** are . . .

- Leaders will understand how an effective volunteer ministry looks.

- Leaders will understand what it takes to create an effective volunteer ministry.

Present a model of an effective volunteer ministry. List the components that are essential (for example, interview each volunteer for placement based on gifts unique to that individual). As you go through the presentation, discuss with the leaders what is already in place and what is necessary to implement in your church.

3. Leaders Share Their Vision for the Church Volunteer Ministry

Your **purpose** is to . . .

- Give leaders the chance to explore what a volunteer ministry would be like for our church.

The desired **outcomes** are . . .

- Leaders will "catch" the vision of the volunteer ministry.

- Leaders begin to "buy in" to the work ahead.

4. Leaders Discuss Their Roles in Relation to the Volunteer Ministry

Your **purpose** is to . . .

- Help leaders understand what activities they'll be responsible for in relation to the volunteer ministry.

The desired **outcome** is . . .

- Leaders will agree on the roles they'll have in relation to the volunteer ministry.

Discuss what reporting and decision-making will be needed within the volunteer ministry. Get agreement about who will be responsible for which actions. Discuss the lines of communication needed among all the ministries and how communication will happen. Discuss expectations the leaders have of each other and the person who will be leading the volunteer ministry.

5. Leaders Will Identify and Discuss Barriers and Concerns
Your **purpose** is to . . .

- Help leaders discuss the barriers they think might impede the progress of the volunteer ministry.

- Help leaders share concerns they have about the volunteer ministry.

The desired **outcomes** are . . .

- Leaders will openly discuss barriers and concerns.

- Leaders will identify actions that will address the identified barriers and concerns.

Create a list of barriers and concerns first. On a flip chart, draw a vertical line down the middle of the page. Label the left-hand column "Barriers" and the right-hand column "Actions." Record the barriers in the left-hand column first. Then go back and ask what actions could be taken to eliminate or minimize the barriers. Assign a name and a date to the actions, if possible.

Create a list of concerns in the same way. If there are any actions that can be taken, list those with a name and a date. Some concerns may just be statements of concern, and no action can be taken.

These two lists will be helpful six months into the implementation to revisit and evaluate. Did the barriers happen? Were the concerns eliminated?

6. Meeting Closure

Your **purpose** is to . . .

- Determine the next steps to take to implement the volunteer ministry.

The desired **outcomes** are . . .

- You'll meet the desired outcomes of the meeting.

- You'll know the next steps to take to establish the volunteer ministry.

Get agreement on the next steps you can take regarding the volunteer ministry, and make them as specific as possible. Close in prayer, thanking God for working through the church leadership and for all the blessings that will flow to the congregation through the volunteer ministry.

Sample Completed Charter Document

Task Force Name: The Volunteer Ministry Task Force

Task Force Mission (Purpose):
Our mission is to explore the scope and possibilities that God intends for an organized volunteer ministry for our church.

Task Force Vision (Desired Outcomes):
When our work is done, we will clearly understand what God calls us to build in the volunteer ministry, and we will have laid the foundation for that ministry.

Task Force Sponsor:
The Church Board

The Sponsor's Role:
Two board members will sit on the task force.

Task Force Authority:
This task force can pray and discern what God intends for the volunteer ministry. This task force can engage the

congregation in what their needs are in a volunteer ministry. This task force can recommend to the board the elements necessary for a viable volunteer ministry including staff, support, space, and financial resources.

This task force cannot—without approval—spend more than $500 on research or materials.

Task Force Member Roles and Responsibilities (What tasks will be accomplished, and by whom—that is, who will call the meetings, who will facilitate the meetings):

- Maria will create and send out the agendas and facilitate the meetings.

- Tom will arrange for the meeting rooms and equipment needed.

- Jose will remind members of refreshment sign-ups.

- Ruth will type meeting notes and distribute via e-mail.

- Devotions will be shared, and members will sign up for meetings.

- Victor will write articles for the newsletter and announcements.

Task Force Time Frame:

This task force will have completed its work when the foundation for the volunteer ministry is complete and others are designated to manage the ministry. This task force may be available for a period to offer support to those who are designated.

Task Force Decision-Making (How will we make decisions?):

We'll make decisions by consensus with a fallback of a vote with a simple majority. (We define consensus as a decision that everyone can "live with" and actively support.)

Task Force Interactions (What are our ground rules?):

- We'll always do full devotions at the beginning of our meetings.

- We'll always end our meetings with prayer.

- We'll speak one at a time and listen carefully to each other.

- We'll check out assumptions before we leap to conclusions.

- We'll affirm each other for the work we are doing together.

- We'll start our meetings on time and end on time.

Task Force Interface with Others (How will this task force communicate with others?):

We'll list who we need to communicate with at the end of each meeting to ensure we are communicating the right amount of information to the right people in the right way.

Task Force Progress (How will we measure progress on the task force?):

- We'll set specific goals and measure progress on those goals at each meeting.

- We'll assess involvement of other stakeholders.

Task Force Feedback (How will we get feedback on what we are doing?):

- We'll ask for feedback when we are interacting with other groups and individuals in the church.

- We'll acknowledge the support we get from others through prayer and assistance.

Task Force Celebration (How will we celebrate progress on the task force?):

- We'll acknowledge our own achievements on our goals.

- We'll celebrate as we move forward toward our vision.

- We'll celebrate our work together when we sunset.

Title: Task Force Member Job Description

Position Summary: The Volunteer Ministry Task Force exists to explore the scope and possibilities that God intends for an organized volunteer ministry for [name of church]. Members of the task force will be committed to prayer and discernment to this end. Members will work together to assess needs of the congregation and opportunities for an organized volunteer ministry.

The task force will also assist in implementing programming to meet those needs through the creation of a volunteer ministry.

The Strategic Fit: We're called to provide nurture and care to each other as Christians. We're also called to be good stewards of the resources given to us by God. An effective and efficient volunteer ministry will help our church do and be both. Our church's vision is [fill in].

Key Job Responsibilities:

- To pray unceasingly for the volunteer ministry.

- To attend meetings to determine the scope of the volunteer ministry.

- To do work outside of meetings when requested to assess the congregation's needs.

- To assume tasks that will establish the volunteer

ministry. These tasks may include creating job descriptions, interviewing potential volunteers, or other tasks that will help establish the volunteer ministry.

- To follow through with people and activities to achieve the goals of the task force.

- To communicate the work of the task force with others openly and honestly.

Benefits: Being a member on the task force will provide . . .

- The opportunity to interact with other believers in the congregation.

- The chance to grow spiritually through discipline of focused prayer, reading of Scripture, and devotions.

- An opportunity to impact this ministry from the beginning.

- The opportunity to be a significant contributor to the church's vision.

Qualifications:

- It would be helpful if the task force member had some experience with this congregation.

- It will be important that the task force member has the ability and willingness to commit and follow through.

- It would be helpful if the task force member has been a volunteer within the church before.

Supervision: The task force member is responsible to the task force chair and/or the sponsor of the task force. The task force member is also responsible to honor the ground rules of the task force.

Signature of Task Force Member_____
Date _____
(Note: You can have individual members sign a charter, or do it as a group.)

Dialogue about Change Agenda

Purpose

- To explore the impact of creating a new volunteer program in our church.

Desired Outcomes

- Everyone will understand the concept of volunteer ministry you're proposing to implement.

- You will create a list of benefits of implementing the program.

- You will create a list of reasons why we need to change what we're doing now.

- You will create a list of changes/losses that people might experience.

Before the Meeting

Prior to the meeting, write the following on a flip chart page:

- Name

- How long you've attended this church

- What volunteer jobs you've held at this church

- A pleasant surprise you once received while serving in a volunteer role

Have nametags and pens to fill them out available, and ask each person to fill out and wear a nametag as he or she enters the room. Don't assume everyone knows the name of each person at the meeting. If nothing else, nametags might save you from making an embarrassing mistake!

Prepare refreshments. Use refreshments that are easy to eat while walking around talking with other people.

Introduction (15 minutes)
Begin by thanking everyone for coming.

Then ask people to introduce themselves by sharing the information on the flip chart sheet. Go first so people know how much detail you're expecting from each participant.

After each person has been introduced, offer a brief prayer in which you thank God for the volunteer contributions of the people in the room. Ask for guidance as together you all consider the future and how to best serve both God and the congregation.

Volunteer Program Overview (25 minutes)
Give a brief overview about volunteer ministry. Define it and share some context of how it plays a role in God's church. Volume 1 of this series can provide you with some thoughts to share. Be sure you include the three theologies identified in volume 1, and explain how implementing them more fully is part of your church's faithfulness in discipleship.

Ask participants to share their responses to this question:

How could our church benefit from having a better-organized volunteer program?

Record their answers on a flip chart. Be careful to accurately represent what people say. If you're unsure about something, ask.

After collecting a page or two of comments, or when the flow of comments seems to be slowing considerably, tape the comments page or pages to the wall where participants can see them.

Dialogue Prompting (30 minutes)
Indicate the suggestions and ask: **Why can't we stay here? Why can't we just keep things the way they are indefinitely?**

Again, record participants' observations. Tape the flip chart paper on the wall where participants can see them.

Say: **There's pain in making changes, but there can also be pain in staying where we are. There are consequences either way. What are the consequences of our staying where we are? We've summarized some of them on this sheet I just hung up.**

Ask for a volunteer to read through the list, framing the comments in the form of consequences. For instance, "We don't have enough nursery staff" might translate to "We won't have enough nursery workers to care for the babies of visitors."

Jot down the consequences—both positive and negative—identified by participants on a separate sheet of flip chart paper.

When you've finished, hang this consequence sheet next to the benefit sheet you created earlier.

Say: **It looks like our church could benefit from making changes in how we handle volunteer recruitment and service. Those changes will certainly stretch us, and they may be painful in some ways. But the pain we feel will be growing pains, and in time we'll find ourselves better able to serve God and our church.**

The people in this room are instrumental in deciding how volunteers are used in our church. God has used your vision and skills to accomplish much. I know we'll continue to accomplish much. As the leaders of the volunteer leadership program consider what changes to make, and what timeline to use in making them, I hope you'll continue to be active and involved . . . and available to give counsel and direction.

Refreshments (20 minutes)
Invite people to stay for refreshments, and to continue talking. Point out that your 90-minute meeting wrapped up early so there would be time for this less formal discussion time.

Be available to listen and answer questions.

Sample Volunteer Ministry Vision and Mission Statements

Sample Vision Statements

We will be a volunteer community that:

- Attracts people

- Creates a volunteer experience that enables the discovery and sharing of spiritual gifts

- Keeps volunteers connected and interested

- Meets the people's needs of the church's identified programs

Our vision is to guarantee that every volunteer is empowered, equipped to use his or her gifts, valued, trained, utilized, and appreciated.

We will increasingly become a uniquely compassionate community reflecting Christ's presence by actively serving others, actively receiving and sharing God's Word of Law and gospel, and actively lifting up prayer as the heartbeat for our daily living and for the daily life of our church.

Sample Mission Statements

The Volunteer Ministry exists to show God's love by giving of ourselves to meet the many needs of Living Hope Baptist Church.
(Living Hope Baptist Church, Bowling Green, Kentucky)

The Volunteer Services Ministry at Southeast exists to make it easy for people to connect with God, the church, and one another through volunteer service to Christ.

(Southeast Christian Church, Louisville, Kentucky)

Helping people in need and following Christ's command that we love one another lies at the heart of our Christian faith.

(Bedford Presbyterian Church, Bedford, New York)

Creating Vision and Mission Statements

Steps for Creating a Mission Statement Worksheet

1. Whom do we serve?

   _____
   _____
   _____

2. What services do we provide?

   _____
   _____
   _____

3. What's unique about us within this church?

   _____
   _____
   _____

Now, craft a simple statement:

What's the most important phrase from everything you wrote above? (*It goes first.*)

Then follow this first phrase with the remaining phrases.

   _____
   _____
   _____
   _____

After you have a statement, review it again and see if you can cut out any text. You want to be as brief and clear as possible. Simplify where you can.

Agenda for Mission/Vision Meeting

(est. duration of meeting: 4 hours)

Purpose of the Meeting

To create a shared mission and shared vision for the volunteer ministry

Desired Outcome of the Meeting

To reach agreement on a shared mission and shared vision

Meeting Topic	Desired Outcome	Time
Meeting Opening: Pray, introductions, and review agenda	Everyone understands why we're here and how we'll proceed for the meeting	10 min.
Introduction to volunteer ministry	Everyone understands what a volunteer ministry is	20 min.
Create a shared vision	Agreement on, at minimum, a draft of the shared vision	90 min.
Break		10 min.
Create a shared mission	Agreement on a draft of the shared mission	90 min.
Meeting closure: Thanks to all, next steps for the volunteer ministry	Meeting closure complete	20 min.

Logistics for Vision/Mission Meeting
Setting up for the meeting:

- Select a comfortable room appropriate for the anticipated number of participants.

- If possible, set up tables in a workable U-shape.

- Place flip charts where participants can easily see them.

- If serving food, put the food where it won't be a distraction.

- Make sure there's wall space for hanging individual flip chart pages.

Supplies needed for the meeting:

- Prepared flip chart pages (See pages 106-108 for content of flip charts)

- Facilitator script

- Name tent cards with participants' names printed on them

- Markers

- Masking tape for taping flip chart pages on the wall

- At least one full pad of flip chart paper

- Extra pens and pencils

- Dot stickers to use while voting

Meeting Facilitator Information and Script
1. Meeting Opening
Your **purpose** is to . . .

- Focus on God's intent for the volunteer ministry.

- Warm up the group, as some participants may have reservations and apprehension about the four hours they'll be together.

- See that people understand the purpose and desired outcomes of the meeting.

The desired **outcomes** are:

- Participants will experience the tone for the day as informal but organized.

- Everyone will understand the purpose and desired outcomes of the meeting.

Introduce yourself and your investment in the volunteer ministry. Do this by sharing your name tent, which is already filled out.

Say: **In front of you is a name tent. On the front of the tent card write the following: your name** (center), **what your volunteer role is in the church (if you have one), and the number of years you've been in this congregation.**

Lead all participants in briefly introducing themselves using the information written on their tent cards.

Say: **We have a full agenda that has room for lots of discussion. I'll make sure we stay on task and move through the agenda. Our purpose today is to come to agreement on a mission and a vision for the volunteer ministry of our church. Our desired outcomes are agreements on our statements of mission and vision.**

Lead a brief prayer asking God for wisdom and a spirit of peace and cooperation.

2. Introduction to Volunteer Ministry

Your **purpose** is to . . .

- Give all participants an understanding of what a church volunteer ministry is.

- Identify essential components of an effective volunteer ministry.

The desired **outcomes** are . . .

- Participants will understand what's included in a church volunteer ministry.

Make notes from volume 1 regarding the definition of volunteer ministry, and what elements are part of an effective ministry. Describe some success stories. You might choose to invite a member from another church that has a successful volunteer ministry to make a brief presentation at this point.

3. Create a Shared Vision
Your **purpose** is to . . .

• come to agreement on the shared vision.

The desired **outcomes** are . . .

• Participants will build a vision

• Participants will reach a consensus agreement on a draft of the vision

Present flip chart page 1.

Say: **We want to come to an agreement about why this volunteer ministry exists. We may not come out with a polished, final statement. Let me request that we follow this ground rule: If I hear you debating over words about intent, I'll let the discussion continue. If I hear you debating semantics or language preferences, we may have to stop and defer this to a smaller group to do the wordsmithing. Is this okay with you?**

Say: **Here's a definition of "vision." It's a word with many meanings, but the one that will be useful to us is "Where You're Heading."**

Present flip chart page 2, then say: **A statement of vision is important to have for a number of reasons. Consider these . . .**

Read the bulleted points aloud.

Say: **We're ready to build our vision statement. Let me create a scenario for you in order to get started. We're going to fast-forward to get to the future. We are** fast-forwarding all the way to [year], five years from now. We've stopped the tape, and here we are—it's [year].

And check this out—it seems our church is now nationally recognized for our volunteer ministry. I'm a reporter assigned to your story. I need to ask you these questions: "What did you focus on to get where you are today? What did you spend your time doing?"

Present flip chart page 3.

Say: **Let's continue with the interview as I ask these questions, too. Let's work through them as I take notes on flip chart pages.**

Record participants' description of the future as they give it to you. You will most likely fill several flip chart pages with information as participants describe the future. Make sure they continue to describe something the church does *not yet have today*.

When the discussion wanes, review the list for common themes. Circle main themes with different color markers.

Say: **We're now ready to begin drafting vision statements. For this step, you'll form into small groups** [or pairs].

Form participants into different groups or pairs. Give each grouping another piece of flip chart paper and a marker.

Say: **Here are your instructions: Based on the descriptions of [year] that you came up with, give us your best shot at a vision statement. Stay concise rather than verbose. Choose a format that works for you. It can be a page, a list, a statement, symbols, graphics, art, whatever. You have about 15 minutes.**

Give a three-, two-, and one-minute countdown.

Hang the drafts in front. Stand at the wall, and have a spokesperson from each group read their group's vision statement. With *gusto*. Twice! Listen for reactions from the larger group as the statements are read. There may be one statement that has broad appeal, so it will be a good starting place for creating a common statement from the collection.

Circle common phrases, each set in a different color, or record them on a blank flip chart page, leaving spaces between phrases.

Say: **We need to come up with a combined statement that we can all live with. Give me the phrases for this combined statement.**

Record phrases on a blank flip chart page, leaving spaces between phrases. Ask participants to complete the statement with linking words. If it's taking longer than the time allotted in the agenda, you may want to assign a couple of people to finish word-smithing the statement later.

If participants *are* able to get to one statement, as a group check it against the criteria on the Checking Our Vision flip chart page. (Present flip chart page 4.)

Also, if your church has a vision statement, put that up next to the volunteer ministry statement to ensure the volunteer ministry statement aligns with the overall church statement.

Ask: **Is our vision statement one you can live with? One you can actively support?**

4. Break
Be sure you remind participants that you'll start promptly in ten minutes. Remind participants where they can find restrooms. Have snacks available.

5. Create a Shared Mission
Your **purpose** is to . . .

• come to agreement on the shared mission.

The desired **outcomes** are . . .

• Participants will build a mission

• Participants will reach a consensus agreement on a draft of the mission

Present flip chart page 5.
Say: **Here's a definition of "mission." The dictionary**

suggests several meanings, but the one that gets at what we want is "why you exist."

Present flip chart page 6.

Read the bulleted points, then say: **When we craft a mission statement, the statement is more than words. It represents the debate and discussion we've gone through to write it. It gets pulled out and used regularly. It helps us make good decisions.**

Now I'd like you to answer three questions I'll ask you one at a time. As you give me your answers, I'll write them on a page. The first question is: Who does our volunteer ministry exist to serve?

Present flip chart page 7.

Record participants' answers on the page. When participants are running out of suggestions, or they've finished the list, ask each person to select the three items on the list that he or she feels are the most important. Give each person three dots with which to vote. Tell them to put one dot next to each of their top three choices. (Note: This approach gives participants the chance to move around.)

When voting has ended, record the number of votes next to each item. Circle those with the highest votes. Hang that flip chart on a side wall.

Present flip chart page 8.

Say: **The second question that will help us create our mission is "What products and services does the volunteer ministry provide to people it serves?"**

Record participants' answers using the same voting technique you used before. Hang this flip chart next to the first flip chart on the side wall.

Present flip chart page 9.

Say: **What makes the volunteer ministry unique?**

Again, record participants' answers. This question might

take them a little longer to answer. There's no need to vote or prioritize this list. When participants are finished, hang this flip chart next to flip chart page 8.

Say: **We're now ready to begin drafting mission statements. For this step, we'll form into smaller groups** [or into pairs] **to begin writing a statement of mission.**

Form the groups and provide them with a piece of flip chart paper and a marker.

Say: **Here are your instructions: Based on these three lists, give us your best shot at a mission statement. Please write your drafts on a piece of flip chart paper, and write large enough that the group can see it when we hang it up. If you have trouble getting started, you can start with the words, "The mission of our volunteer ministry is to . . . " You have about 15 minutes.**

Give a three-, two-, and one-minute countdown.

Hang the drafts in front. Stand at the wall, and have a spokesperson from each group read their group's mission statement. With *gusto*. Twice! Listen for reactions from the larger group as the statements are read. There may be one statement that has broad appeal, so it will be a good starting place for creating a common statement from the collection.

Ask: **What common phrases do you see that are being repeated from statement to statement?** Draw a circle around common phrases, each in a different color, or record them on a blank flip chart page, leaving spaces between phrases.

Say: **We need to come up with a combined statement that we can all live with. Could we start with one of these statements** [the one that got the most positive reaction] **and add, change, or delete to create your shared mission?**

If so, start on a clean sheet. If not, suggest to the group the following . . . **Look at the common phrases and tell me what's the most important of these? Let's begin with that. Give me the other phrases for this combined statement.**

Ask participants to complete the statement with linking words. If it looks like they'll not be able to arrive at a shared statement within the time allotted in the agenda, suggest that a smaller team continue to word-smith the statement.

If participants *are* able to get to one statement, as a group check it against the criteria on the Checking Our Mission flip chart page. (Present flip chart page 10.)

Also, if your church has a mission statement, put that up next to the volunteer ministry statement to ensure the volunteer ministry statement aligns with the overall church statement.

Ask: **Is our mission statement one you can live with? One you can actively support?**

6. Meeting Closure
Thank everyone for coming and investing their time in the volunteer ministry. Explain the next steps you'll be taking to launch or rekindle the volunteer ministry.

Prepared Flip Charts for Mission/Vision Meeting

Flip chart page 1
Vision: Where you're headed

Flip chart page 2
Why vision?

- It embodies the tension between today and desired future.

- It provides a sense of direction.

- It's a tool that communicates where the organization wants to be.

- It provides a framework for opportunity and selection.

- It allows members to be energized about what is yet to happen.

Flip chart page 3
What's Happening Five Years from Now?

- What are clients getting from our organization?

- What do we see going on in and around here?

- What does our organization look like?

- What do our clients look like?

- Who does our organization have relationships (partnerships) with?

- What new needs are we meeting?

- Where are we spending our time?

- Where are we spending our money?

- How would we describe what has changed most in the last five years?

Flip chart page 4
Checking Our Vision Statement
Is our statement of vision . . .

- Outcome focused, describing where we want to be in five years?

- Actionable—can we write goals and vision priorities based on it?

- Simple, yet compelling?

Flip chart page 5
Mission: Why we exist

Flip chart page 6
Why mission?

- Allows the volunteer ministry to focus on what's truly important.

- The ministry can prioritize which problems to address.

- Allows for conflict resolution.

- Prioritizes where people spend time, energy, and resources for the volunteer ministry.

- Creates synergy.

Flip chart page 7
Who does our volunteer ministry exist to serve?

Flip chart page 8
What products and services does the volunteer ministry provide to people it serves?

Flip chart page 9
What makes the volunteer ministry unique?

Flip chart page 10
Checking Our Mission Statement

- Does our statement of mission clearly describe why we exist?

- Is our statement of mission inspiring to all of us?

- Is it demonstrable? Can we see how our assets have been used toward the mission?

- As written, does our statement of mission provide us with clarity for making decisions?

- As written, will our statement of mission keep us focused on what's truly important?

Volunteer Ministry Manager Sample Job Descriptions

Sample 1

Position Description

Membership Ministries Coordinator
First Presbyterian Church of Granville, Ohio

Job Summary

The Membership Ministries Coordinator helps members and friends of the church to identify and claim their gifts, talents, and areas of interest for personal growth, and helps them to identify areas of ministry. The Membership Ministries Coordinator identifies and profiles needs of the church and its ministry, both within the congregation and outside of the church in mission areas.

Purpose of the Position

An important but often neglected spiritual ministry of the church is to call forth, name, and encourage the use of the gifts of members. These gifts have their source in God and are best expressed in some form of Christian service. The Membership Ministries Coordinator takes the lead in coordinating this ministry of gifts and assisting members and friends in linking their interests and abilities with the needs of the church and the world.

Authority

The Membership Ministries Coordinator reports to the pastor who has responsibility for membership, and is a member of the staff, attending one staff meeting per month.

Responsibilities

- Develop goals, actions, and budget at least annually.

- Develop, or supervise the development of, job descriptions for volunteer positions.

- Regularly interview and assist members and friends of the church to identify their gifts and talents, areas for personal growth, and their sense of calling.

- Maintain a current database containing this information. Assist with their integration into service.

- Maintain support systems for volunteers: placement, training, supervision, feedback, and recognition.

- Regularly profile the needs of the church, both within the congregation and outside of the church in its areas of mission. Maintain a current database containing this information.

- Assist church leaders as they recruit volunteers for their needs.

- Communicate regularly throughout the congregation to keep members and friends informed.

- Keep current on congregational events, issues, initiatives, opportunities, and challenges.

Qualifications for Position
The candidate will possess management skills, will know the congregation, will work well with a variety of people, will be present during worship on Sunday, and will be motivated by the creative possibilities within the life of the congregation.

Terms of the Position
The duties and performance within this position will be reviewed annually by the Head of Staff. The position requires 10 hours per week and is a volunteer position.

Sample 2

Position Description
Title: Coordinator of Volunteer Ministry
Department: Outreach Ministries
Reports To: Associate Pastor of Outreach Ministries

Objective

To increase and maximize the number of volunteer opportunities and match more members to those opportunities. To promote spiritual growth by the concept that each person is serving in ministry when they respond to their faith as members of Christ's church (that is, priesthood of all believers, whole body of Christ, and giftedness of each child of God).

Specific Responsibilities/Duties

- Design and implement volunteer recruitment strategies to encourage more involvement from the congregation.

- Develop, or supervise the development of, job descriptions for volunteer positions.

- Design and implement volunteer retention strategies.

- Develop and maintain appropriate systems (such as one-on-one interviews) to help match members' gifts, talents, and abilities to appropriate and meaningful ministry opportunities.

- Develop procedures to involve the members in ministry opportunities, and follow up on placements of volunteers.

- Develop and maintain up-to-date records concerning volunteer services within the congregation.

- Present information about the volunteer ministry at all New Member classes.

- Serve as a resource person to church staff and lay leaders:

—Help them work with volunteers in designing strategies for the recruitment and retention of volunteers for their respective ministries

—Help them initiate training for volunteers as needed, and

—When necessary (and subject to the approval of the Associate Pastor of Outreach Ministries), personally contact church members to recruit them as volunteers.

• Facilitate recognition and appreciation for volunteers in ongoing and meaningful ways.

• Participate as a team member of staff, including attending staff meetings and regularly attending worship services at [church].

• Be available for other assignments and projects as needed and assigned.

Qualifications:
Faith/Spiritual Life: Committed Christian, with a strong Christian faith. Maintains a Christian lifestyle and active devotional life. Actively demonstrates Christian faith through lifestyle and actions.
Abilities/Skills: Good planning and organizational skills. Good communication skills, both written and verbal. Demonstrates strong teamwork and strong interpersonal skills. Goal-oriented and resourceful. Good knowledge of self and personal and spiritual gifts.
Education/Training: B.A. in Education or related field preferred. Training or experience in volunteer ministries or recruiting volunteers preferred. Experience working with and directing people. Experience working as a volunteer. Experience working with a variety of computer programs.

This is a part-time position. Salary of $1,250/month, 25 hours weekly (average). Hours may include daytime, evening, weekend, and holiday work.

VOLUNTEER JOB DESCRIPTIONS AND ACTION PLANS

Marlene Wilson, Author and General Editor

Group's Volunteer Leadership Series™
Volume 3
Group's Church Volunteer Central™

Loveland, Colorado

Group's Volunteer Leadership Series™, Volume 3

Volunteer Job Descriptions and Action Plans

Copyright © 2004 Group Publishing, Inc.

Visit our Web site: **www.grouppublishing.com**

Credits
Author: Marlene Wilson
Editors: Mikal Keefer and Brad Lewis
General Editor: Marlene Wilson
Chief Creative Officer: Joani Schultz
Art Director: Nathan Hindman
Cover Designer: Jeff Storm
Production Manager: Peggy Naylor

Unless otherwise noted, Scripture taken from the HOLY BIBLE, NEW INTERNATIONAL VERSION®. Copyright © 1973, 1978, 1984 International Bible Society. Used by permission of Zondervan Publishing House. All rights reserved.

Produced with the assistance of The Livingstone Corporation (www.LivingstoneCorp.com). Project staff includes Chris Hudson, Ashley Taylor, Mary Horner Collins, Joel Bartlett, Cheryl Dunlop, Mary Larsen, and Rosalie Krusemark.

Library of Congress Cataloging-in-Publication Data

Wilson, Marlene.
Volunteer job descriptions and action plans / Marlene Wilson.—1st American
        hardbound ed.
    p. cm. — (Group's volunteer leadership series ; v. 3)
    Includes bibliographical references.
    ISBN 0-7644-2747-4 (alk. paper)
    1. Voluntarism—Religious aspects—Christianity. 2. Christian leadership.
3. Church work. I. Title. II. Series.
    BR115.V64W556 2003
    253'.7—dc22   2003022120

10 9 8 7 6 5 4 3 2 1   12 11 10 09 08 07 06 05 04

Printed in the United States of America.

Contents

Introduction

Congratulations!

You've taken the first baby steps—well, maybe *giant* steps—toward launching or re-energizing your church's volunteer ministry. That's exciting, and I'm so glad that through these volumes we're able to come alongside you on your journey.

You've demonstrated that volunteers are valuable—so valuable that it's worth involving them in significant ministry. You've proven that as volunteers get more involved, your church will do a better job being what God wants you to be and doing what God wants you to do.

You have a vision and a mission statement. You've got people praying. You've pulled together a task force. So, *now* what do you do? What are the next steps?

Let me suggest five things you'll want to do now—and you'll learn how to do them in this volume.

First, put your volunteer task force to work creating action plans for the volunteer ministry's goals and objectives. Here's a chance to practice your volunteer management skills! You don't need to do all the work yourself; it's time to get your team busy so there's ownership (and so you can take a break!).

Determine the aspects of your church's ministry where volunteers can effectively and meaningfully serve. Good thing you've gotten your church leaders' approval—you'll need their help here as you identify what volunteers will do—and where.

Create volunteer job descriptions. It's not hard to create these essential forms once you understand how to do it—and we'll walk you through the process so you feel comfortable and prepared.

Explore how to manage risks. Risk-management is something both you and your church leaders are concerned about. Let's make sure you address this issue head-on.

Finally, evaluate all that you're doing well, as well as areas where you can improve. Why? So you can take the process full circle yet again, prayerfully finding ways to create an even more vibrant, God-honoring, people-growing, relationship-building ministry to and through your church members.

ONE
Getting Down to Business

What do you expect volunteers to accomplish in your church? And in which areas of ministry? Here's how great planning—and action plans—will help you nail down those details.

Let's imagine that a well-off, well-loved person in your congregation died a few months ago. A few weeks after the funeral, a lawyer visits your church office with some interesting information.

"Mrs. Anderson left five million dollars to the church," announces the lawyer, "but she stipulated in her will that this money be used for one purpose only: to fund several new staff positions for key ministry areas in the church."

Really? No problem!

Then the lawyer drops the other shoe: "There was one other stipulation: The new staff members have to be brought on board in 60 days, and be successful in their positions for a year."

The odds are your church board would find a way to meet that evening in an emergency session. Inside a week there would be a plan in place outlining where the new staff positions would fit into the organization. Job descriptions would be written, advertising done, interviews arranged, and the new positions would be filled in 60 days—even if it took 18-hour days to fill the last opening.

During their first year the new staffers would receive ample training, get plenty of feedback and mentoring, and be compensated appropriately. They'd know exactly what they were doing well, what needed improvement, and how to go about meeting performance standards.

When that one-year anniversary rolled around and the lawyer came to see if he should sign over the check, he'd find a well-oiled, fully-functioning church staff. Why? Because there was tremendous motivation to see that each staff member had what was needed to be effective and successful.

The bad news is that you probably don't have a Mrs. Anderson waiting in the wings to give you five million dollars. But the good news is that you don't need her. If you'll go through the same careful, thorough planning process you'd go through to bring on paid staff and "hire" volunteers instead, you'll still accomplish an amazing amount of ministry.

> "It's worth planning thoroughly for a volunteer role."

My point: It's worth planning as thoroughly for a volunteer role as it is a paid staff member's role.

We know planning is important. We've gone on vacations. We've survived building programs. We know that failing to plan wastes time, money, and energy, and can result in programs that are disappointing to the people we serve.

Are we planning carefully when it comes to our volunteers?

Even at first blush, it's easy to see that there are many places volunteers can do significant ministry in your church. Later in this volume you and your task force will be pausing to look in detail at volunteer opportunities in your church (these are places volunteers *could* serve, not necessarily where they're *already* serving); for now let it be enough to see that you've just demonstrated the need for a volunteer ministry. You may have to demonstrate it again for your church's paid staff members.

By the way, since we're talking about both paid staff and volunteers, let me mention something to keep in mind as you

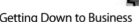
The Five Million Dollar Phone Call

Imagine you've received a phone call from Mrs. Anderson's estate lawyer. You've got five million dollars to fund several new staff positions. What areas of ministry could use extra staff? Where would you spend the money to add staff?

_____

_____

_____

_____

_____

Now, in those ministry areas, how might volunteers fill those same roles and accomplish those same tasks?

_____

_____

_____

_____

_____

(Permission to copy this form from *Volume 3: Volunteer Leadership Series; Volunteer Job Descriptions and Action Plans*, granted for local church use. © 2004 Group Publishing, Inc., P.O. Box 481, Loveland, CO 80539. www.grouppublishing.com)

and your task force move ahead in planning how to use volunteers. If your church (or ministry area) has both paid staff and volunteers, it's important that you emphasize the importance of *both*. While volunteers aren't paid to carry out some aspect of ministry, God calls them to be ministers (see the three theologies discussed in volume 1) just as he calls those who make their paid profession "ministry."

Make sure your volunteers feel like full partners in ministry, a vital part of your church's ministry team. Many of your volunteers are investing in the lives of others—caring for children in the nursery, teaching children in Sunday school or children's church, delving into relationships with middle schoolers and high schoolers, or helping adults grow spiritually in small groups and Sunday school classes. Those efforts are vitally important ministry; don't communicate somehow that volunteers are less significant than paid staff members.

> "Make sure your volunteers feel like full partners in ministry."

One way to help keep equity between paid and unpaid (volunteer) staff is to see that volunteers understand exactly why they're serving. They should agree with, and feel passion for, your church's or ministry's mission statement—as well as your goals and objectives.

Also, help volunteers understand that *you* see them as far more than unpaid labor. Interact with them as front line troops you trust entirely to invest in the lives of others.

You've determined some of the ministry areas in which volunteers could have an impact. Let's say one of those is the church office, where the pastor reports that chaos reigns supreme. It seems correspondence is always behind, the attendance record is six months out of date, and the sole paid secretary is overwhelmed.

You're determined to treat volunteers as full partners in ministry, so your office volunteer will have all the training, tools, and information necessary to be effective. The volunteer will have a comfortable desk, reasonable hours, and an invitation to attend general staff meetings.

So what's next? Do you open the office door, throw a volunteer in, and hope the volunteer thrives? No . . . because you've still got work to do before your volunteer can hope to be useful and effective. The volunteer is needed . . . but you're not sure exactly how. You've got to do some planning.

Creating Action Plans

The idea of creating action plans is pretty simple—your task force decides *what* to do, *how* you'll do it, *when* you'll do it, and exactly *who* will do it. In the context of volunteer leadership, planning is when you decide what things you'll actually *do* to achieve your objectives—and those plans become action plans.

> "You're determined to treat volunteers as full partners in ministry."

Looks simple when I explain it like that, doesn't it?

It *is* simple—but so is moving rocks.

I have a friend who once hired some workmen to shift some of the large boulders on her property so she could make better use of the land near her house. She and the foreman walked around the yard while she pointed to which boulders she wanted moved, and she pointed out exactly where she wanted them deposited. As she talked, the foreman carefully drew a map and drove stakes in the ground.

When they'd finished their stroll my friend looked at the map the foreman had drawn and confirmed that the wooden stakes were in the right spots.

"That," the foreman said with a grin as he tucked the map in his pocket, "was the *easy* part." He knew from experience that actually shifting the stones was difficult. So difficult, in fact, that he didn't want to do it twice—so he took great pains to be sure there was a firm plan in place before the work started.

You need similar plans: careful, thorough, and shared with everyone who either has to do the work or deal with the consequences.

In short, you need action plans.

You need them for your general work as a ministry (for instance, you'll need to meet with paid staff to gather information) and you'll need to create action plans for individual ministry areas (for instance, you may identify the need for a church office volunteer to accomplish key tasks). Those action plans for individual volunteers are the beginning of a job description, and we'll deal with those in depth shortly.

> **"You need action plans."**

Action Plans Defined

As I mentioned in volume 1, an "action plan" is where you determine specific steps to get you to each goal. You think through tactics and sequences of activities, what will happen and when, and what the budget will be.

Each of your volunteer ministry's goals needs a complete action plan, including (and I can't emphasize this enough) *to whom you are delegating the responsibility to achieve the goal.* (We'll explore *what* to delegate later in this volume.)

Through the years I've seen many voluntary efforts launched for worthy causes, but they lacked a plan. People saw a need and decided to do something about it, but because they didn't plan how they'd tackle the problem or implement a service, their efforts flourished briefly and then faded.

Volunteers who signed on to help those causes felt burned, and probably thought twice before volunteering again. People who were going to benefit from the efforts had their hopes temporarily raised, then felt less hopeful than before.

Nobody emerged a winner.

Action plans would have helped those good causes determine how to not just start strong, but also to finish strong. And any shortfalls in money, time, or expertise would have become obvious before reaching a critical point. If you're going to run out of gas, it's good to know that before you're out on the highway.

How Do You Find a Few Good Men—and Women?

When you're creating and implementing a volunteer ministry action plan, be sure to choose people to help you who have some competence in areas related to the goal. You need more than just willingness. Enthusiasm can carry you just so far.

If you were planning to remodel the church kitchen, wouldn't you feel more comfortable if a plumber or an electrician were sitting in on the meeting? They bring practical knowledge to the table, and that can help you keep from making wonderful plans that have no hope of ever being implemented.

It's a balance as you ask your task force to do planning with you. You want to have the enthusiasm of the uninformed ("Let's put the sink on an island in the center of the room—it will let more people help clean dishes") as well as the seasoned advice of the informed ("If we move the sink there, we'll have to put the plumbing straight through the pastor's study downstairs").

If you have experts on your task force, people tend to quickly defer to them. There's less brainstorming and "possibility thinking." But in reality, you did most of that possibility thinking back when you were generating a vision and mission statement. Now it's time to zero in on your goals and be practical in how you'll achieve them.

Your task force includes people who are representing constituencies, so give task force members permission to speak on behalf of their groups as plans unfold. A church staff member may have almost no preference about how the kitchen is remodeled apart from the budget involved, but the hospitality committee representative (who knows the ins and outs of potluck dinners) will have a *lot* to say.

> "Now it's time to zero in on your goals and be practical in how you'll achieve them."

Remind task force members that their expertise and experience is valued as action plans are developed. Encourage people to speak their minds.

As part of your action planning (remember, you'll design an action plan for each goal), let the person(s) responsible for that area help define the details. You've got a task force of the right people pulled together, so let them take the wheel on this process. Remember: Most people are far more committed to plans *they* help make than to plans *you* made. A suggestion you make that might be quickly dismissed as impractical will often, if suggested by a task force member, be given careful consideration. Modifications will be made. Compromises reached.

> "Action plans are useful only if you follow through."

And a notion that was initially thought impossible will eventually be transformed into a goal that's very reachable.

Action plans are useful only if you follow through and identify all the information you need. . .

Who will take responsibility for implementing the plan? You need a name. It may be a committee who completes the work, but you need the name of the person spearheading the effort.

How will the action be implemented? Be specific-break the action into steps that make sense and can be tracked.

When will each step be taken? Without a deadline you can't measure progress, so be specific.

The cost matters, too-especially if there are discounts or savings available if the plan is implemented in a timely fashion.

If you're a person who likes charts, those that follow might be helpful as you pull together your action plans. The first is bare-bones, and the second one on pages 16 and 17 allows you to plan in greater detail.

ACTION PLAN FOR THE FOLLOWING GOAL:

Who	How	When	Cost

ACTION PLAN FOR THE FOLLOWING GOAL:

Action Steps	Review Date	Risk	How to Measure Results

Obstacles Expected	Ideas to Avoid/ Lessen Obstacles	Our Success Confidence Level?

When Should You Plan?

Knowing precisely when to do your planning can be tough in church settings.

I've seen many ministries rolling along full steam, burning through people, money, and time, yet without a clear definition of exactly what the ministry is supposed to be doing. Somehow, the ministry leaders never turned an overarching purpose into measurable goals and objectives.

I've also seen that happen with new areas of ministry. Good people pull together to start a ministry to singles or to seniors. They jump in, but their lack of planning inevitably causes them to run into problems keeping support from church leadership, getting funds from the church budget, or even retaining the people they want to serve. Good volunteers get lost in the process. Potential volunteers don't see any promise for their own growth by being involved in a failing ministry. It becomes a mess because planning didn't happen in a timely fashion.

> "Planning needs to be an ongoing and constant process in your ministry."

Clearly, it's not a good idea to do planning too late. But it's also not a good idea to plan early on, then quit planning. When should you plan? A short answer: *Always* be planning.

Planning needs to be an ongoing and constant process in your ministry. That's one reason to loop the evaluation process back into the planning process. As you evaluate where you've been, you can see how needs have changed, workers have developed new interests, or your church has changed. As you evaluate and come up with new goals and objectives, you'll be aware of and be responsive to those changes.

How Do You Write Action Plans?

You can approach creating action plans in any number of ways, but I'd like to suggest a simple, four-step method. I'll briefly walk you through the steps, then provide an example of how it looks in the real world.

Step 1. Prepare

- State your goals and objectives clearly and specifically.
- Collect facts, opinions, and the experience of others that may bear on the situation at hand.
- Consult with everyone who may be involved—directly or indirectly.

Step 2. Decide

- Analyze all the data you've collected, and think through possible consequences.
- Develop alternative courses of action.
- Evaluate the alternatives and choose the best one.
- Set standards.

Step 3. Communicate, Communicate, Communicate

- Determine who'll be affected by the action plan—directly and indirectly.
- Select and implement the best methods for communicating the action plan to those people.
- Check to be sure everyone understands and accepts the action plan.

Step 4. Control

- Set checkpoints to evaluate progress on the action plan—key dates and steps.
- Compare actual with anticipated results.
- Take remedial action when necessary (change the current plan or even change plans altogether).

Four steps—it looks easy on paper, but we all know how simple things can become complex when you start to add people. The good news is that even when you add people, this really *is* a straightforward process.

Let's take a look at how these planning steps might look in a volunteer ministry setting. Suppose a preschool director is considering adding volunteers from the church to help with a weekday preschool/daycare ministry. The volunteers will work alongside paid staff caregivers.

Now let's run through those four planning steps again . . .

1. Prepare

- Goal: Add five volunteers from First Community Church to assist paid staff in preschool ministry.

- Check with state licensing board for limitations or restrictions on using volunteers, training requirements, and background checks required. Call other churches with similar programs to see if they use volunteers, and ask them to assess the strengths and weaknesses of volunteer involvement.

- Ask the preschool director and current paid staff to identify the busiest times of day when volunteers could help most.

2. Decide

- Ask the preschool director, one or two present staff members, and the church's Christian Education Director to form a committee to help make decisions.

- The committee reviews data and information collected in Step 1 and weighs the pros and cons of using volunteers.

Possible alternatives:

(1) Recruit five volunteers who will assist for two-hour blocks, one each morning of the week, during the busy child-drop-off time (7 to 9 A.M.).

(2) Recruit ten volunteers who will assist for two-hour blocks, one each morning of the week, and one each afternoon

of the week, during the busy child-drop-off time (7 to 9 A.M.) and child-pick-up time (4 to 6 P.M.).

(3) To meet state licensing requirements, volunteers will need intensive training. Before we invest in training a large number of volunteers, recruit two people and train them, and start a pilot program two mornings per week. Determine whether, because of licensing restrictions and requirements, a program using volunteers in preschool ministry will work at this time.

3. Communicate

- The committee decides the best method for communicating the plan to potential volunteers and to others who are affected (such as staff, or parents). Options for communication include a newsletter, group meetings, personal meetings and interviews, newspaper announcements, memos in children's diaper bags, and posting on the church web site.

- Once the final decision is implemented, the committee will make sure everyone is informed appropriately.

4. Control

- The committee realizes that part of the original plan in section 2 should include evaluation. The committee will become an advisory board and continue to meet monthly. They'll ask for verbal or written reports from the preschool director to evaluate if the program is meeting agreed-upon objectives.

- The committee will develop written surveys that will be completed every six months by parents of preschoolers in the program and by the volunteers involved.

- If there are any problems, the preschool director can call a special meeting to determine if there's a need to change the plan (for example, add additional volunteers or do additional training).

• After one year, the committee will evaluate the entire program and recommend whether to expand, drop, change, or leave it as is.

Do you see how the objective has been sharpened and focused into clear steps in an action plan? There's no painful detail, but enough information to let everyone make decisions that make sense—and that are based on a written plan.

Why You Need to Stay Flexible

Action plans can be very fluid. Small wonder, considering how quickly circumstances can change!

Once a volunteer is in place, be open to changing your action plans. Agree up front that you'll change anything that you both agree to, and that you'll always do so in writing. This is good practice if you only have a few volunteers; it's *essential* if you have a large number of volunteers. Putting things in writing builds trust because both you and your volunteers know you're on the same page.

> "All of these steps build on each other."

Remember that all of these steps build on each other up to this point.

If your vision changes, your mission statement will need to be reworked. If that happens, you need to revisit your goals and sharpen them into solid objectives. If you change objectives, you need to revise your action plan. It's like a line of dominoes; if the first one falls, the rest will be impacted, too.

While this sounds like it could be a lot of work, don't be discouraged. Chances are, if things change quickly, it means you're headed in good directions. If other changes happen—for example, you set an objective to recruit three adult Sunday school teachers before fall classes start, and your new volunteers quit before they finish their assignment—you need to revise your plans to reflect how you'll retain future volunteers.

And please don't view changing plans as failure. That's very often not the case.

Plans change when you work with people—especially when you work with people in a ministry setting where you need to be sensitive to God's leading and to the people with whom you're working. That's part of the landscape. Flexibility isn't a luxury—it's a necessity.

Consider the Apostle Paul. His epistles are peppered with references like this passage written to the church in Rome:

> *I do not want you to be unaware, brothers, that I planned many times to come to you (but have been prevented from doing so until now) in order that I might have a harvest among you, just as I have had among the other Gentiles. (Romans 1:13)*

Paul was an apostle. You'd think if *anyone* could do long-range planning with some insight, it would be Paul. But time and time again we see him changing plans, rolling with circumstances that appear, and pursuing opportunities that present themselves.

Stay flexible. It allows you to stay faithful.

> "Stay flexible. It allows you to stay faithful."

We haven't covered all the steps yet in what I call the Volunteer Leadership Planning Loop, but let me share all ten steps with you below. You'll be able to see how the steps flow, and it's a linear process.

I should point out that for existing volunteer positions the process is easier because as you loop through the planning—evaluation—planning process you may not need to make any changes at all.

The Volunteer Leadership Planning Loop

1. What's your *vision?*
   (Refer to your vision statement.)

2. What's your *mission?*
   (Refer to your mission statement.)

3. What are the major *goals and objectives* that will help you fulfill your mission and support your vision?

4. What's your *action plan* for each objective?

5. Write a *job description* for the key person you'll need to recruit to complete the action plan.

6. Decide where and how you can *recruit* appropriate people to take on these jobs based on the skills and time commitment required. Remember: The abilities, skills, and passions of the volunteers must align with what the jobs require.

7. Craft a *message* to communicate as you recruit people.

8. What *training and orientation* will volunteers need based on their experience and the requirements of the job? How will you provide the training?

9. What *supervision* will the volunteers require? (This step includes evaluating your own or the ministry leader's leadership style, as well as the supervisory style the volunteer needs.)

10. How will you recognize and evaluate your volunteers? (Keep in mind it's recognition and evaluation that keep volunteers recruited!)

Notice how step 10—recognizing and evaluating volunteers—is the primary way you keep volunteers on board, motivated, and effective. This planning process is a loop; you're never finished looking ahead. And this process recognizes that the best way to retain volunteers is to do an excellent job delivering on the fundamentals such as planning, creating job descriptions, and communicating.

Here's a secret we'll explore later in other volumes of this leadership series: *Volunteer retention isn't something you do as a separate campaign.* It's the logical outcome of doing other things correctly, including recognizing and evaluating volunteers. Note also that action plans (step 4) play a key role in the process. Until you've written action plans, you can't craft job descriptions or find appropriate volunteers. Action plans are *essential.*

We'll talk about job descriptions later in this volume, but until you have action plans you're not ready to write them. You don't know what you're trying to accomplish, so you don't know who you might need to get the job done.

Here's another secret for action plan success: *Don't treat all volunteers the same.* This is going to feel awkward, so promise you'll stick with me until I finish explaining . . .

If you want to see your action plans actually get implemented, make the volunteers who are responsible for shaping and carrying out those action plans your top ministry priority. If they phone, take the call. If they want to meet for coffee, get with them this week instead of next. If they email, reply within 24 hours.

Wait a minute, I hear you protesting. You want to treat everyone fairly, so *all* your volunteers are a top priority!

If you're leading five volunteers, that's probably possible. But as your ministry grows and you're looking at a list of ten, twenty, or a hundred volunteers, they can't all be your top priority. It's physically impossible.

What do you do?

I'd suggest you decide to not treat every volunteer the same.

While you're available to any volunteer who truly needs to see you, intentionally work through those volunteers who are responsible for overseeing other volunteers. If you've placed Tricia in charge of the nursery and she has fifteen volunteers reporting to her, *work through Tricia.* Pour your time and energy into Tricia, and let her handle issues that arise with those fifteen nursery volunteers.

You're not being mean or arrogant. You're being wise. After all, Jesus himself directed the majority of his teaching to a handful of disciples, then let them spread the word from there. Jesus was available to interact with the lepers, the ill, and the crowds of people who flocked to see him, but at the end of the day when he was providing mentoring, he sat with just a small group of disciples.

I sometimes refer to top volunteers—the people to whom we delegate significant responsibility and authority—as "achievers." They *love* achieving goals. They *love* achieving success. They do their jobs well, and they're creative, energetic, and action-oriented. They want to get moving and stay moving.

If you don't make achievers your top priority, they may very well move on without you, and perhaps head off in the wrong direction. Or they may simply lose motivation and momentum.

If achievers find you unavailable (and *they'll* define what that term means, by the way) too often, they'll switch to another ministry assignment or even another church to find a new assignment. Treat these people well! Don't hold them back. Keep their motivation high and creativity going by never becoming an obstacle on their sprint toward progress.

> "Every construction site needs a bulldozer or two now and then."

Are there volunteer leaders in your church whom you've neglected in the past? Perhaps you've actually *resented* these people because their enthusiasm pushed you along faster than you wanted to go. How can you communicate with those sorts of achievers that you don't want to lose them? that they're your top priority?

Not every volunteer you have will be an achiever—but those who are may be your next level of leadership. You don't want to lose them.

Remember: Every construction site needs a bulldozer or two now and then.

TWO
Deciding Where Volunteers Can Serve in Your Church

Before you sign up volunteers, you need to know where you'll use them. Which jobs are best? Which are off-limits? Here are the guidelines.

The phone is ringing. The bell choir director wants eight volunteers by next Wednesday. The outreach ministry team leader needs fifteen people to do follow-up after an area evangelistic rally. But the treasurer, who's always complaining she has too much to do, doesn't want *any* volunteers.

And the pastor wonders who you can rustle up to run the annual all-church picnic. The pastor wants anyone *but* Mrs. Eresman, who unexpectedly substituted soy burgers for the hamburgers last year because she's a vegetarian.

Or maybe the phone *isn't* ringing. Other than in Sunday school and vacation Bible school, there's no place volunteers are welcome to serve in your church. The other jobs are done by paid staff who have made it clear: Off Limits to Volunteers.

So as you recruit people with great abilities and skills, people who want to serve in areas of ministry they're passionate about, there's no room for them. They aren't welcome.

What do you do? Where do you place volunteers?

Three Guidelines for Placing Volunteers

In light of the three theologies we discussed in volume 1 of this series—the priesthood of all believers, the giftedness of each child of God, and the whole body of Christ—and in light of my experience, I'd like to suggest these three guidelines when it comes to placing volunteers in your church.

1. Place volunteers where they're wanted.

If you place volunteers where they aren't truly wanted, the experience will be negative for everyone involved. The volunteers' expectations won't be met, adequate supervision won't be provided, and nobody will emerge a winner.

If you're in a church where volunteers haven't been used much, let me suggest this: Look for ministry leaders who are willing to work with volunteers. Start there. Let your success build based on the glowing reports that come from busy staffers who now have more time, more energy, and more opportunity to expand the scope of their ministries because volunteers are shouldering some of the load.

2. Place volunteers where they want to go.

Put people in roles that match their unique, God-given abilities, skills, and passions for ministry. Dropping someone into the wrong job is a recipe for disaster.

3. Place volunteers in expanded placement opportunities.

Okay, you've never had a volunteer do premarital counseling. But could a volunteer handle that role? Absolutely. There's not a job at your church that a volunteer can't potentially fill. Even if the role requires ordination, I've seen many churches where retired clergy are ready and available to step in if needed—or wanted.

> "There are no limitations on where God can use volunteers in your church."

From filling the pulpit to filing the tax forms, there are often people who have the ability to make meaningful contributions. God has given them the requisite gifts; it's up to your church to provide the requisite opportunities.

The bottom line: There are no limitations on where God can use volunteers in your church.

The only obstacles are the willingness of your leadership to use volunteers and the abilities, skills, and passions of the volunteers themselves.

So we're really asking the wrong question if we ask "Where can we place volunteers?"

The questions we *should* be asking are:

- *Is there truly a need for a volunteer ministry at your church?* (The answer is "yes," by the way, for all the reasons explained in volume 1.)

- *Is that need felt by your church leadership?* (This may be true of some ministry area leaders and not others.)

- *Where are the places that ministry need and volunteer abilities, skills, and passion overlap?* (To get this information you'll need to interview both the ministry leaders and volunteers—there's no shortcut on this process.)

Some leaders of ministry areas like children's church and youth ministry have a long history of incorporating volunteers. Even the curriculum available for some ministry areas assumes that volunteers will be leading the programs, and it is written accordingly.

Other areas of ministry have less history—or none at all. Often the pastoral aspects of ministry are delivered by paid staff only. True, performing marriage ceremonies is a matter of licensing; not just anyone can do it. But premarital counseling can be done by volunteers, and so can other types of counseling and emotional care. Sermons can be delivered by volunteers, too.

You can't force a ministry leader to take on volunteers; you need the leader's support and enthusiasm for the volunteer placement to thrive.

But you *can* look for ministry leaders who are clearly too busy. They're ripe for a discussion about what volunteers can—and can't—do for them.

In this chapter I'll tell you about how to approach the maxed-out ministry leader and identify the one skill that's absolutely essential for working with volunteers—delegation. No matter what a leader is willing to do to accommodate volunteers, if the leader won't do *this*—run away. Don't place a volunteer with that leader.

Approaching the Maxed-out Ministry Leader

I've met many people—in corporations, non-profit agencies, and churches—who feel overworked, understaffed, and underfunded. Of course, in many churches, those feelings are completely justified. They *are* overworked . . . understaffed . . . *and* underfunded!

Especially when the economy takes a turn for the worse, churches have to watch the purse strings. Although a church may not technically "lay off" a staff member, sometimes open positions aren't filled and the remaining staff is spread thinner.

Other times, a staff member may see the need to expand the ministry and he or she deeply desires to add a bus route, open a food pantry, or make sure each visitor gets a personal phone call as a follow-up gesture.

But without more people, those dreams go unrealized.

Perhaps that's where some of your ministry leaders are now—stretched thin and maxed-out. They feel too busy, as if they're rowing as fast as they can but still they can't make headway upstream. They need more hands and more feet.

If you're directing a ministry area in your church, perhaps *you* feel that way about your corner of the world. You're frustrated. You need more volunteers. And you're *willing* to work with qualified volunteers. Bring them on!

Great—because establishing the volunteer leadership system described in this book series will help you . . . but first you've got to invest the time to make it happen.

And that may be the biggest hurdle for a maxed-out ministry leader. That leader has to pause long enough to actually train a volunteer. And nothing sounds less appealing to someone frantically stamping out a grass fire than to stop stamping long enough to explain to someone *else* how to stamp out fires.

So recognize that not every ministry leader in your church may be ready to use volunteers. That's okay—place volunteers in the soil where they'll be welcome and where they'll bloom. Start with the ministry areas where the leaders *are* ready and the volunteers will thrive.

Don't miss that point: *Place volunteers only where they're wanted and valued.* If a leader doesn't want volunteers, don't force the issue. It's the volunteers who will pay for your insistence.

And as you talk with leaders who show an enthusiasm for using volunteers, I urge you to gently test their true readiness by working through the following questionnaire with them.

> "Not every ministry leader in your church may be ready to use volunteers."

Ministry Leader Questionnaire

- Do you believe in the priesthood of believers in 1 Peter 2:9?

- Do you truly believe that all Christians are called to be active in ministry?

- Do you believe that God gives each of his children a unique set of abilities, skills, and passions—a giftedness—to use for serving others and to glorify God?

(Okay, maybe you can agree with those questions—they're biblical and it's pretty easy to nod your head to them in theory. But let's bring it down another level.)

- Do you believe that because of their giftedness, the people in your church have something valuable to contribute?

- Are you willing to help people in your church learn where to use their abilities, skills, and passions?

- Are you willing to examine your own areas of responsibility so that you'll begin to use volunteers to do ministry alongside you?

(The questions keep getting harder, don't they? We're not finished yet. If you're truly serious about working effectively with volunteers, then you finally need to ask yourself these questions.)

- Do you have enough confidence in *yourself* to not only accept, but actually to look for people who know more about something than you do in an area where you need help?

- Are you willing to delegate major parts of your ministry to gifted and qualified volunteers—and be thrilled, not threatened, when they succeed?

- Are you willing to offer jobs that match the volunteers you find, including ones with a high level of involvement— jobs that make sense as a logical "whole" and fulfilling position, that go beyond busywork, and that truly offer volunteers the opportunity for satisfaction and growth?

- Are you willing to move from being a "doer" of everything to being an "enabler"? Can you become a good manager and find satisfaction in that?

I feel comfortable asking leaders these kinds of questions, because in my years of leading volunteer programs, I've had to ask *myself* the same questions many times.

There have been times when I've been so busy helping organizations and churches start volunteer programs—putting together volunteer task forces, developing mission statements, setting goals and objectives, developing action plans, designing great job descriptions—that I was too blind to see that I needed to recruit a volunteer to assist *me*.

The single most helpful thing for me in those situations was being honest and realistic about my own limitations. I can't know everything. I certainly don't have time to accomplish everything. Once I admit that, it's easy to see the need to bring in capable and knowledgeable volunteers to help.

I'm guessing that you as a leader also occasionally trip up because of your own blind spots. You think you can do it all, or that only you can do it right. Sound familiar? That's because you're human, just like me.

That's why I ask you to now pause and read through the Ministry Leader Questionnaire again—this time with a pencil in your hand. Answer these questions for and about yourself.

Or—if you're *really* brave—go through them with someone you trust who knows your work style and values. Make notes about your attitudes. Start thinking of tasks within the volunteer ministry of which you're protective and that you might need to delegate to a volunteer. Do any people in your church come to mind who might step in to help you in those areas?

Remember: You've got to walk the talk. You've got to model the behavior you want to see in other leaders. If *you* won't trust volunteers to do significant ministry, why would you expect other leaders to do so?

> "Answer these questions for and about yourself."

And there's another reason for you to make the volunteer ministry the poster child for how volunteers can be effective: It will help you know what other ministry leaders think and feel. You've worked so hard on this volunteer initiative—are you really going to turn it over to a bunch of . . . *volunteers?*

Yes. And because you do, that means the children's pastor who has labored to create a vacation Bible school that pulls in kids from all over town can entrust that effort to a volunteer. And the pastor can trust a volunteer to visit a church member in the hospital. And the youth director can trust a volunteer to pull together the fall retreat.

Placing volunteers doesn't happen in a vacuum. Each of those volunteers is placed in a ministry and will most likely report to and be supervised by someone. You go a long way toward helping volunteers succeed by making certain those

> "Placing
> volunteers
> doesn't happen
> in a vacuum."

leaders and supervisors are ready and prepared to work with the volunteers in their ministry areas.

And two things you can do to assure a successful placement are to help leaders work through creating job descriptions and to learn to delegate well.

Let's start with job descriptions.

THREE
Designing Job Descriptions That Work

What? Job descriptions in the church? You bet—and here's why this step in the volunteer placement process is worth its weight in gold. Plus you'll get step-by-step help creating crisp, clear job descriptions.

I was flipping channels one day and happened on a show that fascinated me. The premise of the show was that a team went into someone's home and in just a few hours completely redecorated a room or two.

Maybe you've seen the show, or maybe you're thinking I'm too easily entertained. Let me explain: I've lived in the same house for more than 30 years. I've done some things with it, but in many ways it's the same place I walked into way back then. I've got to wonder what a team of my friends or family would do if they were unleashed with paint rollers and the chance to move furniture around, knock down a wall, or install a new kitchen sink.

Here's hoping I never find out.

Anyway, when you're watching the team of remodelers get started, it's frantic activity. They've got a limited amount of time, so they're hurrying along as fast as they can. Maybe they already knew what they planned to do, or perhaps they're just wired to plunge right into projects. And of course, they want the best for their friend or family member—the person in whose home they're working.

But once in a while, you'll catch a glimpse of someone in the background who's just standing around, looking lost. This person probably has some skills or he wouldn't be there. And his passion for getting the job done is just as high as the others who are helping—he wants his homeowner-friend to be pleased when the surprise is revealed. So why is this person standing in the midst of the chaos, surrounded by others panicked that they might not finish on time, yet appearing to have nothing to do?

I'm guessing that no one has said, "You're good at sewing? Here, make these new draperies." Or "You know how to use power tools and read a plan? Here, build a desk for the den."

People in churches are a lot like the people on that television show. Some—the ones that seem to be doing everything—are what I call the "Pillars" of the church. Other people who don't seem to be doing anything I refer to as the "Pewsitters." The Pewsitters *always* outnumber the Pillars.

> "The Pewsitters *always* outnumber the Pillars."

Unfortunately, the Pillars in most churches are burning out (maybe you've been one in the past and you've changed churches or "gone underground" for awhile to get a break). Meanwhile, the Pewsitters wander off, feeling left out and unneeded.

It's a terrible cycle, and it totally undermines the three theologies we explored in volume 1. People with something to offer aren't involved. People who have one set of skills are forced into inappropriate jobs because *someone* has to do it. And one after another, the Pillars topple out of exhaustion.

What's a Pewsitter to Do?

Pastors and other church leaders like to blame the vast majority of the people in their churches—those pesky Pewsitters—for not volunteering to help with the church's overall ministry, or serve in any church programs. Of course, sometimes the reason is as simple as the fact no one has asked.

But beyond that, many Pewsitters just don't *know* what

they'd do if they volunteered. They come to church week after week, and they see mostly the same people doing the visible tasks. The same people sing. The same people teach. The same people collect the offering and make the announcements.

And it can be hard for people to describe if they're being left out. It can be tough to express something that may just seem to be an indescribable feeling. They can't put into words:

> "Many Pewsitters just don't know *what* they'd do if they volunteered."

- what they think they're good at,

- what they got tired of doing when they volunteered before,

- what they know they don't like to do,

- what they want to learn,

- where they're being led to grow.

The following is an all-too-familiar occurrence at many churches. . .

Jack had attended First Church for a few years and had decided it was time he found a place to serve. Jack was a banker by trade, and one thing he knew was that he *didn't* want to serve in a financial role. He did that all week long.

But Jack was intrigued by the idea of teaching in the preschool department. Jack loved the years his own children were preschoolers, and he's the big-teddy-bear kind of guy preschoolers instinctively love.

So Jack filled out a survey and eagerly described his interest, his education, and his experience working with preschoolers. He even indicated a willingness to help each week in the preschool class, since he knew how important it is for preschoolers to have consistency.

About a month later, Jack still hadn't heard from anyone at church about his volunteer interests. Yet as he sat down for the worship service and opened his bulletin, he saw an announcement that shocked him. Rita—who already was the president of the women's ministry at church, helped organize the annual missions festival, and sang in the church choir— was being recognized as the new volunteer serving weekly in the church's preschool class.

Of course, probably no one meant to overlook Jack. But the message he likely received was "They just want me for my money" or "I guess they don't want men working as volunteers in Christian education."

And no one meant to overuse Rita, who's clearly a Pillar. But churches seem to burn people like Rita out and let people like Jack stay on the sidelines.

How are you doing with connecting people with ministry opportunities? Have you delegated an appropriate task to everyone who's willing to do something? You may think the answer is "yes," since your appeals for volunteers seem to fall on deaf ears.

But check your assumption using the survey below. Politely talk with people as they leave your church's services. Ask, "Do you currently volunteer to help with any ministries in our church?" For those who say "yes," you can politely ask about their involvement and thank them. Affirm them—they deserve it!

> "Affirm them— they deserve it!"

But for those who say "no," ask them which of the listed choices describe why they don't volunteer.

Please *don't* use this as an opportunity to sign people up for existing volunteer openings. You'll need to interview each person and place them according to their aptitudes, skills, and passions to be effective.

Your goal is to find out why Pewsitters are sitting instead of plugging into church programs as volunteers. Position your survey-takers where they can interview people without creating a bottleneck or delay parents picking their children up from classrooms. And if someone doesn't want to participate, respect that.

Volunteer Survey

Ask the following question of every person that passes. Please indicate whether the person you're interviewing is a child (12 or under), a teenager (13-19), or an adult.

"Do you currently volunteer to help with any ministries in the church?"

If the answer is *yes*, politely ask about their involvement and affirm the person.

If the answer is no, ask which of the following choices describes why they don't volunteer:

____ I'm new, so I don't know where I fit in yet.

____ I've volunteered in the past, but I'm taking some time off right now.

____ I've never been asked.

____ I don't know what ministries need volunteers.

____ I've indicated that I'm available, but no one has contacted me.

____ Other: _____.

___ Child ___ Teenager ___ Adult

How Do We Get People Out of the Pews?

You've discovered a lot about yourself and your ministry. Maybe you're now aware that if you had some volunteer help you could be more effective in your area of ministry. You might find people who are even more gifted than you are to accomplish some of the responsibilities in your job.

And that would let you do two things: Focus on the parts of your ministry you really enjoy, and expand the scope of your ministry as you take on new tasks—and as you delegate new responsibilities to volunteers.

And now you hear that many people in your church would volunteer if they knew what to do and knew that someone was needed to do it!

So . . . why don't they sign up?

Let's explore at least part of the solution to this problem. It's the next step in the process of a volunteer ministry: designing jobs for volunteers to do.

My use of the word "design" is intentional. I'm not just trying to use a sophisticated term for writing job descriptions (although it's also okay to use that term). But I like to keep the word "design" in mind because it helps keep the central focus on artistically and skillfully planning jobs that your volunteers will do—and enjoy doing! The more creative and detailed you can be, the more likely the volunteer who fills the job will be content—even joyful—about serving in it.

> "A well-designed job description is an invaluable tool for recruiting the right volunteers."

Essentially, you'll list all the work that needs to be done—the responsibilities and tasks that can be accomplished by volunteers. Then you'll divide those responsibilities and tasks into jobs that are appropriate for various volunteers.

Take this task seriously. A well-designed job description is an invaluable tool for recruiting the right volunteers.

This tool allows you or your recruitment interviewers to do a better job of interviewing potential volunteers. A well-designed job description will help you determine if the volunteer needs any training. And it will help you evaluate the volunteer's performance and measure whether or not using volunteers in your ministry is successful.

What's so important about designing jobs?

Until you can explain what a volunteer is supposed to do, most potential volunteers won't agree to come on board to give you a hand. Nor *should* they—because you aren't ready to put them to work doing something significant.

Unfortunately, when you have 47 kids running around at your youth group meeting or a bursting-at-the-seams Sunday school, it's tempting to recruit volunteers just to gain some manpower. But if they don't know what to do—what you expect of them or how they can make a difference with the people they're serving—you'll quickly lose many of those volunteers.

Recruiting volunteers before you design jobs is like trying to dance before the music starts. Sure, you can start dancing, but there's a good chance that you'll end up out of step once the music begins.

Years ago, when I came out of the corporate world and started leading volunteers in non-profit organizations, I interviewed dozens of volunteers who were leaving agencies.

When asked why they'd quit, they often answered, "I was never really clear on what I was supposed to do, and I didn't even know who to ask for help."

> "Recruiting volunteers before you design jobs is like trying to dance before the music starts."

Agencies had been driven by their need to fill a certain number of volunteer slots. They thought they could simply get people into place and then figure out what to do. Most often, that didn't work well.

It *still* doesn't work well. Not at agencies, and not at your church.

What do volunteers want—and need?

When I started designing jobs for volunteers and writing job descriptions, leaders in non-profit agencies were resistant. They felt that giving volunteers job descriptions took the "magic" out of volunteering.

That one puzzled me. I didn't consider keeping people in the dark about exactly what was expected of them "magical." It was confusing for the paid staff and frustrating for the volunteers.

Some church leaders feel it's too business-like to have job

descriptions for volunteer roles. They seem to think that getting organized by designing jobs for volunteers is somehow not trusting God. But without job descriptions volunteers are miserable. They're ineffective. They're unsure they're doing the right stuff.

When you make sure people's abilities, skills, and passions match the volunteer position, you demonstrate that you care more about your volunteers than your own need to fill jobs. You show you're not willing to toss volunteers into jobs and then watch to see whether they sink or swim.

This might not seem overly important to some leaders in churches. But think how many people get hurt, and even leave the church, because of wounds they receive while volunteering in the wrong place. They fill a job, but they aren't recognized for it. They may even be criticized because they're failing at a job that wasn't an appropriate fit for them in the first place.

> "Volunteers want the benefits that come from having job descriptions."

Volunteers want the benefits that come from having job descriptions. They need the clarity and the knowledge that the position they're signing up to handle has been thought through and defined.

Job descriptions can help you be sure that you're providing consistent service in your church or ministry. They help you evaluate whether volunteers are meeting the standards and providing the quality the job requires. They demonstrate to volunteers that you take what they do seriously and that you don't see them as frivolous contributors to your church or ministry. They help your volunteers understand exactly what you expect from them—what you'll hold them accountable for.

When you put job descriptions in place your volunteers know that you value them, that you trust them, and that they're making a difference in the lives of the people your church or area of ministry serves.

How do you design jobs that fit both you and your volunteers?

So, as you start to design jobs, realize that this process is part of the total fabric of what you're doing with volunteers within your ministry or as a whole within your church.

Take your leadership style, for example. If you're a rather loose manager of people, you can't design jobs that require constant and close supervision. If you do, both you and your volunteers will fail. You might recruit the right kind of person, someone who needs a lot of supervision. Yet your style won't provide enough encouragement, correction, and feedback, and the volunteer will probably feel lost.

Or, if you could be described as rather controlling and autocratic in your management style, don't design jobs or recruit people who are creative or achievement-oriented. You'll only hold them back, and again, both you and the volunteers will be frustrated.

It's fairly easy to keep your management style in mind when you're designing jobs for volunteers who report to you, but what about a job that reports to another person? What do you do then? Does it makes sense to build in that consideration for volunteers who report to the head custodian, a job that seems to be filled by a different person every six months?

Do this: Make certain you cover supervisors' management styles in the interview process. If it's a significant factor, deal with it in the job description. Typically that's not the case, and the issue can be explored in the context of an interview.

Levels of Involvement

When you create job descriptions for volunteers in your church or area of ministry, you're going to discover that some volunteers want very light involvement. Other volunteers desire intense involvement, and still others are looking for every level in between.

To help everyone find a way to contribute, and to successfully recruit the right volunteers to fill the right positions, you'll need to come up with several levels of involvement for various jobs or tasks. For example, if you run a food pantry as part of your ministry, you might have job responsibilities that include:

Lightest involvement: Donate money or food to food pantry.

Moderate involvement: Work in food distribution center sorting donated items and assembling grocery bags.

Heavier involvement: Coordinate the work of volunteers to deliver food to needy families in community. (See also page 83, "Sample Job Descriptions.")

Creating several levels of involvement allows volunteers to find jobs that match their skills, desires, and the level of commitment they can offer. Due to time limitations, family responsibilities, and low self-confidence, some volunteers want to do routine or sporadic tasks.

But volunteers who wish to commit more time and who have the appropriate skills may be looking for more. Also, some volunteers who start at the lightest level of commitment may want to move to a higher level of commitment after testing the waters. Knowing they have this option can be comforting and motivating.

> "It's wise to stay flexible in the types of jobs you offer and how you define those jobs."

It's wise to stay flexible in the types of jobs you offer and how you define those jobs.

Some volunteers are willing to assume very responsible assignments, and for those sorts of positions I urge you to design "volunteer professional" level positions.

A "volunteer professional" position is one that defines the broad areas of responsibility but doesn't spell out every specific task required to fulfill these responsibilities. It also won't specify the time and manpower needed, because it's up to the volunteer to decide how to best fulfill the responsibility. The volunteer selects his or her own staff from the potential volunteers who have been interviewed.

Often, the less responsible the job, the more specific you

need to be with your job descriptions. The volunteers who consider these jobs need to know exactly what you expect of them in terms of time requirements, duties, and details. Also, be clear about what skills are required. These detailed descriptions help volunteers determine if the job fits the realities of their lives.

Remember: If a volunteer has a good experience at a less-demanding level, he or she might take an interest in assuming more responsibility.

When determining levels of responsibility, it helps me if I imagine an inverted pyramid.

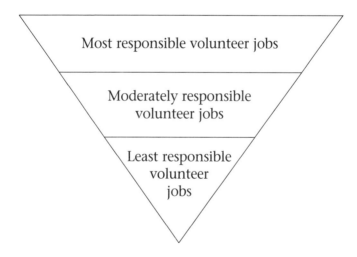

Most responsible volunteer jobs (for example, design Sunday worship experiences)

- Define broad areas of responsibility and authority.

- Assign responsibility rather than specific and detailed tasks.

- Allow volunteer to determine and negotiate needs.

- Define skills and abilities required for the job.

- Leave room for initiative and creativity in how reponsibility is carried out.

Moderately responsible volunteer jobs (for example, create skit to illustrate sermon)

- Spell out tasks fairly well.

- List time requirements and define levels of skill required.

- Indicate lines of responsibility and authority.

Least responsible volunteer jobs (for example, pass offering plates)

- Clearly define duties, time, and skills required.

- List specific tasks.

- Spell out exactly what needs to be done and when.

What Motivates People?

One other thing to keep in mind about designing jobs for volunteers is that the job descriptions need to include motivators or benefits. Do the jobs allow volunteers the opportunity to develop new skills or learn something new about themselves? The worst jobs are ones that are so rigidly constructed that the volunteers feel that they either need to fit into that box, or they'll just have to move on. And clarity counts: I think that the best job descriptions are precise and concise, rather than elaborate or complicated.

> "The best job descriptions are precise and concise, rather than elaborate or complicated."

We dig deeply into what motivates volunteers in volume 4 of this series, but let me briefly introduce a few concepts here. I think they'll be helpful to keep in mind as you work with crafting job descriptions.

When you match the motivational needs of volunteers to appropriate job descriptions, you'll see both motivation and performance improve. And don't guess what motivates people; you can know for sure if you ask them or observe them.

I don't think you can overestimate the motivational power of lining up a job with people's goals for themselves. Why does each volunteer want to be involved in your ministry? Most volunteers will have at least two goals:

1. They want to use their abilities to grow or develop.
2. They want to answer their call to serve others.

As you work with individual volunteers in your ministry, you'll have opportunity to help them stretch. You want them to be realistic about their abilities and involvement, but you also want them to move at least a bit out of their comfort zone. It's a balance—and one you'll need to keep for your overall ministry goals and objectives, as well.

A note: If you lead a large volunteer program, you may be able to provide this level of care only for the volunteers who report directly to you. If that's the case, model how to connect jobs with motivations and encourage these volunteer supervisors to do the same for the people who report to them.

The following worksheet can help potential volunteers learn a little more about themselves and help them understand why they're volunteering. Feel free to copy it and use in interviews or give it to volunteers for self-assessments.

Why I Volunteer

1. As I'm involved in my volunteer role, I want to achieve the following goals:

_____

_____

_____

_____

_____

2. What are some of the positive things that might happen if I reach theses goals?

_____

_____

_____

_____

3. What are my chances for success?
   (Place a mark on the following line for each goal you identified)

Very good————————good————————fair————————poor————————very poor

4. Why do I feel this way?

_____

_____

_____

_____

5. What are some of the negative things that might happen if I reach these goals?

_____

_____

_____

_____

6. What could keep me from reaching my goal(s)?

_____ I don't really have the skills, ability, and/or knowledge needed.

_____ I don't want it badly enough to really work for it.

_____ I'm afraid that I might fail.

_____ I'm afraid of what others might think.

_____ Others don't want me to reach this goal.

_____ This goal is really too difficult to ever accomplish.

_____ Other reasons:

7. What are some things I could do so the obstacles listed above don't prevent me from reaching my goals?

_____

_____

_____

_____

8. Do I still want to try to reach these goals?

_____ Yes

_____ No

_____ Undecided

9. Who can help me reach these goals?

Name:

_____

Kind of help:

_____

_____

_____

_____

10. What are some first steps I can take to reach these goals?

_____

_____

_____

_____

11. What else do I need to do if I really want to succeed?

_____

_____

_____

12. Will I take the above steps?

_____ Yes

_____ No

_____ Undecided

13. If you answered yes to item 12, make the following self-contract. Write a self-contract for each goal you've decided to meet.

Self-Contract
I've decided to try to achieve the goal of _____. The first step I'll take to reach my goal is _____. My target date for reaching my goal is _____.

Signed:

Date:

Witnessed by:

(Permission to copy this form from *Volume 3: Volunteer Leadership Series; Volunteer Job Descriptions and Action Plans,* granted for local church use. Copyright © 2004 Group Publishing, Inc., P.O. Box 481, Loveland, CO 80539. www.grouppublishing.com)

How Can You Make Existing Jobs Better?

What should you do about jobs that volunteers are already filling? As long as someone is accomplishing those tasks, should you leave them alone and assume that everything is fine?

That's a dangerous assumption. Most jobs can be improved if you examine them closely.

If someone is filling a volunteer position and is content in the job, you can simply match the job description to the person. But if you have positions that have been tough to fill, or that are plagued with repeated volunteer turnover, designing new descriptions will help solve those problems.

> "Most jobs can be improved if you examine them closely."

Ask yourself if the volunteer jobs in your area of ministry are interesting and challenging enough to hold people in them. Ask your current volunteers what they think of their job descriptions and how they'd improve their jobs. Together with your current volunteers, go through your job descriptions and see if you can come up with ways to enlarge, enrich, or just make them more fun.

The following process can help you revise a job description that's not working.

How to Fix a Broken Job Description

Start with a volunteer job description that's tough to fill, or that has suffered from frequent turnover. Use one or more of the following techniques to make it more appealing.

1. Enlarge the job—list additional tasks that you could include in this position.

2. Enrich the job—list functions that might be more managerial that a volunteer could take over.

3. Simplify the job—List tasks that have turned out to be menial and remove them from the job, or combine tasks that could be done more easily by one volunteer.

4. Add variety to the job—Add tasks that spice up a position to make dull or routine tasks more appealing.

5. Create continuity in the job—Add steps that make a job feel more whole; this can add appeal to a position that requires a single task to be done over and over.

Nuts and Bolts of Writing Job Descriptions

Let's assume the worst: You've inherited a volunteer ministry that has dozens of volunteers already serving (that's good!) and you're in need of another dozen volunteers (that's less good) and you have exactly zero job descriptions on file. All the current volunteers were recruited with verbal descriptions of what they'd do, and for the most part they've adapted.

The volunteers you still need are waiting to hear what you want them to do, and job descriptions would certainly help. So you need to work two directions: Create job descriptions for the people who are already serving, and create them for the positions you need to fill so you can place the right people in those positions.

Don't worry—creating job descriptions isn't really all that complicated. It requires focus and information, but you can develop the first and gather the second. And as you'll see from the sample job descriptions below, you don't have to worry about the format of the forms. You can create an outline, use bullet points, or simply write descriptions in paragraph form. Nobody is going to grade you on format or font selection.

> "Creating job descriptions isn't really all that complicated."

Just make certain that each job description clearly contains the following:

- Job title

- Goal of the position

- Who the volunteer is responsible to or reports to

- A two or three sentence summary (or list of points) describing the job

- The approximate time required per week or month

- The "term" of the commitment, stated in days, months, or years

- A description of the training that will be provided

- A list of any special qualifications or unique skills the position requires

- The benefits that the volunteer will receive for doing and completing the job.

Use these items as a checklist to be sure job descriptions you write include all the relevant information. Again, writing style and format matter far less than clarity!

Here's an exercise for you to do before you create job descriptions for positions in your volunteer ministry.

Using that checklist, design a job description for your own position. When you're finished, look for areas of your job that could be delegated to volunteers.

If you'd like to see some sample job descriptions, check out those starting on page 83. Note that there are several approaches, and the job descriptions needn't be multi-page essays.

The list of "action verbs" on page 89 may be helpful, too, as you craft your job descriptions.

If you'd like a template that defines what each of the information areas in a job description should cover, see page 90, where you'll find a Volunteer Position Description Cheat Sheet that was developed by my friends and colleagues, Sue Waechter and Deb Kocsis.

And if your church is a member of Group's Church Volunteer Central, visit Group Publishing at www.grouppublishing.com and link to dozens of already-prepared, easily tailored job descriptions for nearly any volunteer position you can imagine.

Gathering Information

If you're working on a job description for a position that will report to you, gathering the necessary information is no problem. You know who the volunteer will report to and what the volunteer is expected to do.

But what if you're in a huge church where you aren't even certain what some volunteers do? What if the volunteer will serve as the associate choirmaster? You may have exactly zero idea of what an associate choirmaster does, and be uncertain if the volunteer will report to the choirmaster, the choir director, or the choir coordinator.

How can you write a job description when you're in the dark about details? The short answer is: You can't. Instead, you need to sit down with the person who will be supervising the volunteer and help *that* person write the job description.

> "Sit down with the person who will be supervising the volunteer and help *that* person write the job description."

That's why it's so important that you become comfortable creating job descriptions; the odds are good that you'll be coaching others on how to do it. I'd like to suggest this quick process for getting busy ministry area leaders to stop and focus on creating solid job descriptions.

Refuse to place volunteers until job descriptions are complete. It's important that ministry leaders understand that job descriptions aren't just paperwork. They're essential for the placement process—and you can't work without them. Stand firm on your need for both the written job description and the clarity and thought that went into crafting it. You're being an advocate for the success of your volunteers and the volunteer ministry if you insist on volunteer supervisors having a clear understanding of what—and who—they need.

Give volunteer supervisors the checklist you used to create your own job description. You're delegating the responsibility to create job descriptions. That means you've got to provide all the information necessary to complete the job.

Give volunteer supervisors sample job descriptions. Use those I've provided or samples from your church. The task of creating job descriptions is less intimidating when you've got a short stack of samples to use as models.

Review job descriptions with the ministry leaders who create them. This brief meeting allows you to clear up any uncertainty you may have about what was written and make sure the job descriptions reflect what's really desired. Plus, you'll be able to thank and affirm the leaders who take time to create job descriptions.

Revisit job descriptions after volunteers have been placed. Six weeks to six months after a volunteer is actually doing the job, it's a good idea to talk with both the volunteer and the volunteer's supervisor. Is the volunteer actually doing what was anticipated when the job description was written? If not, make adjustments to reflect reality.

"Thank and affirm the leaders who take time to create job descriptions."

Clear, crisp job descriptions go a long way toward getting the right people in the right spots—and making volunteering fulfilling and a boost to spiritual growth.

But another piece of the puzzle is equally important and something the volunteer really can't control. It's the willingness of a volunteer's supervisor to *delegate*. Without the ability to delegate, ministry leaders don't allow volunteers to do anything significant.

Until your ministry leaders master the skill of delegation, your volunteers won't find their ministry experiences as rich as expected, and ministry leaders will struggle with managing volunteers.

Let's deal with delegation next—before you place the volunteers in the care of supervisors who aren't sure how to make the best use of their willingness to serve!

FOUR
Delegation

Before you place a volunteer, make sure a ministry leader is ready to give that volunteer a significant role. These fundamentals of delegation will help your ministry leaders—and you—work well with volunteers.

Delegation is the process of identifying a responsibility and transferring it, and the authority to meet it, to another person. It's thinking through—ahead of time—how to share work.

And that seems so simple—until you try to actually *do* it.

The problem is that it's one thing to assign a responsibility to another person. It's another thing to also transfer the power required to accomplish that responsibility. Most of us are good at giving away the job, but not so good at giving away the power to do it.

When the responsibility and necessary power travel together, that's delegation. When the responsibility is given without the power to do it, that's not delegation. It's dumping. Here's an example of the difference . . .

Suppose Jack is a volunteer in the youth department. The youth pastor approaches Jack and explains that there's a youth group lock-in on the calendar in two months. The pastor wants Jack to plan the program and run with it.

Jack asks questions about budget, schedule, and programming. The youth pastor has already gathered all that information, and he passes the file over with a warm "thank you" and a promise to check in weekly to keep up with progress. The youth pastor tells Jack to pull together the program and recruit helpers; he's got the authority to call any youth volunteer who's been screened and certified and ask that person to help.

Jack has been delegated a task, and he's excited about making the next lock-in both fun and spiritually significant. He understands the goals and has the information he needs to get started. Plus, he's got a weekly "touch base" to get questions answered.

That's delegation.

Now suppose instead that the youth pastor catches Jack in the hallway after church Sunday morning and explains that nothing has been done about the youth group lock-in that's scheduled next Friday. The youth pastor had intended to get things started earlier, but other commitments kept getting in the way. The youth pastor begs Jack to take on the project, and after some arm-twisting Jack agrees.

It's not until after the youth pastor says, "Thanks for saving me, Jack!" and slips away that Jack realizes he doesn't really understand what the point of a lock-in is. He doesn't know how much money he has to spend, or how to go about organizing the event. He's not sure where he'll be able to get information or help.

> ### "There's way too much dumping when it comes to volunteers."

That's *not* delegation—it's dumping.

There's way too much dumping when it comes to volunteers.

If Jack survives his first lock-in, do you think he'll be back? He will if the task was delegated to him, but if it was dumped on him he'd be crazy to ever take another assignment.

Delegation will make or break your volunteer ministry. You must do it well—and do it wisely. Following are some things I've learned about delegation that will help you as you forge ahead . . . and they're helpful things to teach any leader who works with volunteers.

1. Choose appropriate people for assignments.

Interview and place paid and volunteer staff carefully. This is your chance to maximize strengths and compensate for weaknesses. Seek out skills and knowledge that each person needs to do his or her assignment successfully.

2. Define responsibilities clearly and creatively.

Each person needs to know what he or she is doing. It helps some people to think of the assignment as a framed blank canvas. You describe what the basic finished painting will look like, and that you expect it to fit on the canvas and within the frame you've provided. But the colors, the brush marks, and the decision about who helps finish the painting are up to the artist. This can help the person you're delegating to know where he or she can function freely, and where there are limits.

3. Delegate segments of a job that make sense.

Some positions can be divided more than others; don't assign bits and pieces of a role that won't feel significant to the volunteer. You might function best by delegating a whole area of your ministry to a volunteer. That person then recruits other volunteers to work under him or her. Make sure that those people report to your volunteer leader rather than to you. You want simply to hold the leader accountable for a whole segment, rather than multiple people accountable for bits and pieces of that area.

4. Set goals and standards of performance mutually.

As you develop performance standards be sure to get the buy in of the people who'll actually supervise the ministry area in which the volunteer works. Does the Music Minister care if choir rehearsals start on time? If so, have that reflected in the choir director's job description. And when it's time to place someone in the choir director role, be sure the expectation is clear.

5. Agree on deadlines and ways the volunteer can report progress or problems.

Nothing stalls progress faster than a volunteer being unable to work out problems promptly. Also, reports build momentum for volunteers when they can communicate progress being made, and reporting lets ministry supervisors encourage or correct volunteers.

6. Give accurate and honest feedback.

People want to know how they're doing. They deserve to know. When you delegate, tell people you'll be evaluating their performance and then do so. Communicate that your intent isn't to catch them doing something wrong, but to encourage them to take appropriate risks and even make honest mistakes.

7. Share knowledge, information, and plans.

While you want to allow room for growth, don't let avoidable errors happen simply because others don't have information you could easily share. Let people know you'll be doing this—and how you'll be doing it.

8. Provide necessary orientation, training, and recognition to the volunteers who report to you.

This is the frame part of the blank canvas. Make sure volunteers know their boundaries, but then free them to work within those boundaries by arming them with the tools they need. Look over their shoulders once in a while and say "good job." Talk up their good efforts and accomplishments in front of others.

9. Give volunteers who are capable of accomplishing significant portions of the ministry a voice in the decision making.

Remember, they may know more about that area of your program than you do.

10. Truly delegate.

Most people, when they receive responsibility for a project, don't want you checking up on every step or taking back part of the assignment before they've had a chance to do it. Learn to let go.

By the way, as you think about delegating you'll inevitably begin thinking of people who might be great at assuming some of *your* tasks. When I've served as a volunteer coordinator in different settings, I've made an effort to find volunteers who knew more about a topic or an area than I did. Those sort of volunteers make you look better! If they do a great job implementing a more efficient process, or effective ministry area, you look like a genius because you put them in charge and supported their efforts.

> "Never be afraid of delegating to sharp people."

Never be afraid of delegating to sharp people.

What Should You Delegate?

One reason many leaders have trouble delegating is that they simply don't know what they should let go of. If you're the leader of a ministry area in your church, these questions will help you determine what you can delegate when you find the right person.

This is one of those rare moments when you have a perfect excuse to spend an afternoon alone in a coffee shop or sitting under a tree in the park. You need time to think, with no interruptions. If that appeals to you and you do your best thinking in that sort of setting, go find that park bench.

Another approach is to jot down the specific jobs you do in your ministry work for a few weeks. Use that log to give you the information you need to fill out the form.

If you're not a church leader who'll be delegating jobs to volunteers, by all means have those leaders who will be keep a log of what they do. That will give you the information you need to create volunteer positions that report to those leaders. Or have *those* folks go sit under a tree for half a day as they work through the following form.

And no, they won't *have* a half-day to do this. But remind them that a half-day invested now will pay huge dividends down the road, and if they're feeling over-busy and burned out, this is the first step to their getting help.

Delegation Worksheet

1. What functions—the major pieces or elements of your job—are you responsible for?

2. From this list, what is it essential that you do personally? Put an asterisk next to each of those items.

3. What other things would you like to get done or see done but haven't managed to get to yet?

4. From this list, which of these would you like to do yourself if you had the time? Put an asterisk next to each of those items.

5. Which of the remaining items from these two lists would you be willing to delegate if you could find the right person? Are any of them similar enough to each other that they could be combined into a larger job—something that could be delegated as a whole to give you more relief, as well as provide a volunteer with a meaningful role? What might those job titles be?

6. Considering those job titles, what would the ideal person for each of these jobs look like? What skills, experience, aptitudes, and spiritual maturity would he or she have?

Levels of delegation

Question 5 in the worksheet suggests that you think about how you could combine similar responsibilities to create a larger volunteer job. One advantage of this arrangement is that the volunteer you recruit for the larger job can then recruit others to help fulfill that job. Those volunteers then report to the volunteer leader rather than directly to you. Only the volunteer leader reports to you.

Think of it this way: If it takes ten people to lead small groups in your church, would you rather have all ten of them call you to report how the weekly meetings went, or call someone you recruit to run that ministry? Wouldn't it be handy to have a small group team leader?

If you're like me, you'll opt for a weekly call from your small group team leader. If that volunteer is trained and capable, your ten small group leaders will get great encouragement and support—and you'll get one call instead of ten.

A system that has volunteers managing volunteers requires you to train not just volunteers, but volunteer *supervisors*. If you want to have people in those roles, create job descriptions for those spots. You must be intentional about creating those positions.

Check out the samples of job descriptions with different levels of involvement on page 93.

The Cost of Delegation

For ministry leaders, delegation can feel costly. It requires doing the preparation so a meaningful responsibility can be passed along. It demands thought and planning.

And, frankly, it requires giving up some power. We don't do that easily or comfortably. What happens if you hand over a job to someone who fails to do it—or do it well? How will that reflect on you? How will you relate to the person who let you down?

"For ministry leaders, delegation can feel costly."

The call to delegate raises some questions in the minds of leaders—including you. How would you answer these?

Can you value administration as well as doing the work yourself? Some leaders find their personal value and worth in being able to do things well. Some fear that if they delegate certain areas of their ministry or program, people might not think they're doing their job.

Will your job be as fun if you just do administration? Many church leaders went into professional ministry because they enjoy the activities associated with the role. Some tasks are fun, and giving them away to volunteers will make the job far less rewarding and enjoyable.

Will things get done right? In the church it's important that things get done properly. After all, if the new members' class is boring, families might choose to leave the church before they form enough relationships to be grafted into the congregation. But is it true that you're the only person who could do an adequate job in that class?

Can you share power? This is the bottom line for many leaders, because delegating is more than assigning a task. It's assigning a responsibility, with sufficient authority to fulfill that responsibility. If you want to delegate well, you must delegate the authority or empowerment that allows someone to do a meaningful job. How do you feel about that?

Good delegation involves trust.

It's a two-way street: The volunteer must trust that sufficient information and power has been transferred. Otherwise the volunteer role will be difficult and will probably end in failure—and nobody likes being set up to fail.

> "My experience is that volunteers want to do their best."

The ministry leader must trust the volunteer to fulfill the responsibility with excellence as it was described in the job description. Otherwise the people depending on the responsibility to be met will be disappointed—and the job may fall back on the ministry leader.

Here's the thing about trusting volunteers: You can generally err on the side of trusting too much. My experience is that volunteers want to do their best, and they'll rise to meet your expectations . . . *if* you're clear about what those expectations are. There's another reason you want to make your job descriptions clear, concise, and achievable!

Help is on the way.

If the notion of delegating areas of ministry feels *odd* to you, don't worry: There are plenty of biblical examples of leaders doing precisely that.

Moses found that it was more than a full-time job just settling squabbles between people, and at his father-in-law's advice he turned over a significant piece of his mediation responsibility to carefully chosen men.

And then there's this example of delegation described in the book of Acts:

> *In those days when the number of disciples was increasing, the Grecian Jews among them complained against the Hebraic Jews because their widows were being overlooked in the daily distribution of food. So the Twelve gathered all the disciples together and said, "It would not be right for us to neglect the ministry of the word of God in order to wait on tables. Brothers, choose seven men from among you who are known to be full of the Spirit and wisdom. We will turn this responsibility over to them and will give our attention to prayer and the ministry of the word." (Acts 6:1-4)*

Seven men were chosen whose qualifications matched the job description, and the responsibility became theirs. That freed the apostles to focus on doing what was most important in their ministry: prayer and preaching. Caring for widows wasn't a job that was dumped—it was delegated. And the results were predictably positive as the church grew.

The apostles realized something that perhaps is dawning on you and other ministry leaders in your church, too: You can't do it all. At least, you can't do it all *well*. It's time to delegate.

It takes some work to delegate—to adequately identify the task, create the job description, and locate the proper people who will fulfill the responsibility. But making the effort can breathe new life into your ministry because at last you'll be able to *catch* your breath.

Delegate well and you'll be surrounded by top-notch people who are there to help. You'll have time to dream of new ways your ministry can develop—and you'll have time to do something about those dreams.

And if the current pace of ministry is burning you out, you'll be able to lean on other people who understand and who have a stake in your being successful.

And you'll have an additional benefit: You'll personally witness God using volunteers who are growing spiritually, finding meaning, and sensing fulfillment as they live out their faith by serving others.

FIVE

The Risk of Using Volunteers

The days of pretending bad things don't happen at church—or to the people our volunteers serve—have long since ended. How can you protect your church, your volunteers, and the people you serve?

It's a call no pastor wants to receive. Color drained from the pastor's face as he heard the news that for more than three years a volunteer in the children's ministry had been abusing children in his care.

It's a call no volunteer wants to receive. A boy in the church-sponsored midweek program claimed that the volunteer had exposed himself to the boy. Although the volunteer knew it wasn't true, a police investigation was underway.

Some risks you face in your ministry are obvious: Your building might burn down. You might have a budget crunch that takes some of your programs off-line. You might find that your attendance doubles (or triples) and suddenly your facilities must be replaced.

Because your church is growing and alive, there are risks. It comes with the territory. That's also true of your volunteer ministry.

But if one of your volunteers does something to a person he or she is serving . . . or if a claim is made against a volunteer you've placed in ministry . . . the losses are more than just a building.

Reputations crumble. Ministry is derailed. Trust is destroyed.

I'm not trying to scare you, but I do want to instill a sense of urgency so you take immediate and decisive action. If you're not protecting every constituency in your ministry—the volunteers, the people they serve, and the church itself—*now* is the time to correct that oversight.

What Are the Risks You Face?

This slim volume can't pretend to provide the last word in how you should proceed, but I can point you in the right direction. I'll help you think through the possibilities and decide on some next steps in your process. And I'll pay extra attention to how you can protect your volunteer ministry and your volunteers.

The topic is "risk management," and it needs to be on your radar screen.

Risk management

Perhaps you've not thought much about risk management. But quickly answer these questions:

- Can a volunteer's acts make your church liable if another person is harmed? (The answer is yes!)

- Are your volunteers protected by law from any liability, or can your volunteers be held liable for certain actions? (The answer is that liability protection laws in most jurisdictions don't fully protect your volunteers.)

- Could your church face significant loss because of expenses incurred from a lawsuit? (Absolutely. And the financial losses are just part of the price you'd pay.)

- Are there potential volunteers who will shy away from signing up to volunteer if you're unable to describe the steps you've taken to protect them and the people they serve? (Yes. It's probably happening already.)

Enough scare tactics

Rather than dwelling on what *could* happen in the area of risk and liability, let's try to come up with some ways to manage and minimize those risks and liabilities.

I think the following is a pretty good definition of risk management: Risk management includes all management efforts aimed at minimizing the adverse impact that losses may have on an organization. The goal is to put in place systematic, organized processes that avoid, eliminate, or lower the chances that a loss will occur.

What's required of you to do risk management is that you identify what processes will accomplish eliminating or lowering your risks, then put those processes in place. Where risk management is concerned, talk is a great place to start, but action is required.

> "Where risk management is concerned, talk is a great place to start, but action is required."

The consequences of not initiating risk management procedures and policies are potentially severe. Not only will your church and ministry be impacted, but individual lives of volunteers (or members of your congregation) can be tragically damaged.

Why Do You Need to Manage Risk?

There's a cost associated with managing risk, both in time and dollars. But as noted above, there's a cost associated with not managing risk, too.

Being found negligent just one time could result in financial damage your church or ministry couldn't survive. With the decline of "charitable immunity"—the legal doctrine that at one time protected charitable organizations from financial responsibility for causing harm—liability for most non-profit organizations is the same as it is in for-profit businesses. So, the primary goal of managing risk in your volunteer program is to create a relatively safe environment where your volunteers can carry out the mission of your church or area of ministry.

How Can You Manage Risk?

Of course, you can't completely eliminate risk in your church or area of ministry. That's why I keep referring to "managing risk." Probably every volunteer and volunteer position brings some level of liability right inside your facility. Since you can't completely eliminate risks, you need to use your judgment and start by focusing on the ones that matter most.

Also, please again note that this brief chapter is just a primer on risk management. My goal is to bring this topic to your attention, to help you measure where you are in terms of risk management, and to nudge you along to get started on being proactive. But you'll probably need additional resources.

If you choose to use some, I strongly recommend *Beyond Police Checks: The Definitive Volunteer and Employee Screening Guidebook* by Linda L. Graff (Dundas, Ontario, Canada: Linda Graff and Associates, Inc., 1999). I also recommend workshops conducted by Sue Waechter and Deb Kocsis (info@cornerstoneconsultingassociates.com).

Where do you start? I recommend that you take these four steps.

1. Look at each volunteer position and identify any potential areas for liability. Again, use your judgment and concentrate on reducing risk in the areas that matter most. These will probably be areas where the people served are the most vulnerable: children and teenagers, people with disabilities, and senior adults.

2. Evaluate the ways you can manage those risks. What can you do to protect the people you serve—and your volunteers? Are you willing to proactively take steps to raise awareness and make changes?

3. Choose the means and implement your strategy. Here's where you actually do something. Be aware that in any risk management strategy, the volunteer recruitment and placement process is thoroughly investigated. Practically speaking, that means when you're in the interview phase of volunteer recruitment (see volume 4 for details) you'll have to decide when to initiate police screenings of volunteers.

4. Monitor your ministries and determine whether the means of managing the risk is meeting your church's needs and the needs of the people you're serving. Make sure the steps you've put in place are truly managing the risks you've identified.

Complete the self-assessment on page 72 through 74 to gauge how well your church or your particular area of ministry currently recognizes and manages risk. The assessment looks long, but you'll cruise through it in about ten minutes.

*Please choose one of the three answers; Yes, No, and Unsure (?).
Put a check mark in the box of your choice.*

General Liability and Risk Management	Yes	No	?
Does our church have an ongoing risk management committee?			
Have we examined the activities performed by volunteers and taken action to manage the risks?			
Do we have a policy and procedure manual for our volunteer program?			
Do we formally review the manual every year?			
Do we have general liability coverage for the volunteer program?			
Is one person responsible to review and update the liability coverage?			
Do we have events throughout the year that put us at greater risk for liability; if so, do we obtain coverage?			
Managing the Risks of Interviewing, Screening, and Terminating Volunteers			
Do we have current job descriptions for each volunteer position in our church, including board members?			
Do volunteer job descriptions clearly indicate what qualifications are needed to fill each position?			
Do our job descriptions specify what physical requirements are required for the position?			
Do we protect ourselves against discrimination in the way we write our position descriptions?			
Do we complete a background check on volunteers?			

	Yes	No	?
Do we regularly review job performance with volunteers and document it?			
Do we tell volunteers in their initial orientation that they'll have performance reviews? When? What will be covered?			
Do we immediately handle complaints or concerns about volunteers' behavior?			
Do we have written procedures for terminating volunteers?			
Do we provide volunteers with a written handbook regarding the policies and procedures?			
Do we clearly explain who will supervise volunteers and to whom they are responsible?			
Do we ask volunteers to sign a statement that they've received orientation and training and understand our expectations of them?			
Do volunteers understand the boundaries of their job descriptions; what they can and cannot do; where they should or should not be?			
Managing the Risk of Confidentiality			
Do volunteers understand how our church defines confidentiality and privacy?			
Do volunteers understand what they can and cannot say?			
Do volunteers know the consequences of breaking confidentiality?			
Managing the Risk of Personal Injury Liability			
Do we explain safety procedures in working with people?			

	Yes	No	?
Do we adequately post safety warnings for volunteers?			
Do we explain safety in their physical workspace?			
Do we provide general safety training for volunteers?			
Do we have an incident report process for volunteers?			
Do we require volunteers to report any incident that is not consistent with routine activities?			
Do we abide by the Right to Know Act and provide information regarding it? (Contact the U.S. Environmental Protection Agency for info.)			
Managing the Risks of Volunteer Drivers			
Do we have insurance that covers volunteer drivers?			
Do we have certificates of insurance on file for volunteers driving their own vehicles?			
Are volunteers made aware that they must notify us of any changes in their insurance policy?			
Do we need or have automobile insurance above and beyond the volunteer's own coverage?			
Are volunteers made aware that they may need to notify their personal auto insurance carrier of the volunteer driving activities?			
Do we check for a current, valid driver's license?			
Do we check driving records?			
Do we provide special driving training for volunteer drivers?			

If you ended up with mostly "no" answers, a few "unsure" answers, and just a handful of "yes" answers, don't be surprised.

Many ministries and churches utterly flunk this assessment. Don't be discouraged if you see lots of room for improvement; feel motivated. The fact that you're reading this chapter and that you want to do something about risk management probably puts you ahead of most churches!

I strongly suggest that you go through this assessment with other staff members at your church. Bring it to the attention of your senior pastor and your church board. Although they might prefer to just look the other way on risk issues, having them take part in filling out the assessment will help them see how much work there is to do.

What Are Your Options?

Keep in mind that there's no way you'll ever be completely free from liability unless you close the church doors and cease ministry. In our society, anyone can sue anyone, at any time, and for just about any reason. So even if you apply every one of the following methods and many others, you won't be completely secure. But here's a start at how you can minimize your church's liability.

Eliminate the risk.

This is pretty much what I just mentioned—closing your doors and ceasing to do ministry. But before you dismiss this idea, do some thinking. There might actually *be* some ministries in your church that you believe are too risky. There may be a program or area of ministry where volunteers serve, and it somewhat supports your mission, but you could live without it. If considerable risk is involved in that program, you might choose to eliminate that program entirely.

For example, perhaps your church offers a free medical screening clinic to your neighborhood. Volunteer medical professionals use the church facilities and receive financial support to screen for certain health issues of low-income residents. Think about the risks. Professionals are providing the care, and they likely have malpractice insurance. But what about your church?

Could something happen in your facility that you'd be liable for? You might decide that the risk in this situation isn't worth it and eliminate the program entirely. Or if you're very committed to the ministry, you might instead financially support an off-site independent clinic to provide the same services, but with that independent organization assuming the liability in writing. A tough call—but it may be a wise one.

Of course, you probably won't eliminate your youth ministry simply because it fosters relationships between adults and kids. Relationship is a key part of why your church and various ministries in the church exist at all. Instead, you'll want to have enough screening, training, and supervision in place to show that you and/or your volunteers weren't negligent in the event of a negative situation.

> "A tough call— but it may be a wise one."

Transfer the risk.

This essentially means buying insurance. Or you could use some sort of contract that holds you harmless. Of course, the reality is that even with a contract, you may not be held harmless. Why? Because—as I've just stated—in our society, anyone can sue anyone, at any time, and for just about any reason. And negligence is negligence; no contract removes your obligation to take customary precautions.

But a signed contract, properly reviewed by legal counsel, may help reduce your liability. See page 95 for information that one church requires from its volunteers: a covenant agreement, consent forms, reference forms, interest forms, and a signed contract.

Is it overkill? This church doesn't think so . . . and neither does its lawyer. You'll need to decide for yourself. I'm personally uncomfortable using contracts with volunteers and don't use them—but they are a tool at your disposal.

Reduce the risk.

This means looking at ways to minimize your liabilities by having more comprehensive and up-to-date job descriptions for volunteers, policies and procedures for volunteers, supervision of volunteers, and documented training and orientation of volunteers. You can do this and tremendously decrease your risk without spending a cent. It's doing what you already do (or should be doing)—better.

Some examples of policies that reduce risk are:

- A volunteer driver who takes children under 18 on an activity must have another nonrelated adult along.

- Adults can never be alone with a minor.

- No snacks or food that include nuts or nut oils can be served.

- All children must have signed medical release forms to participate in programs that involve travel or overnight stays.

- Only drivers over the age of 25 can serve as volunteer drivers, because 16- to 25-year-olds have a statistically greater chance of getting into accidents.

Retain the risk.

This means that your church decides to accept and retain the risk involved in the volunteer program, though you do what you can to reduce the risks. This category indicates that your board or church leadership has gone through the process of determining what risks are involved in the volunteer ministry, and your church leadership has formally decided to retain the risk. You'll want to document that your leadership reached this decision.

The good news is that the more you're proactive about minimizing your volunteer program's risk, the less problems you'll face.

The bad news is—I've already said it—anyone can sue anyone, at any time, and for just about any reason. Yet the more you document and record what you've done to be vigilant, the harder it is to prove you were negligent.

Monitor and evaluate.

Periodically check to be sure that whatever risk management procedures and policies you've set into place are still effectively getting the job done.

Times Are Changing

The whole area of managing risks among volunteers is constantly changing. At one time, churches and other nonprofit groups had charitable immunity. But that protection has eroded. In the present, your church or ministry probably would face the same liability as any other organization or business.

> "All it takes is one lawsuit—perhaps even one allegation—to close down your ministry."

Because the answer to "What should we do about risk?" continues to change, probably the best tool you can have is a set of guidelines that help you decide what's reasonable to do about risk management.

Here are some guidelines you might want to incorporate into the list you develop.

• **Recognize that the accountability we shoulder is heavier than ever.**

Have there always been cases of abuse by staff members in positions of trust? Clearly that's the case—but now we're in a position to use technology and our policy books to do a better job of preventing people who shouldn't be volunteering from being in positions where they can abuse others on our volunteer staffs. And it's not only *right* for us to take whatever steps we can to ensure safety, it's *smart*. All it takes is one lawsuit—perhaps even one allegation—to close down your ministry.

- **Acknowledge that not every volunteer position requires the same scrutiny.**

If a volunteer will be working at home making phone calls to notify church members about an upcoming business meeting, you probably don't need to do any background checks at all. But if the volunteer's job involves making contact with others while on duty, that's a completely different situation. If those people are children, teenagers, or others who are vulnerable, use the strictest screening protocol you can practically put in place.

- **Get free advice.**

Typically, one question raised in court is whether your church was negligent in providing background screening. Did you do what was prudent and customary? You probably don't need an Interpol screening, but if it's typical for churches and other ministries in your area to do a certain level of screening for positions, do at least as much. Talk with your peers and find out what they're doing. Share that information when others call you.

- **Expect changes.**

Personnel screening is a dynamic field, and the rules keep changing. Investigate and re-investigate at least once per year what's happening. What's prudent and customary is driven by technology and the law; new standards appear with amazing frequency. Determine that for the benefit of your volunteers and those you serve, you will reflect excellence in this issue. If you want to do what's best for your volunteers and the people you serve, you'll stay on top of what's new and changing. Check with the experts now and then by consulting legal counsel and attending some workshops.

- **Establish a paper trail.**

Document every screening effort. Keep information in volunteers' files, and keep files secure.

• **Be consistent.**

Whatever you establish as your protocol, be consistent and apply it to everyone. Make no exceptions—including yourself. Have you put yourself through the screening procedure? Until you do, it's going to be difficult for you to convince others. And remember: If your church is a member of Group's Church Volunteer Central, you may qualify for discounts on background screenings. Call to find out (800-447-1070).

Risk Management Benefits Us All

There are many reasons to be intentional about managing risk.

There are the financial considerations: Your insurance provider may give you a discount if you have certain protocols in place. And you may avoid a devastating lawsuit.

But there's an even more important reason: Risk management protects people . . . including your volunteers.

> "There are many reasons to be intentional about managing risk."

Risk management is often viewed as an effort to weed out predators who might volunteer in your programs to gain access to children, teenagers, or others. And your efforts *will* help deny those people access to your church members.

Yet you're also protecting your volunteers. By adding some risk management guidelines to your training, you keep volunteers from accidentally ending up in compromising—though innocent—positions. If a teenage girl tells her adult male youth sponsor she has something private to tell him, that adult may innocently step into a room and close the door behind them so they can speak in private.

When a parent rounds the corner looking for her daughter and discovers them sitting alone in a dim room behind closed doors, the assumptions aren't pretty, even if the topic of discussion was how the teenager could be more supportive of her parents.

I urge you to create a policy handbook for your volunteers. It's a good idea anyway—an *essential* idea, as you'll discover in volume 5—and it should include material that covers risk management. Be sure you include a statement about which positions require background or police record checks. List what other screening, training, and supervision your church provides. Outline safety procedures. And include a church policy statement on confidentiality and privacy.

You can't be too proactive when it comes to risk management!

(I'm greatly indebted to Sue Waechter and Deb Kocsis for helping with much of the information and content of chapter 5. This chapter is largely adapted from their "Managing Risks in Your Volunteer Program" workshop. For more information, contact Cornerstone Consulting Associates, LLC, P.O. Box 265 Midland, Michigan 48640; Phone: (989) 631-3380; Fax: (646) 349-4985; Web site: www.peopleprocessproduct.com; Email: info@cornerstoneconsultingassociates.com)

Sample Job Descriptions

The following sample job descriptions are from several churches and reflect several levels of commitment. You'll notice they're each slightly different in format, but each spells out basic responsibilities, the essential skills a volunteer needs, and a projected time commitment.

Greeting Card Mailer

Importance to our church: An appropriate greeting card can lift the spirits of someone who is experiencing grief, illness, or loneliness.

Responsibilities: You will contact the church office weekly on Wednesday afternoon to receive the names of those to be mailed cards. You will purchase appropriate greeting cards—preferably with a Christian message—add a personal message, and mail the cards. Costs for cards and postage may be reimbursed, if desired.

Time frame: The volunteer will arrange according to his/her schedule the one hour needed each week.

Skills to be used/developed: This position requires only that you care about people.

Number of volunteers: We need one volunteer.

Benefit for the volunteer: You'll receive satisfaction from letting others know you care during a stressful time in their lives.[1]

(Cross of Christ Lutheran Church, Bellevue, Washington)

Membership and Renewal Committee

Purpose: To integrate an evangelistic spirit into all facets of our church life: children, youth, adults, and worship. Work toward the goal of seeing more people come to know and trust Jesus Christ as Lord and Savior and commit to become members of our church. Give oversight to new member visitations, classes, and integration into our church.

Role of committee member: To ensure that all aspects of our church community reach out to our members and the greater community to invite and encourage men, women, and children to commit their lives to Jesus Christ. To encourage new believers and attenders to become committed to our church by becoming members.

Time commitment: Two hour meeting once a month; committee serves a two to four month term.

Skills needed: A desire to see our church become more effective in witnessing and concern in rendering needed service that may do much to bring people to Christ and deepen the faith of the entire congregation

Benefit to the Volunteer: You'll interact with people who are interested in our church and have the opportunity to share your faith.[2]

(First Presbyterian Church, Bellevue, Washington)

Sunday School Activities Coordinator

Importance to our church: Activities that reinforce the Bible lessons and truths are exciting for children and provide them with opportunities to discover or develop creative expressions.

Responsibilities: You will plan, coordinate, and explain creative activities/crafts designed to enhance the Sunday lessons being taught. You will work with teachers, department coordinator, and resource center coordinator to make sure needed items are available. Attendance at teachers' meetings is necessary.

Time frame: Summertime is a good time for planning, and coordinating is from September to May. You need to be present during Sunday school, 9:30 – 10:40 A.M., every other Sunday. Teachers' meetings are held approximately once every six weeks.

Skills to be used/developed: Volunteer needs activities/crafts skills. An understanding of skill levels for different age groups will help you select appropriate activities and crafts.

Training/resources: Attendance at teachers' workshops, curriculum/activities displays, and browsing through Christian bookstores will provide a wealth of ideas.

Number of volunteers: We need one or more volunteers.

Benefit for the volunteer: You will have the personal satisfaction of using your creative talents in a ministry that reinforces the story of God's love for His children.[3]

(Cross of Christ Lutheran Church, Bellevue, Washington)

Volunteerism Committee

The purpose of the volunteerism committee is to create a more effective ministry of volunteers. A Volunteer Coordinator and Assistant Volunteer Coordinator—who serve for two-year terms—will coordinate and continuously bring together volunteers with committees that have needs for volunteer service.

The volunteerism committee is divided into subcommittees to implement and share volunteerism techniques. The various duties of the committee are:

1. To prepare volunteer ministry position descriptions so every committee member has a clear expectation of what the committee will accomplish.

2. To identify volunteers in the congregation and keep a central record available for committee use.

3. To match volunteers and ministry positions while maximizing the use of all who wish to volunteer and integrating them into the mainstream of church life.

4. To orient and train volunteers.

5. To recognize volunteer service work in the congregation and in the community.

6. To help volunteers experience growth by moving from one volunteer commitment to another through evaluation.

7. To be alert to volunteerism needs and opportunities in the congregation and bring these to the attention of the Church Council and various church committees.

The Volunteer Coordinator will be the primary contact for any ministry leader who has volunteer needs in his or her area. Whatever interest a person may have in the various opportunities in church volunteer ministry, the Volunteer Coordinator will put them in touch with the right person. The church newsletter will regularly list the Volunteer Coordinator's phone numbers.[4]

(Our Saviour's Lutheran Church, Merrill, Wisconsin)

Children's Ministry Welcome Center Greeter

Position Purpose: To provide general Children's Ministry and classroom location information to parents and visitors.

Responsibilities: To staff the Children's Ministry information center during a weekend service. To be familiar with the various ministries available to children weekly and seasonally.

Weekly responsibilities: Arrive at the Welcome Center thirty minutes prior to the start of the service and remain for at least twenty minutes after the service has begun. Place classroom charts, registration cards, and other information on the tables for parents to pick up. Greet parents and children as they come by the counter, direct them to the appropriate classroom, answer their questions, or provide other information as requested. If unable to answer a question, direct the guest to a LifeKids Children's Ministry staff member.

Requirements: A warm and friendly individual who is comfortable meeting new people. An individual who interacts effectively with other people and who desires to be a member of a dynamic ministry team. Acquainted with the expectations of, benefits to, and commitment that the Children's Ministry has to our teachers.

Benefit to the volunteer: The person serving in this ministry position will enjoy seeing how God uses his or her engaging personality to welcome people to our church and to initiate an ongoing relationship with the Children's Ministry, the church, and the Lord.[5]

(Lifebridge Christian Church, Longmont, Colorado)

Action Words for Dynamic Job Descriptions

Use the following list of action words to add action to your job descriptions.

Administer	Interact
Advise	Lead
Arrange	Listen
Build	Mail
Call	Model
Care for	Observe
Check	Organize
Communicate	Participate
Contact	Plan
Coordinate	Prepare
Create	Provide
Demonstrate	Purchase
Design	Repair
Encourage	Research
Ensure	Review
Evaluate	Schedule
Experiment	Set up
Foster	Supervise
Guide	Teach
Help	Train
Improve	Visit
Initiate	Write
Innovate	

Volunteer Position Description Cheat Sheet

An alternative "blank" form for designing job descriptions

Position title: A specific, descriptive title that neither exceeds nor diminishes the work of this position. It should give the volunteer a sense of identity, and it should define the position for other volunteers and staff. The title shouldn't distinguish whether the person is paid or unpaid; instead, it should simply reflect the work he or she will do.

Position impact: The purpose and desired outcome of this position should be tied directly to the mission and vision of the church or area of ministry. The impact statement should define how the work of this position will bring positive outcomes for those the church or area of ministry serves.

Performance standards: Responsibilities and duties should be listed as performance standards to be clear about the expectations of the person who fills the position. The list should not only include the activities or accomplishments, but the way the duties are carried out.

Qualifications: The list of qualifications should be clear and explicit. Communicate what is minimally required for this position, as well as what would be beneficial. Include education, personal characteristics, skills, abilities, and experience.

Benefits: This should describe the benefits to the volunteer in this position. State the benefits from the volunteer's perspective, not what the church or area of ministry will receive. Be sure to state benefits, not features.

Commitment required: With the people your church or ministry serves in mind, be explicit about what the requirements are for a person's commitment. How long do you expect a volunteer to serve in this position? How many hours per week, month, year? Address the issue of absenteeism.

Training: Specify the nature and length of all general and position-specific training required for this position. Be clear about what training is mandatory and what is optional.

Responsible to/responsible for: Define who the volunteer is responsible to in the church or area of ministry; define who the volunteer is responsible for if he or she serves as a volunteer leader.

Contract for Volunteering

Volunteer:

I, _____, agree to serve in a volunteer capacity for the above responsibilities for the above specified amount of time and in accordance with the above outlined performance standards.

Volunteer signature_____

Date _____

Volunteer Ministry:

I, _____, agree to provide you with the information and tools to successfully accomplish the responsibilities of this position for our organization and clients. I agree to support you in your efforts.

Staff signature _____

Date _____

Term of this contract:

From_____/_____/_____to _____/_____/_____

Adapted from a handout by Sue Waechter and Deb Kocsis, "Managing Risks in Your Volunteer Program" workshop (Midland, Mich.: Cornerstone Consulting Associates, LLC).

Examples of Job Descriptions with Different Levels of Involvement

Most Responsible Volunteer Position

Title: Volunteer Recruitment Task Force Leader (or Chairperson)

Responsible to: Director of Volunteers

Area of Responsibility: To be responsible for the recruitment of volunteers for this ministry. This includes the organization of other volunteers to assist in this effort as needed; the design of recruitment materials; and the implementation of recruitment objectives, as defined together with the Director of Volunteers and approved by the Advisory Committee

Length of Commitment: One (1) year.

Qualifications: Organizational skills, knowledge of public relations and ability to work well with staff and other volunteers. Knowledge of church and community is helpful.

Comments: This position carries a good deal of responsibility and thus it is recommended that it be your only (or at least, major) volunteer commitment for this year.

Moderately Responsible Volunteer Position

Title: Speaker's Bureau Volunteer

Responsible to: Volunteer Recruitment Task Force Leader

Definition of Duties: Give presentations on behalf of this ministry for the purpose of recruiting more volunteers and encouraging church support of our ministry and its goals. Presentations to be given at adult Sunday school classes, small group meetings, worship services, and at other opportunities as assigned by Recruitment Task Force Leader.

Time Required: 2-4 hours per month. Generally audiences meet on Sundays, but not always.

Qualifications: Public speaking; ability to operate visual aid equipment helpful. Commitment to ministry goals and objectives and a belief in the value of volunteers. Enthusiasm is a must!

Training Provided: Orientation sessions will be arranged with staff and volunteers to thoroughly acquaint volunteer with the ministry and its needs.

Least Responsible Volunteer Position

Title: Telephone Aide

Responsible to: Volunteer Recruitment Task Force Leader and Secretary

Definition of Duties: Telephone prospective volunteers from lists obtained at speeches and presentations to set up interviews with the staff. Phoning should be done from the Office of Volunteers.

Time Required: 2 hours a week. Monday morning preferred.

Qualifications: Pleasant phone personality and ability to work congenially with staff and volunteers.

Comments: This volunteer must have transportation available, as our church office is not accessible by public transportation.

Sample Forms for Volunteer Leaders

First Methodist Church Leadership Covenant

PURPOSE

To agree, as a spiritual leader of FMC, to be "above reproach" so that the world will see, hear, and respond to our leadership in directing them toward the grace of Jesus Christ, and to seek a careful, exemplary Christian lifestyle to encourage other believers and strengthen the church.

PARTICIPANTS

This agreement is for all in regular teaching positions or pastoral care positions, all staff, interns, coordinators, lay ministers, and other positions designated by pastoral leadership.

SPECIFIC AGREEMENTS

1. You have accepted Jesus Christ as your personal Savior.

2. You are a member of (or actively pursuing membership at) FMC.

3. You will work in harmony with the said policies and statement of faith of FMC.

4. You support FMC with your time, money, and loyalty, including participating in the ministries and worship services on a weekly basis.

5. You are known for a dedicated Christian life, according to the standards of God's Word, and you shall purpose to put any sin out of your life that your influence on others might be helpful and not a hindrance (Romans 14; 1 Timothy 3; Titus 1).

6. You are committed to unity, church teamwork, and biblical respect for church leadership (Philippians 2:1-4; Hebrews 13:7, 17).

7. You recognize, accept, pursue, and hold in highest regard the biblical instruction concerning family and marriage responsibility (Ephesians 5:22–6:4; Colossians 3:18-24; 1 Peter 3:1-7).

8. You are careful even in areas of Christian liberty or where the Bible is silent.

THE FMC LEADERSHIP COVENANT

Explanation Concerning the Principle of Influence

Recognizing the responsibilities of both individuals and the community of believers, it is necessary that there be a mutual commitment within the body to certain standards of behavior in order to effectively accomplish the church's purpose (Philippians 3:15-17).

Although certain practices and attitudes are clearly prohibited in Scripture, others are simply matters of taste and discretion (Romans 14:1-6). The church recognizes the problems of Christian liberty, especially within the sphere of those things which may not, of themselves, be either good or bad. Even committed Christians may disagree in these areas.

We want to focus on the positive. Our message is Christ, the cross, and what is clear in Scripture. Concentrating on side issues could sideline us. But we do believe spiritual leaders should show extra care because of their influence on others. We ask that those in leadership and influential positions be obedient to the Lord and growing in maturity. That is the main thing. Then even in areas of debate or Christian liberty, we ask leaders to live with Paul's attitude of concern to build and not hurt others (Romans 14:19-20).

Leaders are asked to abstain from the use of tobacco and the use of non-medicinal narcotic or hallucinogenic drugs and intoxicating alcoholic beverages (because of the principle to guard one's physical body as God's temple) and to avoid the connection with habits considered inappropriate for people in leadership in a church like ours. It is expected of our leaders to live within their means and practice financial integrity.

In other areas of choice such as music or entertainment, eating habits, movies, television, or reading material, those in spiritual leadership at FMC are asked to exercise careful Christian discretion.

Choices should be guided by these principles: done in faith

(Roman 14:22-23) with clear conscience (Acts 24:16), for the glory of God (1 Corinthians 10:31), and to build, not offend others (Romans 14:21).

In areas of possible question not covered here, spiritual leaders are to abide by the direction of the pastoral leadership.

Of course, the observing of these principles does not comprise the whole of one's responsibility to God and therefore does not indicate that one is living under the Lordship of Christ. FMC, however, appreciates the willingness to follow these guidelines because it shows a maturity and spiritual concern for the whole Christian community, and that is a special and larger issue.

NAME (Please Print)_____

DATE _____

SIGNATURE_____

First Methodist Church

BACKGROUND INVESTIGATION CONSENT

I, (Print Name) _____

hereby authorize First Methodist Church's pastor in the area of requested employment or volunteering, and the Director of Finance and Administration Office, to make an independent investigation of my background, references, character, past employment, education, criminal or police records, including those by both public and private organizations and all public records for the purpose of confirming the information contained on my application or volunteer form(s), and/or obtaining other information which may be material to my qualifications for employment or as a volunteer now and, if applicable, during the tenure of my employment or as a volunteer with First Methodist Church.

I release FMC, and any person or entity which provides information pursuant to this authorization, from any and all liabilities, claims or lawsuits in regards to the information obtained from any and all of the above referenced sources used.

The following is my true and *complete* legal name, and all information is true and correct to the best of my knowledge:

Full Name (Printed)

Phone #

Maiden Name or Other Names Used

Present Address

Length of time at present address

City/State

ZIP

Former Address

Length of time at former address

City/State

Zip

Date of Birth

Social Security Number

Driver's License #

State of License

Signature

Date

NOTE: The above information is required for identification purposes only, and is in no manner used as qualifications for employment or placement.

First Methodist Church

What Floats Your Boat Sheet

Your supervisor wants to get to know you! Give us some insight by completing this fun sheet, please.

Name:

1. What motivates you? (Write three or four lines on how you like to be encouraged.)

   _____

   _____

   _____

2. A daily encouragement for me would be:

   _____

   _____

3. If I could select a gift for myself for under $20, it would be:

   _____

   _____

4. If I had all day to do something for myself, I would:

   _____

   _____

5. The most fun I ever had was when:

   _____

   _____

6. My favorite hobby is:

_____

_____

_____

7. My greatest passion in life is:

_____

_____

_____

_____

8. One area where I am growing is:

_____

_____

_____

9. The greatest strength I possess is:

_____

_____

_____

_____

First Methodist Church

Children and Youth Ministry Volunteer Team Questionnaire

Legal Name (Last, First, Middle)

Nickname

Home phone

Work phone

Cell/pager

Best time/place to call

E-mail address

Street address

City/State/ZIP

How long at your present address?

If less than five years, give previous address and number of years:

Previous address

Years there

__Male __Female

Date of birth ____/____/____

Marital status

If married, spouse's name

Number of children

Ages

Emergency Contact
Name

Relationship

Phone number

Occupation

Place of employment

Number of years

Employment history for last five years:
Employer's name/phone

Employer's name/phone

Employer's name/phone

Do you have a personal relationship with Jesus Christ? Describe briefly.

_____

_____

_____

_____

How long have you attended First Methodist Church (FMC)?

_____

List any leadership/volunteer experience you've had with children/youth:

_____

_____

_____

List any training/education that has prepared you to work with children/youth:

_____

_____

_____

List any other FMC ministries you're involved in:

_____

_____

Age/grade preference

Hour preference

Local Personal References
(must be 18 years old and not related to you)

Name

Relationship

Address

Phone

Comments (staff use)

_____

_____

Name

Relationship

Address

Phone

Comments (staff use)

_____

_____

Name

Relationship

Address

Phone

Comments (staff use)

_____

_____

Applicant's Statement

I hereby authorize FMC to verify all information contained in this application with any references, my past or present employers, or any other appropriate personnel at my present or past employers, churches, or other organizations and any individuals to disclose any and all information to FMC. I release all such persons or entities from liability that may result or arise from FMC's collections of all such evaluations or information or its consideration of my application.

Should my application be accepted, I agree to follow the policies of FMC and to refrain from unscriptural conduct in the performance of my services on behalf of the church.

I understand that the personal information will be held confidential by the church staff.

Applicant's signature

Date

How to Establish a Volunteer Ministry Budget

What does it cost to create and maintain a volunteer ministry? You may well be asked, and this handy worksheet will help you determine what your church can expect to spend. Keep in mind that even if you're using an office in the church and the church copier, there are costs associated with that overhead. Play fair: Roll the appropriate prorated expenses into your budget.

And to keep things simple, figure annual costs. That's typically how church budgets are figured—though it's smart to check.

Personnel

Volunteer manager   _____

Secretary   _____

Additional staff   _____

_____   _____

_____   _____

Benefits (estimate at _____% of total salaries)   _____

Subtotal—Personnel $_____

Overhead

Some of the items below are one-time purchases you'll need to make to set up an office. Others are line items you'll carry throughout the year.

Office furniture and equipment

Desks, chairs, lamps, etc.

    File cabinets   _____

    Bulletin boards, white boards   _____

    Computer equipment   _____

    Audio-visual equipment   _____

    Additional equipment   _____

    _____   _____

    _____   _____

    _____   _____

Subtotal—Office furniture and equipment $_____

Telephone

    Installation $_____

    Monthly service charge (x12)   _____

    Long distance (x12)   _____

    Message service charges   _____

Subtotal—Telephone $_____

Office Supplies/Expenses

Rent   _____

Utilities   _____

Office & maintenance supplies   _____

Photocopying   _____

Printing   _____
    (stationery, brochures, etc.)

Postage   _____

        Subtotal—Office supplies/Expenses $_____

Travel

Local   _____
    (Mileage reimbursement, etc.)

Long distance travel   _____
    (conferences, professional development)

        Subtotal—Travel $_____

Risk Management Screenings

Subtotal—Risk Management $_____

Development and Training

Registration fees   _____

    (for conferences, seminars, etc.)

Journal subscriptions, books, etc.   _____

Membership fees   _____

    (for professional associations)

Handouts/books for training   _____

Refreshments   _____

Other training materials   _____

    (slides, films, etc.)

Other _____   _____

Subtotal—Development Training $ _____

Sources

I'm deeply indebted to Augsburg Publishing House for its willingness to let me draw material from my book, *How to Mobilize Church Volunteers* (Minneapolis: Augsburg Publishing House, 1983) for this volume. I also frequently referred to my book, *The Effective Management of Volunteer Programs* (Boulder, Colo.: Volunteer Management Associates, 1976).

Happily, the principles I thought timeless years ago still apply—but I've taken the liberty of updating the information and filtering it through my subsequent years of experience.

1. *Volunteer Ministry: Your Gift of Christian Service* (Bellevue, Wash.: Cross of Christ Lutheran Church, 1988), p. 61.

2. *Serve God by Sharing, Caring, Serving* (Bellevue, Wash.: First Presbyterian Church of Bellevue), p. 10.

3. *Volunteer Ministry: Your Gift of Christian Service,* p. 33.

4. *Volunteers in Christ Reference Guide* (Merrill, Wis.: Our Saviour's Lutheran Church, 1984), p. 17.

5. Lifebridge Christian Church, Longmont, Colorado.

VOLUNTEER RECRUITMENT, INTERVIEWING, AND PLACEMENT

Marlene Wilson, General Editor

Group's Volunteer Leadership Series™
Volume 4
Group's Church Volunteer Central™

Loveland, Colorado

Group's Volunteer Leadership Series™, Volume 4

Volunteer Recruitment, Interviewing, and Placement

Visit our Web site: **www.grouppublishing.com**

Credits
Writer: Mikal Keefer
Editor: Mikal Keefer
General Editor: Marlene Wilson
Chief Creative Officer: Joani Schultz
Art Director: Nathan Hindman
Cover Designer: Jeff Storm
Production Manager: Peggy Naylor

Unless otherwise noted, Scripture taken from the HOLY BIBLE, NEW INTERNATIONAL VERSION®. Copyright © 1973, 1978, 1984 International Bible Society. Used by permission of Zondervan Publishing House. All rights reserved.

Produced with the assistance of The Livingstone Corporation (www.LivingstoneCorp.com). Project staff includes Chris Hudson, Ashley Taylor, Mary Horner Collins, Joel Bartlett, Cheryl Dunlop, Mary Larsen, and Rosalie Krusemark.

Library of Congress Cataloging-in-Publication Data

Volunteer recruitment, interviewing, and placement / Marlene Wilson, general
        editor.—1st American hardbound ed.
    p. cm. — (Group's volunteer leadership
    series ; v. 4)
    ISBN 0-7644-2748-2 (alk. paper)
    1. Voluntarism—Religious aspects—Christianity. 2. Christian leadership. 3. Church work. 4. Volunteers—Recruiting. I. Wilson, Marlene. II. Series.
BR115.V64V655 2003
253'.7—dc22   2003022121

10 9 8 7 6 5 4 3 2 1   12 11 10 09 08 07 06 05 04

Printed in the United States of America.

Contents

Introduction

Take a look at these four recruitment techniques. If they look familiar, you're in trouble . . .

When it comes to recruiting volunteers, there's a long list of ideas that simply don't work. Maybe you've tried one of these . . .

- You have the pastor hold the Sunday morning service hostage until someone signs up for nursery duty next week.

- You place inserts in the Sunday morning bulletins week after week after week until you get enough names to staff the Sunday school.

- You stand the cutest little girl you can find up front in the worship service asking for someone—*anyone*—to come help her understand Jesus. Extra points if her lower lip is quivering and there's a single tear creeping slowly down one cheek.

- You send letters home with all the fourth-grade boys demanding their parents take turns serving as helpers—or else. It's not until later you realize all the letters wound up as ammunition in a paper wad fight out in the parking lot.

It's no surprise that those techniques of volunteer recruitment are destined to fail. Anyone who's made a compelling announcement asking for volunteers and then stood at a lonely sign-up table suspects there *must* be a better way.

There is.

The remainder of this Volunteer Leadership Series will help you create a volunteer ministry that makes use of the best possible recruitment techniques. You'll learn new, proven approaches to getting the right people in the right spots. You'll gain new skills that make recruitment easier. You'll learn to think about volunteers and managing volunteers in a new way.

And your new way of thinking begins here. It starts with a new definition of what it means to "recruit" a volunteer.

Recruitment Redefined

A new way of thinking about recruitment. Trends in volunteerism. Why people do—and don't—volunteer. And what *really* motivates volunteers.

Many people think that recruiting volunteers is a matter of crafting a sales message and then putting the people who respond to work. We tuck those warm bodies into open volunteer slots and then move on.

The problem with that approach is that volunteers who enter a ministry that way don't stick. They aren't fulfilled and they usually aren't effective. You end up right back on the same old treadmill, trying to replace people who you got to replace other people who themselves were replacements.

A certain amount of turnover will happen no matter what you do. But you can shrink turnover and increase volunteer satisfaction (yours with the volunteers, and the volunteers with their roles) by thinking of recruitment as *more* than a sales job. And by determining that just any warm body *won't* do for your volunteer ministry.

Think of recruitment this way:

Recruitment is an invitation to come discuss a volunteer role.

It doesn't mean the person responding will necessarily get the job.

Notice that when you recruit with this definition in mind, the process is like a job interview, where a company selects from among a talented pool of applicants. It's not a desperate attempt to get somebody doing a job that needs to be done.

But you might be thinking: *I AM desperately seeking people to do jobs that need to be done! I can't AFFORD to be selective.*

Not only can you afford to be selective, you *must* be selective. To do anything else is to shortchange everyone in the process—the volunteers, your church, and the people who will benefit from the volunteers' involvement.

Consider what happened to a youth minister who was short a youth sponsor and was then introduced to someone who wanted the job . . .

> **"You *must* be selective."**

"The guy looked perfect for the role," says John, the youth minister. "He was good-looking, high energy, and related well with the kids. Plus, I had so many parents telling me he'd make a wonderful youth sponsor that I felt I had to try him out."

Mistake.

After a month of stellar service, the new 25-year-old youth sponsor decided to date one of the senior high girls.

The good news is that John happened to walk into the conversation while the sponsor was telling the girl what time he'd pick her up for their date—so the date never happened.

"I was shocked," says John. "My heart went to my throat, my stomach fell to my feet, and I thought, "am I *hearing* this? I wanted to *kill* the guy."

Nothing on the security screening had indicated the new volunteer abused children. Or sexually molested teenage girls. Or even drove too fast in a school zone. And in fact the volunteer never *had* done any of those things.

"He just met a nice girl and wanted to take her out," remembers John. "When I told him he couldn't date the kids, he was baffled. He didn't see what the problem was. He didn't have a clue."

Would it have been worth John's time to be more selective about whom he placed in the youth sponsor role? Absolutely.

And would he have been smart to sit down with the sponsor and cover the bases about what was—and wasn't—appropriate behavior? You bet.

But John was desperate for staff and wasn't sure he'd do any better if he kept looking. So he took a shortcut and bypassed the orientation and training—something he will no longer do.

"Nothing happened, but it easily could have," says John, who still serves in a position where he's responsible for finding volunteers. "I learned a *lot* from that experience."

When you live in a world of too many jobs and too few volunteers, how can you turn down people who are willing? The harsh reality is this: Sometimes you have to go with the people you have available. The *good* people—the people you *wish* you had—aren't the ones signing up when you pass around the sign-up sheet.

> "How can you turn down people who are willing?"

What's wrong with people these days? Why isn't anyone volunteering anymore?

Trends in Volunteerism

The fact is that people *are* volunteering—just not in the ways you may remember.

Back in the Good Old Days, when relatively few women worked outside the home, you could sign up volunteers by simply announcing a need. Back in the Good Old Days, when the work week was 40 hours long and families played badminton in the backyard after dinner, men had time to get together on Saturday afternoon to do yard work at the church building.

But those Good Old Days are gone—if they ever existed at all.

These days you're facing trends that shape how much time people are willing to volunteer, and how they want their volunteer commitments structured. Your community may differ somewhat, but in general, you'll need to consider these following 12 trends when you're creating your volunteer ministry.

• **Work life is expanding—and varied.**

How many people do you know who still work the hours of 9 to 5, Monday through Friday? Some studies indicate that only about a third of employees work those once-normal hours.

Part-time jobs, jobs that demand travel and long hours, service jobs with irregular hours, health-care jobs that require night shifts, extra jobs, home-based jobs that blur the lines between "family time" and "work time"; these are common today. So are long commutes that consume extra hours each day.

> "People staffing your volunteer roles will be juggling jobs, families, friends, and their volunteer duties."

Many churches want to find people who'll commit for several months at exactly the time many volunteers are seeking short-term, one-shot volunteer assignments.

According to Independent Sector's *Giving and Volunteering in the United States* (Washington, D.C., 1999), 61 percent of persons who are employed part-time volunteer, and 58 percent of persons who work full-time volunteer. That means the majority of people staffing your volunteer roles will be juggling jobs, families, friends, and their volunteer duties.

• **Families are changing.**

In many homes, grandparents are now raising their grandchildren. Single-parent households are far more common than they once were. The traditional definition of "family" is being stretched and redefined in many directions, and there are unique stresses with each definition. Woe be to the organization that assumes stay-at-home moms will sign up to be Den Mothers, recess chaperones, or Sunday school teachers because those moms want to contribute to organizations that benefit children.

- **People seek balanced lives—and that may eliminate volunteering.**

In an effort to live lives that include family, friends, work, and worship, many church members are opting to intentionally *not* volunteer for tasks. This isn't a lack of concern or unawareness. It's a deliberate decision to limit the number of their obligations, and for these potential volunteers a "no" is a non-negotiable "no."

- **There's increased competition for volunteers.**

Organizations that were once well funded by government agencies are experiencing budget reductions. Every organization is trying to do more with less. The demand for volunteer labor is increasing, which means your church members might very well have full volunteer schedules at the United Way, Homeless Shelter, or SPCA before you ever contact them about serving on a church committee.

- **The motivation for volunteering is shifting.**

In the 1950s and before, the value behind volunteering was commitment. When you signed on to teach Sunday school, you did so because you were expressing a commitment to God, the church, and the children.

Today the values behind volunteerism seem to be compassion (I want to help and make a difference) and community (I want to be part of something bigger than myself. I want to belong and to be in a network of caring people).

Motivation impacts *everything* in a volunteer setting, from how you recruit volunteers to how you assign them to how you recognize them.

- **Volunteers expect more.**

Maybe they used to settle for that "good feeling" that came from helping others, but now they're expecting the organizations that use them to be professional, flexible, and responsive. Good enough isn't good enough anymore. If a volunteer experience is disorganized, frustrating, or wastes the volunteer's time, that volunteer won't be back.

- **There's a changing pool of volunteers available.**

As Baby Boomers reach the age of wanting to do something significant in addition to something lucrative, highly trained and highly skilled people are becoming volunteers. The ranks of volunteers are also growing because of layoffs. Teenagers are entering the volunteer pool because of experience with school "service learning" projects and to bolster resumés for college applications and job searches.

- **Volunteers want to shoulder responsibility, not just tasks.**

Many volunteers bring significant management experience with them when they show up to volunteer. They want to be actively engaged in their roles, which means they want to use all of their skills. Electrical engineers won't be satisfied for long stuffing envelopes. Volunteers are seeking meaningful, interesting work.

- **There are more volunteer options available in churches.**

As churches grow in size, the number of "niche" ministries grows. It used to be a volunteer could work in Christian Education or serve on a board. Now a volunteer can help direct traffic, handle finances, play bass in the worship band, or serve coffee in the café.

- **Guilt is gone as a motivator.**

"Because you should" isn't a reason people willingly accept any longer. Rather, volunteers are motivated for other reasons and they're more willing to explicitly ask what benefits will come to them as a result of their volunteering.

Volunteer managers must be able to answer the question "What's in it for me?" with clear, definite benefits that will flow to the volunteer.

- **Technology is changing volunteering.**

It's now possible to write, edit, and produce the church's monthly newsletter without ever setting foot in the church office. Balancing the books requires software, not board meetings. And the list of technology-related volunteer roles—handling lights and sound, computer consulting, and preparing PowerPoint presentations among others—is growing rapidly. Some volunteer positions require specialized knowledge and thorough training.

- **The cost of training and maintaining volunteers is rising.**

It's more expensive than ever to bring a volunteer on board at your church. The cost of a security screening, the training needed to make a volunteer proficient in a role, insurance to protect the church and volunteer—even the paperwork for tracking volunteers is more extensive than ever before.

> "These trends aren't good or bad; they simply exist."

It's unlikely this trend will reverse direction anytime soon, if ever.

Please note that these trends aren't good or bad; they simply exist. They're reality. And as you plan how to initiate a volunteer management ministry or fine-tune the one that's already in place in your church, you've got to keep them in mind. Wishing there were more stay-at-home moms who want to donate a day per week to your project won't make it come true.

Why Won't People Volunteer?

Everyone who's attempted to staff a ministry with volunteers has a top-ten list of excuses they hear again and again. But the items on those lists usually boil down to two basic issues: a perceived lack of time and fear.

The perceived lack of time

Fact: We all get 24 hours in a day, and 168 hours in a week. The amount of time available to volunteers and non-volunteers is precisely the same.

The concern about having enough time to volunteer really isn't about time. It's about the number of obligations a potential volunteer has that make a claim on his or her time.

If a person is pulled in many different directions and rushes through a nonstop hectic schedule, it's going to feel as if there's no time to spare, . . . and there isn't. One unforeseen incident sets off a domino effect that leaves the next ten appointments missed or delayed. There's no margin in this person's life.

For each potential volunteer, there is a critical issue you must settle before you place the volunteer in a role: Will this person dedicate enough time to the role to be successful? And can the volunteer provide the *right* time? Is the volunteer available when the volunteer job needs to be done?

"Will this person dedicate enough time to the role to be successful?"

A busy sales professional decided to join the Big Brothers. Following the necessary interview and screening process, a first meeting was set up to introduce the volunteer to a potential match. An agency representative was present, as was the volunteer, the eight-year-old boy who was seeking a big brother, and the boy's mother.

The agency representative laid out the agency's expectations again. The big and little brother would meet once a week for three to four hours, meetings would be confirmed by phone 24 hours in advance, outings would be inexpensive, and all parties would stay in touch with the agency. Everything was exactly as described in earlier communications with the individual parties.

Then the mother casually mentioned that the meetings would have to be on Mondays between 3:00 and 6:00 P.M. Weekends were already booked with activities and her work schedule was set.

The connection between the boy and volunteer never developed. For the volunteer, Mondays were busy—especially during work hours. He could meet with the boy on weekends and evenings, but not during work hours.

The volunteer experience failed to develop, but *not* because the volunteer lacked time. It failed to develop because the time the volunteer *had available* didn't match the task.

As you seek to match busy people with volunteer roles, what can you do to overcome the barrier of a perceived lack of time?

Some suggestions:

- **Segment volunteer roles so there are more, but less time-consuming, roles to fill.**

For instance, rather than ask a Sunday school teacher to gather supplies, prepare the lesson, and teach the lesson, you might have another volunteer do the gathering of supplies. Divide volunteer roles into contained tasks and recruit more volunteers who each do less.

- **Connect the volunteer role with another valued activity.**

For instance, if a potential volunteer wants to spend more time with family, suggest a volunteer role that can be accomplished by a family. If the potential volunteer wants to get more exercise suggest the volunteer mow a yard, weed a garden, or do another exercise-oriented task.

- **Suggest that the potential volunteer sign up for a one-shot project rather than an ongoing role.**

An airline pilot whose flight schedule won't allow her to consistently lead a small group on Wednesday night might very well be willing to give a full day some weekend when she's off. Sometimes it's not the amount of time that's a problem; it's the expectation that the same hour will be available each week.

Short-term missions are growing in popularity because they're short term—and can be accomplished by someone who's not willing to completely change his or her life. Habitat for Humanity (www.habitat.org) and Group Workcamps (www.groupworkcamps.com) have found ways to recruit thousands of volunteers who do remarkable amounts of ministry in short-term settings.

- **Create flexible volunteer positions that are less time sensitive.**

It doesn't really matter if someone creates a form on your church web site at 9:00 in the morning or at midnight. And if you're planning ahead, stocking up on animal crackers for VBS can happen anytime during the week before VBS begins. Be intentional about structuring volunteer opportunities so they have the maximum time flexibility possible. This won't be possible with some roles—such as leading a class that meets from 9:30 to 10:30 on Sunday mornings, but it will be possible elsewhere.

- **Create volunteer positions that don't require travel.**

Especially for older volunteers who might be homebound or have issues with travel at night or in bad weather, look for volunteer tasks and roles that don't require travel. Some examples: making phone calls, creating follow-up packets for visitors, and creating craft packets from materials delivered to the volunteers' homes.

When "I don't have time" emerges as an issue in dealing with volunteers, don't assume you understand what the potential volunteer means by those words. It's worth probing to see if one of the strategies listed above can manage the issue and make it possible for the potential volunteer to sign up for a role.

Fear of volunteering

Some people shy away from volunteering because of fear. Not necessarily fear of your organization or the specific opportunities you're offering, but rather three other things . . .

- **They're afraid they'll fail.**

If a volunteer role is poorly defined or lacks training and resources, failure is an almost certain outcome. If volunteers sense they're set up for failure, they won't feel excited about participation.

Volunteers dislike crashing and burning on projects, or disappointing themselves and you. It's up to you to design the volunteer role so you can provide reassurance that no volunteer will be sent out on a limb that will then be cut off.

- **They're afraid of being abused.**

Abuse is a strong word and may overstate the case—but not by much. When a volunteer is given an impossible task, it feels like abuse.

Jim Wideman, in his book *Children's Ministry Leadership: The You-Can-Do-It Guide* (Group Publishing, 2003), describes what sometimes happens to people who sign up to teach Sunday school. "In many churches, new Sunday school teachers are trained by getting a little lecture, handed a book, thrown in a classroom, and told to not come out until Jesus returns."

Jim describes what happens to new volunteer teachers this way: "We tell them they'll get some help and in a couple years we *do* find them a helper. That's when we open the classroom door and are amazed when the teacher comes screaming out, quits on the spot, and disappears forever. So what do we do? We hand the book to the helper we found and throw *that* person in the room."

> "When a volunteer is given an impossible task, it feels like abuse."

Small wonder someone in a church like that would be afraid to sign up to teach Sunday school. You can't quit and there's no training. It's a volunteer's nightmare . . . and it's abusive.

A volunteer would only have to be mistreated that way once before deciding: *never again*. And the only way to be *sure* it never again happens would be to avoid all volunteer roles.

By the way: Volunteers consider it equally abusive to take them on and then give them nothing worthwhile to do.

• **They're afraid they're not "good enough."**

On a typical Sunday morning a church member will see someone preach, teach, and lead music. There may be solo instrumentalists, a band, or a choir. There may be people ushering. Perhaps there are greeters and people staffing an information desk.

And depending on the size of the church and the church's emphasis on excellence in programming, the people serving in visible roles might be demonstrating professional-level skills. They're not just singing—they're singing remarkably well. They're not just playing piano—they're playing at a level you'd expect to hear in a concert hall. They're not just ushering, they look like the concierge at the five-star hotel downtown.

The unintended message: If you're going to serve here, you've got to have the skill and polish of a pro. In our choir, only music majors need apply.

Is that true? Probably not . . . or maybe it *is* true.

A church's desire to have excellent programming creates a smoother, more enjoyable worship service. But it also discourages potential volunteers who know they can't hit the high notes or deliver a top-notch lesson. It can seem there's no place for a nonprofessional to participate.

Here are ways you can banish fear when it comes to volunteering:

- **Define roles carefully—with a full job description in writing.**

Job descriptions provide reassurance to potential volunteers in that they know what they're getting into—and you've thought through what you want. Solid information tends to help people see a challenge as an opportunity or adventure rather than a threat.

See volume 3 for information about how to create job descriptions.

- **Listen carefully to concerns about the volunteer role and the volunteer's fit with the role.**

What's behind the concern? Has the volunteer failed in another volunteer role? Has a friend failed in the role you're proposing? Is there a question of trust about how thoroughly you've described what's expected? What history is the potential volunteer carrying into the discussion? If you detect fear or suspicion, gently probe to get to the root of it.

- **Remove uncertainty.**

Volunteers can be less than confident about participating because they know they're being "sold" on a project. Sure, you're here now—when the volunteer hasn't yet been reeled in—but will you be around when there's a problem to be solved?

Let potential volunteers know what you'll do to help them in their volunteer efforts. Describe the support and involvement they can expect from you and other leaders. Then do what you say you'll do.

The Unspoken Barrier to Volunteering

There's another common reason people don't volunteer, though you'll never hear people actually say it: tradition.

In many churches it's a *tradition* to simply sit in the pew. Few people ever volunteer for anything. It's a *tradition* to pay the soloists who sing on Sunday morning, the nursery workers who care for children on Wednesday night, and the caterers who've replaced the potlucks.

Recruiting volunteers in a church culture that doesn't honor or encourage volunteerism is a challenge of Olympian proportions. And at heart, it's a spiritual matter.

> "Another common reason people don't volunteer: tradition."

If you're in a church where volunteering "just isn't done," consider doing the following:

Meet with the leadership.

Determine if your assessment is accurate. Is it true that most people won't volunteer, or is that true just of one ministry area? If the children's ministry area can't beg, borrow, or steal a volunteer but the adult ministry has a waiting list for involvement, the problem may be with the reputation or administration of the children's ministry area. Be sure you see things clearly, and that you're fixing the right problem.

And if most members of your congregation *are* volunteering in service but only outside your church, that's helpful to know.

Ask leadership to provide teaching about the biblical expectation for involvement.

If people truly aren't serving anywhere, ask for clear teaching about the biblical mandate to serve others. Volume 1 of this series will provide your leadership an excellent starting place for researching that mandate.

Remove every barrier you can find to volunteering.

Some have been identified already, but consider these possibly hidden barriers, too:

- *Do staff members discourage volunteers?* It can be done by failing to design roles that can be filled by volunteers, or refusing to provide information that allows volunteers to function effectively.

- *Is there such competition for volunteers that it frightens volunteers away?* If the new members' class is stalked by the youth pastor, children's pastor, and other staffers who are all pitching the importance of their different ministries, it may create an environment that actually repels volunteerism. To say "yes" to one staffer creates hard feelings with other staffers.

- *Is there a "volunteer toxic" environment that combines a refusal to delegate with vague or nonexistent job descriptions?* It may be so difficult to come on board as a volunteer that it's truly not worth the effort.

- *Are volunteers ignored?* Find out when the last volunteer recognition effort was organized. If the year starts with "19–" then you've identified one problem to overcome.

In volume 1 of this series we identify the common obstacles to volunteerism . . . be sure they're whittled down or cleared out altogether before you start a recruitment campaign.

Pray—and invite others to pray with you.

Is your church one that's discouraged—and as a congregation you have no vision for the future?

Is your church one that's defeated? Perhaps your "glory days" of attendance and impact were 20 or 50 years ago, and those who remain see themselves as defenders of a glorious tradition. Your leadership has dug in and is holding on . . . and that's all.

Is your church dead? There's no spark of life anywhere you look?

Pray for your church and what God wants to do with you. Ask others whose hearts align with yours about wanting to see people involved to join you in regular times of lifting your church up to God.

A bonus: the single best-kept secret of effective recruitment revealed!

There's a simple technique that will revolutionize your recruitment efforts. It's powerful, simple, and you can do it without having to invest in additional books, conferences, or consultants.

And you even get immediate feedback when this technique is used.

Ready?

Here it is: Ask people to serve.

It's that simple. Honest.

> "Ask people to serve."

One of the reasons most frequently cited by volunteers as to why they didn't get involved sooner is that nobody asked them to do so.

That *doesn't* mean they weren't subjected to countless recruitment campaigns. They may have walked past sign-up tables, sat through announcements, and flipped past the pleas for help written in the church newsletter and bulletin.

But nobody *asked* them, face to face, by name, to fill a volunteer role.

If it's increasingly difficult for you to get volunteers, consider how large a role person-to-person recruitment plays in your approach. It is far, *far* more effective than "paper-to-people" recruitment efforts.

What *Really* Motivates Volunteers

First, a disclaimer: You can't motivate a volunteer. It's simply not within your power. But you can discover what already motivates individual volunteers and try to scratch those particular itches.

Everyone has what Marlene Wilson calls a "motivational preference." If you can identify it, you can help each volunteer have a meaningful experience while volunteering through your program.

David McClelland and John W. Atkinson did groundbreaking research at Harvard University and the University of Michigan, respectively, which led to a theory that goes a long way toward helping you identify what motivates your volunteers. A brief listing of their seminal studies is given at the end of this chapter.[1]

Fortunately, Harvard professor George Litwin and his research assistant, Robert Stringer, Jr., helped translate the McClelland-Atkinson theory and applied it to organizations in their book, *Motivation and Organizational Climate*. Marlene Wilson adapted these ideas to working with volunteers in her book, *The Effective Management of Volunteer Programs,* and the following synopsis appears courtesy of Harvard Division of Research, Graduate School of Business and Volunteer Man-agement Associates.

> "A disclaimer: You can't motivate a volunteer."

McClelland and Atkinson were curious about why one person's favorite job was another person's least favorite, and why some people liked to figure things out on their own while others wanted clear directions.

Starting with the premise that "people spend their time thinking about what motivates them," they conducted extensive studies checking out what people thought while walking, eating, working, studying, and even sleeping. They discovered people *do* think about what motivates them, and they identified three distinct motivational types: Achievers, Affiliators, and Power (or Influence) people.

Let's take a closer look at those three motivational types.

Achievers value accomplishments and results.

They like to set goals and solve problems. They want to know where they're headed and want things to happen in a timely way. They *hate* having their time wasted.

Achievers tend to be well-organized, prefer deadlines, are

moderate risk takers, and are often articulate. They like "to-do" lists. They depend on their pocket-calendars and electronic organizers. And if achievers have a leader who's poor at delegation, they'll go crazy.

If an achiever responds to a project they think is significant and they discover it's just a small task, the achiever's motivation immediately deflates. In fact, unless they're extremely committed to the cause, you'll lose them.

In churches resistant to change, where achievers have no room to grow and stretch, you'll find them coming in one door and going out another. You can utilize and attract achievers by learning how to use task forces effectively (see volume 2). Search for achievers with good delegation skills, and they'll form excellent teams around themselves.

Affiliators are "people people."

They're sensitive, nurturing, and caring. Interacting with others and being part of a community is what motivates them. They care less about the work being done than about the people they're doing it with. They're easily hurt, so leaders need to know that affiliators will require more of their time. However, it's time well spent because affiliators make church a good place to be. They're the ones walking up to visitors and striking up conversations.

Affiliators are good barometers about how things are going in your volunteer program. They know how people are feeling about things. They're also good persuaders, listeners, and public speakers. They make excellent interviewers, members of listen-care teams, or leaders of small groups.

And they're great choices for projects like mass mailings. Get a group of affiliators together with a pot of coffee, and they'll have the mailing done before you know it—and enjoy the process because they chatted the entire time.

Power People come in two varieties: McClelland categorized them as *personal* and *social*.

Both types like to think about having impact on people and outcomes. They think long-term and are good strategists.

If you want to enact change, find some power-motivated people and get them on your side. If you convince them, they'll spend their time thinking about who they need to influence and how they need to do it.

Personal Power People use their power on *people*, usually through manipulation and intimidation. They think in terms of win-lose, and if they perceive someone else is "winning," they instantly assume they're losing. They're comfortable with conflict—and tend to create a lot of it!

In the church, these people can be toxic. If someone has left your church bleeding, there was probably a personal power person involved. These are also the people who can quickly crush programs and new ideas.

Social Power People like to influence and impact others in a win-win way. Convince a social power person of your vision, and they'll move mountains to see your project happen. The reason they can do this is because they see power as infinite and self-renewable. The more power they give away, the more they get. Therefore, they aren't threatened by the success of others. Their goal is *your* success. How the church needs these people!

> "In the church, personal power people can be toxic."

By the way, social power people are the best at dealing with personal power people because they aren't intimidated by them. *Never* send an affiliator to deal with a personal power person.

Please understand that most people have some characteristics from each of these motivational types, and an individual's primary motivational style may change over time and within differing situations. Marlene Wilson reports that she has exhibited all three styles.

When she was a homemaker while her children were young, she was an affiliator. When she became a program director, she shifted into achievement. She used to enjoy thinking about program goals, or how to write a book or produce a video series. Now she sees herself as a social power person. She finds herself thinking, *"How do I influence things that matter? How do I use whatever time and energy I have left to have the most impact on the things I care most about?"*

You can motivate people with these three styles by placing them in appropriate settings. For instance, an affiliator may make a wonderful receptionist, so long as the job doesn't also require a great deal of pressure to get filing and typing done on a tight schedule.

And you can use insights drawn from these types to create appropriate recognition for individual volunteers, too. You'll find a detailed list of suggestions in volume 6, on pages 94-95.

1. Seminal studies contributing to this paradigm include: David C. McClelland, *The Achieving Society* (Princeton, NJ: D. Van Nostrand Company, 1961); John W. Atkinson, *An Introduction to Motivation* (Princeton, NJ: D. Van Nostrand Company, 1964); John W. Atkinson and N. T. Feather, *A Theory of Achievement Motivation* (New York: John Wiley and Sons, 1966).

TWO
Marketing Your Volunteer Ministry

How to effectively craft a message and attract people to your volunteer ministry. Ten critical questions. The most effective marketing campaign ever.

Marketing your volunteer ministry simply means this: deliberately telling your target audience the benefits your volunteer ministry can provide to them.

The term "marketing" sometimes has a negative association because it's the same word used to describe how tobacco companies create smokers, whiskey companies create drinkers, and car manufacturers put their super-sized models in garages.

It would seem that in the church, where it's understood that everyone has an ability, interest, or passion to share for the common good, where everyone is called to be active in ministry, and where discipleship is an expectation, there would be no need for "marketing" service opportunities.

> "'Marketing' sometimes has a negative association."

After all, shouldn't church people be *looking* for volunteer opportunities?

Well . . . yes. But people often *aren't* looking. And if they are, there's lots of competition for the slice of time they have available for volunteering.

If you want to be heard and have people respond, it's important that you target an audience you want to address. Be intentional about crafting a message that cuts through daily clutter and makes an impression.

The best way to be sure that you are effectively communicating with people you want to address is to create a "marketing plan." With a marketing plan, you won't waste time and resources talking to yourself, to the wrong people, or to nobody at all. You'll make the critical decisions up front that will direct how, when, and where you communicate about the volunteer opportunities in your church. You won't find yourself answering the questions a marketing plan addresses when it's a crunch time and you're stressed.

> **"You already have the information and resources you need to create a marketing plan."**

Here's the good news: You already have the information and resources you need to create a marketing plan. You won't need to go hide out for a month digging through church records, or hire an expensive expert to pull together a serviceable plan. You can do it.

And we'll walk you through the steps.

How to Create a Marketing Plan

First, let's clear up a couple of misunderstandings about marketing.

Marketing is *not* selling.

Marketing is simply a deliberate process of getting your message out to the people you want to hear it in a clear, concise manner.

Marketing is *not* manipulation.

The goal of your communication should never be to somehow trick people into volunteering. That's completely counterproductive. You end up with people you don't want as volunteers, and your volunteer ministry gains a reputation that will keep good people away.

Marketing is *not* just for people with MBAs.

There's nothing terribly complicated about what you'll be

doing, but it will require your making decisions. Since you can't do everything ("Let's take out a full page ad in the newspaper announcing we need nursery workers!"), you've got to decide what you *will* do—and your marketing plan is where you narrow down your communication options.

Marketing is *not* a once-per-year event.

If your church limits marketing and recruiting to a few weeks per year, perhaps as you head into the fall, you're limiting your effectiveness. You need volunteers all year, and people enter your congregation all year. So why wait to put those new people to work?

Plus, if every volunteer position comes up for renewal at the same time, you're almost guaranteeing a training nightmare as you have a large percentage of staff exit and other people come on board.

Finally, remember the wise words shared by an unknown marketing genius: *out of sight, out of mind.* If the volunteer ministry falls off the congregation's radar screen the majority of the year, it will be treated like a temporary distraction—not an integral part of the congregational life.

To create a marketing plan, you must answer ten critical questions. Let's look at these carefully.

1. What is the purpose of your volunteer ministry?

You will want to create a purpose statement, but before you tackle that, be sure you've got a mission statement in place. It's best if you create one in the context of a task force, and you'll find step-by-step help in volume 2 about how to craft a mission statement.

But here's a quick explanation: A mission statement communicates who you are, what you do, what you stand for, and why you do what you do. It's clearly articulated, widely understood, and truly supported by your church leadership, your volunteers, and by you. Your mission statement is the banner you hold up to rally the troops and to let potential volunteers know what you're about.

Before you market your "product" (presumably connecting people with volunteer opportunities and helping people be successful in those opportunities), you've got to be able to describe what you're doing. The clearer you are, the better you'll communicate with your target audience.

Your mission statement is an integral part of your marketing plan. If you *don't* have a mission statement—or the mission statement you have is vague or not compelling—take time to revisit it or to create a statement when you've assembled your task force.

> "The clearer you are, the better you'll communicate."

Your volunteer ministry's *purpose* is tucked away in your mission statement. It's the problem you want to solve, or the thing you want to accomplish. It's the reason you exist as an organization or a ministry.

Some questions that might help you get at your purpose in order to craft a purpose statement are:

- Who does your volunteer ministry serve?

- What services does your volunteer ministry provide to those you serve?

- What is unique about your ministry?

Be sure your purpose clearly identifies why your ministry exists and is inspirational to your paid staff, volunteers, and the people you're serving. A test: Run the purpose statement past your most dedicated volunteers—the ones you wish you could clone. How do they respond to it? Does it capture what motivates them to be involved?

And be sure your purpose statement can keep everyone focused on what's truly important in your ministry.

2. What can you say—in a "sound bite"—about your volunteer ministry?

You probably won't be interviewed by a national news network this week, but if you were and you had to sum up what you do in just a few seconds, could you do it?

A "sound bite" is a short statement that captures the spirit of what you're doing in your volunteer ministry. It's a quick, catchy phrase that a news story would run on the air. And it's the sort of phrase that will stick with people who hear about your volunteer ministry.

When creating a sound bite for your marketing, make sure it's brief, catchy, and packed with exciting, descriptive words. Make it memorable, and have it tell the essence of what your ministry does.

These sample sound bites will give you a taste of what you're after:

> "Lend an ear, gain a friend."

> "Help us grow kids who care."

> "Make a friend for life."

> "Serve a child, serve the Savior."

There will be many times that you have a brief opportunity to market your volunteer ministry. Be able to do so in ten seconds or less.

Some professional salespeople actually prepare what they call "elevator presentations," brief pitches that can be delivered in an elevator as it travels from the tenth floor to the ground

> "A 'sound bite' is the sort of phrase that will stick with people . . . . Go borrow an elevator and give your sound bites a try."

floor. There's no room to show visuals, so it's the power and focus of the words that have to connect. Go borrow an elevator and give your sound bites a try. You'll be ready when the pastor points to you and says, "Let's let our Volunteer Ministry Leader take 20 seconds to tell you about it."

3. Who is your target audience?

There was a time when most volunteer recruiting messages were aimed squarely at stay-at-home moms. As noted earlier, that's a shrinking percentage of the population. These days you'd better think again about whom you want to reach with your marketing message.

This isn't a small thing. You must communicate your message in words that the audience understands, and highlight

Words to Avoid at All Costs

When crafting your marketing message, there are words you'll want to avoid. Good news: Here's a short list you can delete from your vocabulary before they get you in trouble! (Bad news: You'll probably discover other things to avoid as you work with volunteers.)

Worker. Who wants to be a "worker" in a ministry? The term denotes one of those bees who hauls pollen around all day so the Queen Bee can live in luxury. Call people volunteers, or staffers, or by their first names—but *don't* call them "workers."

Should. If this is your answer when people ask you why they might volunteer, you're dead in the water. Nothing turns off most people more than being told they *should* do something. That's a "push" word. Dig a little deeper and cast a "pull" vision that draws people *toward* the decision to volunteer.

Obviously. Okay, it's clear to you that people need to volunteer. But don't assume it's clear to them. They've not volunteered in the bell choir for 40 years and haven't run out of oxygen yet, thank you very much.

Duty. Ouch. This is a cousin to *should*. The clear implication is that failing to do what you've been asked to do is not just saying "no." It's *shirking* your duty.

Desperate. That you're desperate for a volunteer raises some questions you'd rather not raise: Why are you desperate? What do other people know that has convinced them to refuse? What aren't you telling me?

Anyone could do it. Do you mean it's so easy that it's meaningless, or that someone with the skills of a houseplant could accomplish the task? Either way, it's insulting.

What would Jesus do? Well, he might just ask you to wait until he was finished teaching to help you change the flat tire on the church bus. Or he might delegate the job to someone else. Jesus was a remarkable servant, but he *didn't* let himself be sidetracked from what was most important for him to accomplish in his ministry. Are you sure that your volunteer request is the most important thing the potential volunteer could be doing with his or her time?

benefits that the audience cares about. The language you select must connect with that audience.

Please note that you may have several campaigns running at the same time. You may be targeting:

Internal audiences—such as your pastor, board, or other governing body. Your message might be that there's a need for their support, endorsement, and involvement. You might also be building enthusiasm among the paid church staff for working with volunteers. You might be soliciting leadership's help in fundraising.

External audiences—as you recruit for additional volunteers, or a specific type of volunteer. You may be asking for time from people, or goods and materials from businesses. You might be asking young drivers to sign organ donor cards, or elderly people to donate used eyeglasses. You might want a volunteer to take over the Junior High youth group, or someone to help coordinate weddings scheduled at your church building.

Who's your audience? What do you know about those people? What do they care about? What's their situation in life—are they likelier to be married or single? Parents or not parents? Working, retired, or between jobs? Young or old? Do they have transportation or are they homebound? Are they leaders or followers? Are they conservative or liberal? Do they value stability and tradition or innovation and change?

And are there times they're so involved with other things that they simply won't pay attention to your message? For instance, if you're recruiting Sunday school teachers on Christmas morning, your timing is way, way off.

> "You want to speak their language."

The more you can identify the people you want to reach, the easier it is to reach them. You want to speak their language.

And don't think that this sort of market segmentation communication is something new. Consider what the Apostle Paul said about sharing the gospel:

> *Though I am free and belong to no man, I make myself a*
> *slave to everyone, to win as many as possible. To the Jews*
> *I became like a Jew, to win the Jews. To those under the law*
> *I became like one under the law (though I myself am not*
> *under the law), so as to win those under the law. To those*
> *not having the law I became like one not having the law*
> *(though I am not free from God's law but am under Christ's*
> *law), so as to win those not having the law. To the weak I*
> *became weak, to win the weak. I have become all things to*
> *all men so that by all possible means I might save some. I*
> *do all this for the sake of the gospel, that I may share in its*
> *blessings. (1 Corinthians 9:19-23)*

Of course, you may be designing a marketing campaign that you want to reach everyone in your church. They're all over the map when it comes to age, health, and employment status. How can you target a message when there's no specific group of people to whom you want to aim your message?

Think again. There *are* commonalities in your church.

For starters, they all go to your church. They've accepted some common truths and beliefs. They probably all live in relatively close proximity. Many of them may know each other. They may agree on fundamental doctrinal issues. If you want to recruit five people to paint the Christian education classrooms, they've all seen the peeling paint. If you want to recruit ten people to do a community outreach program, they all know the neighborhood. If you want to recruit twenty people to feed and house members of a visiting choir, they all know their way back to church when it's time to deliver the choir members for a performance.

The nature of what you're trying to accomplish will help you find the common traits in potential volunteers, and help you select which volunteers to target.

Which leads to the next question . . .

4. What are your assumptions about your audience?

You aren't communicating in a vacuum. People in your audience already have feelings and beliefs about volunteering. They already have feelings and beliefs about themselves as volunteers, about you as a volunteer recruiter, about how volunteerism fits in your church, and about volunteerism itself.

Depending on how people feel and think, you may need to tailor your marketing message. For instance, if you're the sixth person this year who's tried to break through apathy and get some-one—*anyone*—to volunteer, it's prob-ably not a good idea to start with a pulpit announcement. Why? Be-cause that's what all five of the other people did—and everyone in the audience has already said "no" five times.

> "People in your audience already have feelings and beliefs about volunteering."

You need to start somewhere else.

What can you discover or surmise about your audience? What do they know about the volunteer ministry? Is it posi-tive or otherwise? Where did they get the information they have? How would they describe what a typical volunteer experience is like in your church?

Describe how you believe people feel and think about vol-unteering in your church. One description might be as fol-lows:

> *Volunteering is for the old people in our church because they have lots of discretionary time. Once you sign up for a volun-teer role, you're stuck in it until you die or Jesus comes back. Volunteers get honored once a year at a banquet, but that's about it—you never see them being thanked other than that. I should volunteer—I feel bad that I don't—but I'm a volunteer in other places like the Scouts and the kids' school. Except I don't think the pastor would count that as real volunteering because it's not at church.*

If those are thoughts running through your audience's mind, shouldn't your marketing message take these thoughts into consideration and address them?

It's not just the thoughts and feelings of the audience that impact your message; your thoughts, feelings, and assumptions play a part, too. Some of your assumptions might include . . .

- People are willing to give their time and resources if they're invested in a specific church program such as Sunday school, youth group, home visitation, or outreach.

- People expect to get something of value from their volunteer experience.

- People volunteer because they're asked directly.

- Volunteers are important people who have tremendous value.

- The church staff assumes that most volunteers aren't well trained or very reliable.

- The church staff thinks volunteers are nice to have, but aren't to be included in decision making.

- Some church staff thinks volunteers are more trouble than they're worth.

- Volunteers tend to quit unless their egos are stroked continuously.

What do you assume about volunteers? How do those assumptions aid or hinder your marketing message?

Four Tips for Creating an Effective Recruitment Message

1. **Communicate a vision.**

It's one thing to ask someone to be a worker in vacation Bible school. It's another to ask if someone would like to have the privilege of having an eternal impact for Christ in a child's life.

Communicating your need for volunteers won't motivate people; that's *your* problem. But inviting someone to join you in doing something important that will have an impact—*that's* worth doing.

2. Test your message.

What you easily understand may not be easily understood by others. Avoid slang, insider information, and abbreviations (for instance, not everyone knows that "VBS" stands for Vacation Bible School)—unless you use them strategically to connect with your target audience.

3. Communicate benefits without dwelling on them.

People want to feel noble when volunteering, not as if they're signing up just to get something in return.

4. Make it easy to respond.

How can someone get more information? Make it simple to follow up with a contact point. Provide a phone number, web site, brochure, physical information table—several options that provide the same simple, clear information. Make it easy to take the next step, and the more personal you can make the contact point, the better.

That said, sometimes there's value in making it *difficult* to respond.

At a local church, two sign-ups were under way after each worship service. One table was for the parish blood drive, and the recruiter was as close to the main door as possible so he could speak to everyone passing by. He had a sign-up sheet and schedule with him.

The woman recruiting teachers for an upcoming catechism class set her table up across the parking lot, inside the parish school, down the hallway in a classroom.

The blood donor recruiter told the woman, "You know, if you move your table over here by mine, you'll get a lot more people to sign up."

The woman smiled sweetly and said, "I'm not after people who need it to be convenient to sign up. I want people who are motivated enough to find me. You're after large numbers, so you're recruiting with a net. I'm after a very special sort of volunteer, so I'm fishing with a line."

What approach best suits your recruitment effort: a net or a line?

A rule of thumb: Spend more time on vision than logistics—it's the vision that will convince a potential volunteer that the role is both doable and worth doing.

5. What goals do you have for your marketing?

You need to define the outcomes of your marketing efforts if you hope to achieve them. And the more specific you are, the better you'll be able to determine if your plan got you where you wanted to go.

When you've finished your marketing efforts, what do you want people to know about your volunteer ministry? To say about it? What will your target audience be doing differently than what they're doing now? How many new volunteers will you have recruited or will you have reenlist? What evidence will point to the fact that your message was heard?

> "Be definite about your goals and write them clearly."

Keep in mind that if your marketing plan calls for you to bring people on board gradually, your plan should reflect that outcome in an appropriate timeline. It does you no good to recruit one hundred people today if you have nowhere for them to serve. If you expect to have one hundred positions gradually open throughout the coming year, write your marketing plan in such a way that it calls for you to recruit people at gradual intervals so nobody's time is wasted.

Be definite about your goals and write them clearly. If you don't aim at something specific, you won't know if you've accomplished what you set out to do—and that makes evaluating your efforts all but impossible.

When setting marketing goals—or any goals—include these elements:

• Make marketing goals specific.

"I want people in our church to know there are lots of ways they can volunteer" is too vague to be of any practical use. Force yourself to become more specific by determining *which* people you want to have knowledge . . . *what* they'll do to demonstrate they have knowledge . . . *where* they'll go as a result of having knowledge (to a volunteer orientation, hopefully!) . . . *when* they'll take action based on their knowledge

. . . and *why* they'll care about the knowledge they've gained.

Anything you can do to sharpen and focus a general marketing goal helps you accomplish it—because you know what you're aiming at.

A more specific way to phrase the goal presented above might be: "25 members of our church will attend a volunteer orientation program on February 10th, and 21 will be placed in volunteer roles by February 25."

• **Create marketing goals that are possible to attain.**

"Everyone in our church will be serving in a volunteer role this year" is a great goal. It's a *wonderful* goal. But is it likely you'll attain it?

Probably not.

There's nothing wrong with aiming high, but if you aim *too* high you'll just get discouraged. It's not necessarily a failure of your faith to set a goal that's more attainable. Should it be a challenge? Yes. Should it require faith? Certainly. But should it be realistic and attainable? Absolutely.

Goals must be achievements you're willing and able to work toward. If you set the bar high, that's motivational. If you set the bar so high there's no hope of your reaching it, that's unfair to you and anyone who's willing to help you.

> "Only you can determine if a goal is too high, too low, or just right."

If you have 45 people serving in volunteer roles this year, perhaps it would be a more realistic—yet challenging—goal to write, "As of April 10, 75 members of our church will be actively involved in volunteer roles."

Only you can determine if a goal is too high, too low, or just right. Do you believe that with God's help and hard work you just might reach it? Then it's probably a good goal.

• **Create marketing goals that have measurable outcomes.**

One measurement is time—set deadlines for the various steps in your marketing plan. If you intend to make an announcement from the pulpit on Sunday, which Sunday will it be? If you'll be personally contacting everyone in the church directory, when will you get to all the "A's?" All the "B's?" When will you finally be calling Zack Zuckerelli?

How many volunteers do you want to sign on? By when?

Marketing goals need observable results. You can count noses when it's time for a volunteer training event—so count noses. You can count the number of phone calls or personal visits you make, so count them.

One reason you make marketing goals measurable is to be able to track progress toward meeting them. Be sure to include time deadlines with each goal and sub-goal. The accountability is necessary.

Also, put a *name* next to each observable goal and sub-goal. Who is responsible for making it happen? If it's everybody, you're in trouble. Only when someone specific is accountable for achieving a goal will it actually happen.

> "Marketing goals need observable results."

As you move forward over time, it's likely you'll have to adjust your timing, tweak your budget, and reconsider which parts of your marketing plan require revision. Having observable goals lets you know where you are in the process.

A note: If you adjust your plan, keep track of those changes and update your written marketing plan. It's your master-planning document. Take time to document why and when you made adjustments—that information will help you do a better job of planning in future marketing cycles.

6. **What are the benefits your volunteers can expect to receive?**

Let's start by differentiating between features and benefits.

A feature is a *characteristic* of a product or service that's inherent in that service or product. For example, in a new car there are many features—power steering, air conditioning, and a gas gauge are among them.

A benefit is the *advantage* the user of the car receives because of the features. Power steering allows the driver to maneuver the car more easily. Air conditioning allows the driver to be comfortable in hot weather. And the gas gauge lets the driver avoid running out of gas and having to hike to the closest gas station!

What are the benefits your volunteers can anticipate receiving that you can include in your marketing message?

> "What are the benefits your volunteers can anticipate receiving?"

There was a time that few people would admit to volunteering for any reason other than pure altruism or discipleship. It was all about helping those less fortunate, and serving God.

Now the "What's in it for me?" question is raised more directly. It's not that people are no longer altruistic, but they're quicker to acknowledge that they have other motivations for volunteering as well. They're comfortable with the notion that it's okay to profit in some way from volunteer service.

This kind of profitability seldom comes in the form of money, though some volunteer service qualifies for tax breaks. Rather, volunteers also want to receive a nontangible benefit from their hours of service.

Not every volunteer role provides the same benefits. Not all benefits are equally desirable to each volunteer. But if you can present a variety of possible benefits for volunteers to consider, it may sweeten the deal when it comes to recruitment.

Among other benefits, these are some that may be available to volunteers:

Increased skills—If a teenager is planning to babysit for extra money, it never hurts to say that she's a regular volunteer in a church nursery.

Increased contacts—When someone volunteers, he or she makes contacts that can be leveraged for business or social opportunities. And in addition to those pragmatic concerns, friendships can quickly develop in a volunteer setting.

Volunteering is a way for those new to a church to be more quickly integrated into the faith community.

Increased knowledge—Someone who wishes to grow in a skill set may gain valuable experience in graphic design, sound engineering, or another area of expertise.

Increasing career potential—Networking that happens in a church volunteer setting can lead to new employment, or a reference that will enhance a resume.

Increasing self-awareness—By interacting with people in a volunteer setting, volunteers can expand their personal horizons and explore new situations and challenges. Volunteers often learn much about themselves.

Feeling accomplishment—Playing guitar in the worship band or serving in the church drama ministry might well satisfy a desire to perform that can't be met apart from joining the local community theater.

Satisfying a desire to give something back to the community or church—It's possible that someone who's volunteering at a homeless shelter today may have been a resident there just a few months ago. It's not uncommon for someone who's a tutor today to have benefited from a tutor's help in the past. There's a tremendous sense of satisfaction in helping another person.

Changing a volunteer's focus—If a volunteer is ill, depressed, lonely, or adjusting to loss in life, helping others can provide relief.

Raised self-esteem—Volunteers may feel better about themselves and their abilities because they're helping others. Also, they'll feel they are making a valuable contribution and may feel needed.

Recognition—A plaque or pin—something to hang on the wall of the study or wear on a lapel—may be the extrinsic reward that a volunteer craves.

What are the benefits that will be available to volunteers participating in your volunteer ministry? How have you made that information available?

Note that some volunteers consider it crass for you to

recruit on the strength of what's in it for the volunteers themselves. They want to think of themselves as primarily altruistic even as they consider which benefits might flow back to them. It's a wise volunteer manager who delivers the benefits that volunteers desire, but who treats those volunteers as if they're acting on the most noble motives possible.

7. How do you intend to deliver your marketing message to the target audience?

There are nearly endless possibilities for how to deliver your message.

You might attend scheduled church meetings and speak to people in groups such as worship services, committee meetings, and classes. Or you might send literature to people at home. You could call everyone directly. Then there's the face-to-face meeting, which is normally far more effective than any other technique at sharing your enthusiasm about the volunteer ministry—and recruiting additional volunteers.

Some factors that might influence which communication channels you select include . . .

The task for which you're recruiting volunteers. If your goal is to recruit enough people to move chairs out of the church sanctuary after the morning worship service this weekend, you won't need to provide much training—or seek a long-term commitment. In that case, an announcement and call for a show of hands will probably do the job, especially if the call for volunteers comes at the end of the worship service in question.

Do you need one eye surgeon willing to go on a medical mission trip, or twenty people willing to bake two dozen cookies for the next potluck? Generally speaking, the more complicated the task or rare the volunteer skill set, the more direct your communication will need to be.

The number of volunteers you need. If you're in a church of five thousand people and you need three volunteers for a fairly simple role, stopping into one adult class to recruit volunteers may accomplish the goal.

If you're seeking hundreds of volunteers, you'll need to

contact lots of people. A mailing is one option, but so is training a team of volunteer recruiters who will make personal contacts on your behalf.

Your budget. Your marketing plan will cost more than just time, though staff time and volunteer hours may be the most expensive item on your budget. Every activity will have a financial cost associated with it.

If you expect to do mailings, contact the post office or a mail center to determine the most cost-efficient way to make use of letters, brochures, or newsletters. If you intend to create teams to do marketing activities, then also figure in food and other reasonable costs.

Make the budget information available to people who are responsible for marketing activities, by the way. They need to know how much money—and time—they have to spend.

The time available. When you're planning the Christmas cantata and it's July, that's one thing. When the river's hit flood stage and Civil Defense needs people to haul sandbags, that's another situation altogether.

> "Your marketing plan will cost more than just time."

There are times a "phone tree" can be effective because the need for volunteers is immediate, and the cause so compelling very little explanation is needed.

Seek to plan far enough ahead when recruiting and using volunteers that you do *not* need to make use of instantaneous recruitment strategies. They may work once, but there's a diminishing return. Remember what happened to the proverbial boy who called "wolf" once too often: He lost the ear of his audience and suffered for it.

And when it comes to getting the most "bang for your buck," there's one way to reach your target audience that has far more impact than any other: word of mouth.

Word of Mouth Marketing

There's no more powerful way to market your volunteer ministry than through current volunteers. When a current volunteer tells friends that it's a great thing to sign up, that's a recruitment message that no number of slick brochures can equal.

Your current volunteers are your absolute best recruiters. They know the positions, they know your culture, and they know people like themselves.

Be intentional about word of mouth advertising. It may not occur to your current volunteers that they can recruit additional volunteers unless you encourage them to do so.

Here's how to create a successful Word of Mouth Marketing Campaign. It costs you nothing . . . but brings huge returns!

- **Create a super volunteer environment.**

Unless current volunteers love spending time in their roles, they'll never recommend a friend to do the same. Ask yourself: "Is what we do worthy of praise? Is how we do it worthy of praise? Are the results we're seeing worthy of praise?" If the answer to any of those questions is less than an enthusiastic "yes," you're not ready for a word of mouth marketing campaign.

Why? Because what is being said won't be positive.

When your process is praiseworthy (ask your volunteers to let you know when that happens), then it's time to go to the next step.

- **Find and thank champions.**

Not every volunteer will be willing to talk up your volunteer ministry. Identify those who will—and those who are effective at bringing in new referrals and volunteers. Go out of your way to thank them and encourage them to keep up the effort!

- **Bring your champions into the information loop.**

You don't want them giving misinformation—or old information. Be sure you brief them and provide every possible reason that they could recruit a new volunteer for you.

8. What marketing content do you want to deliver?

You have a purpose statement. You've written your sound bites. You've identified what matters to your target audience.

You know which benefits you can offer to your volunteers. You have an idea how you might want to connect with your target audience.

But all that makes very little difference if you have nothing to say.

Firm up the content you'll deliver in your marketing message. What is the central message you want to deliver?

When marketing your volunteer ministry, there are some things you simply *can't* say.

- Volunteering won't necessarily make participants rich—at least monetarily.

- Volunteering won't necessarily make participants younger—at least on the outside.

- Volunteering won't necessarily make participants more attractive to the opposite sex—but it certainly couldn't hurt!

The fact is that most of the benefit-promising marketing messages used to sell investments, skin cream, and baldness remedies just aren't available to you . . . but it's no real loss.

You *can* with integrity communicate that in volunteering there's deep fulfillment and meaning. That through volunteering a person can impact lives forever—and for the good. That through the touch of volunteers people who have no homes can find housing, people who seldom smile can find joy, and people who were once unable to read now can be employable.

> "In volunteering there's deep fulfillment and meaning."

You can craft a message that talks about significance, not sensuality. That's a message Coca-Cola® would love to own—but they don't. They never will. It's *your* message to share because the work you do connects people with people at a profound level.

Don't focus on what you can't say and promise. Focus on what *only* you can say.

As you craft your message, remain mindful of these points . . .

Keep your message simple.

No one wants to have to decipher your message. Be sure your audience never has to work hard to sort out what you're saying. And make responding to your message very, very easy.

For instance, rather than making volunteers figure out that to sign up they can call the church office and leave a message at 555-CARE, just list the phone number. Especially among older volunteers whose bifocal vision no longer appreciates small print, being forced to peck out the right buttons on a phone isn't appreciated.

Keeping your message simple sounds easy, but in fact it's very difficult to resist the temptation to complicate things. The benefit of simplicity is that it focuses on the quality and truth of your presentation, not on the gee-whiz theatrics of PowerPoint text swinging in from every possible direction on the screen.

> "Keeping your message simple sounds easy, but in fact it's very difficult."

Simplicity eliminates distractions and lets your audience focus on the central message.

Make sure your message reflects the tone of your volunteer ministry.

If it's fun to volunteer, say so. Show happy people interacting with other happy people in brochures and video clips. Talk about the friendships that have developed.

At one church in a northern state, the youth group got together after each heavy snowfall and shoveled the walks and driveways of elderly church members. The goal was to get to a home and shovel it—always at night, when the youth group members could meet—without being detected by the resident.

"Operation Snow" was a successful volunteer service project, but few in the youth group would have described it as such. To them it was the chance for buddies to pile into a station wagon and have fun while sneaking around at night. Friendships were the big draw; helping others by shoveling was a secondary outcome.

When recruiting for new volunteers, Operation Snow crew members talked about the sneaking—not the shoveling.

Be accurate in crafting your message.

While it's true that some volunteer positions save lives and make the world a better place, some volunteer positions fall a bit short of that. Folding bulletin covers is not quite as heroic as teaching the toddlers. Both roles are important; but don't portray the bulletin-folding job as on a par with taking the gospel to China. Never exaggerate, because people aren't fooled and you'll only diminish your credibility.

> "If it's fun to volunteer, say so."

Rather, describe the benefits of folding bulletin covers when you do it weekly with three friends around a table at the church building. It's a social time that includes fun, friendship, and donuts.

Grab the attention of your target audience.

That's easier said than done, but here are three tips for creating marketing messages that cut through the clutter of information overload and impact audiences.

• **Make the message personally relevant.**

If you're an 81-year-old widow, it's unlikely any marketing effort on behalf of the Young Marrieds Bible study group will motivate you to attend a meeting.

People tend to pay attention to things that have implications in their own lives, especially if what's being marketed appeals to their own personal goals, values, or felt needs.

One need felt by almost everyone everywhere is the need for more time. If you can honestly portray your volunteer ministry as making a huge impact in a limited amount of time, that's going to be well received. Don't ask people to "set aside a full week to support missions in Haiti by going to serve people."

Instead, ask them to "impact lives in a short-term, one-week missions trip."

See the difference? The first message sounds like a huge

investment. A *full week*? Who's got a *full week* to spare? The second message sounds like less of a time commitment, though both messages refer to the same seven days.

We also tend to pay attention when people portrayed in marketing efforts look like us, act like us, and seem to care about the things we care about.

Here's how you can put that tendency to use: On your volunteer web page and in your announcements use people who resemble the folks you're trying to reach. If you're after building attendance in your family night activities, show families. If you want leaders for the men's group rafting trip, show men who look like they could handle a raft.

• **Make the message enjoyable.**

People are drawn to things that make them feel good. That's one reason guilt is a poor marketing tool—it simply doesn't feel good. People avoid it.

You can make your marketing message enjoyable in several ways:

Excellent visuals. Don't settle for dark or muddy pictures, or static visuals. Take the time to capture images that are attractive, fun, and are of top-notch quality. It's worth the investment. And don't forget the power of showing your volunteers in action.

Engaging sound. If someone is doing a voice-over for a prerecorded announcement or recruitment video, use a voice that's easy to understand and sounds attractive. That's not to say you have to hire an expensive voice-over artist; using too "slick" a voice might actually backfire and alienate your audience. You don't need a voice professional—just someone who can speak with enthusiasm and clarity.

If you use music in your marketing, be sure the music you select is appropriate to your message and your audience. Music hooks emotions; be sensitive to what emotions you might be snagging. And respect copyrights when you select music—if it's illegal to use a song and you do so anyway, you signal to your audience that you aren't to be trusted. After all, you've just broken the law.

Easy readability. If you do a print piece, make it easy to read. Don't let a designer overpower your message with creative design. In the same way, use simple words in a straightforward fashion. Never make your audience work hard to decode what you're saying.

And a word about humor. Avoid it. It's dangerous, and a joke or cartoon in your brochure grows tiresome after a few readings. Can humor be used effectively and make a marketing message enjoyable? Absolutely. But realize that what's funny to one person isn't funny to the next person. Why take the risk?

- **Make the message unpredictable.**

It's predictable to *you*, of course, but it shouldn't be easily predicted by the person on the receiving end of the message.

If a message is novel, odd, or unexpected, it grabs attention because it's involving and new. Those two qualities require a great deal of creativity, of course, but the impact is worth the effort—*so long as the novelty doesn't obscure the message.*

Use this approach sparingly, and always test it before incorporating it widely in your marketing. It has great potential to confuse as well as amuse.

- **Use testimonials.**

In every brochure, video, PowerPoint presentation, and announcement about volunteer opportunities, include a testimonial. Why? Because people are skeptical when *you* tell them about a volunteer position. As the person recruiting volunteers, *you* need volunteers, right? So it stands to reason you'll say anything to recruit someone and solve your problem.

That means you have low credibility simply because it's perceived that you will benefit when someone raises a hand and volunteers.

But when someone *else* says that volunteering is rewarding—someone perceived to be objective—then the words carry more weight.

Is this fair? No. Is it necessarily accurate? Of course not—but it's real. Why do you think that companies selling weight loss programs always show you a happy customer who rec-ommends the program?

Take this a step further. When it's time to make an announcement about volunteering, be sure it's a *volunteer* who makes the announcement.

Collect testimonials from your dedicated volunteers and keep them on file. Start now. You can use them when the opportunity presents itself, but not if you haven't got them in hand.

And here's a bonus: When a volun-teer gives you permission to use his or her testimonial, it builds greater loy-alty in the volunteer providing the glowing words.

Here are five tips for using testimo-nials effectively in your marketing:

> "Collect testimo-nials from your dedicated volun-teers and keep them on file."

1. The time to ask for testimonials is toward the *begin-ning* of a volunteer's experience. There's a "honey-moon period" in most volunteers' involvement. That's the time when volunteers are likely to be most positive, and when the volunteer is most in touch with the benefits the experience is bringing to his or her life.

2. The more specific the testimonial, the better. It's one thing to say, "Serving in the nursery is good" and another to say, "Serving in the nursery let's me help families build a spiritual foundation in the precious children the families entrust to me."

3. Ask volunteers to make mention of your purpose or mission in their testimonial. If your ministry to spe-cial needs children is designed to build relationships as well as provide education, ask the volunteer to say so—if it's true in the volunteer's experience.

4. If the person giving the testimonial is credentialed in a relevant way, include the credentials. It's great

that a parent likes your Sunday school. It's especially great if a parent who's *also* a professional educator likes your Sunday school.

5. Always, always, *always* get permission to use testimonials. Never assume.

9. How will you evaluate your marketing efforts?

Your marketing efforts will grow stronger if you incorporate the classic feedback loop used by businesses when they track marketing impact: Action, Observation, Adjustment, Next Action.

Here's how it works . . .

Action describes the effort you make to market your volunteer ministry. For example, you launch a campaign to staff the choir with capable singers.

Observation describes your checking back to see if you were successful in meeting your marketing objectives. Are there enough sopranos in the first pew?

Adjustment describes the tweaking you'll do in light of ·the results of your marketing efforts. If you were able to recruit all the women singers you needed but you didn't land any men, you might want to redefine your target audience, or at least adjust the channels of communication you're using.

> "Some evaluation is built right into the system."

Next Action describes the new approach you're using. After giving it time to have an effect, you'll again observe the outcome . . . make adjustments . . . and act again.

Note that some evaluation is built right into the system because you identified desired marketing objectives that are observable and easily checked. (Good for you! Here's where the hard work is paying off!)

However, some other information will require digging.

Your budget, for instance—how are you doing? Are you under, on, or over? And how are you doing when measured against your timeline?

10. What trends and realities threaten your success?

When motion pictures transitioned from silent films to "talkies," even some top actors and actresses found their careers were suddenly over. Why? Because now that their voices could be heard, they lost their appeal.

Clara Bow, who had enjoyed a hugely successful career in silent films, fared less well on the silver screen when her thick Brooklyn accent was audible. Within a few short years, her film career was over. Technology had killed it.

Technology impacts your volunteer ministry, too—but how? Is it helping you or hindering you? How can you harness it to use it to your advantage? Consider not just the trends discussed at the beginning of this volume, but the following threats and opportunities listed below:

- **What trends in your community are working for or against volunteerism?**

If your local high schools require volunteer service for students in a civics class, how can you position your church so it is a recipient of volunteer hours? You wouldn't use part-time unchurched teenagers in your midweek program, but you can leverage the class requirement with your own teenagers to let them fulfill the requirement as they explore church ministries.

And perhaps the new swing set you want built in the play area could be constructed by unchurched kids?

The economy also has an impact as adults find they're either more—or less—available to volunteer hours for projects.

- **What organizations are competing with you for volunteer hours?**

Perhaps it seems uncharitable to think of other worthwhile organizations as competition, but you're all looking for volunteer involvement, and there's a limited pool of volunteer hours.

What organizations are your primary competitors? When you talk to people who tell you they're already involved in service, where are they volunteering? You may discover that the local hospital auxiliary or library board is staffed with people you'd love to have leading small groups in your church.

The questions you need answered are these: Why is volunteering for your competition so attractive? What are the benefits received by those volunteers? What can you learn from other organizations about how to structure your volunteer ministry?

- **Are changes happening in your community or church?**

Things change—and your marketing message may need to change with them to match a shifting demographic or environment.

Has your church had a large influx of older people? younger people? homeschoolers? people who are wealthier or less wealthy than your existing membership? Is your leadership shifting direction regarding worship style, number of services, or approach to Christian education? Change isn't a bad thing, but it can certainly impact your volunteer ministry.

> "Things change—and your marketing message may need to change with them."

The pastor of a church in the West came up with a great solution to fix the problem of an overcrowded sanctuary: Go to two services. The parking lot congestion would be lessened, the congregation wouldn't be sardined into the pews—it seemed like a "no-brainer" when he suggested it to the church board. The pastor wanted to make the change in 30 days.

Fortunately, several board members happened to be people who have volunteer recruitment functions in the church. Both the children's church and Sunday school superintendents pressed the pastor for details: What would happen to their programs?

The pastor thought for a moment and then shrugged. "You'll do two Sunday schools and two children's church programs, I guess."

The church did make the change—not in 30 days, but eventually—and the superintendents did double their volunteer staffs to accommodate the change. But had the change been made in just a few weeks, as the pastor proposed, it would have been chaos.

Stay abreast of changes that will impact your volunteer ministry. For community information, talk with local business reporters and local chambers of commerce. Real estate agents often see trends develop early on as well.

To stay in touch with changes in your church, become an active participant on decision-making boards. Volunteer to serve there and you'll be amazed how quickly you get in the information loop!

A Brief Summary

Creating a marketing plan is the best way to be assured that your marketing efforts will be coordinated, focused, and consistent. And to create that plan you need to answer these ten questions:

1. What's the *purpose* of your volunteer ministry?

2. What can you *say*—in a "sound bite"—about your volunteer ministry?

3. Who is your *target audience*?

4. What are your *assumptions* about your audience?

5. What *goals* do you have for your marketing?

6. What are the *benefits* your volunteers can anticipate receiving?

7. How do you intend to *deliver* your marketing message to the target audience?

8. What marketing *content* do you want to deliver?

9. How will you *evaluate* your marketing efforts?

10. What *trends and realities* threaten your success?

Don't rush the process of answering these questions. Any time you invest in creating a marketing plan will be returned many times over as you avoid off-target campaigns, last-minute decisions, and wasted efforts.

Keep your written marketing plan where you can refer to it often. It's your blueprint for marketing success. You'll want it handy.

Though there's no particular format a marketing plan should follow, we've provided some worksheets on pages 98-103. Use them to help you walk through the process described above.

Communicating about your volunteer ministry clearly and regularly is a key to successfully involving people in ministry opportunities. But *which* ministry opportunities? There may be no shortage of people in your church willing to help out with the Easter Festival, but when the Missions Fair rolls around, there's a distinct echo in the room when you ask for volunteers. Nobody responds. You're talking to yourself.

> "Are people in the right jobs?"

And why is it that your volunteers in one area of ministry seem to stick forever, effectively serving others and glorifying God, when you can't keep a Sunday school teacher for more than six months?

The answers to those questions can become complex, but there's an obvious place to start: Are people in the right jobs? If they aren't, you can count on frequent turnover, burned out volunteers, and a distinct lack of enthusiasm for volunteerism in your church. When a square peg is pounded into a round hole, it's no fun for either the peg *or* the hole.

The solution: Place the right people in the right jobs.

And you can accomplish that with interviews.

THREE
Interviewing Prospective Volunteers

How to get yourself and your church ready. Building a team of interviewers. The four-step interview process explained.

The context in which most of us have encountered interviews is when we've tried to land a job. And with few exceptions, the interviews have been nerve-wracking experiences.

We spend the days leading into the interview composing answers to the questions we most expect to hear from the Personnel Manager who's sitting behind a desk, pencil in hand as she fires off one question after another.

My biggest weakness? *That's probably my tendency toward being a work-a-holic* (a trait we secretly hope will be viewed as a virtue by a potential employer), *and maybe my near-obsession for excellence.*

The reason I left my last position? *It was a mutual decision, based on the changing demands of the marketplace* (I'd have had to learn to actually touch-type, but I won't mention *that*).

Interviews tend to be carefully choreographed experiences, with the person being interviewed determined to reveal only what's most positive and likely to impress the interviewer. For the person being interviewed, it's a sales presentation with the sole goal of getting a job offer.

> "Interviews tend to be carefully choreographed experiences."

Meanwhile, the person doing the interviewing is attempting

to kick over rocks and see what's hidden beneath. Does the interviewee have the skills needed to be successful? Will he fit into the corporate culture? Is there something lurking just beneath the surface that would be helpful to know—but is being concealed?

What's missing in many interviews is a desire to understand and be understood—to lay cards on the table and see if there's a good combination.

No wonder that when many churches hear that interviews are essential for a well-run volunteer ministry, eyebrows shoot up. After all, if people want to volunteer, why not just let them? They already know what they want to do, right?

Not necessarily.

Let's take a look at what volunteer interviews are—and what they aren't.

The Volunteer Interview

Volunteer interviews aren't an experience in which the involved parties are trying to avoid being honest and open. Just the opposite—they're helpful *only* if everyone at the table is seeking the same goal: *to put the right person in the right job.*

Here's the rub: Potential volunteers—people who've decided to commit time and energy to serving in and through your church—often don't know what's really involved in each volunteer role. And they usually don't know the complete range of volunteer roles available to them.

Consider: On a typical Sunday morning a typical church member—let's call him Bob—may see only a few roles being filled by volunteers. The greeter, usher, and people who take up the offering are probably all volunteers, as is Bob's Sunday school teacher. And it's probable the people in the worship band are volunteers, too, but that's about it. If Bob doesn't see himself in any of those specific roles, he may decide there's nowhere he fits as a volunteer.

What Bob *doesn't* see is the administrative assistant in the church office on Monday morning. The altar care coordinator who organizes a team that keeps the front of the sanctuary visually interesting. He never sees all the boards meet to do the business of the church, and the follow-up and visitation teams aren't on Bob's radar. The people who write and prepare the bulletins and newsletters aren't obvious, nor are the six guys who keep the building and grounds in tip-top shape.

The youth sponsors are serving elsewhere in the building, as are most of the children's ministry leaders. And someone's going to count the money in the offering plates and handle church finances on Sunday afternoon—though Bob won't see that happen.

Bob isn't even aware that the church has periodic short-term mission trips, or that the big room downstairs with all the groceries in it is a food pantry for the community.

> "Potential volunteers . . . usually don't know the complete range of volunteer roles available to them."

Had Bob turned around to look, he'd have seen Susan running the sound board and John recording the pastor's sermon for distribution to shut-ins, who will be visited on Monday evening. Dale and Patty deliver those tapes and a healthy dose of encouragement every week.

There are search and personnel committees, small group ministries, singles ministries, and college ministries Bob knows nothing about—and they're all run by volunteers. A prayer team is praying for the morning worship experience even as Bob sits in church, but he doesn't know it.

The wedding Bob will attend next Saturday at the church will be coordinated by a volunteer, but Bob won't be aware of the hours Nancy has put into making sure everything is just right for the bride—and the bride's mother.

Bob has placed himself on the sidelines as a volunteer not because he's apathetic, but because he has no vision for the scope of your church's volunteer ministries.

You think Bob's a slacker. After all, he's an elementary teacher who refuses to teach Sunday school, although he's a natural. After asking him twice to take over the second-grade class and being turned down flat, you're wondering about Bob's salvation. How can a Christian be so callous about serving God?

Here's what you don't know about Bob: He's tired of teaching. After 23 years in the classroom the last thing he wants to do is spend weekends doing the same thing he does all week long.

But he *is* an avid photographer. He often wonders why the church doesn't do more with the projection unit that's hanging from the ceiling, but he's never thought to ask. And he's just gotten a grant from the State to develop a training program for the teachers in the district. Bob's a Master Teacher who actually enjoys helping teachers fresh out of college master the real-world skills they need to deal with challenging kids.

You don't know Bob—and he doesn't know the volunteer opportunities in his own church. Not the ones that would excite him and give him the chance to pursue his passions.

So Bob sits. Week after week. And your corporate worship experience isn't blessed with visually dynamic photographs to accompany the singing. Your struggling Sunday school teachers don't receive a seminar that would build their skills and increase their effectiveness.

How many Bobs are there in your church?

Would you like to get them involved?

The interview process is one way to do it. At an interview Bob would be able to express what he's passionate about—photography, training, and whatever else God has wired him to get jazzed about—and to hear the range of places he could put that passion to use. He'd get connected.

> "Volunteer interviews help put the right people in the right jobs."

That's what volunteer interviews do—connect people with volunteer roles. They help put the right people in the right jobs—to the benefit of the volunteers, for the good of the church, and to glorify God.

Volunteer interviews *are* about placing volunteers in the

right spots. Volunteer interviews *aren't* about judging people in an effort to eliminate them from service opportunities.

Volunteer interviews are also a wonderful place to do ministry. At church we spend much of our time listening. We hear sermons, teaching, and music. Plenty of information gets beamed our way. But how often do we get to be *heard*?

In the setting of a one-on-one interview with potential volunteers, you have the privilege of entering into the lives of brothers and sisters in Christ. You get to ask questions that get at what matters most to people, and then hearing what they have to say. The potential volunteers get valued and *heard*—and that's ministry.

How to Get Started with Volunteer Interviews

Before you dive into doing interviews, there are some things you need to do. Building an effective volunteer ministry is a process, and you'll sabotage your efforts if you do things out of order.

For the interview process to be effective, you need to be ready in two ways . . .

You need to be ready personally.

A question to consider: Do you *really* believe that everyone has something to offer in ministry? Truly, down deep, cross-your-heart-and-hope-to-die believe that God has gifted everyone with a skill, passion, talent, or ability that can be used to bless others and glorify God?

Because if you have any doubts about that, it's going to show in your ability to interview potential volunteers.

If you haven't reviewed carefully the Scripture passages outlined in volume 1 of this Volunteer Leadership Series, do so now. Ask God to impress on your heart *his* heart for letting very imperfect people do ministry in his name. It's one of the ways God shows us grace: He lets us do significant things that have eternal consequences.

Not one of the people you interview as potential volunteers will be perfect. Their skills won't be perfect. Their experience won't be perfect. Their thinking and demeanor won't be perfect. And that's as it should be—because *we aren't perfect people*.

So adjust your expectations and proceed accordingly. You're going to have to see people as God sees them, and place them accordingly. You (and/or your team of volunteer interviewers) must understand the goal of the process: *to get the right people into the right jobs*.

It's that simple.

You won't be attempting to sell anyone on a particular job that desperately needs to be filled. God already knows that position is open and he has someone in mind for it—but not necessarily the person you're interviewing. It's far, far better to leave a volunteer job empty than to fill it with the wrong person.

> "You're going to have to see people as God sees them."

You won't be offering career counseling or spiritually admonishing people to "name and claim" abilities, skills, or passions they don't currently have. God may choose to develop new attributes in people, but that's between them and God.

You *will* be carefully, prayerfully attempting to discover the uniqueness in each person you interview. You'll be presenting a variety of volunteer positions that might be of interest to the person you're interviewing. You'll seek to be clear, nonjudgmental, and reassuring.

Your goal is to get the right people into the right jobs. Are you ready to put that goal first in your interactions with potential volunteers?

Your church needs to be ready.

If 25 people raised their hands today and volunteered to show up next Sunday morning to help, where would you use them? Are you ready to give them the information they need to be effective? What would you do with a flood of volunteers?

A flood is exactly what might happen if you proactively interview people in your church and unleash the volunteer potential that's simmering out there in the pews.

We've long sighed and lamented how the old "80/20 rule"

seems to be the eleventh commandment in the church. We congratulate the 20 percent of the people who do 80 percent of the work, then wonder what could ignite a fire under the other 80 percent of the people who just show up and sit there.

Well, there's no sense getting people recruited if you're not ready to follow up. That will frustrate everyone.

Here are eight ways you'll want your church to be ready before you begin interviewing volunteers:

1. Your church leaders must be ready to share responsibility and power.

Not every church truly wants volunteers in significant positions. Sometimes it's fine if "new people" set up chairs and tables for the church social hour, but to make a suggestion about how to revitalize that event you have to have been born into the church. The advice of "newbies" isn't welcome.

If you've asked leaders of ministry areas to tell you what volunteer positions they want filled, and each position you've received is an entry level slot, that tells you something: Apparently there's not a willingness to share power. Or there's a deeply held belief that volunteers can do tasks, but not supervise people.

Those are not good signs that your church will be a culture where volunteers can grow in their skills and abilities. Before you continue with implementing volunteer interviews, meet with church leadership and explore any issues that might be fueling their concern about giving volunteers power and authority.

2. You have job descriptions in hand.

Until you have completed job descriptions—preferably written by the leaders who will supervise the volunteer roles described—you're not ready to interview volunteers. Why? Because you aren't ready to put the right people in the right jobs. You don't truly know what's involved in the jobs. You can't answer volunteers' questions.

And you aren't absolutely sure you have the buy-in from the leaders in every ministry area. A hesitation to fill out job descriptions can be one indicator of a lack of enthusiasm for the volunteer placement process.

Job descriptions are vitally important. A sample job description is on page 104. Use it as a template to teach your leaders how to create job descriptions for existing and proposed volunteer positions.

3. You have a team of volunteer interviewers.

Depending on how many interviews you need to conduct, a team approach to the task is essential. For the role of volunteer interviewer, it may actually be best *not* to ask for volunteers to fill the role. It's such a specific role that you may do better to handpick people to do the task.

When Marlene Wilson wanted to build a team of volunteer interviewers in her church, she sat down with her pastor and they looked through a church directory.

"We checked the ten to twelve people we individually felt would be the best candidates," says Marlene. After determining who had the skills to be effective, the candidates were contacted individually and asked to consider taking on the role. Each candidate agreed.

May you have a similarly happy result!

Here are the qualities Marlene Wilson suggests you look for in appropriate candidates . . .

Someone who is a genuinely friendly and approachable person.

The ideal candidate is likely someone who has a broad network of friendships and acquaintanceships already. They're engaging and warm.

Someone who cares about people.

Your top candidates may be serving in people-helping roles already, or working in the social sciences. The value of caring about people can be expressed in many ways, but it should be in evidence.

Someone who is a good listener.

Test this for yourself. Engage a potential candidate in

conversation, and pay attention to how the individual communicates empathy, warmth, and respect. Does it *feel* as if the person is listening? Do you hear follow-up questions that signal comprehension? Does it *look* like the person is listening? Is the candidate focused and attentive? Leaning forward and making eye contact?

Listening skills can be taught (and should be!), but you may not have time to do so before the interviews begin. Look for candidates who have a high degree of competence in this area already.

Someone who is trustworthy and with whom people will feel comfortable sharing personal information.

This is really a two-fold requirement. The person must in fact be able to be trusted with information. Someone who is a gossip won't make a good volunteer interviewer. And the person must be *perceived* as trustworthy by others. Otherwise interviews won't reveal much because interviewees won't be open. See page 104 for a sample job description for this role.

4. You've decided whom to interview.

Churches approach this issue in a variety of ways.

Some churches begin with a church-wide interview, connecting with every member. That's the ideal, but depending on the size of your congregation it may be impractical.

Other churches interview people who pass through the new members class, and build a base of information that way. Still other churches begin the process with current leaders and those who aspire to leadership positions.

Mindful that your goal is to identify the abilities, skills, and passions that are available to do ministry in your church, and that you want everyone to have the opportunity to be effectively involved in ministry, the more people you interview the better.

Start small if necessary, but look forward to including as many people as possible. And don't forget that you are interviewing *all* the membership—*including* youth and children.

Young people have been given God-given abilities, skills, and passions, too. Don't forget to help them find significant, meaningful ministry opportunities.

5. You're ready to collect and safeguard information.

As you do interviews you'll be collecting personal information. Generally speaking, you need to treat it as confidential personnel information.

Before you begin interviewing, know where hard copies of the interview sheets can be kept in a secure environment. Know who will have access to the information—electronically or in hard copy. It may seem like a minor detail, but where *will* you put hundreds (or thousands) of pieces of information so they're secure and still available to the right people?

Decide now on what information storage and retrieval system you will use, *before* you collect information. If you're the person functioning as the Director of Volunteer Ministries—at least in part of your church's programming—let this be your responsibility. You'll reap the benefits if you see that it's done well.

If possible, use computer software to record and retrieve information. It requires keying in data, but once you've captured it, you've got it forever. Updating addresses and phone numbers is simple, as is sorting information.

You may already have a software program designed to track pledges, contributions, attendance, and other administrative functions. See if that program can be adapted. If not, conduct a quick web search for programs—there are dozens of them, always being updated. Visit Group's Church Volunteer Central at www.churchvolunteercentral.org for reviews of possible software selections.

Remember to set up different security levels so more than one user can utilize the software, and only appropriate people can get at sensitive data.

Sound too expensive? If you buy a software program and don't use it, it's very expensive. *Buy only what you'll use . . . and then use it*. Nothing is more expensive that a needless technology purchase.

If you want an inexpensive, down-and-dirty approach and you don't intend to ask for sensitive information, ask a computer savvy volunteer to set up a simple database in Microsoft Access or another database software. Even Excel spreadsheets are sufficient for small churches.

Some questions for you to consider before purchasing software:

> "Buy only what you'll use . . . and then use it."

- Does the proposed software meet our present needs, exceed our needs, or greatly exceed our needs?

- Can the software meet our needs if the size of our church doubles?

- Is it easy to use?

- Who'll use the software? What do those people think of the choice?

- Is training provided? By whom? When? How often?

- What kind of on-going support does the vendor provide? At what cost?

- Can multiple users access the software at varying security levels? How?

- Is our current computer hardware adequate to use the software? What upgrades might be required? Are we willing to make them? At what cost?

- Does purchasing this software contribute to our ability to fulfill our mission and meet our goals? In what ways?

6. You're ready to respond when unexpected information is revealed.

It may not happen often, but it will happen: You or one of your team of volunteer interviewers will discover uncomfortable information about a church member.

Generally, you aren't required to divulge what you discover to a local law enforcement agency unless you discover the individual is being hurt, is hurting or plans to hurt someone else, or is doing something illegal. Those are broad guidelines, though.

Determine what your approach will be before you begin interviewing people. What is your church policy? The policy recommended by your insurance carrier? What does the law require in your area? Do the homework now, mindful that interviews conducted with potential volunteers are an official function of your church's program.

Not every piece of unexpected information will necessarily trigger a call to law enforcement or social service authorities. But sometimes it *should* trigger a referral to a capable, qualified people-helper like a pastor or counselor.

> "Determine what your approach will be before you begin interviewing."

It was during an interview with a potential children's worker that one interviewer, Kim, asked the question, "What is it about this church that attracted you?"

The woman being interviewed became quiet and stared at her hands as a long moment passed. "At least here the pastor hasn't made a pass at me yet," she said finally, in a still, small voice. Then, eyes on fire, she leaned toward Kim and hissed, "That's what happened in my last church. I hope he rots in hell."

"It was like she turned into a different person," Kim remembers. "She took a couple of long breaths, shook her head, then with a smile, looked back up at me said, 'Well, then, any more questions?'"

Oh, yeah. Kim had a *lot* more questions—but none she was qualified to ask and process with the potential volunteer.

They finished the interview, then Kim suggested that before the woman enter into ministry at the new church she consider addressing the issues that she had with her experience at the last church.

"I told her that we'd walk through the process with her

every step of the way, and I looked forward to offering her a choice of volunteer positions. But she couldn't serve joyfully out of an abundant life when she wasn't experiencing one."

The woman heeded Kim's counsel and accepted a referral to the church's counseling ministry. A year later she was on board as a volunteer.

"She's doing great," Kim says, "But she wouldn't have been if we hadn't interviewed her and given her some direction. She'd just have *appeared* to be doing great."

What would you do in a similar situation? How would you refer her? Decide now so that you are ready.

7. Your church is ready to provide background screenings for potential volunteers.

The days when screening volunteers was the ultimate "extra mile" effort of ultra-careful churches are over. It's now something that needs to be part of your standard procedure. It protects your church, the volunteers who serve through your church, and most importantly, it protects children and youth.

Three decisions you need to make:

• What level of screening do you need?

In this world of computers you can arrange to have someone screened for practically anything. And not every volunteer position needs the same sort of background screening.

For instance, if Jerri is going to be handling the church checkbook, you'll want to know that her credit history and her use of money have been screened. Has she proven to be a capable steward in the past?

If Dave wants to work with a small group of children on Wednesday night, his use of credit is probably less important than whether he's been convicted of a crime, and if so, which crime.

You can arrange for background screenings in each of the following areas, and more:

Identification—Is the person operating under an alias?

Criminal records—Has the person been convicted of a crime?

Credit checks—Is the volunteer on a solid financial footing? This can be a general indicator of responsibility and financial skills.

Education and employment verification—Has the person lied about credentials or previous employment?

Department of Motor Vehicles—Is the person to be trusted transporting children or teenagers on trips?

Bankruptcies, liens, and judgments—Is the person in financial straits?

Civil lawsuits—Has the person been a plaintiff and/or a defendant, and if so, how many times? Is the person prone to settling conflict through litigation?

Screening—at a price—can also uncover real estate holdings, marital history, residences, and bank assets. Almost anything that someone wants to hide can be dragged into the light.

And the screenings can be conducted just for your local area, your state (or province), your country, or internationally. It's all available—at a cost.

You want to strike a balance that makes background searches affordable and effective. It's doubtful that Bill, who you've known for years and who grew up in the church, has shady international business dealings in Dubai.

Contact your insurance provider and ask for guidelines. That will let you know what level of screening is generally recommended, and may also qualify you for a rate discount because you've put the procedure in place. Contact other churches in your area, too. What sort of screening do they require? Why did they settle on that level?

What happens if you find that someone has been convicted of a crime? What crimes will disqualify someone from volunteering in a specific area, and which crimes aren't a problem? After all, getting three speeding tickets in a year is one thing if Larry wants to volunteer in the bulletin stuffing ministry, and quite another if he wants to drive the church bus.

And get in touch with several screening providers. If you're a member of Group's Church Volunteer Central, you can get screenings at a variety of levels at a significant discount. Take advantage of this opportunity—the savings on screenings alone can more than pay for your membership each year.

- **Who will you screen?**

Not every volunteer role involves the same risks. Generally speaking, if a volunteer has contact with children or youth, that volunteer needs to be screened. Discuss other guidelines with your insurance carrier, other churches, and the screening provider you hire. And again, if you're a member of Group's Church Volunteer Central, ask for guidelines from that organization, too.

You'll need to decide what to do if a potential volunteer is new to your area. Will you screen both locally and in that person's previous place of residence? What if, after several years of service, a volunteer switches from a role where there's been no contact with children to the role of fourth-grade Sunday school teacher?

It's critical that you put policy decisions in place before you begin interviewing volunteers, and that once those policies are in place you *never make an exception*. Perhaps Mrs. Wazniak *has* been teaching children's church for 35 years. That's wonderful—give her a certificate of appreciation . . . and a screening.

- **How will you advertise that you screen volunteers—and when?**

Screening is a safety net—your last chance to keep someone who has already lied to you twice (you asked about convictions on your application and in the interview, right?) from having access to the people you serve, and to your other volunteers.

People who have been convicted of a crime tend to fear screenings. They know if they're listed in a sexual offender database that their names will pop up. They know if they've been imprisoned or involved in the court system that it's going to come out. So if they know you're going to screen them, they tend to not even attempt to volunteer.

So announce that you'll be screening at the interview stage

of your recruitment and placement process. Why? So people have a chance to tell you about their issues, rather than hiding them from you.

If a potential volunteer says, "Look—I can tell you right now that if you screen my records you'll find out I spent a year in jail for car theft when I was 19 years old. That was 23 years ago and I've long ago repented. I've not taken so much as a stick of gum that wasn't mine since, and I never will. God has changed my life."

That's a very different situation than someone who chooses to remain silent, waiting to see if your screening turns up a past conviction.

> "Let potential volunteers know early on that screening is mandatory."

Let potential volunteers know early on that screening is mandatory if you intend to screen them. You'll need their approval, and if someone refuses, you may have kept a wolf out of the sheep pen.

What's your plan for screening potential volunteers? Is it in place? And have you and your team already gone through the process?

It may be that to do what you're doing you don't need to be screened. It would save your church money if you weren't screened. You've never been arrested or convicted of a crime and you know for a fact you'll come up clean when you're screened.

Do it anyway, and here's why: You'll be able to tell anyone who is offended by being asked to go through a police screening that you've been through the same procedure. That fact will stop a lot of arguments before they start.

Yet, you may find that if you *start* screening volunteers, you offend the faithful volunteers who have served for years. How can you navigate that quagmire?

- Explain that everyone will be screened—and include *everyone*.

- Explain that results are confidential, and detail how information will be safeguarded.

- Be clear on what levels of screening you're including for various volunteer positions. This will reduce fear among people who have had ancient run-ins with the law, or who fear embarrassment about past decisions.

- Talk about the church's need to be viewed as a safe place by visitors who don't know the character of long-term volunteers. It's not a personal thing; it's a sign-of-the-times thing.

- Stand firm. Seek to understand a volunteer's concerns, but if the decision is that everyone will be screened, everyone will be screened.

- Determine how you'll go about responding if someone is found to have a criminal background. Will you separate volunteers from service? Will you keep volunteers in place if they've demonstrated healing and repentance? Will you offer volunteers who are screened out of one position the chance to serve elsewhere?

8. You're ready to make a handoff to the appropriate volunteer leader.

Once a potential volunteer is interviewed, where will you send the person? In each area of ministry where a volunteer will be used there must be someone designated to do the follow-up interview. As you'll see in the next section, *you* won't actually offer anyone a volunteer position. You'll simply refer a volunteer to an area where you think they'll flourish. It's up to someone in that area to determine if the volunteer and a volunteer role are a fit.

If in your best judgment you think someone would make a great youth volunteer, is the Youth Ministry Director ready to follow up? If not, don't send anyone to the youth department until that leader *is* ready.

Being "ready" comes down to this: Are resources in place for training and orientation that will make the volunteer successful? Have you removed as many institutional and personal obstacles to volunteering as possible? Do you have a compelling vision for what God will do through and in you as volunteers grow involved in new ways?

Is your marketing message tight and focused? Your strategy for marketing set? Your planning finished?

Yes? Then contact the people whom you think will make good interviewers, get them on board, and begin training them.

How to Train Your Interview Team

First, a principle to embrace: The more your interviewers do at the front end of your interview and placement process, the less you will have to fix later.

It's true. Interviewers are key players in the process. They have an enormous influence on whether potential volunteers eventually become practicing volunteers. You want your team of interviewers to be as effective as possible.

And to be effective, your team must have both information and skills. The data you can pass along in printed form, and it's probably best to do so in a three-ring binder. Why? Because you'll be updating it frequently. Whether you have a team of one or one hundred, decide how you'll go about getting updates into the hands of your team and formalize that process.

Here's what your team must know . . .

Interviewers must know about your church.

Give your interviewers a copy of your church's mission statement and vision statement. Provide copies of your volunteer ministry's mission and purpose statements, too. Discuss them thoroughly, and how the interviewers will be cooperating in helping bring those missions and purposes to life.

Be sure your interviewers know about the major ministry areas and initiatives in your church and how those ministries wish to be described. Your interviewers are gateways for volunteers entering church ministries; if their information is spotty or incomplete, it will show in the quality of referrals made.

If at all practical, have the leaders in those ministry areas meet your interviewers. As a potential volunteer is interviewed and then referred for a follow-up interview and placement, you want the process to be as seamless as possible. It all works best when there's at least some relationship between the people in the process.

Consider creating a notebook of information for your volunteers, and make sure information is consistent across every volunteer's notebook. While different interviewers will have different styles, the experience should be equally informative.

Interviewers must know relevant policies and procedures.

Where do surveys go when they're completed? What tools are available for introducing potential volunteers to possible job matches? What's the timeline from the completion of the first interview to the next step? What *is* the next step? How do you make a referral? Those are the sorts of practical questions your interviewers will have—and they'll need answers.

You'll enhance interviewers' comfort level if you anticipate at least some of the questions they'll have and proactively provide information. Then ask what other questions they have and provide that, too. One church leader has this philosophy: "Any time I hear the same question twice, I create a policy and print a brochure."

You may not want to go to the trouble of creating a brochure, but the information should certainly go onto an updated "Frequent Questions" sheet in your interviewers' notebooks.

Interviewers must have skills, and among these are three skills that are essential for a successful interview. Here's what your team must be able to do . . .

1. Interviewers must be able to put people at ease.

Part of this skill is to conduct interviews in a setting that's free of interruptions and that's physically comfortable. It may be a room or office at your church, but it can just as easily be a coffee shop where you can sit in a quiet corner booth. The chief requirement is that you find a place you can talk for 30 or 40 minutes without the flow of the conversation being broken, and without being overheard.

If you *do* use an office, avoid having a desk separate the interviewer and potential volunteer. Set the phone so it won't ring. Communicate in every way throughout the duration of the interview that nothing is more important than the person being interviewed.

But even if the lighting is fine, the temperature perfect, and the chairs comfy, people being interviewed may still feel ill at ease.

What *really* relaxes people is how interviewers conduct themselves. Is the interviewer rushed, or relaxed? Is the interviewer open and respectful? Is the interviewer able to converse easily and listen carefully? Does the person being interviewed feel important and heard, or perceive that the interviewer is just plodding through paperwork?

> "What *really* relaxes people is how interviewers conduct themselves."

Remember: The interview is an opportunity for the interviewer to minister to the potential volunteer. Your interviewers must be primarily people-focused, not task-oriented, as they conduct interviews. As they master the interview process they may in fact choose to not even take notes unless it's absolutely necessary. Note-taking breaks eye contact and may make the potential volunteer uneasy. It's best if interviewers can remember what was said well enough to fill in the paperwork immediately after the interview ends.

Also, coach interviewers to speak clearly and explain things patiently, preferably without using coded language. It's easy in a church setting to assume that everyone knows when "Advent" is, or what "Communion preparation" means. A potential volunteer may nod politely as if understanding but in fact be totally in the dark. It's better to over-explain than assume comprehension.

2. Interviewers must be able to ask appropriate and meaningful questions.

This takes practice to interview with grace, so plan to train your interviewers even if they have strong people skills. In fact, *especially* if they have strong people skills.

Sometimes interviewers who love spending time with people tend to fill the first half of any interview time with chit-chat, sharing stories from their own lives. Establishing rapport is fine, but it can't take over an interview session. Nor can selling the potential volunteer on the wisdom of signing up to volunteer, or reviewing facts that aren't really relevant until a potential volunteer is offered a position.

Some interview skills to sharpen in your volunteer team . . .

- *Ask open-ended questions and make open-ended statements.*

An open-ended question or statement is one that can't be answered with a simple "yes" or "no" and usually reveals far more information than a directive, closed-ended question.

For instance, a closed-ended, directive question might be, "Do you have a family?" You'll get an answer, but it might very well be just "yes" or "no." Instead, ask for family information in the form of an open-ended question or statement such as, "Tell me about your family." The answer will likely be something along the lines of "Yes, a husband and two children," followed by details.

One simple way to train your volunteers to use open-ended questions naturally is to have them form trios and practice on each other by assigning three roles: Interviewer, Interviewee, and Observer. Select a subject such as "My Last Vacation" and have the members of each trio take turns in the different roles.

Using open-ended questions is a habit your interviewers must form. And it *is* a habit—practice is essential.

- *Ask linking questions.*

A linking question is one that ties to something the person being interviewed has just said. It's an invitation to go deeper, to explain and explore more fully. A linking question communicates that the interviewer is actively listening, not just running down a list of questions and gathering the least amount of data needed.

Here's an example of linking questions following an open-ended statement:

Interviewer: Tell me about your favorite volunteer experience.

Potential Volunteer: That would have to be when I was the Cub Scout leader for my son's Webelo Pack. We had a great time together. I did that for two years.

Interviewer: What was it about being a pack leader that was so much fun?

Potential Volunteer: Part of it was being with my son and having that time with him. And part of it is that kids that age are just great. Lots of energy and creativity, and sometimes they even listened to me.

Interviewer: It sounds like you enjoy being with children.

Potential Volunteer: I love it. I was going to be a teacher, but ended up not finishing college. In my last church I got to teach in Sunday school, too.

Interviewer: But Cub Scouts was your favorite volunteer experience. I'm wondering why it ranked higher than teaching Sunday school.

Potential Volunteer: I think it's because the person running our Sunday school was so strict with the children. I had a hard time thinking it was so important they memorize a verse each week, and that only the kids who did got treats. I didn't think that was fair to the kids who don't memorize well.

See how much more information was revealed by using an open-ended approach and linking questions than by firing off a series of closed-ended questions? And yet the discussion wasn't confrontational or stilted. That natural flow comes with practice—help your interviewers get plenty of it.

• *Use body language to make a connection.*

The vast majority of communication is nonverbal, so train interviewers to maintain comfortable eye-contact with potential volunteers, and physically demonstrate they're listening by sitting in an open, attentive pose.

There are many, many resources to assist you in training interviewers to be more effective listeners, but the most effective one may be a member of your church or community who's a professional counselor. Most counselors have highly developed listening skills and could help your team become competent in those skills listed above. Invite such a person to sit down with you and plan a training session or two, or to provide on-going coaching.

> "Your interviewers are *not* counselors."

A caution: Your interviewers are *not* counselors. They're not equipped to provide the care a trained counselor can provide. If you provide listening skills training, be clear about how to use those skills within the confines of the interview process.

The goal of an interview isn't to do therapy. It's to gather appropriate information to determine where to refer the volunteer, and to provide a listening ear. That's all. If something more is revealed and requires follow-up, train your interviewers in how to refer potential volunteers to a more qualified person.

A 90-minute training session is provided for you on page 85. It will increase the readiness of your volunteers to be effective listeners. You may also wish to have a training session to familiarize your interviewers with policies and procedures related to interviewing volunteers.

Develop Tools for Your Interviewers

Which tools you need depends on what process you use. I'd like to suggest a process for you to follow. It's one that's been used successfully in a variety of churches—large and small—and will be easy for you to adapt. It assumes you have trained interviewers, a system in place to capture and use information you gather, and people you can hand potential volunteers to for an additional interview and job offer.

This four-step process involves:

1. Sending a letter to confirm interviews you have scheduled (include with the letter a Discovering My Abilities, Skills, and Passions form that interviewees will complete prior to their interviews).

2. Conducting an interview using the Sample Interview Form as a guide.

3. Referring the potential volunteer to a ministry leader for a follow-up interview.

4. Confirming the placement was successful.

The tools you will need are the confirmation letter, the Discovering My Abilities, Skills, and Passions form, an Interview Form, and a follow-up letter.

And good news—there are samples of these forms for your use at the end of this volume! Let me walk you through the four steps . . .

Confirm the appointment.

Your marketing plan has been a success. People are interested in meeting with you or a member of your interview team to explore volunteering through the church.

It's helpful if potential volunteers give some thought to what they're good at doing before they arrive. They may be limiting their thinking about volunteering to only what they've done in church, and as a result eliminating their ability to serve in an area of ability, skill, or passion.

The Reach Out—Renew—Rejoice letter on page 106 is an invitation to think more holistically and to prepare for a personal interview. Send the letter and a copy of the Discovering My Abilities, Skills, and Passions form on page 108 to each person you will interview about a week before the scheduled interview. That's enough time to thoughtfully, prayerfully consider the questions, but not so much time that people set aside the letter and form.

You may choose to underscore the importance of thinking about the questions presented in the letter and form by calling the person a few days before the appointment to confirm the time and place, and to inquire if the letter and form arrived. Ask again that interviewees bring the completed form with them to their interviews.

There's a "hidden agenda" in making the confirmation call: It communicates that this is a serious appointment. Doctors' offices call to confirm appointments—you should, too.

Conduct the interview.

Here's where you and your team of interviewers put your training to use. God bless you as you bless others in your volunteer management ministry!

Refer the potential volunteer to a ministry leader for an additional interview.

Assuming no red flag arose to indicate the potential volunteer should *not* serve as a volunteer, you'll now recommend one or more ministries in which the interviewee could serve.

Please remember that *you will not offer the interviewee a position*. It's up to the person who will supervise the interviewee to bring the volunteer on board. You'll be in a position to show the interviewee job descriptions and suggest placement . . . but that's all.

The moment you want to reach is the one where you present ministry opportunities and ask, "Does this appeal to you?" What drives the opportunities you present isn't a list of open positions. Rather, it's which positions include abilities, talents, skills, and passions that align with those expressed by the interviewee.

The following chart summarizes how the interview process unfolds. It may be a handy tool to photocopy and place where you'll see it often.

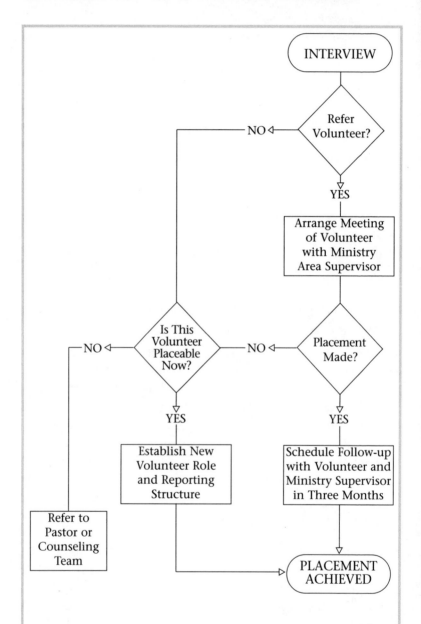

Confirm the placement was successful.

After suggesting a volunteer role for the interviewee, contact the person who supervises that position and ask him or her to schedule a follow-up interview with the person you or your team just interviewed. Then, a week later, follow up again with that supervisor to see if an appointment has been set.

It's this step where too often the ball is dropped and potential volunteers lose heart that there's a place for them to serve. Even if there's no current open position in the preschool ministry, if a potential volunteer expresses interest, the Preschool Director *must follow up promptly.* Timing is everything.

Also send the person you've interviewed a letter reminding him or her to expect a call for a follow-up interview. If a law enforcement screening will be required for the desired position, say so in the letter. Again, that's not something to hide.

Three months after the placement has been made, schedule a follow-up meeting or phone call with both the supervisor and the volunteer. Find out how things are going and whether the placement is working. Seek to resolve any misunderstandings and conflicts. If a volunteer isn't thriving in his or her volunteer role, go through the interview process again and provide another, more appropriate role.

There's another part of the volunteer placement that deserves a closer look: orientation. It's where you have the opportunity to ensure that volunteers get connected with the information and people they need to be successful.

You can't overestimate the need for outstanding volunteer orientation and training—and you'll learn how to provide them in the next volume of this Volunteer Leadership Series, *Volunteer Orientation and Training.*

Active Listening Training Workshop

A 90-minute workship that will help you equip your team of interviewers.

In this hands-on workshop you will accomplish the following:

- Expose participants to five skills associated with active listening.

- Lead participants in practicing those five skills.

- Facilitate evaluation of participants in those five skills.

Supplies needed: Chairs, pens or pencils, a whiteboard or piece of posterboard and markers, one copy of the Active Listening Encouragement and Evaluation Sheet per participant (see end of this chapter), Bible, nametags.

Introduction

Welcome participants as they arrive. Even if you believe everyone knows the name of each other person, ask everyone to fill out a nametag as people arrive. On the nametag ask people to write their first and last name, and the name of a childhood pet, if they had a pet.

Encourage people to mingle and attempt to guess what sort of animal the other participants' pets were, based on the pets' names.

When the announced start time has arrived, gather participants together and say:

Welcome to this Active Listening Training Workshop. In the next 90 minutes we'll discover how the five skills associated with active listening can help us become better interviewers. We'll get a chance to practice those skills, too.

Let me admit right up front that all of us have room to grow in our listening skills—including me. This is a safe place to learn new things and to stumble a bit as we learn new things.

Open your Bible and read aloud 1 Peter 4:10, printed here for your convenience:

"Each one should use whatever gift he has received to serve others, faithfully administering God's grace in its various forms" (1 Peter 4:10).

Say: We can choose to become better interviewers for lots of reasons. It can be the challenge that intrigues us, or that getting better at this will help us professionally. It's a valuable skill. Maybe it's because we're the sort of people who, if we do something, want to do it with excellence.

Let me suggest this as a motivation: so we can cooperate with the purposes of God. It's clear in the passage I read and elsewhere in Scripture that each person in our church is designed by God to have a place in service. We're made to serve God in unique ways that we may not understand ourselves. The interviewing we'll do will help people find appropriate, rewarding places to serve. That makes what you do an important ministry!

And the skills you'll learn or have reinforced in this workshop are a big part of what will make you an effective interviewer.

Let's commit this time to God.

Lead in a prayer dedicating the workshop to God, and ask his blessing on your learning and application of what you're learning.

The Workshop

Say: Listening is more than just waiting for your turn to speak. It's more than a way to gather information. When we truly listen, we communicate warmth that allows interviewees to open up and share what—and who—they really are. We help the people we're interviewing feel worthy and respected.

Listening is a gift we give others.

In the next hour we'll identify and practice several techniques that help us actively listen to others. Active listening is simply this: listening to others, and letting them know we're listening. Sounds simple, doesn't it?

It's not. Most listening is passive, not active. The two types of listening differ in some important ways:

- *Active* listening requires us to be engaged and patient; passive listening demands nothing more than simply staying quiet.

- *Active* listening communicates concern, interest, and empathy; passive listening falls far short of that.

- *Active* listening often builds a relationship; passive listening usually doesn't.

- Finally, *active* listening is rare; passive listening isn't.

Turn to a partner and share about a time you talked with someone—maybe a friend or partner—and when you were done sharing, you felt truly heard. What was that like? You've got two minutes.

Allow two minutes, then call attention back to yourself by gently sounding a whistle or clapping.

Say: Now share about a time when someone was hearing you, but not really listening. What was that like? Again, you've got two minutes.

Allow two more minutes, then call attention back to yourself by gently sounding a whistle or clapping.

Say: Quite a difference, wasn't there? Please call out a few words that describe how you felt when someone was *truly* listening to you—and let us know that. How did you feel? Jot the descriptive words you hear on the whiteboard or piece of poster paper.

Say: **Now call out some words that describe how you felt when someone was not really listening. How did you feel?** Jot the descriptive words you hear on the whiteboard or piece of poster paper.

Say: **Here's what's sad: If we talked to the people who were with us in our second situations—where someone was with us but not hearing us—those people would probably say they *were* listening.**

Listening can be done well—or poorly. We're going to identify and practice some skills that make it likelier that someone we're interviewing will describe the experience with the *first* list of words.

Here's what we'll do: I'll briefly describe five active listening skills that we each need to master, then we'll get in teams and practice them. Please know that you don't need to become an expert in these to be effective. What you need is to listen to others in the way you want to be listened to; it's like the Golden Rule of Listening.

Here are the skills . . .

Skill #1: Help the interviewee feel comfortable.

Some of this is what you do physically. (Demonstrate as you continue.) For instance, be sure you place chairs so there's no barrier between you, but don't have chairs face-to-face—that's confrontational. Sit at a slight angle, so you can talk comfortably. Sit up straight, leaning slightly forward so you appear attentive and focused. Maintain eye contact that's comfortable, but not a stare-down. And minimize distractions by turning off your cell phone, and any radio or television that might snag your attention or the attention of the interviewee.

Also, speak in a pleasant, relaxed tone. Don't rush through your questions or speak loudly.

Skill #2: Communicate that you're listening.

React to what you're being told by nodding, raising your eyebrows, or responding in another nonverbal way

to the emotion and content you're hearing. The idea isn't to become a mime, but to provide clues that you're attentive and listening carefully.

Occasionally saying something like "I see" or "uh-huh" will provide verbal clues you're listening, too, but use them sparingly.

One great way to communicate you're listening is to use linking questions and provide an opportunity for the interviewee to elaborate.

Skill #3: Focus on what you're hearing.

Listening is *hard work*. It requires us to do things we don't normally do . . .

- *Keep an open mind.* It's hard to wait until the interviewee is finished talking before you decide if you agree or disagree, or form an opinion. We often listen just long enough to reach a conclusion, then express ourselves. The problem with this approach is that an interviewee may not know what she thinks about something until she's done sharing. And *we* certainly don't know. We must keep an open mind.

- *Focus only on the speaker.* Try to not think about what you're going to say next or about your own concerns. You can't be thinking about whether you rolled up your car windows and what an interviewee is saying at the same time.

- *Don't do too much sharing.* It may seem odd to say, but although you're trying to develop a relationship, it is usually counterproductive to disclose too much about yourself. The purpose of the interview isn't for you to share your volunteer experiences, but to draw out the interviewee. Disclose who you are, but only as it encourages the interviewee to share. If the interviewee asks you questions about yourself, respond—but redirect the interview back to the person being interviewed.

Skill #5: Reflect back what you hear.

This is perhaps the most difficult skill to master. You want to be able to reflect what you've heard by paraphrasing what you've been told. This allows you to know if you've listened accurately and to give interviewees the chance to correct you.

Here's what's tricky: You need to reflect *both* parts of the message you've received—the content and the emotion.

Here's an example of something you might hear from Mary when you're interviewing her: "When I was a volunteer at First Church, it was a good experience." (Deliver this line calmly and in a straightforward manner.)

Pretty straightforward, right? You might paraphrase that remark by saying, "Sounds like when you were at First Church you enjoyed being a volunteer."

Notice that my reflection paraphrase sums up both the *content* of what she said: she was a volunteer at First Church—and what I understood that she *felt* about being a volunteer: she *enjoyed* it. She never said she enjoyed it, she implied she enjoyed it. I put a word in her mouth to make sure I'm clear about how she felt.

If I was right, Mary may say, "Oh, yes, I loved getting together with the other volunteers and we became friends. I hope the same thing happens here." That's some valuable information about what motivates Mary to volunteer.

If I was wrong about how she felt, Mary will correct me. She might say, "No, I really hated it. It was good because it helped me be less shy, but I couldn't stand the people I was with." That's helpful to know, too!

Think of each message you receive as having two parts: content and emotion. Sometimes the content is really big and there's hardly any emotion. A lecture about cellular biology in science class is usually like that. The teacher sends you tons of content, but it isn't that emotional.

Other times a message has very little content, but lots of emotion. When you tell someone you want to marry "I love you" for the first time, there's not much content—but a *lot* of emotion.

When you reflect back to people what you're hearing, reflect both content and emotion. That can be tough because we're used to thinking we "get it" when people tell us things; that we don't have any cause to check if our assumptions are correct.

That's dangerous. Communication is so complex that it's amazing we ever understand each other at all. And where we misunderstand each other is often about how we feel. If you tell me your grandmother died, it means something very different if she was a big part of your life than if she was someone you'd never met who refused to see you. The content is the same, the emotion completely different.

So what happens if you reflect to someone that you think they're sad, when they're not? They're really angry, but they look sad.

Here's what happens: They correct you and move on. As long as your reflection is tentative, nonjudgmental, and it's obvious you want to understand, people don't hold it against you that you read them wrong. They straighten you out and move on.

How do you reflect? Here's a simple formula you can use until the process feels more natural and you can substitute wording of your own:

"Let me be sure I understand. You were a volunteer at your former church (there's the content) and you feel good about the experience (there's the emotion)."

And if you're stuck for a word that sums up the emotion, consider using one of these words: mad, sad, glad, or scared. They pretty much capture everything someone can feel.

See how challenging active listening can be? You need to listen not just to the words but also to the emotions. You have to focus. You try not to jump in or make judgments, and you want to encourage someone else to keep talking. It's hard!

Let's practice some of those skills right now. Believe it or not, it's fun—and you'll see huge improvement in your skills as you practice.

Form trios and ask the person in each trio who has the next birthday to be the Interviewer. The person with the next birthday will be the Interviewee. The last person in each trio will be the Observer. Trios will need to sit far enough apart from each other that conversations can happen easily, but it will be helpful if you can see each trio. That will help you signal stop times and let you see if a trio gets stuck.

Ask the Interviewer to arrange the chairs so they're angled and it's comfortable to talk. The Observer should sit off to one side where she can hear but won't be in the direct line of vision. Give the Observer a copy of the Active Listening Encouragement and Evaluation Sheet (found at the end of this chapter) and a pencil or pen. Tell participants they'll interview for eight minutes, but they don't need to watch the clock. You'll interrupt to call the session to a close. Encourage the Observer to take notes of times they see examples of what's on the sheet. And be specific—the more specific the feedback, the more helpful it is.

You'll have six rounds of interviews, and you need to provide topics that elicit both content and emotion but don't turn into deeper sessions than your trios are prepared to handle. Use one of these topics, or develop your own:

- Describe a family vacation from your youth.

- Describe a time from your childhood when you struggled in school.

- Describe a time in your life you were frightened.

- Describe a time you took on a challenge and were successful.

- Describe something you'd change about your house or apartment if you could.

- Describe something you'd do if you had 50 million dollars.

Once you've announced the topic and given the interviewee 30 seconds to think about it, start the interviews. Expect a lot of nervous laughter the first few times you have practice sessions; you're pulling people out of their comfort zones.

At the five-minute mark, blow a whistle gently or clap your hands. Ask everyone to take a deep breath, stretch their muscles, and then move the chairs so both the Interviewer and Interviewee face the Observer. Then ask the Observer to go through the Encouragement and Evaluation Sheet and give examples of what the Interviewer did well. The sheet also directs the Observer to ask the Interviewer and Interviewee how the process felt. Allow time for this discussion, then quickly move on.

Ask members of each trio to rotate chairs and do the exercise again with a new topic. Each member of the trio will have each role once. The way trios decide who goes next is up to them.

After you've participated in three interviews, tell participants they'll do another three interviews in round-robin fashion, with one change: Observers will now also take notes on how the Interviewer can improve. Instead of just encouragement, there will also be critique and evaluation. The goal will be to help Interviewers identify what skills they need to practice in the context of additional conversations at home or work.

You Should Be in Pictures

A Note: If you have the technology, or you are working with a very small group, another way to provide feedback is to videotape each session and include the Interviewer in viewing the tape. Nothing shows us more clearly how we're actually behaving than a video of ourselves. Interviewers will tend to see only their shortcomings, so be careful to be especially affirming.

After the second round of interviews, gather participants together. Ask participants how they feel about their practice sessions and how they'll put the five active learning skills to use elsewhere in their lives.

Suggest each participant take an Active Listening Encouragement and Evaluation Sheet home to keep handy. If you intend to hold another training or orientation session regarding procedures and policies, announce it at this point.

Active Listening Encouragement and Evaluation Sheet

As you observe the interview, make notes about the following interview skills. Your candid feedback will help the Interviewer grow in ministry effectiveness. Remember to be specific in your feedback and to offer compliments as well as critique.

Helps the Interviewee feel comfortable.
❏ Removes physical barriers to conversation.
❏ Sits up straight or leans slightly forward.
❏ Makes consistent eye contact.
❏ Speaks in pleasant, relaxed tone.
❏ Doesn't appear to be distracted or rushed.

Communicates listening.
❏ Is physically responsive with nods or facial movements.
❏ Provides sparing verbal cues.
❏ Uses open-ended questions.
❏ Uses linking questions.

Focuses on Interviewee.
❏ Displays nonjudgmental attitude.
❏ Displays patience.
❏ Appropriately self-disclosing.

Reflects back what Interviewee communicates.
❏ Paraphrases content.
❏ Paraphrases emotion.

After giving your feedback, ask both the Interviewer and Interviewee how they felt about the interview. What feedback does the Interviewee have for the Interviewer? What does the Interviewer think are his or her strengths . . . and weaknesses?

FIVE
Photocopiable Forms

Here's everything you need to launch your recruitment and interview campaign—from idea-generating marketing forms to follow-up letters to new volunteers.

Copy and adapt any of the forms you find here. They're yours for the taking, so long as you use them in your local church setting. Keep in mind that no form is truly a "one-size-fits-all" solution, so give serious thought to personalizing these forms for your unique situation. Ask someone in your church who has a writing background to work with you to tweak what you find here until it perfectly reflects your church's values and personality.

Defining the Purpose of Your Volunteer Ministry

Your Mission Statement:

Who does your volunteer ministry serve?

What services or products does your ministry provide to those you serve?

What is unique about your ministry?

Your Purpose Statement:

Checklist:

❑ Our statement of purpose clearly identifies why our volunteer ministry exists.

❑ The statement of purpose is inspiring to paid staff, volunteers, and clients.

❑ The statement of purpose provides clarity for decision-making.

Determining Your Target Audiences

Internal audiences:

What we *know* about these audiences:

What we *assume* about these audiences:

External audiences:

What we *know* about these audiences:

What we *assume* about these audiences:

Checklist:

❑ You've identified each audience your volunteer ministry needs to address.

❑ You've checked what you know against unbiased data (demographic information, church profiles, discussions with church leaders).

❑ You've checked what you assume with at least two members of each audience you've identified.

Setting Marketing Goals

Marketing campaign:_____

As a result of our marketing efforts, what do we want people to *know*?

How will we know we've accomplished this goal?

Who is primarily responsible for making this goal happen?

As a result of our marketing efforts, what do we want people to *believe*?

How will we know we've accomplished this goal?

Who is primarily responsible for making this goal happen?

As a result of our marketing efforts, what do we want people to *do*?

How will we know we've accomplished this goal?

Who is primarily responsible for making this goal happen?

Checklist:
- ❑ Be sure each goal is specific.
- ❑ Be sure each goal is challenging, but attainable.
- ❑ Be sure each goal is measurable.
- ❑ Be sure each goal is connected to a calendar date.
- ❑ Be sure each goal is connected to a person's name.

Volunteer Benefit Analysis Sheet

Marketing campaign: _____

Volunteer role being filled:_____

What benefits are likely to flow to volunteers who fill this position?

Skill set benefits:

Social benefits:

Knowledge benefits:

Emotional benefits:

Spiritual benefits:

Recognition benefits:

Checklist:

❑ Each benefit area has at least one benefit flowing from the job description for the role.

Note that if a benefit area is not represented, it may be perceived as a weakness by potential volunteers.

Marketing Message Delivery Planning Sheet

Synopsis of marketing content (*state in two or three sentences*):

Goal of campaign:

Target audience:

Proposed channels of communication (*How do you intend to deliver your campaign message to your target audience?*):

Resources available:
- Finances (*What's your budget?*):

- Time (*When do you need to finish? start?*):

- Influencers (*Champions who'll give testimonials or support*):

- Free forums (*Worship services, newsletters. . . Anything you can use without it impacting your budget?*):

Checklist:
- ❏ Be sure your plan is attainable using available resources.
- ❏ Be sure your plan focuses on the campaign goal and each part of your plan makes sense in light of the goal.
- ❏ Be sure you've identified a person who is responsible for each element of your plan.

Volunteer Ministries Placement Interviewer
Sample Job Description

Job Title: One-to-one Interviewer

Responsible to: Director of Volunteer Ministries
                                   and Volunteer Ministry
                                   Task Force

Desired Commitment: 6 months
                         4-6 interviews (approximately 30
                         minutes each), attend training
                         session (2 hours) and follow-up
                         meetings (2 hours)

Duties: Attend interview training workshop.
                                   Make appointments with those
                                   members you will interview.
                                   Conduct one-to-one interviews as
                                   assigned by Task Force.
                                   Fill out interview follow-up form
                                   after each interview.
                                   Feed appropriate information back
                                   to church staff or volunteer director.
                                   Attend follow-up meeting to provide
                                   feedback to task force regarding
                                   interview process.

Desired Qualifications: Ability to handle confidential
                            information.
                            Experience as a volunteer.
                            Genuine, caring, "people person"
                            attitude, and having an excited
                            commitment to the concept of
                            volunteer ministry.

Good listener.
Familiarity with church programs,
or willing to learn about those
programs.
Interviewing experience is helpful,
but not necessary.

Training: Interview training workshop is
provided and required.

Sample Interview Confirmation Letter

Reach Out—Renew—Rejoice!
"Each one should use whatever gift he has received to serve others, faithfully administering God's grace in its various forms." *(1 Peter 4:10)*

Dear Jack:

Thank you for our conversation about the volunteer ministries available through <u>First Church</u>.

We place a high priority on involving members in appropriate, fulfilling ministry. We believe the Bible teaches that all of us are unique and important, and that we've each got something valuable to offer in service to others.

It would help me get to know you better if we could talk about some of the following things when we meet <u>on Saturday, July 26 at 2:00 P.M. in the church office</u> . . .

- What have you done that's given you the greatest satisfaction here at <u>First Church</u>? At another church? In the community?

- What have you always wished you could do?

- What do you enjoy doing in your leisure time?

- Is there a skill you wish you could learn or try?

- What are your hobbies?

- What do you feel you're good at? that you might be good at? that you're not good at?

- What have you done as a volunteer that you enjoyed the least?

And here's a question I'd love to explore with you . . .

- What would you like to see happen here at <u>First Church</u> that would have significance for you and/or your family?

That's a lot to think about, but we value your ideas, dreams, opinions, and suggestions. We welcome any questions or concerns you might have about the volunteer opportunities here at <u>First Church</u>.

I look forward to meeting with you, <u>Jack</u>. It's a visit with a wonderful purpose: As members in the body of Christ we'll be able to better know each other, support each other, and encourage each other in service to others and God.

Sincerely,

<u>Nancy Johnson</u>
<u>Director, Volunteer Ministries</u>
<u>First Church</u>

Discovering My Abilities, Skills, and Passions

Answer the following questions, while thinking of any area of your life that's currently exciting for you—church, career, home, family, school, your social life, leisure time, hobbies, or any other part of your life that energizes you.

1. Some things I believe I do well are:

2. Some things I think I'm not very good at are:

3. If given the chance, I think I might be good at:

4. One new thing I've tried recently that went well was:

5. Who encouraged me to do what I listed in #4? What made the person or persons think I could do it? Does this person or these people encourage me to try new things often?

6. Who are my mentors (my loyal, wise advisors) in life?

Sample Interview Form

First Church Interview Questionnaire

Name: _____   Spouse: _____

Home Phone: _____   Work Phone: _____

Cell Phone: _____   E-mail: _____

Address: _____

Birthdate:_____ Gender:_____ Marital status: _____

Church member since: _____   Is spouse member? _____

Children at home (*please list*)   Birthdate   Church member?

Other children not at home, or family ties to <u>First Church.</u>

Have you served in any of the following capacities? (*please check*)
___ Church board or other congregational leadership
___ Christian education   ___ Youth ministry
___ Committee work   ___ Usher ministry
___ Other:
Where and when?

Leadership training received at church or work (*please explain*):

_____

_____

Other training received (*such as child abuse training, Stephen Ministries, and other training*):

_____

_____

Are there times of the day or week you are not available?

_____

Worship service you prefer to attend:

_____

Notes:

Permission for information to be entered into the church database (*please sign*):

_____   _____
Signature   Printed name

Today's date: _____   Interviewer: _____

Sample Interview Follow-Up Letter

Dear <u>Jack,</u>
Thanks so much for meeting with me and agreeing to consider being a volunteer in <u>First Church's Preschool Christian Education Department.</u>
That role is supervised by <u>Karen Hedges.</u>
<u>Ms. Hedges</u> will be contacting you by phone in the next week to arrange to meet with you to further explore your volunteering in that ministry. Though it appears that your God-given abilities, interests, and passions for service would be well-used in that ministry, it's a good idea to be sure. Additional discussion will help confirm our thinking.
Again—thank you, <u>Jack.</u> It's exciting to see you step out and serve. God will bless your efforts and help you grow as you serve others!
Though you'll be talking with <u>Ms. Hedges,</u> please call on me if at any time I can be of service to you.
Sincerely,

<u>Nancy Johnson</u>
<u>Director, Volunteer Ministries</u>
<u>First Church</u>

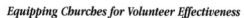

VOLUNTEER ORIENTATION AND TRAINING

Marlene Wilson, General Editor

Group's Volunteer Leadership Series™
Volume 5
Group's Church Volunteer Central™

Loveland, Colorado

Group's Volunteer Leadership Series™, Volume 5

Volunteer Orientation and Training

Visit our Web site: **www.grouppublishing.com**

Credits
Writer: Mikal Keefer
Editors: Mikal Keefer and Scott Kinner
General Editor: Marlene Wilson
Chief Creative Officer: Joani Schultz
Art Director: Nathan Hindman
Cover Designer: Jeff Storm
Production Manager: Peggy Naylor

Produced with the assistance of The Livingstone Corporation (www.LivingstoneCorp.com). Project staff includes Chris Hudson, Ashley Taylor, Mary Horner Collins, Joel Bartlett, Cheryl Dunlop, Mary Larsen, and Rosalie Krusemark.

Library of Congress Cataloging-in-Publication Data

Volunteer orientation and training / Marlene Wilson, general editor.—1st
        American hardbound ed.
    p. cm. — (Group's volunteer leadership series ; v. 5)
    ISBN 0-7644-2749-0 (alk. paper)
    1. Voluntarism—Religious aspects—Christianity. 2. Christian
leadership. 3. Church work. 4. Volunteers—Training of. I. Wilson, Marlene. II. Series.
BR115.V64V65 2003
253'.7–dc22   2003022122

10 9 8 7 6 5 4 3 2 1   12 11 10 09 08 07 06 05 04

Printed in the United States of America.

Contents

Contents

Introduction

Why being intentional about setting up an orientation program and training program makes sense for your ministry.

Remember how the first day on a new job feels?

You want to make a great impression, so you show up exactly on time—or early. You're nervous about the work, whether it'll be something you master quickly or something that leaves you baffled.

Will your job be as described during the interview, or are you walking into something bigger than you expected? Where will you sit? Will you be able to use the new computer programs? Have you dressed appropriately? Will you fit in? Are people friendly?

You have a hundred questions, but they all boil down to this: Will I be successful?

Starting a new job—as a paid employee or a volunteer—can be intimidating. There's so much information to learn . . . so many logistics to master . . . so many people to get to know. It's all a bit overwhelming.

And through it all there's a steady drumbeat of desire to do the job well—to be successful.

That means your volunteers want precisely what you want: for them to hit the ground running when they start their volunteer jobs, and to accomplish great things. You want for them to be successful.

You're well on your way to creating a successful volunteer ministry. You've drafted job descriptions, recruited great people, carefully interviewed, and placed people in volunteer jobs that fit like a glove.

Now it's time to take the next step by providing intentional, targeted orientation and training programs.

In a nutshell, an orientation program answers the question: What is it like to live or work here? A training program answers the next question that usually follows: What does it take to be successful here?

When a volunteer has the answers to both those questions, you dramatically increase that volunteer's comfort . . . effectiveness . . . and likelihood of sticking in the job.

You win. The volunteer wins. The ministry wins. The people your ministry serves win. And everyone gets to be successful.

ONE
Orientation Defined

Orientation is a process, not a one-shot program. Here's how to create a process that meets the needs of your volunteers—and your paid ministry staff, too.

For years you've entered your name in contests, filling out little cards and sending in box tops for drawings, and for years your name has never been drawn—until now.

The knock on your door was official notification that you're the Grand Prize Winner, and your all-expenses-paid trip to Italy will begin immediately. You've got just enough time to stuff two suitcases full of the clothes you think you'll need for your week in beautiful Tuscany, where you'll stay at a private villa.

Within an hour you're whisked away by limousine to the airport, where a chartered jet wings you away on your whirlwind journey.

On the way, you use the complimentary phone to call everyone you can think of: family, friends, even people you hardly know. A private secretary is at your house, cleaning, filling the dishwasher, and phoning the Curl Up & Dye Hair Salon to cancel your appointment since Giuliano (who coifs all the Italian movie stars) will visit the villa to give you a complete makeover.

The jet lands and you're given your choice of any rental car you want, including the sporty red convertible you've long wished you could afford back home. You hop in, a map spread out on the seat beside you, and with the radio blaring opera you're soon winding your way through the rolling hills of Tuscany, the landscape lush with vineyards, olive trees, and cypress groves.

Unfortunately, as you approach a medieval town carved into a hillside, you find the road growing narrow—too narrow for your car. Your villa, unfortunately, rests high above the town on a rocky outcrop. There's no way to reach the villa except through the town's center, where cobbled streets were designed for horses, not horsepower. You should have taken a scooter instead of a car.

> "You're soon winding your way through the rolling hills of Tuscany."

You schlep your suitcases up through town, smiling and nodding as you go. This is the Tuscany of your dreams, but it's also the Tuscany that's off the beaten tourist path. Few people can give you directions in English, so your search for the specific road that will take you to the villa is long, torturous, and extremely uphill.

You no sooner reach the villa (the view is *magnifico,* by the way) when you toss your laptop on the marble desktop. You dig the adaptor you bought when you were hoping to visit another country someday out of your computer case, plug it in, and immediately fry your computer. Nobody told you that household current is 220 volts in Italy, not the 110 your trusty laptop was wired to lovingly accept. You won't be e-mailing home to tell people about the wonderful time you're having.

Nor will you be doing much walking through the charming town, as you brought sandals and you're already feeling blisters form. You had no idea that the main form of transportation in this town was walking.

So sitting in Tuscany, in a villa that would be right at home in *Italian Dream Vacations* magazine, you stamp your foot (which pops a blister) and shout, "Why didn't someone tell me about this place?"

What you needed—and didn't get—was an orientation.

When you don't have enough information about an environment where you'll spend time—even wonderful Tuscany—the experience can be horrible. You're unprepared for the terrain. You don't know what to expect from the people you'll meet. You don't know the culture, how to accomplish things, or who to call for help. You feel alone and vulnerable.

And to a volunteer walking into a junior high boys Sunday school class for the first time, that's exactly how it feels.

You've invested a great deal of time and energy in finding, interviewing, and placing volunteers. If you fail to orient those volunteers into your ministry and their unique roles in it, you may well undo all you've accomplished.

There's tremendous power in a well-run orientation process. Not only can it salvage a Tuscan vacation, it can also keep your volunteers happy and on board.

The Power and Benefits of an Orientation Process

Notice that orientation is being referred to as a *process,* not just a *program.* That's because to be effective, an orientation will take more than a one-shot program—even if that program stretches over several days.

> "An orientation answers the question, 'What's life like around here?'"

Remember: An orientation answers the question, "What's life like around here?" That's not a question that can usually be answered quickly, or in one session. It's something a new volunteer discovers over the course of time.

You can help that discovery process along, and in this volume we'll tell you how. It's good to have a formal orientation program as a kickoff, but don't make the mistake of thinking that will be enough. It won't, at least for most volunteers.

The nuts and bolts of a volunteer's job are described on his or her job description . . . but job descriptions tell new volunteers what they'll be doing, not what life is like. Job descriptions leave lots of questions unanswered, such as . . .

- "Where's the closest bathroom?"

- "If I leave my lunch in the church refrigerator, will someone steal it?"

- "Is it okay to tell jokes and laugh around here?"

Deliver a great orientation for your volunteers and you'll answer their questions. You'll put them at ease. And . . .

You'll reassure volunteers they made a good decision by volunteering.

If the orientation is positive and helpful, it reinforces the volunteer's decision to be involved. It's not the first impression your volunteer ministry has made, but it's the first significant taste of the actual job. In a world where promises are often made ("you'll enjoy this volunteer role—sign up and find out for yourself!") and then broken, your follow-up will be noticeable and appreciated.

Scott, a volunteer in an Indiana church, describes his first volunteer role at the church he attended: "I was asked by a ministry leader to direct the Wednesday evening children's program for a period of three months. I checked to make sure my schedule was clear, then jumped on the opportunity.

"After I accepted, the ministry leader looked at me, patted me on the back, and said, 'I'm so sorry. Good luck.'

"That leader didn't reassure me at all. Basically he told me I'd made a mistake by taking the bait, that I'd soon regret it, and that heading up that program was the most difficult thing I'd ever do."

Fortunately, Scott immediately recruited a few close friends to help him with the program, and the three months were a blast for the leaders and the kids. But if Scott hadn't been the enthusiastic guy he is, he could easily have quit before he ever reached his first Wednesday night.

You'll connect the volunteer ministry to the larger purpose of the church.

Here's your chance to cement in a volunteer's mind how his or her job contributes to the larger mission of the church.

There are a dozen versions of a story that communicates this concept well. Here's one version you can share with your volunteers. Consider including it in your orientation programs to help volunteers catch a vision for how every job is important and contributes to the cause. One manager gives each new person on his team a copy of this story and a cobblestone to use as a paperweight.

During the middle ages, a Swiss bishop made the long journey to Germany to see the Frankfurt Cathedral. Still under construction after a hundred years, the cathedral would someday be the largest in Europe, a magnificent monument to God. A place where thousands would gather and worship.

The portly cleric rode through mountain passes into Germany. Miles from Frankfurt, the bishop could see the unfinished cathedral towering over the town, an enormous skeleton of supports and timbers. Massive gray walls rose where stone masons slowly fitted together row after row of huge blocks.

Eventually, the bishop stood in the very shadow of the cathedral. Around him swarmed an army of engineers, stonecutters, and carpenters. Crew chiefs shouted orders, pulleys creaked as stones were pushed and pulled into position, and the pounding of chisels and hammers echoed off soaring walls.

The bishop touched the arm of a man hurrying past. "Tell me what you're doing," the bishop said.

"I've got to recalculate the angle of the nave roof before we all get crushed," snapped the man. "Step aside!" And with that the man huffed away.

The bishop noticed a half-dozen laborers holding a rope that wound up into the distant darkness above, then back down where it was tied around a large stone block.

"What are you doing?" asked the bishop.

The workers exchanged annoyed glances. "Well, Father," said one, "we're hoisting this block up to the top—unless you can talk God into floating it there." The men laughed, squared their grip on the thick rope, then leaned into their backbreaking task.

The bishop saw a small, elderly man sitting near a doorway. He was hunched over, chiseling cobblestones. The bishop's heart went out to the man—obviously a stonemason whose age and failing eyesight made him good for nothing but this thankless task. A craftsman whose life had been reduced to chiseling stones for a walkway in some forgotten corner.

"And you," said the bishop. "Tell me what you're doing."

The old man looked up without missing a beat. "Me? I'm doing the same as everyone else—to God's glory, I'm building a cathedral."

A well-crafted orientation program helps volunteers see the importance of what they're doing. It's an opportunity for them to discover how their roles serve God, advance the work of the church, and have eternal significance.

You'll reduce volunteer turnover.

There's a direct correlation between orientation and retention. You've placed volunteers where their abilities, skills, and passions connect with a volunteer role, but they're not yet at home in that role. During their orientation you'll help them feel comfortable—and a volunteer who's comfortable, challenged, and growing is one who's likely to stick.

On the other hand, if a volunteer feels unwelcome—for any reason—that volunteer isn't likely to be with you long.

You'll help volunteers be successful in two ways—culture and information.

Matching a volunteer with the right job is only part of what sets a person up for success. The volunteer also has to match up with the culture where she's serving and master the information that's required for her to be successful.

Let's start by considering what happens when the culture of the volunteer collides with the culture of the ministry area . . .

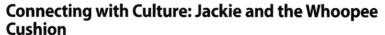

Connecting with Culture: Jackie and the Whoopee Cushion

Jackie is a quiet, serious musician who wants to join her church's music ministry. She's sung in choirs since she was a girl, and she has a high regard for the dignity and majesty of choral music. Her choir experience has always been in choirs that prepared thoroughly and performed complicated choral pieces brilliantly.

She's gifted, skilled, and eager to sign on as a volunteer vocalist. To Jackie, serving in this spot seems like a match made in heaven. She can't wait for the first practice session.

Except the church's approach to music ministry is to lead worship, not to perform. And the music team isn't all that worried about hitting every note perfectly, or choosing challenging choral pieces. By intent the group selects easy-to-sing worship choruses and plays in an accessible, simple way so everyone can join in.

Plus, it's a tight-knit group that has fun as well as does ministry. During Jackie's first practice session the bass player leaves a whoopee cushion under the pad on the piano stool. The loud "pfffffffft" that echoes around the sanctuary when the keyboard player sits down prompts so much laughter that even the music director is howling hysterically.

What are the odds that Jackie will last as a member of the music ministry? that she'll even survive her first night of practice with the team?

In spite of her many musical gifts, there's a total disconnect when it comes to culture. In Jackie's case the distance might be so great that nothing could help her bridge the gap—but an orientation would be helpful. And it might be enough.

> "What are the odds that Jackie will last?"

At the very least, an orientation to the music ministry and its culture would keep Jackie from being scandalized and angry.

Granted, Jackie's case is extreme. But even for people who don't have to figure out how to transition from the Mormon

Tabernacle Choir to the Mostly Tentative Choir, culture can be a problem.

And it's a problem you can solve by taking volunteers through an orientation.

Orientation is where you cover culture—and help volunteers decide how they'll fit in. You'll give new volunteers the understanding and tools they need to effectively enter into new roles, surrounded by new people, working on new teams.

> **"Orientation is where you cover culture."**

You can't overstate the impact of culture on a volunteer's experience. If volunteers don't understand how people communicate, or embrace the values of your ministry, they'll never feel at home.

But how do you communicate culture? Let's answer that question by first examining what components combine to create our culture at church, and in our ministry.

Communication

There's probably a distinct approach to how you connect with other people in your church. Are titles important? Do you speak to each other directly, or is there a fair amount of caution in expressing opinions? Is there a "chain of command" to be respected, or can a volunteer speak to anyone about anything? How are messages and ideas shared?

Information

How is it distributed? Is it widely shared, or does confidentiality play a role that must be respected? How does a volunteer go about learning things?

Technology

How highly regarded is the latest technology? What does a volunteer need to know—and why?

Power

Who's in charge? What's their style of sharing—or not sharing—

power? How is power expressed? What are volunteers allowed to decide on their own? For what must they seek approval, and from whom?

Economics

How is money viewed in the ministry? What's scarce and must be used carefully, and what seems to be always available in abundance? How do people go about getting what they need?

Values

What does the ministry hold in high regard? What does it believe? How are those beliefs expressed? How thoroughly are the values integrated in the culture—is everyone on board? How clear are the preferred values?

Tradition

What traditions are part of how things are done? Who's the keeper of the flame for the traditions? Are the traditions embraced, tolerated, or somewhere in between? How are the traditions celebrated?

Rules and regulations

What are the rules that maintain order in the culture? How are those rules structured? What are the penalties for breaking the rules?

Tone

What's the emotional tone of the culture? Is it okay to have fun? How much fun? How do people have fun? Are there times the culture demands solemnity? When and why?

Change

How open is the culture to changing things? What sort of things are changeable, and which are "sacred cows" that seem immune to change? How does one go about instigating change?

Pecking order

Who's important and who's less important? How is that demonstrated? How are segments of people divided—and why?

Who is "the enemy"?

Is there a cause that the culture seeks to promote, or a group or cause that has been identified as the enemy? What cause will encourage the culture to circle the wagons or send out the sentries?

> "Acclimating to a new culture is an ongoing process."

Watering holes

Where does the culture gather for support and sustenance? Where is the culture in evidence and celebrated?

Acclimating to a new culture is an ongoing process. Allow time and opportunity for it to happen. It's simply not possible to work through a list of cultural elements like those listed above in one brief meeting.

And a word of caution: You might think that because someone was raised in your church and already knows the people with whom he or she will be serving, there's no need for an orientation. You would be wrong. There's a huge difference between being a student in a class and teaching the class. And what's valued in the high school youth group will vary dramatically from what's valued in the preschool ministry.

In addition to covering culture, orientations will help volunteers in another way . . .

Connecting with Information: Mrs. Brown and the Missing Envelopes

Orientation is also where you can shorten the learning curve for volunteers. You can tell them what they need to know instead of hoping they'll figure it out on their own . . . something that may never happen.

At one church, the Sunday school superintendent received

a complaint from the offering usher about Mrs. Brown, a Sunday school teacher who failed to turn in the offering collected in her second grade classroom. Other teachers placed the change they collected in envelopes, then slid the envelopes under their classroom doors. The designated offering usher went down the hallway collecting envelopes while classes were underway.

There was never an envelope outside Mrs. Brown's door.

Theories were floated. Was she pocketing the estimated two dollars in change each Sunday? spending it on classroom supplies? failing to take an offering at all? What could be done? What should be done? Did the pastor know?

Finally, the supervisor asked Mrs. Brown about the class offering. She replied that no one had ever told her about any envelope procedure. She'd been collecting the money in Sunday school, then dropping it in the offering plate an hour later when a collection was taken during church.

Mrs. Brown had circumvented the offering envelope procedure, but still accomplished the goal: Offering money was collected and turned in. Once the process was explained, without fail an envelope scooted out from under her door each Sunday. Satisfied, the offering usher declared Mrs. Brown a success.

What information you share in an orientation meeting depends on what you want to accomplish. Do you have a clear purpose and set of objectives? Without them, you don't have much chance of having a meaningful orientation meeting. Nor will you know if you were effective in meeting your objectives.

"What information you share depends on what you want to accomplish."

Whatever you settle on as objectives for your orientation process, be sure you're hitting them by measuring results. It may be a year or more before you have enough volunteers entering or leaving the program to be able to determine impact, but it's important to begin now. The sooner you start, the sooner you'll know how to tweak volunteer orientations so you're making the most of the program.

- If your objective was to transmit information, administer a test to be sure volunteers are learning and retaining the information.

- If your objective was to reduce volunteer turnover, track whether volunteers exposed to the orientation program stayed longer than other volunteers.

- If your objective was to help volunteers become effective sooner, do interviews with volunteers six weeks into their volunteer experience. Ask how what they covered in orientation helped—or hindered—their ability to master their jobs.

Whatever your objectives, it's likely you'll be sharing information at orientation meetings. Since that's a given, be careful about selecting what information you'll include. Ask yourself and, perhaps, your task force:

> "As you answer these questions, three things will quickly become obvious."

- What information has proven to be most useful to new volunteers?

- Who is best suited to present the information?

- When is the information most appropriately presented?

- What logistical information do new volunteers need?

- What problems and challenges are typically encountered by new volunteers?

- What policies and procedures do new volunteers need to know?

As you answer these questions, three things will quickly become obvious . . .

Not every volunteer needs precisely the same information.

For instance, a Sunday morning greeter might need a far more detailed awareness of how the building is laid out than the volunteer who's in charge of mowing the yard.

This reality suggests that some orientation is task specific and needs to be done later, when the entire group isn't assembled. To force a bus driver to sit through a discussion about the proper cleaning of the communion cups is a waste of time—and guarantees the bus driver won't be back for more meetings.

There is some information every volunteer needs.

Where to park, what standards of conduct are expected, where the first aid kit is located—that's information that's universally needed.

This reality suggests that truly universal information is so important that it needs to be written down and accessible. A volunteer handbook and volunteer web site are two good places for this information to reside even after an orientation meeting.

There's some information you may not have.

You may have suspicions about what problems are most often encountered by new volunteers, but do you really know? You probably only hear about a fraction of the challenges faced by new volunteers; you're guessing about the rest.

This reality suggests that if you want to have a relevant orientation, you need to be asking volunteers to recommend what to include in the orientation. A survey of both current and new volunteers will provide agenda items.

And be sure that paid and unpaid staff who supervise volunteers have input, too. You want the orientation to meet their needs as well as the needs of the volunteers.

No matter what content you include, the initial meeting should be brief, relevant, and direct. Especially if you want volunteers to be back for more orientation, or ongoing training meetings, demonstrate that you can run a purposeful meeting that doesn't drag on forever.

Whatever else your orientation covers, these items are generally a good idea to include:

- The organizational chart (with no names listed next to titles)

- The church history, vision statement, and mission statement

- Your ministry's history, vision statement, and mission statement

- Training opportunities: who, what, when, where, why, and how

- Performance expectations and appraisal

- Safety information: evacuation plans, severe storm plans, and first aid kit location.

- Logistics: where to park, where to find the coffee pot, among others.

- And in every orientation meeting, be open for questions, comments, and observations from volunteers. Volunteers are absorbing information and assimilating into the culture; provide every opportunity for them to ask questions and get answers.

When Should You Schedule the Formal Orientation Program?

There's often a formal orientation event for new volunteers, an initial meeting where general information is shared and administrative matters are addressed. This has great value, as it helps volunteers assimilate quickly and easily.

But that initial event often results in a severe case of information overload. The new volunteer is inundated with details that can't possibly all be absorbed. Eyes glaze over. People fidget. So much data is pushed at volunteers that it's amazing any of it is retained at all.

A better solution is to give new volunteers less information, but to come back to talk with them several times. An initial meeting is worthwhile, but to avoid overload be careful to provide the right information at the right time.

> "Provide the right information at the right time."

At your initial meeting be certain to:

- Warmly, sincerely welcome new volunteers and ease their transition into new volunteer roles,

- Communicate essential information—but only essential information,

- Remind volunteers of the ministry's expectations about their conduct and contributions,

- Distribute and review any orientation handbooks that are needed by volunteers, and

- Offer to answer general questions that are of interest to everyone present. If a question is job-specific, respond to the interested volunteer after the meeting, or refer the volunteer to his or her ministry supervisor.

That's all you need to do at an initial, formal orientation meeting.

Is there more information volunteers need to know? Absolutely—but in a one-shot, group setting that's probably all anyone can take in. The rest of the material you can cover later in smaller groups organized around volunteer assignments, or in a one-on-one setting.

The fact is that at an orientation meeting volunteers probably don't yet know what they need to know. They won't have a clear picture of what's truly important information to master until they dive into their jobs and hit a few snags.

Remember the trip you won to Tuscany? You didn't know what you needed to know about Italian electrical current until you'd toasted your computer, or that walking is the standard mode of travel in small Tuscan villages until your toes were blistered and sore.

You learned from experience—and in some ways you want your orientation program to save your volunteers from a similar fate. Some things are great to learn from experience . . . but why make the same mistakes others have made?

Jim Wideman, a children's pastor who has more than a thousand volunteers involved in his program, says it well: "Experience is the best teacher . . . but it doesn't have to be *your* experience."

> "Effective orientation is an ongoing process."

The secret of an effective orientation program doesn't lie in hosting a tremendous formal meeting anyway. It's this: Effective orientation is an ongoing process. You can't hold one orientation meeting and then cross it off your list forever.

Remember: The purpose of orientation is to answer the question, "What's it like to live or work here?" Every time a volunteer changes jobs, or the job the volunteer is doing changes, or the culture or rules change—it's time for more orientation. The process never actually stops. Never.

Who Should Lead the Orientation Program and Process?

At the risk of sounding ungrateful, let us suggest that you may not be the best candidate for the job.

Not that you haven't done great work in connecting the new volunteers with appropriate service opportunities. And not that you wouldn't do a stellar job of facilitating the orientation. After all, you're probably the one who pulled the information together.

But you probably aren't the person who will be supervising the volunteers, or being in a primary relationship with them. If you have enough volunteers entering into a particular area of ministry, it's a good idea to let the person who will be supervising them do the orientation.

Of course, maybe the new crop of volunteers will report to you, or your volunteer ministry is small enough that you can be in relationship with everyone. If that's the case, go to it. Lead the orientation program yourself—but still involve others in the overall process.

And have people who will be working with the volunteers at the formal orientation. From the very start you can help volunteers find buddies who know the ropes, who serve in the ministry roles in which the new volunteers will serve.

> "Have people who will be working with the volunteers at the formal orientation."

A case study: the Group Workcamps orientation program.

Each summer, Group Workcamps organizes more than 60 week-long, short-term mission programs where teenagers repair homes of the elderly and disadvantaged. The vast majority of the leaders at those Workcamps—each of which is housed in a community school and involves an average of 350 teenagers and youth leaders—are volunteers.

More than a thousand volunteers are needed each summer, and because of the program's reputation and excellence, each year that number of volunteers is recruited, screened, placed, and trained. Workcamp volunteers do everything from manage the school kitchens, to coordinate travel, to work alongside teenagers as together they roof a house or paint a porch.

Note the scope of this volunteer program—it's huge. The Workcamps themselves are scattered in communities all over the continent. There are more than a dozen volunteer roles at each camp, and one of the more challenging is the job of "director."

Directors are the people ultimately responsible for running the Workcamps. If a youth leader falls through a ceiling, or the food vendor fails to deliver the lettuce, or a teenager drifts away from a worksite, the director gets involved.

Because of the complexity of preparing for the role, there's an orientation for Workcamp directors in Colorado each May. Volunteers who will direct camps are flown in, housed at a YMCA high in the Rockies, and given three days of orientation and training.

And during those three days, what do you think is the single most energetically received session?

It's this: a several-hour meeting where new directors get the opportunity to ask veteran directors what to expect. There's no agenda other than to connect first-time volunteers with people who've dealt with the same responsibilities before.

> "The orientation is relational, not agenda-driven."

The orientation is relational, not agenda-driven, and relationships that form continue through e-mails, phone calls, and encouraging notes between peers. The session sets an expectation that directors will be helpful to each other and responsive when there's a question or concern.

The inch-thick orientation and training manual every director receives is packed with helpful information. It's useful. It's referred to often. It's practical and well organized.

But the manual isn't the magic.

Something else happens during that three-day orientation and training meeting that shapes volunteers into directors who will embrace a week-long Workcamp experience that keeps them up into the wee hours of the morning day after day. That requires them to be servants even if they're tired. That inspires them to deliver top-flight customer service to teenagers and youth leaders alike.

Here's what happens during those three days that makes the difference—and you can reap similar rewards if you can build these elements into your orientation program, too . . .

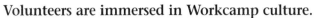

Volunteers are immersed in Workcamp culture.

The staff hosting the orientation doesn't just talk about serving others; they model it in a hundred ways to the new volunteers. Meetings start and end promptly. Questions are answered clearly. Requested information is tracked down and reported. The needs of volunteers are taken seriously—which is exactly what will be expected of the directors when they're running their own camps.

For three solid days, the Group Workcamp vision, mission, and values are soaked up by volunteers.

Anything that will be expected of directors at their Workcamps is modeled during the orientation. That way there's never a question as to what's meant by "service" or "leadership." Everyone has experienced it.

Top people lead the orientation program.

When the Senior Pastor or CEO shows up to lead an orientation session, that communicates the significance of the orientation process. At the Group Workcamp orientation new volunteers hear from—and have dinner with—the founder of the program. And the people leading sessions are front-line staff.

Be sure you have your best people leading your orientation programs, too. And having your Senior Pastor show up to personally thank your volunteers for their commitment and servant hearts will fire up your team.

Stories are shared.

There's power in stories. The stories we share carry the DNA of our values and culture. The stories highlight what's important and lift up heroes to emulate.

> "There's power in stories."

At the Group Workcamp orientation, stories play a central role. They're told to illustrate what works—and doesn't work. What's wise—and what's foolish. What matters—and what's not important. Stories are shared with humor and laughter, but never is the point missed: There's truth in these stories. Let those with ears hear and understand.

In your orientation process, tell the story of how your volunteer ministry came into being. In the process you'll share what vision motivated your founders to persevere until the ministry was born. Tell stories about volunteers who've made you proud—they embody the attributes that are considered virtues in your culture.

And never miss the opportunity to capture stories as they unfold in your ministry. The best stories you could tell next year may well be happening right now.

New volunteers are celebrated.

There's always a temptation for veterans to form cliques. It's just natural: They're friends who've shared experiences, and perhaps they seldom see each other between annual orientation sessions.

Although it's natural, it's toxic for new volunteers.

At the Group Workcamp orientation, newcomers are intentionally integrated into sessions with veteran volunteers. Past experience is applauded and appreciated, but in many ways it's irrelevant. The focus is preparing for the summer ahead, not reminiscing about past Workcamps. New volunteers are given high honor for their willingness to serve and celebrated as legitimate members of the team.

How do you handle cliques among your volunteers—especially among groups of long-term volunteers? Where is there an opportunity for newcomers to be heard, accepted, and endorsed?

Evaluations are filled out.

How do you know what's preparing your volunteers for their roles and what's not helping? You ask your volunteers. They know—at least, the experienced volunteers know.

Don't let a formal orientation program in your church go past without designing in an evaluation of the program and the process. For your convenience, a Program Evaluation Form is on page 100. Adapt it to use at your formal orientation programs. You'll also be asking volunteers to fill out the same form after three to six months; comparing their answers will let you know what they remember and what was most and least helpful.

You probably won't be flying your volunteers to a remote mountain getaway for three days anytime soon. But you can pull together a one-day retreat . . . or even a half-day retreat. It's a chance for you to transform volunteers into servants who will rise above even their own expectations.

TWO
The Volunteer Orientation Staff Handbook

Most companies provide a handbook to staff members during orientation—and you should, too. Here's why . . . and what you need to include.

Denise's first day at her new job wasn't quite what she expected.

"First we had a tour of the facility," she reports. "I saw where I'd be sitting, and figured out where to hang my coat and stash my purse. I had lunch with one of the people on my team. That stuff I pretty much knew was coming."

What took Denise by surprise was how she spent the afternoon.

"Six of us sat in a little conference room for three hours," she says in amazement. "We opened up an employee handbook and took turns reading through it—out loud. Then we had to sign a form that said we'd read the handbook. I was bored out of my mind."

Denise shakes her head as she remembers what felt like a wasted afternoon. "I just can't believe that was the best use of our time. We had a million things we could have done, and they had us reading out loud like we were in first grade. Somebody must really care about that handbook," she says.

It probably was the best use of Denise's time to read through the handbook. While the presentation style was at best mind-numbing, it did expose Denise and the other new hires to critical information they need to know.

And because everyone walked out of the conference room with a copy of the handbook, Denise knows where to find the details she's forgotten when she's wondering how to schedule vacation time or wondering what the company's policy is about snow days.

But that's a for-profit company. They need orientation handbooks for new hires, right? Does your volunteer ministry really require you to create one?

Yes . . . and here's why.

Five Reasons You Need a Volunteer Ministry Orientation Handbook

Creating a handbook can be a time-consuming task, even if you start with another church's handbook as a model. But without question developing a handbook is worth the investment—for at least five reasons:

1. Orientation handbooks compensate for information overload.

Volunteers can absorb just so much information at a time. Trying to cram too many policies and procedures into their heads at one time is like continuing to pour milk into a glass that's already full: There's no more room.

A handbook provides the details in a handy reference guide. The volunteer may not recall exactly what the policy is about appropriate clothing, but she knows where to look it up.

2. Orientation handbooks are open 24/7.

Who are the volunteers going to call if they can't remember the procedure for lining up a substitute Sunday school teacher? You—of course. Do you really want that to happen again and again?

If you've outlined the procedure in a handbook, volunteers can find the needed information anytime . . . without phoning you at 10:30 on a Saturday night. A well-written, clear handbook intercepts and answers many questions before they reach you.

3. Orientation handbooks are empowering.

Giving volunteers information in written form empowers them to make many decisions without having to ask for information. They'll know the church's philosophy of discipline and how they'll be reviewed.

4. Orientation handbooks require you to set policies.

Orientation handbooks force you—and other ministry leaders—to think through policies and procedures that affect volunteers. What should volunteers do if a tornado warning sounds while they're working with children at church? What are appropriate boundaries to respect in the adult-teenager mentoring program? How will volunteers be evaluated?

You can't write policies until you've made hard decisions about how situations should generally be handled, and that often takes some discussion among church leaders. But that's a good thing: The time and energy you invest in creating policies is time and energy volunteers don't have to exert wondering what to do when situations arise.

By the way, if you're a member of Group's Church Volunteer Central, visit www.churchvolunteercentral.com for examples of brief, clear policies. Not a member of Group's Church Volunteer Central? Call 1-800-447-1070 for information about what it can do for you and your volunteer ministry.

5. Orientation handbooks establish expectations.

If you expect volunteers to uphold standards, you've got to make clear what those standards are. If you don't want to see gossip, have a conflict resolution system established. If you expect all volunteers to attend worship services regularly, say so.

> "If you expect something of paid staff, expect it from unpaid staff, too."

And a word about standards: If you expect something of paid staff, expect it from unpaid staff, too. It's a double standard to insist that no staff members smoke on church property, but then put out ashtrays for volunteers. Hold everyone to the same high standards. Doing less will confuse church members who don't see all that much difference between the Associate Pastor of Christian Education (a paid staff position) and the Sunday School Superintendent (an unpaid staff position).

Besides, when you expect less of unpaid staff than paid staff, you demean your volunteers. Treat them like professionals, too.

So you need a volunteer handbook. Does that mean you have to have it ready for that first, formal orientation meeting? And do you really have to sit there and read it out loud?

The fact is that reading a long list of policies to volunteers accomplishes little. Volunteers won't remember what you said, and the policies won't impact their behavior. It's largely a waste of time if you're trying to teach volunteers information.

"Everyone knows this stuff counts."

But here's what it does accomplish (and even our friend Denise noticed it on her first day at the new job): *When you stop and read the handbook it communicates how very important the material in the handbook is to the organization—and to the new volunteer or employee.* You draw attention to it. You shine a spotlight on it. And everyone knows that no matter what, this stuff counts.

Many companies and churches don't go to the lengths Denise's company did—they don't expect employees to read handbook policies aloud. Instead, they distribute handbooks and set a deadline by which employees must return a form stating the handbook has been read.

We'd like to suggest you adapt that procedure slightly. Distribute handbooks at your first formal orientation meeting. Also distribute a Volunteer Handbook Acknowledgement Form (page 99) that volunteers must sign and return before they're allowed to serve in their volunteer role.

But what if you're a small church? Everyone knows everyone, and it's easy to explain to people how things work and what to do. Why bother with creating a handbook full of policies everyone already knows?

Even if you're in a church of 50 members, your volunteer ministry needs written policies in a handbook. Here's why . . .

- **Policies help resolve problems and eliminate hazards.**

A friend of ours is a lifeguard at a city pool. When he was hired he thought his job would be to sit on a platform diligently watching the water, ever prepared to toss aside his whistle and clipboard and dive in to drag out a drowning swimmer.

His supervisor straightened the young man out.

"Your job is first and foremost not to rescue people who are victims of accidents or stupidity," the supervisor said. "Your job is to keep people from having accidents or doing anything stupid."

During the course of his summer the young man never once dove in to save someone. But more times than he could count he kept children from running on the slick cement around the pool and enforced rules that kept weak swimmers out of the deep water. The lifeguard discovered that the pool policies he'd at first thought were silly actually kept people safe.

Your volunteer ministry policies can accomplish the same thing: Keep volunteers from getting into deep water without realizing it.

It may seem like a perfectly logical thing for Jack Smith to drop off a couple kids from the youth group after the meeting, and since Alisa's house is near his it just stands to reason Jack will take Alisa, a 17-year-old girl, home last.

> "Your volunteer ministry policies can keep volunteers from getting into deep water."

So there Jack is in the car at night, alone with a high school junior. Not smart.

A written policy about never having an adult with a minor in a car alone could have prevented Jack from ever making this mistake by setting a boundary beyond which he couldn't go.

- **Policies clarify responsibilities.**

Knowing who is responsible to make decisions when the roof leaks is a good thing for the Sunday school teacher who stops by the building on a Saturday afternoon to pick up curriculum and notices an inch of water in the church basement.

If your volunteer handbook doesn't have a page titled, "Who You Gonna Call?" add one—fast. But do it by the title of the person responsible, not the name. When the Sunday school teacher sees she should call the "building and grounds deacon," she can then check the phone list to see who that is. Remember: Keeping the phone list and the handbook separate saves you from having to constantly update the handbook when people fill new roles or phone numbers change.

- **Policies provide stability and continuity.**

Over the course of a few years you may have a complete turnover in volunteer staff in some area of ministry. You'll still be able to deliver a consistent level of service if everyone is on the same page concerning expectations—and the policies in your volunteer handbook can deliver those expectations.

- **Handbooks will help you provide a thorough orientation.**

Encourage volunteers to highlight items as they read through their handbooks. Then, at your next team meeting, discuss the policies—answering questions and highlighting the policies that you think are most important.

You'll be able to move through the material more quickly if everyone has read the handbook, and you'll know if something in the handbook is unclear because those are the sections that will generate the most questions.

Be sure volunteers write their names in their handbooks, too. Be clear that every volunteer is to have a copy of the handbook, to read it, and to affirm that he or she has read the entire document.

And make sure you keep track of who's read the handbook. You'll need that information when it's time to update or add a policy and issue a new handbook or replace selected pages in handbooks.

Also, your insurance company may offer discounts on liability coverage if you can demonstrate that no volunteer is placed until after having read policies about issues like child safety, sexual harassment, and confidentiality. Check with your insurance provider to see if any such discount is available to you.

When volunteers turn in their Volunteer Handbook Acknowledgment Form, keep the signed forms in their files. This documentation may be helpful should your church ever face civil litigation.

Feel free to adapt the Volunteer Handbook Acknowledgment Form to fit your unique situation. It's merely a template; have it reviewed by your legal counsel and make whatever changes are appropriate. Also, be mindful a signed form may have no impact whatsoever in the case of litigation . . . but it is one way to prove you attempted to communicate important policies.

Still not convinced? Then think about this . . .

• **Policies make managing a program easier.**

Because policies include the "what," often the "why," and occasionally the "how" of a decision, you don't have to rethink situations each time they arise. Some of that has already been done and formalized; you can simply determine if circumstances warrant making an exception.

Look—every volunteer ministry makes policy decisions frequently. They just don't call them "policy decisions" or write them down. It may be that your developing policies is as easy as reviewing the decisions your leadership has made lately, and getting those decisions down on paper. One example of how that might look is on page 107. It's a list of policies related to the nursery at First Christian Church—see how many decisions have been captured in simple policy statements.

Be proactive, too. Lots of policies are developed because

something has gone wrong and nobody wants it to happen again. So do this: Think about what might reasonably be expected to go wrong and decide how you'll handle it now—before the bus breaks down, the power goes out, or the hurricane hits. Put your plan in writing.

Your handbook of policies won't be an imposition on your volunteers. In fact, your volunteers will welcome having the clarity and reassurance of the handbook.

Types of Policies

A word about policies before you begin writing them for your handbook: Policies are not all created equal. Some are non-negotiable, and others are very negotiable. Let's take a look at both categories.

> "You need to always be meeting or exceeding the requirements of the law."

Non-negotiable policies

Some policies reflect local or federal laws. That you're working with volunteers rather than paid staff, or operating in a church rather than a company, doesn't change the law. It's real—and you need to always be meeting or exceeding the requirements of the law.

In Romans 13 we read,

Everyone must submit himself to the governing authorities, for there is no authority except that which God has established. The authorities that exist have been established by God. Consequently, he who rebels against the authority is rebelling against what God has instituted, and those who do so will bring judgment on themselves. (Romans 13:1-2)

If local building codes require you to not have more than 120 people in a room, don't let the 121st person through the door. If the Health Department insists you maintain your church kitchen at a certain level of cleanliness because you serve meals to the homeless twice per week, amaze the Health Inspector with how the floor sparkles and the food preparation meets every requirement.

And if federal law says you shouldn't sexually harass someone, don't do it. Ever. Period.

In some cases churches are able to bypass or be exempted from statutes that apply elsewhere—but why would you want to not measure up? If civil policies are about respecting the rights and dignity of people, be very, very careful about deciding they don't apply to you.

When you create your handbook and review it with volunteers, be clear that non-negotiable policies are just that: non-negotiable. Breaking them will result in being separated from volunteer opportunities in the church at minimum, and in some cases civil prosecution.

Negotiable policies

Some policies are simply principles you've put in place to guide action. They're not laws. They can be bent or broken without dramatic consequences.

For instance, if your policy is to have Sunday school teachers sign on for six-month terms of service, that's a decision you've already made. You might have created that policy to help ensure consistency for the children in the Sunday school.

But if a woman who's taught Sunday school for just four months were to suddenly lose her husband, you wouldn't try to force her to complete her term of service. You could easily make an exception—and probably should make an exception.

The point: These policies are set in wet cement. Exceptions can be made, but be judicious about how often and for what reasons you make exceptions. In general, make exceptions rarely and only for good cause. A policy that's not applied fairly and consistently will quickly become a point of conflict.

Here are categories of negotiable policies you'll want to include in your handbook:

How-to-get-things-done policies

These policies concern themselves with how tasks are completed. For example, the volunteer serving as the church secretary will undoubtedly get phone calls—and those calls need to be handled professionally. One policy you might put in place for your entire volunteer ministry is that every phone call, e-mail, or other message must be responded to within 24 hours.

If the volunteer serving in the church office happens to miss the mark and returns a call two days late, will the volunteer be fired? No—but it will be cause for a discussion and review of the job expectation so the volunteer understands the importance of the policy.

When-to-get-things-done policies

If your volunteers are reimbursed for expenses, someone in the accounting office wants those expense reports on time so he or she can close out the month.

Don't expect volunteers to have the same sense of urgency about your deadlines that you have—unless you tell them those deadlines are important.

What-to-do-and-not-do policies

These policies explain what volunteers can and cannot do. They set boundaries that help define what appropriate relationships look like.

These policies may be negotiable or non-negotiable; it depends on what boundary will be crossed.

A negotiable policy may involve whether a Sunday school teacher can buy a child a birthday present. The answer: Certainly—but only if it's small, and only if it's something the teacher does for every child in his class.

These policies may also identify a boundary that a volunteer cannot cross, such as "borrowing" offering money as a short-term loan, or inviting a student to go on a date. Crossing that sort of boundary elevates the issue to a non-negotiable policy.

What Should Be in Your Volunteer Orientation Handbook?

First, here's what *shouldn't* be there . . .

- Don't include organizational charts with names attached, phone lists, or anything else that's likely to need frequent updating. Ideally, you'll make changes in the handbook infrequently, and only when there's an addition or change in policies.

- Don't include anything that you don't intend to enforce. Companies have found that if they're lax about enforcing one part of an employee handbook (drug testing, for instance) then employees can be justified in assuming that other policies (taking unannounced vacations, for example) won't be enforced, either. You won't find yourself in court trying to fire volunteers because they didn't give two weeks' notice before heading off to Montana to go elk hunting, but the principle has merit. If you aren't going to take something in your handbook seriously, don't include it.

- Don't include the little stuff. If your pet peeve is when nursery workers forget to empty the diaper pail on Sundays, the place to deal with that is in a training session with nursery workers. Don't add a separate section in the handbook about WHAT TO DO WITH STINKY STUFF. Use your handbook to focus on the larger, more general issues.

> "Anything vague or cute should be cut."

- Anything vague or cute should be cut from your handbook. Humor is fine, and if it's part of your culture and you encourage it, you'll want to let it shine through. But don't let humor or cuteness interfere with the clarity of your handbook. Write to ensure you're not misunderstood. Use crisp, definite language. Say what you mean.

- Any specifics that are covered in job descriptions. Keep things simple: Let job descriptions speak for themselves.

That's what shouldn't clutter up a handbook.

But what should be in a handbook? And how do you keep your handbook from becoming a 300-page manual that few can lift and no one will read?

You'll greatly increase the value of your handbook if you use it to communicate the information that doesn't change—and you communicate the information briefly.

That is, you don't need to deliver the last word on who brings the donuts on Sunday mornings, and how you really should bring a variety that includes cream filled, nut covered, glazed, and also plain donuts; that a box of glazed donuts might be easy but will fail to please some of the teachers—and you can probably guess which ones they are, isn't it obvious?—and, by the way, don't forget the cinnamon twists: They're the director's favorites.

Just say snacks are available in the teachers' prep room on Sundays. Be brief. Be clear.

Here are eleven areas you should address in your policy handbook. They're in no particular order; they're all important.

1. Your ministry's mission, vision, and values

Include the mission statement, vision statement, and a brief description of what you value. Be sure what you include is consistent with your overall church's values, mission, and vision.

If your ministry places a special emphasis on teamwork, communication, diversity, quality, or another value, briefly define that value and describe what it looks like in your setting.

2. The general organizational structure of your ministry

Without naming names, describe who reports to whom. This is your chance to proactively re-route most phone calls away from yourself, so be thorough!

Provide the organizational chart here; the easily updated phone list you hand out with the handbook will supply the details. You did remember to identify each person on your phone list by ministry role, too, didn't you? If not, add that information. It doesn't help if in the handbook you instruct teachers to call their section supervisors as identified on the phone list and then the phone list doesn't say who does what.

3. Dress codes and other behavior standards

If staff members aren't to use tobacco or alcohol while serving a term as a volunteer, say so. If that prohibition extends only to the times volunteers are actually serving, say that instead. Be clear where you can be, especially on behaviors that are black and white, done or not done.

Some of those standards may be abundantly clear, such as . . .

- No pierced body parts visible (other than simple earrings),

- No visible tattoos, and

- No fad clothing (for example, grunge or gothic).

It's trickier when the behaviors involve interpretation, such as what constitutes "modest" apparel. Imprecise terms such as "modestly" and "professionally" leave a lot of gray area.

How high can a skirt go and still be modest? How tight can jeans be and still be professional? Who decides if someone has violated the policy, and who's going to tell the offender? How should it be resolved?

Your policy isn't the place to nit-pick about the number of inches a hemline can rise above the knee, or precisely what a T-shirt slogan can or can't say. Your goal isn't to create a comprehensive rulebook, but to briefly communicate standards.

Most volunteers are ready and eager to cheerfully comply with standards—once the standards are clear. So if you use vague words, supply a couple of examples of what you mean. Volunteers will get the message.

And here's a tip: Should someone show up to teach in clothing that's inappropriate, ask a leader of the same sex to take the offender aside and calmly suggest that the individual change clothes and then return to the volunteer role. Be careful not to communicate condemnation or spiritual superiority, but instead a gentle, caring redirection to what "modest" means in the context of the volunteer setting.

4. Equipment and facility usage

Is it okay to use the church's copier to make a copy of your son's social studies report? Is it okay to use the computer in the accounting office to look up possible condo rentals in Vail for next winter? to look up stock prices? to look up porno sites?

What exactly are your policies regarding the use of the church's equipment and facilities? Your handbook is a great place to explain them.

5. The performance evaluation system

When and how do you evaluate volunteers? Describe the process so there are no surprises later. Having this spelled out is reassuring to volunteers because it communicates you care enough to actually come see what they're doing and to help them improve. A performance evaluation system says you value them and their work.

6. Safety information

Include evacuation plans, severe storm plans, the location of first aid kits, and a notification system to use in case someone is hurt. Be especially brief here; when there's blood on the floor the average person will remember just one or two things, not a complex maze of instructions.

And don't forget to include standards about the situations in which adults can be with teenagers or children. What seems harmless at the time can take on sinister tones when viewed under the harsh light of a police inquiry or the direct questions of parents. Your policies can keep volunteers from getting themselves into trouble.

7. Security information

Do children need to be checked in and out? What's your system for that? Must outside doors be secured in some areas? Who has permission to activate or deactivate an alarm system? Spell out—briefly and clearly—what principles and standards you're maintaining in the effort to keep people secure.

Include a statement about which positions require background or police record checks and never, ever fail to enforce this policy. List what other screening, training, and supervision your church provides, too. And include a church policy statement on confidentiality and privacy.

8. Logistics

Are volunteers to park in a certain spot so visitors can have the closest parking spots? Is there a specific system for reserving audio-visual equipment or getting a broken chair repaired? Where are mops and buckets kept? A brief review of this information will help volunteers fit into the church's procedures.

9. Grievance procedures

Not everything will go smoothly 100 percent of the time. When a volunteer feels he or she has a legitimate complaint against a supervisor, what should the volunteer do?

Jesus provides some excellent guidelines for conflict resolution in the book of Matthew.

Consider . . .

> But I tell you that anyone who is angry with his brother will be subject to judgment. Again, anyone who says to his brother, "Raca," is answerable to the Sanhedrin. But anyone who says, "You fool!" will be in danger of the fire of hell. Therefore, if you are offering your gift at the altar and there remember that your brother has something against you, leave your gift there in front of the altar. First go and be reconciled to your brother; then come and offer your gift. (Matthew 5:22-23)

> But I tell you: Love your enemies and pray for those who persecute you. (Matthew 5:44)

> If your brother sins against you, go and show him his fault, just between the two of you. If he listens to you, you have won your brother over. But if he will not listen, take one or two others along, so that "every matter may be established by the testimony of two or three witnesses." If he refuses to listen to them, tell it to the church; and if he refuses to listen even to the church, treat him as you would a pagan or a tax collector. (Matthew 18:15-17)

In short: Forgive, confront, seek resolution. It's a good idea to apply those principles to your situation if there's dissent in the ranks. If your policy about conflict specifies that volunteers should talk first to someone who can actually do something to resolve the situation, you'll eliminate a great deal of gossip.

10. Career development opportunities

Volunteers have careers, too. Some volunteers have several of them—one inside the church, and one outside the walls of your building.

> "In short: Forgive, confront, seek resolution."

Take Eddie for instance. On Sunday morning he's an adult class leader, taking a group of parents through a study of good parenting habits. But on Monday morning he's a medical doctor explaining to patients why they should exercise.

Eddie has two careers—one as a teacher and one as a doctor—and he wants to grow in both of them.

What opportunities can you offer Eddie that will help him grow? A master teacher mentor who will assess his teaching and facilitating skills? That will help Eddie in both his careers, so you'll find him eager to sign on.

If you can offer mentoring, training courses, a library of useful training materials, or any other development opportunities, tell volunteers about them.

11. Scheduled events and activities

Do you have quarterly training meetings? an annual banquet? staff meetings on Sunday mornings? If you have regular programming, identify it and be clear about whether attendance is encouraged, optional, or mandatory.

Handbooks Are Not All That's Needed

Don't think distributing a handbook of policies completes the orientation process. Handbooks are helpful—but they aren't the last word in orientation.

In addition to orienting new volunteers, be sure to let existing volunteers who will work alongside the new faces know that someone is coming. Make introductions, and encourage existing volunteers to connect with new people over a cup of coffee or a donut.

Informal orientation will happen only if volunteer peers are talking. True, you don't know what the veteran volunteers might say, but they'll say it anyway—you might as well encourage the process.

Also, see that the paid or unpaid staff members who will supervise the new volunteers quickly arrange individual meetings with their new reports. The relationship volunteers have with their supervisors will make or break the volunteers' experience. It's the supervisors who will shape the volunteers' work flow and are positioned to best provide training and encouragement.

Some churches have found it helpful to create a video that includes orientation material. If done well, this can be a benefit—but it shouldn't (and can't) replace person-to-person contact.

Finally, arrange for a follow-up program in three to six months. Get the same group of volunteers back together for a "reunion" and see how they're doing in their roles. If you're in a large church it's possible they haven't talked since their formal orientation program. They'll enjoy seeing each other again and swapping stories, and you'll have the chance to administer the same test you gave them after the first orientation program.

Compare test scores and comments. You may find that something the new volunteers rated poorly on their first test is ranked highly on the second test. Use what you learn to shape future orientation programs and processes.

And here's a challenge for you to consider taking: When you've completed your orientation process, give each volunteer a copy of the Volunteer Bill of Rights you'll find on page 110. It summarizes the basic expectations volunteers should see met. Are you delivering them? Some have to do with orientation and training, some with the design of your volunteer ministry.

Transition to Training

The formal orientation program covers the big picture issues, but most of your volunteers' questions will be about their specific tasks. You probably aren't prepared to answer those questions; that's up to the volunteers' supervisors.

We'll focus on training next, and it's a piece of the puzzle that you'll find challenges you like few other areas of volunteer leadership. Training requires you to set aside your preconceptions and do a great deal of listening well before you ever begin talking.

Training Volunteers

The benefits of providing training—for you, your church, and your volunteers. Plus a great story about a hospital you won't want to visit anytime soon.

The administrator at a large hospital in the Midwest had a problem.

The hospital's maternity unit was bursting at the seams—thousands of women gave birth at the hospital each year. Business was booming, and referrals were at an all-time high. Beds were constantly full, and the nursery was constantly packed with babies.

That wasn't the problem.

The problem, the administrator nervously admitted to a researcher, was the orientation program hosted by the hospital on the first Thursday of each month. It had been organized for nearly ten years by the maternity floor Head Nurse and her assistants, and hundreds of women and their partners filled the hospital auditorium each month to be oriented about how to have a baby at the hospital.

The information was clear: what door to come in, how to fill out paperwork, what the visiting hours were, where cars could be parked after dropping off the women in labor. The audience even got a tour of the Maternity Unit, including a peek at the newborns in the nursery. And everyone left with a bag piled high with sample packs of diapers, formula, and wipes. Some lucky moms won door prizes that included new car seats and other expensive baby gear.

The problem, said the hospital administrator, was that in spite of the orientation program the admission procedure for women in labor was chaotic at best. Nobody knew how to fill out the forms or could remember which elevator took them straight to the Maternity Unit. There was no discernable difference between patients who had attended the orientation and those who hadn't.

> "The orientation was expensive, but was it working?"

The orientation was expensive, but was it working? Should it be expanded? modified? dropped altogether?

And to further complicate matters, the Head Nurse was convinced that her orientation program was the only thing keeping anarchy from breaking out on the Maternity Unit. When the administrator inquired about tweaking the program, she'd announced she had no intention of changing one word of what she considered to be a perfect program. Case closed.

So evaluating the orientation program had to happen very, very delicately.

Six weeks and a hundred interviews later, here's what was discovered: The women and partners who presented themselves at the hospital doors wanted to know just two things . . .

What's the fastest way to the Maternity Unit? Patients knew there was a dedicated elevator, but in the grips of contractions nobody could remember where it was. Nor did they care. They wanted someone—anyone—to personally escort them where they needed to go.

How can I get painkillers? Enough with the small talk and forms. Where's the anesthesiologist?

The problem with the hospital's orientation program was that it centered on what the hospital wanted people to know. It answered questions patients weren't asking. It covered material patients ultimately decided was unimportant.

Patients didn't care if it was inconvenient when they left their cars parked on the sidewalk by the emergency room entrance. Patients didn't care if forms had to be filled out singly or in triplicate. Those are things that mattered to the hospital, not the patients.

The researcher suggested that a team of volunteers should provide escorts and valet parking services to supplement or replace the orientation program. Satisfaction with the hospital would rise, and the cost of the orientation could potentially disappear.

The suggestion was never implemented.

Notice that the hospital was doing good things. The nurses stayed late once each month to meet with expectant moms and their partners—that's a good thing. They convinced hospital vendors to donate sample packs of baby stuff—that's a good thing, too. The nurses gave tours and handed out flyers and brochures by the dozen—and that's a good thing.

But they missed the mark.

Why? Because the hospital staff didn't start by identifying what the patients wanted to know.

The patients wanted to know the bare minimum a panicked person can retain about how to get to a doctor and an epidural. From the patient's perspective, that was the training material that mattered. Everything else was irrelevant.

If there's a moral to this story it would be this: Good intentions aren't enough when it comes to training. It requires careful attention to what's really needed—and not just from your perspective.

"Good intentions aren't enough when it comes to training."

The Cost of Training

We couldn't track down who said it first, but we spotted the saying on a bumper sticker: "If you think education is expensive, try ignorance."

It's true, isn't it? Education is expensive. Educating your

volunteers through carefully designed training sessions is expensive—but consider what it costs if you let them operate in the dark.

- What might happen if a nursery attendant doesn't understand the proper ways to provide security for babies?

- What might happen if an elementary teacher doesn't know how to apply loving correction?

- What might happen if a youth volunteer doesn't see anything wrong with letting the kids go unchaperoned at the youth lock-in?

- What might happen if someone ushering thinks nobody will notice if he slips away from his post to grab a cup of coffee with friends over in the Hospitality Café?

- What might happen if . . . ?

Clearly ignorance is not bliss—not when it comes to working with volunteers.

Why Training Is Worth the Effort—and Cost

It's how you build in excellence.

When you embrace the idea of training, you get to decide how excellent your programming will be. If you don't do training, you take what you can get.

Think about it: If you've placed appropriate people in volunteer roles, you know they're capable. There's at least a good chance they can accomplish the job set before them.

And they're motivated—they signed up, went through interviewing and placement, and completed orientation. They want to deliver great service.

But there's a lot they don't know, and in any volunteer role what you don't know can hurt you—or at least hurt your performance. Your volunteers will stumble along doing their best, but it's completely possible for them to make the same

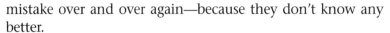

mistake over and over again—because they don't know any better.

If you want excellence, training is worth the effort.

It's how you make volunteers happy.

Training is also worth the effort if you're looking for happy volunteers.

Nobody likes feeling incompetent, especially when the job is important. To you a volunteer stuffing inserts into bulletins may not look like he's doing anything complicated, but you're wrong. He's given up a morning with his wife to be at the church, sitting in a corner of the office, sticking pieces of paper inside a bulletin cover. His back is acting up because he's sardined at a table that isn't really comfortable, but he's not complaining. He's praying for the people who will receive the bulletins on Sunday morning.

He's not doing grunt work. He's doing ministry.

So imagine how happy he'll be if, as he wraps up the 500th bulletin cover, you point out that the yellow insert should have gone in before the brown one.

Want happy volunteers? Training is worth the effort.

It's how you hold down costs.

True, training volunteers can be expensive in terms of preparation time and photocopies. But imagine what it would cost if you had to hire professionals to do everything volunteers do?

People wiser than us have pointed out that if you want to do a job in the most cost-effective way, you need to clearly understand what you're trying to accomplish before you get started and decide how you'll proceed. That's true with building highways, and it's true with trimming the church lawn.

Don't let people learn from trial and error. You'll pay for each error.

Want to hold down costs? Training is worth the effort.

It's how you respect the calling of volunteers.

If you truly believe that God brings volunteers into ministry roles so they can grow closer to him and use their spiritual gifts, abilities, skills, and passions, your job is to help them. You'll want to encourage and equip them. And that means providing training opportunities so they get ever more capable in service.

Want to cooperate with God's purposes? Training is worth the effort.

There's no reason to fail to provide training, just excuses.

If you're directing the volunteer ministry in your church, you'll find yourself in the role of "trainer." You may be training volunteers who report directly to you, or training other ministry leaders how to train the volunteers who report to them. However your church ministries are configured, training will play a significant role in them.

Let's consider your role of trainer.

Trainers—What Do They Do, Exactly?

If your mental image of a trainer is someone who's standing in front of a room, holding a clipboard and speaking to rows of attentive learners, you've got some challenges ahead of you.

That view of training—the expert lecturing students—is both out of date and ultimately ineffective.

Here's the thing: There are talented people who make careers out of becoming ever more expert trainers. They study how people learn, and how to set up environments where adults are best able to focus and retain knowledge. They study learning styles, presentation styles, and what tools can bridge the two. Every day they study what works, what doesn't work, and what could work better.

> "Don't worry—
> you're up to
> the challenge."

And to think: Training is just one of the hats you have to wear!

Don't worry—you're up to the challenge. Training, at heart, is teaching—and if you're like most volunteer ministry leaders you've had considerable experience helping others learn new information and build new skills.

Effective training really breaks down to five key responsibilities, each of which you can handle, and most or all of which you've already mastered.

See for yourself:

Responsibility 1: Prepare and prepare some more.

The first place you'll do preparation is the training material itself.

We'll dig into how to develop appropriate content for training sessions later in this volume, but for now realize that effective training takes considerable effort and focus. It's not something you throw together at the last minute.

Plus, you need to prepare the volunteers themselves. In the sessions you lead you'll put them at ease and share why the training they'll experience is important. As a trainer it's your job to capture the volunteers' attention; don't assume they'll just give it to you. It's your job to create (and maintain) a compelling learning environment.

Responsibility 2: Explain the skill or task you're addressing in training.

Let's say you're showing office volunteers how to operate the photocopy machine. The volunteers are responsible for creating, designing, and copying flyers for an upcoming event. Operating "Ol' Jambox" (as your antiquated machine is affectionately known) is a skill they'll need.

The trick is for you to break down the information into manageable bites and build on information the volunteers already have.

Responsibility 3: Show as well as tell.

It's one thing to hear about how to do a task, and another to see it demonstrated. Help volunteers grasp how to operate the office photocopy machine by actually pulling open drawers and pushing buttons. Show volunteers where the paper goes in, where it comes out, and how to find the fire extinguisher if Ol' Jambox decides to burst into flames—again.

Responsibility 4: Involve volunteers in actually doing the task or skill.

Volunteers' confidence grows when they have the opportunity to perform the tasks or practice using the skill while you're there to coach them through it. A trainer learns to monitor closely at first, then gradually step back as volunteers develop competence and good habits. You'll help volunteers process their newfound information as they work with the copier.

Responsibility 5: Review and retrain.

As volunteers operate Ol' Jambox, give them encouragement and honest feedback. Maybe one of the volunteers seems to have a feel for communicating with the quirky copier, and is able to coax a ream of forms out of the machine before papers start to jam. Perhaps another volunteer needs to quit stabbing the buttons hoping to intimidate the machine into working at all.

Review what volunteers have learned, and provide the tweaking—retraining—that's required to get everyone up to speed.

That's it: a trainer's job in a nutshell.

Trainers are teachers—teachers who work with adults, and who facilitate learning by using hands-on, active learning. That's a win for everyone, because skills and information are more easily learned and retained by volunteers when experienced in a practical, active way.

Plus, it's way more fun to teach!

As we consider how to design a training session, see how interaction and involvement are woven into the process. They're there for a reason.

FOUR
How to Design Training Sessions That Work

Nine strategic steps that let you deliver on-target training sessions—every time.

An effective training session starts long before volunteers walk into the room, fill out their nametags, and mingle by the coffeepot. The actual session is the part of the process people associate with training, but it's only the tip of the iceberg.

If you experience a training session that's informative, effective, and useful, you can bet the trainer began preparing for the session weeks before.

That's the decision you have to make first: Will you be disciplined in preparing for training sessions? If not, seek out someone who will, and delegate the training function of your ministry to that person. Training is too important to hope that when you wing it something good will come out of the experience.

> "Training requires thoughtful preparation."

Training requires thoughtful preparation. There's no shortcut.

Assuming you believe that training is worthy of your best effort, go through the following nine-step process to create on-target sessions that accomplish your goals.

Step 1: Determine the Need

What do people want and need to know? This is the step skipped by the hospital that was providing elaborate—and largely meaningless—training to expectant mothers.

Some experts call it "gap analysis": identifying the space between the existing experience and knowledge of your volunteers, and what experience and knowledge they'll need to accomplish a task.

It's that gap between what they've got and what they'll need that training seeks to fill—so you'd better do a good job identifying the gap. Providing training for the wrong experiences and knowledge is useless.

Consider the experiences of a friend of ours named Brian . . .

Brian was determined to make his school basketball team after failing to make the squad the previous year. "I was the last guy cut," Brian remembers. "It about crushed me."

So Brian attended basketball camps and spent afternoons at city courts where he sharpened his skills in game after game of pick-up ball.

"I'd always been a timid player," Brian says, "afraid to get under the hoop and mix it up. But if you're not willing to throw a few elbows you got eaten alive out on the public courts—especially the ones where the really good street players hung out. Nobody called fouls out there; it was a matter of pride. You either intimidated the other players or you died."

> "Brian watched—and learned."

Brian watched—and learned. He mimicked better players and learned how to shave half-steps while driving to the basket. He practiced moves that eventually had him winning instead of watching, taking high-fives from players he respected.

Brian went from timid to intimidating. "I learned to take it to the bucket," he says. "Get in my way and you were going down. I could usually get around you, over you, under you—something. But if I couldn't—well, I went through you."

So Brian felt strong when he tried out for the varsity team his junior year.

"I put on a show for them right off the start," he says. "Once I had the ball I angled and cut my way to the basket.

Every time. I smoked the defense during our first scrimmage. Scored 28 points."

Brian went home sure he had impressed the coaches. And he had—they cut him from the tryouts the next day.

Stunned, Brian asked the head coach what had happened. He pointed out that he wasn't the player he'd once been, timid and shy. Now he was a scorer—and he'd proved it.

That's when the coach gave Brian the news: Brian hadn't been cut from the squad the previous year because he lacked the ability to score, or because he'd been weak on hitting the boards and bringing down rebounds. He'd been cut because the coach didn't think he was a team player.

And if anything, Brian was even worse now. He didn't pass, he didn't run plays, he just hot-dogged the ball and left the rest of the team standing around.

Brian had trained hard to improve—but in the wrong skill.

"I never made the team until my senior year," Brian says. "But I was high man on assists that year."

Ouch. Brian had done a poor job with "gap analysis."

Do your needs analysis carefully. Fixing the wrong thing doesn't move volunteers ahead; it leaves them further behind.

And it's important you not confuse activity with accomplishment when it comes to training. Holding training sessions is only useful if there are appropriate outcomes (ones that help fill the gap) that can be demonstrated by the volunteers. Do they know how to operate the photocopy machine after your training session? That's actually easy to determine: Have them show you how to do it.

> "Ask volunteers what they need to know."

Did they truly learn? Also easy: Call them back in a week and ask them to demonstrate their retained skills.

Volunteers themselves may help you with needs analysis. Ask volunteers to tell you what they need to know. Ask their supervisors what they need to know. You may get a glimmer of what's needed when you interview or survey the people served by your volunteers. If Jack thinks he's doing a great job delivering Christian education and his supervisor agrees, but children aren't learning anything, there's a gap—and a need for training!

When thinking about training, start by determining what the volunteers need to be doing differently as a result of the training. Is the need they're experiencing one that can be met through more information? through using a new skill? through a shift in attitude?

How you understand the need sets the course of the entire training session.

Step 2: Establish Objectives

Okay, let's be realistic: A one- or two-hour training session isn't going to completely revolutionize how Jack teaches in the fourth-grade class. One session isn't going to somehow toggle on Jack's effectiveness switch so kids start learning, especially if you're going to present the training to the entire Sunday school teaching staff and can't focus solely on Jack.

But you can do this: Write clear objectives you think you can achieve given the number of learners, the various settings in which they deliver Christian education, and the amount of time you have for the session.

> "Narrow down what you're trying to accomplish."

Narrow down what you're trying to accomplish. Instead of "figure out how to have every teacher become effective in engaging children and doubling students' learning" (lofty, but not probable), zero in on one skill classroom teachers could use to improve their teaching. Classroom management techniques, perhaps, or skills related to using active-learning techniques.

Write behavioral objectives—what volunteers will be able to do at the end of the training session. It may have to be demonstrated through role plays (as in the case of Jack dealing with his students), but be certain that volunteers can do a show and tell with the new skill or information.

And be absolutely certain that possessing the new skill or information will help address the need you identified in step 1.

Step 3: Create the Evaluation Tool

Decide how you'll have volunteers prove they've "gotten it" at the end of the training session, and create that evaluation tool now. Be specific, and design it so it answers the question, "How will volunteers prove they've achieved the session's objectives?"

Seems backward, doesn't it? Why create the test before you've created the training session?

It's because the evaluation tool pinpoints your destination. It identifies where you want to end up at the end of the session when volunteers are walking out the door. It measures the outcomes you identified in step 2.

Step 4: Brainstorm the Training Session

"Arrange your outline in a logical order."

Working alone or with colleagues, think about the evaluation tool you've identified. Write it out and tape it to the far end of a white board. Then, with a marker in hand, ask, "Given where the learners are now, what do they need to learn to let them pass this evaluation exercise?"

The answer to your question—the steps and skills—are the content of the training session. You've created your session outline.

Step 5: Dig in—It's Time to Write a Session

Arrange your outline in a logical order. Before you flesh it out, though, ask yourself the following questions. Your answers will help you shape *how* you deliver the content of the training session to your volunteers.

And be warned: This will take some time.

You're pausing to consider how to tailor the training session so it powerfully connects with your volunteers—all your volunteers.

Think of it this way: Pretty much anyone can wander onto a softball diamond. Anyone can walk to the pitcher's mound. Anyone can stand there, face the catcher crouching behind home plate, and throw a softball to the catcher. It's only 46 feet, so it's not terribly difficult.

You lob the ball, and it gets to the catcher—either in the air, on the bounce, or rolling along in the dirt. If you lower the definition of "pitching" far enough, anyone can do it.

But to sizzle that ball into the strike zone, blistering it into the catcher's mitt—that takes some effort. It requires practice and preparation. And it's the sort of pitch that gets fans up on their feet and cheering.

Don't just settle for lobbing training sessions at your volunteers. Do what's necessary to make each one spectacular, streaking straight across home plate.

> "Without motivation, there's no lasting learning."

It comes down to delivery—and your answers to these questions will help you find and hit the strike zone every time.

- **How will I present this session in such a way that volunteers care?**

Without motivation, there's no lasting learning—so always establish to a volunteer's satisfaction why a skill must be mastered or information learned. What problem of the volunteer's will it solve to enthusiastically embrace the work required to accomplish the outcomes set for this training?

- **How can I build on information volunteers already possess?**

Do you actually know what people already know? You can establish this by using a pretest at the beginning of the training session and then adjusting the session depending on what you discover.

Clearly, this is a risky maneuver. You may discover that half your volunteers could lead the session, and the other half have no clue about the topic. More likely you'll find that volunteers fall along a continuum stretching from incompetent to very competent.

For instance, our Sunday school teacher friend, Jack, probably already knows something about classroom discipline. What he knows may be wrong, or it may be right, but he knows something.

If you're a beginning trainer, you may wish to skip pretests for a few sessions until your confidence builds. But then by all means use them—they'll let you know precisely how to meet the needs of your specific audience.

> "If you're lucky you may find you have a valuable resource in the room."

And—if you're lucky—you may find you have a valuable resource in the room that you can tap to make the training session even stronger.

That's what happened to a colleague of ours who, while he was a sophomore in Bible college 30 years ago, was asked to prepare a two-hour training session for a large multi-college retreat.

Here's his story . . .

The Accidental Professor

"I was leading a training session on hermeneutics, which is the science of interpretation—in this case the interpretation of Scripture. My audience included about a hundred college students, and I assumed that very few of them had even *heard* of hermeneutics. All they knew was that I would be sharing some principles that helped with Bible study.

"On a whim I took a quick poll. I asked how many had ever heard of hermeneutics, and only one hand was raised. When I saw whose hand it was, I nearly fainted.

"That hand was connected to a man I recognized as Lewis Foster, an academic who'd helped translate the New

International Version of the Bible. How could I lead a training session on Bible study with a Harvard Ph.D. sitting in the back of the room? A Harvard Ph.D. who was fluent in every ancient language except cave drawing? Who was I kidding?

"I figured the best thing I could do was have everyone turn their chairs around and I'd let Dr. Foster lead the training," our colleague admits. "I introduced him and made the offer, but he declined and moved to the front row. He encouraged me to continue and, knees shaking, that's what I did.

"Dr. Foster paid careful attention and frequently nodded in agreement as I spoke. My credibility with the audience shot up about four thousand percent every time his head went up and down," says our colleague.

"When there were questions, Dr. Foster let me answer first, and only added something if I'd completely gotten in over my head. When the session was over he shook my hand, congratulated me on a job well done, and walked out. That was an amazingly gracious guy."

Our colleague was fortunate that Dr. Foster chose to support rather than challenge him. Not every expert is so gracious.

If you find yourself in a situation where someone in your audience is truly better informed than you, and is intent on letting everyone know it, defuse the situation by reminding your audience that everyone will have time to speak later in the session. Most people take the hint.

- **How can I address various learning styles during the training?**

There have been several attempts to categorize learning styles, and each of them agrees on this point: Talking at people isn't the way to go.

There are people who learn best by seeing a demonstration, or who learn best by diving in and trying things themselves. There are logical thinkers and people who learn best when they're interacting with others. Still other people learn best through introspection . . . or through music . . . or through experiencing nature.

How can you possibly present all of the information in each of those styles?

You can't . . . but you can make sure there's something for everyone during the training session.

If you're helping Sunday school teachers learn how to handle classroom discipline, include these elements . . .

• Have volunteers tell stories about situations that have arisen. This will snag your verbal and linguistic learners.

> "Make sure there's something for everyone during the training session."

• Ask visual learners to design a classroom setting that would minimize disruptions. Where would the teacher be? the students? What furniture would or wouldn't be in the room?

• Ask musically inclined people to suggest a theme song for the chaotic classroom. What popular song (or classic song) sums up what it's like?

• Recruit kinesthetic learners to act out a skit about a typical classroom discipline challenge.

• Suggest that logical learners brainstorm ideas about what Sunday school teachers can do to overcome the discipline challenges.

• Issue this challenge to the naturalists in your audience: What lessons are there in nature about how to deal with disruptions from children (and no, teachers can't eat their young!)?

• Give interpersonal learners the chance to work together to plan an event where people could find answers around the challenge of classroom discipline. Who would attend? What would happen?

• For intrapersonal learners, ask them to describe how they feel when children sabotage their lessons.

Will all these fit in a single training session? It will help if you have a breakout session that allows people to choose between several of the activities so they can plug in where they're most comfortable. And even if you can't accommodate every learning style, the more you can use, the more people in your audience will think you're speaking directly to them.

• **How can I make this session interactive?**

It's less difficult than you might imagine. Including peer-to-peer discussion in small groups or pair-shares is a great place to start.

Consider breaking out small groups to each tackle a piece of a carefully identified problem, with each group then coming back with its piece of the jigsaw puzzle. This is a great way not only to be interactive, but to build ownership of the solution that eventually emerges.

Look for places to effectively use activities, exercises, discussions of case studies, team building or team work, brainstorming—they're all ways to include interactive learning.

Picture the person who'll attend who's most likely to be thinking of something else. Maybe it's Jerry, who always appears to be taking notes, but you know he is actually filling out work-related expense reports. Or Samantha, who drums her fingers and fidgets if she's forced to sit still for more than ten minutes.

Here's your goal: Design a training session that Samantha can tolerate and that will have Jerry checking his watch when the session ends, wondering where the time went.

• **How can I intentionally encourage volunteers in the context of this training session?**

What will you say or do that affirms volunteers in their service and faithfulness? Saying "thanks for coming" is a good start, but you'll have more opportunity as the training session unfolds. Add to this list . . .

• Know the names of volunteers when they arrive. Greet them by name—before they fill out nametags.

- Know what each volunteer does in ministry so you can ask specific questions and keep the training relevant.

- Affirm individuals for their contributions.

- Pray for individuals, asking God to bless them.

Once volunteers are serving in a ministry role, occasional training sessions may be the only face-to-face time you have with some volunteers. Don't miss the chance to remind them that what they do is ministry, and that their ministry is appreciated.

> **"Affirm individuals for their contributions."**

- **How can I encourage volunteers to grow in their relationship with Jesus in the context of this training session?**

Remember one of the core values of volunteer leadership: One outcome of participating as a volunteer needs to be growth in the volunteer's relationship with Jesus.

Never lose sight of this value! Let it slip from view and you're simply recruiting people to do jobs. You're no longer involving them in significant ministry that changes lives—including the volunteer's own life.

Ways you can encourage relational growth with Jesus at a training session include . . .

- Praying with the volunteers.

- Asking volunteers what impact their volunteer experience is having on their relationship with Jesus. Let them tell you!

- Sharing a devotion together, perhaps one prepared by one of the volunteers.

What else could you do? With your content outline and your answers to the questions listed above, you're ready to finish creating the training session. Keep in mind the limitations you face regarding time and space (no sense planning to illustrate teamwork by playing a full-court volleyball game if you'll meet in a classroom), and go to it. Craft a workshop that covers the material and integrates the insights you gained by thinking about how you'll shape the delivery of your training session.

Step 6: Develop a Great Opening

How you launch into your training session is very important. It's when you reel in your volunteers and get them focused and concentrating, or it's the precise moment you lose them—maybe for the entire session.

Because of that, be very intentional about how you begin your session.

A word of caution: Be wary of humor. If your joke falls flat, or your humor somehow offends a volunteer, you're sunk.

A stronger opening will be some way to illustrate the point that the subject matter you'll cover together will solve a problem experienced in the volunteers' lives. Establish that the training is relevant and there's a benefit, and you're home free.

> "Be wary of humor."

Step 7: Decide on an Icebreaker to Use in Your Session

Even if you suspect all your volunteers know each other, icebreakers are a good idea at the beginning of your session. Why? Because they do three important things:

- They focus attention. Your volunteers are tired, busy, and at least partially wishing they could be doing other things. When you get them actively involved you force volunteers to be present in the moment.

- They're fun. Ask most volunteers what they expect to experience at a training session and you'll wait a long time before you hear "fun." That's because the expectation is that training is boring. Not true! Start your session out on the right foot by exceeding volunteers' expectations immediately with a few minutes of good, clean fun!

- And, if the volunteers truly hate icebreakers, you unite them against a common enemy: you! Perhaps this is a bit overstated, but if you're enthusiastically asking volunteers to do something that stretches them past their comfort level, they'll all be on the same page. You can build from there by acknowledging their willingness to try new things, and promising you'll never again ask each person to sing a verse of his or her favorite show tune.

Four Fool-Proof, Easy-Prep, No-Fail Icebreakers

Enjoy!

Find the Fib

Ask each volunteer to tell three stories about his or her life that highlight something nobody at the meeting knows—except one of the stories is a fib.

This is easier for new people whose history is largely unknown, but everyone has something from their childhood that isn't generally known. A first job, an unusual skill, an odd experience while on vacation; they're all grist for the mill.

Have volunteers form groups of three or four and take turns sharing stories. Then, after a volunteer talks, ask the other group members to vote on which story was a fib. Following the vote, let the storyteller reveal the truth.

Guess the Pet

This is a simple icebreaker that uses nametags. In addition to writing his or her name, ask each volunteer to also write the name of a childhood pet. After all the volunteers have arrived, form volunteers into groups of four and try to guess what sort of animal the pet was.

This icebreaker finally rewards the person who once named a pet boa constrictor "Fluffy."

Decipher the Code

Another nametag icebreaker. In addition to writing his or her name, ask each volunteer to also write a number that has significance in his or her life.

For instance, if a woman was married on May 23, 1987, the number written would be 52387. If a man's childhood home was 1011 Pennway Lane, the number might be 1011. After all the volunteers have arrived, form volunteers into groups of four and try to decipher what the numbers mean by asking yes and no questions.

Brush with Greatness

Amazingly fun—but it takes a bit of explaining.

The goal is to have each volunteer consider some connection he or she has to someone great (or at least famous) and to share it. The vaguer the connection, the better.

For instance, "I used to babysit for George Clooney" is strong, but "My uncle was once knocked out by a stray golf ball hit by President Ford" is stronger. You'll be amazed at the life some of your volunteers have led.

Step 8: Practice

Never let the time you stand up in front of a group of volunteers be the first time you've run completely through a training session. Practice walking through the session at least twice to test the timing of the activities and to be sure your notes are clear to you.

Some ministry leaders actually do the entire training session with peers to get their feedback.

Also, this is a good time to think about how you'll set up the location where you'll be doing the training session. Do you need audio or visual equipment? Will you need to be able to control the lighting? Do the chairs need to be set up in any particular configuration or removed altogether? Are there props for you to gather, or people who will be working with you in presenting the material? snacks or notepads and pens to have available? nametags to fill out before volunteers arrive?

Logistics are part of the practice session. Be sure you know what you'll need, and have it ready to go before the eleventh hour. The eleventh hour is reserved for prayer and whatever crisis comes up to throw you off track.

Step 9: Ask for and Value Feedback

Build two feedback loops into your training sessions. The first is already in place: the ability or inability of the volunteers to do what was set as an objective. If your training was effective, it should have had an impact on their abilities to meet the objective.

But use another feedback loop, too: surveys from volunteers who have gone through the training session.

A sample training session evaluation begins on page 101. Adapt it to suit your situation, but please note that unless you include open-ended questions to prompt a candid evaluation, you won't learn much from surveys. If you train enough volunteers at a time to make it practical for volunteers to believe their responses can be anonymous, remove the opportunity for volunteers to report their names. If you have ten or fewer volunteers in a session, they probably doubt they can stay anonymous anyway, so ask for names.

Those nine steps will guide you through designing on-target training sessions, but there are still things you could profit from knowing. Among them are the two dozen tips for trainers we've gathered from top-notch trainers from around the country and included in the next chapter.

Read through the list with a highlighter in hand. Mark those nuggets that you know would improve your training sessions or your skills as a trainer.

How to Get Volunteers to Actually Show Up for Training Sessions

Frank was busy. Things came up for Sarah. Jeff was unexpectedly called out of town on a job-related trip. Terri was on vacation. Joni's kids got sick. The in-laws dropped by unannounced for a visit at Mike's house. Hannah forgot. Dirk's dog died.

Host training sessions long enough and you'll be convinced there's no such thing as a new excuse—until you hear one. And you will hear one. It's frustrating to prepare training sessions and have people who have agreed to come—and who need the training—not show up.

Here are six things you can do to prompt higher attendance . . .

1. Realize it's true: Sometimes things *do* come up.

Very few of us have perfect attendance for anything. Be graceful when volunteers encounter illnesses, broken water heaters, emergency dental visits, and other schedule-changing events.

2. Be sure training is an up-front expectation.

Outline what's expected in terms of training in the job description. Mention it at meetings. Talk about it in newsletters. And always connect training with the benefits that come from it.

3. Provide lots of advance notice.

Schedule your meetings well in advance, and if possible make them consistent. It's easier to clear a spot on the calendar if it's predictable, such as the last Sunday evening of each month.

4. Remove obstacles.

Provide child care. Include a meal if the session approaches meal time. Be as adaptable and accommodating as possible.

5. Consider alternate training methods.

You probably can't get all your volunteers to set aside a full day for training. It just doesn't happen any more. If attendance for training events is slipping, perhaps you stop asking "When should we meet?" and start asking, "How would you like to receive training?"

Options include:

Mentoring—which can be arranged at the convenience of the mentor and mentoree.

On-line training—(as through Group's Church Volunteer Central) that lets volunteers log on at their convenience.

Independent study opportunities—which could include video courses, workbooks, books to read and review, and audio tapes.

Bite-size training—such as e-mails that address just one teaching skill, an answering machine with a brief training tip that volunteers can call at any hour, or five-minute meetings on Sunday mornings before a worship service or between services.

Observation/coaching—which involves a trainer watching a volunteer in action and then giving specific feedback to the volunteer.

If a volunteer opts for non-traditional training, it will increase the amount of work you—or someone on your task force or board—will have to do. But the result is better trained volunteers.

6. Ask volunteers to write one-year training plans.

Remember: Including people in a process builds buy-in to the process. Let volunteers know what training is available, what level of training is appropriate for their role, and ask them what sessions they wish to take. Hold volunteers accountable with regular check-ins.

Two Dozen Tips for Trainers

Training is art as well as science. Here are things top-notch trainers have discovered to be true—you can put them to use in your own volunteer ministry training sessions today!

Training is a bit like cooking: It involves both science and art.

When you're trying for the perfect lasagna, you've got to master the science first. The temperature of the oven, the acidity of the tomato sauce, the thickness of the noodles; that's the science. It's unforgiving and non-negotiable. Mess up how long you leave the pan in the oven and you've either got lasagna soup or lasagna jerky. Neither is anything close to the perfect lasagna.

But master the science and now you can express your art. Exactly how much cheese do you add? And what kinds of cheese? Ah—that's when you delight people lucky enough to get a dinner invitation to your house. And when you start to develop the secret of your own family recipe.

> "Training is a bit like cooking: It involves both science and art."

We hounded some excellent "cooks" to get their secrets for successful training sessions. Here are the tips they shared. Two dozen that you can serve up to make your perfect training session even better.

1. Multi-sensory learning lasts longer—so never settle for lecturing. Find ways to involve the senses, and wrap stories into your training. Emotional content also touches people in significant ways. You'll notice you can remember the joke the pastor shared as a sermon introduction far longer than you can remember the sermon itself. Take advantage of the power of story.

2. Learning is most successful when stress from environment, emotional factors, and external commitments are reduced. This is one reason that what happens in the first five minutes of your training session is so vitally important. If you can focus volunteers, convincing them to set aside their concerns for the duration of your training session, you'll see more learning happen.

Here's a technique that you can use if all else fails: Open the door into the hallway outside your room and invite all the concerns and worries being experienced by your volunteers to wait outside. Tell volunteers they can pick up their concerns after the training session is over—but for the duration those concerns will be waiting in the hall.

3. Past experience should be part of the present learning. Build on what people already know—how they already think and what they already understand—and you'll find people are quicker to accept what you say.

4. What you present first and last will be retained in a disproportionate degree. It's the way we tend to listen to each other: What's said first and last counts most. So start strong and sum up at the end; those two portions of your training are your best chance to make an impression.

5. Success reinforces learning. It's better to cover something limited and do it so volunteers experience success than to attempt to cover more and fail. Break skill training into bite-size pieces. Dumping a ton of information on volunteers just buries them.

6. Volunteers learn at different speeds. Obvious, huh? So why do we think one training session will have every volunteer emerge from the meeting on the same page and ready to go?

One benefit from having mentors work with volunteers is that there's room for individual coaching.

7. Learning and unlearning are continuous; review and practice are critical. The good news is that people are always learning. The bad news is that they're always forgetting, too. If you want volunteers to sustain learning and stay good at something, provide for practice and review opportunities.

All learning is not like riding a bicycle: You don't automatically remember. Come to think of it, riding a bike isn't like riding a bike, either. Adults who jump back on after 20 years of not riding usually fall down. The learning curve may be shortened, but there's still a learning curve.

8. There's more than one reason to provide training sessions. Here are some possible reasons you might create training sessions:

To impart knowledge—how to fill out an attendance sheet

To develop specific skills—how to share your faith story with a child

To modify attitudes—to motivate a tired team to keep on trying

To help individuals select a task—helping the youth group decide between a short-term mission project in Haiti or a ski retreat in Vail

To enable volunteers to identify with the ministry—sharing your vision and mission

To increase volunteers' self-confidence—to encourage, motivate, and help them see the positive outcomes of their work

To respond to volunteers' personal needs—to give over-busy volunteers a better understanding of time management or life balance

To accord volunteers status—training sessions communicate that volunteers are worth keeping, and keeping current

To offer them an opportunity to opt out—when a new set of expectations is coming, training lets everyone see what's going to be required

What's your purpose in having a training session?

9. Create a culture where growing in skills and knowledge is valued.
If you expect volunteers to be proactive about finding their own ways to grow in their skills and abilities, you've got to be intentional about creating opportunities for that to happen. Many of your volunteers have access to training through their companies, or through purchasing their own books and magazines. They'll be likelier to do so if you . . .

10. Set an expectation that training is part of volunteering. In each job description be clear that training sessions, workshops, and other growth opportunities are part of the job. Ask for attendance at formal sessions you conduct, but suggest that volunteers find other avenues to grow, too.

11. Model behavior you want to see in volunteers. What courses or workshops are you taking? books you're reading? mentoring you're experiencing? Talk about it enthusiastically when you're with volunteers.

12. Make training dollars available. Okay, you can't afford to send everyone to a conference this year. Can you afford to get subscriptions to appropriate magazines for each of your staff? They'll get monthly or bi-monthly reminders that you're supportive of their stretching in their abilities.

13. Make training enjoyable. Don't just drag some chairs into a circle in the church basement. Decorate around a theme. Provide child care. Send invitations. Be creative! The energy you invest will communicate the importance of training and jazz up the experience without spending a fortune to take your team to Hawaii for a beachfront training session.

14. Integrate mentoring into your training process. If a volunteer serves as a teacher, arrange for regular visits from a master teacher who'll observe and provide help reaching the next level. If a volunteer makes hospital visits, ask the hospital chaplain to team up with your volunteer for a visit or two, then talk with your volunteer about how to be even more effective. Training doesn't have to be a separate event hosted quarterly in a special room at church.

15. Build variety into your training. When you're communicating content, use as many media and methods as you're comfortable using. Keep in mind that when people hear information, they retain little of it. When they roll up their sleeves and immediately use that information, it becomes part of who they are.

Use technology that the church already owns. Find out what it takes to plug into the PowerPoint dock, and use the video projector to show film clips.

16. It's okay to repeat yourself. If you do a session on emergency evacuation procedures, consider following up your formal training with a fire drill followed by a refresher course followed by another fire drill. Over the course of a few months the information will sink deep into what your volunteers know—and what they've practiced doing. And a practice evacuation costs nothing.

17. Consider "certifying" some positions. There's nothing wrong with having "usher certification" that demonstrates that the certified usher has been through a training course, been mentored by a certified usher, and has passed a ten-question exam that includes the questions an usher is most likely to be asked.

The cost of developing a certification program? Almost nothing—just the training, the testing, and a certificate designed on your computer.

18. Build feedback loops into your training. If training sessions are characteristically you talking and everyone else listening, you may be surprised how little training is actually taking place.

The goal of training is for volunteers to retain and use information, not just to be exposed to it. Remember that talking isn't necessarily teaching, and listening isn't necessarily learning.

19. Let volunteers apply new knowledge immediately. There's a half-life on learning. Unless volunteers use it fairly quickly, it tends to slip away because it has not been applied. Be intentional about providing opportunities to apply learning quickly!

Best is to actually put new knowledge to use, but a great deal will be retained even if the best you can offer is simulation or practice sessions. Anything that moves theory down to practical application is a plus!

20. Make emotional connections. Use stories as well as statistics. If you fire off a long string of numbers you'll see eyes glaze over—fast. Mix it up, and be sure that even statistics are presented in such a way that there's an emotional response on the part of your training audience. You're looking to make an emotional connection, to build on the material being presented, and to add to other, existing interests of your audience.

21. Keep things interesting. Volunteers who have given up a Saturday for a training session will forgive almost anything except boredom. You forgot to bring a snack—no problem, everyone will live. You ran ten minutes overtime—well, you'll do better next time.

But if you're boring, you're dead. Beat boredom by being interactive; use group projects and discussions. Design your session so more than one learning style is tapped.

And personalize the training to keep it relevant. Volunteers are much more interested when you're helping them solve an immediate problem than when you're passing on information they don't see an immediate need to have.

Find a need and design training to meet it!

> "Beat boredom by being interactive."

22. Training isn't always the solution. If you have a volunteer who seems unable to be successful in a role after training, coaching, and several second chances, it's possible that volunteer will never be successful. The task may be beyond the volunteer's ability. You may have misunderstood the volunteer's abilities, skills, or passions for ministry. Move the volunteer to a new role and start over. Sometimes it's wise to cut your losses.

23. Bring snacks. Always. There's nothing like a plate of homemade chocolate chip cookies to win a training group over.

24. Use experts. A sad fact: Everyone knows you, so you must not know much. But if you find someone in a neighboring church who has the same knowledge you have, that person is an expert!

Dig for resource people willing to provide training at no (or low) cost. They're out there. A professional teacher in your church or a neighboring church can speak to classroom discipline. A counselor can share training about conflict resolution or listening. Who has expertise in your circle of acquaintances? You can often find a true expert at a local college, or involved in a local church, and get the benefit of that person's expertise for the cost of mileage reimbursement and a thank-you gift.

A caution: Knowing something doesn't mean you know how to teach it. You'll need to work with presenters to make sure they design training that's on target.

And a bonus tip:

25. Keep track. What gets measured gets reported, and what gets reported is usually what matters. Know who comes to training events and who doesn't—and keep track of attendance. If attendance is part of the volunteer's job description, immediately follow up with no-shows to find out why they missed and to arrange make-up training.

There's nothing like watching a session on video to convince a no-show that it would have been more fun to be there in person.

The cost of recording the training session? A call to borrow a video camera, asking a teenager to do the taping, and a videotape.

SIX
Training Approaches for Small Churches—and Busy People

How do you keep training sessions from overwhelming your schedule? Here are three ways to keep training in check—but still effective.

Some trainers estimate that preparing a one-hour training session can take up to 10 hours. When you consider how much research is required to do a needs analysis and then work through designing a session, that estimate doesn't seem far-fetched. In fact, it may be conservative.

So here you are, the lone person responsible for your church's volunteer ministry. Where are you going to find time to create and lead training for the dozen different volunteer jobs you have to fill?

And another question: Why should you create a formal youth leader training program when you only need to recruit, place, and train one youth volunteer? It doesn't make sense!

Except it does make sense.

> "There is never a reason for setting a volunteer up for failure."

What doesn't make sense is letting a volunteer enter a job for which he or she isn't prepared, and then letting the volunteer fail for lack of knowledge or skills. Especially when we know we could come alongside the volunteer and help that person flourish in the ministry role.

Stand firm on this point: There is never a reason for setting a volunteer up for failure. Never. If a ministry isn't ready to receive a volunteer, or a volunteer isn't ready to take on the role, don't force it. The result will be disappointment and failure all the way around.

Which means what? That you have to provide all the training?

Not necessarily.

How Specialized Does Your Training Program Need to Be?

You've got volunteers doing everything from accounting to lawn care. How much specific task-related training is worth providing?

Asking these questions will help you make that determination . . .

- Are there volunteers serving in roles that require continuing education units, licensing, or certification by the government? If so, what responsibility does the church feel for helping volunteers maintain their certification? any? all? You probably can't provide the actual training; the decision you need to make is whether you'll pay for any or all of it since the church benefits from it.

- What are logical groupings of volunteers who need training? For instance, do you have fifteen educators who could use training, but just two puppeteers? If you have time to design just a few specialized training sessions, where will you get the "biggest bang for your buck"?

- What new skills and knowledge do volunteers need to master for your ministry to reach a goal that's already in place? For instance, if the church plans to open a day care center and to utilize volunteers in some roles, there are training considerations to address before the day care's doors open for business.

- What funding is available for training?

- Is there expertise your team has developed that can be organized into training that could be provided for other churches? And if so, would charging for that training generate money to support or expand your ministry?

- What incentives are in place to encourage volunteers to seek additional training? What obstacles are in place that interfere with training? You won't be a happy camper if you prepare training sessions and nobody comes.

Here's where you probably landed after answering those questions:

You want trained volunteers, and the benefits that come with training.

Some jobs seem to require very little training.

You don't have time to train everyone.

You aren't sure what to do.

Join Donna

Welcome to the club. That's precisely where Donna found herself when she assumed the role of Director of Volunteers for her church of two hundred.

"We had most of the programs operating that a church of a thousand has," she says, "which meant we were really stretched on covering the jobs."

Donna did what she could, but some jobs went unfilled because there wasn't anyone in the church who was appropriately gifted to fill them. In other cases there were people serving, but only one or two per job category.

> "How could I possibly justify writing a training session for Matt?"

"I found myself wondering how I could possibly justify writing a training session for Matt, who was responsible for stacking chairs in our worship center after Sunday morning worship celebrations. He put the chairs on a rack and rolled the rack into a closet. What was I supposed to train him to do?"

Here's the thing: With the church sitting at an attendance of 200, Matt didn't really need a formal one-hour training session. Doing a five-minute demonstration handled it. But if the church grew to a thousand, and the ten rows of chairs multiplied into a sea of chairs, what then?

Matt would need help. How should he go about recruiting volunteers? scheduling them? supervising them?

Matt would probably need to lock up the building because he and his crew would take longer to accomplish the task. What responsibilities came with having a key to the worship center?

Matt would need to do periodic evaluations of his volunteers. How could he do that without them having a job description? And him having one as well?

Because the church was still small, Donna had the luxury of not creating a formal training session. She still needed to create a job description, provide an orientation, and train Matt to do the task, and for the moment that was enough.

But if the church grew and Matt's role changed, formal training would be needed. And the lack of it would eventually become obvious. Failing to provide in-depth training is like burying a land mine; sooner or later it will be triggered.

Because of demands on her time, Donna has found three innovative ways to provide training—including a technique she used to train Matt.

Decide if these techniques will work for you, too . . .

1. Training Sheila

"A decision to expand our Sunday morning program to include a children's church service threw us for a loop," says Donna. "None of our children's ministry team had ever actually led worship for elementary students."

So Donna called the children's worship team leader at a nearby, larger church. And after identifying who would be leading the new ministry, that person attended a month of services at the other church. "They were incredibly helpful," says Donna. "Sheila got training from their staff, and learned what worked and didn't work for them. It shortened our learning curve dramatically. Our program got up and running far quicker because of what Sheila learned."

Which raises the question: Is your church the best place to get the training your people need? Be open to calling other churches—and being called by other churches in turn. What churches in your community might be willing to help you?

Donna still needed to create job descriptions, but she was able to get some from the other church to adapt. And again—if your church is part of Group's Church Volunteer Central there's a wealth of job descriptions available for your review at www.churchvolunteercentral.com.

> "Donna called the children's worship leader at a larger church."

Donna will also need to eventually create (or have Sheila create) training sessions for additional children's church staff who come into the program, but that can wait until everyone catches their breath.

2. Training Bruce

Donna's church building sat on a corner one block away from a university campus, which meant that you might expect the congregation to have a vibrant outreach to college students.

You'd be wrong.

"Some of our members were students, but given that dorms housing more than two thousand students sat within three blocks, we weren't being very effective reaching them."

The pastor decided to launch a visitation program in the dorms. "We looked around the congregation and found we had a retired military recruiter who was worshiping with us.

He knew all the people who ran the dorms, he was used to knocking on doors, and he was passionate about his faith. Perfect, right?"

Perfect, except he didn't want the job.

"He told us he'd retired from knocking on doors. He had zero interest in doing it again, even for the church."

So Donna shifted her request. Instead of actually going on visits, would the man be willing to pass on what he knew to someone else? Would he become a trainer?

> "Perfect, except he didn't want the job."

After some deliberation, the ex-recruiter agreed, and Donna found Bruce, who was willing to go to the dorms and to build a team to go with him, but who lacked experience connecting with college students and establishing relationships.

The result was a successful program. And once it was up and running the ex-recruiter decided to take an active role after all.

Donna arranged for Bruce to receive the training he needed, but not from her. And if you're willing to isolate training into modules, you may find you don't need to do all the training, either.

Bruce needed two sorts of training: how to share his faith, and how to be comfortable inviting students to participate in a program. Donna knew how to deliver the first sort of training, but not the second. That's where the ex-recruiter came in.

In your congregation are there teachers and principals available who aren't interested in teaching a class—but they'd train teachers? Are there professional salesmen who would be willing to train your ushers how to make eye contact, shake hands, and engage people? Are there counselors who can teach your small group leaders how to actively listen? The possibilities are almost endless.

3. Training Matt

Back to the man with a chair rack and a mission . . .

Donna recognized the need for Matt to have some help, so

she encouraged him to recruit a few chair stackers who could give him a hand, learn the ropes, and then cover for him when he happened to be out of town.

Donna developed a job description, which one of the stackers—the vice-president of a multi-million dollar insurance company whose corporate office was in town—was delighted to receive. He had it framed and hung it in his office as a reminder that service, not status, was the highest calling.

And the formal training session? Donna never developed it.

"I couldn't find a skill gap," Donna reports. "This is a narrow enough task that we can cover it with OTJ—on the job training. Matt can explain the entire procedure to his helpers in about five minutes, so I'm letting orientation take care of the training."

> "Where can you use OTJ training in your volunteer ministry?"

At last look the system is doing fine—chairs get stacked and put away, and nobody has needed a training session to do it.

Where can you use OTJ training in your volunteer ministry? At what point do you need to move past it and structure formal training?

SEVEN
Track Your Training

Training isn't cheap, so get the biggest bang for your buck by tracking your volunteers' training history—and planning ahead.

You're ready to do it: Make sure every volunteer is trained. You're willing to invest time, energy, and even—perhaps—budget on creating effective training sessions. You've got a dozen or two dozen or two *dozen* dozen volunteers moving through your training sessions.

It's beginning to feel like you're running a university, not a volunteer program.

But can you remember which volunteer has taken which seminar, session, or class? Do you know if you have enough CPR-trained volunteers whose certification is current? Are there enough volunteers who've taken the driver safety course that your insurance agency insists on for adults who transport special needs kids? Do you know which training sessions are most useful for someone who's volunteering in Christian education as opposed to, say, the Christmas pageant?

Different programs in your church have different training needs. Volunteers themselves have different training needs depending on the demands of their volunteer roles or their own skill levels. Or new training may be required because somewhere along the way the requirements for being a volunteer receptionist changed, and only those with computer skills need apply.

You need to track the training you provide—on several levels.

- **You need to know which volunteers have completed specific sessions.**

If completion of specific sessions is a prerequisite for serving in certain roles (for example, "Nursery volunteers must complete the nursery orientation and the infant CPR class"), then you'd better be able to know who's done what, and when. And don't count on being able to remember.

Try this: Recite which courses you took during your last semester of high school. Now list the eight people who sat closest to you in homeroom.

Right—we didn't think you could do it. Few people can. And if you'll put a system in place to track your volunteers' ongoing participation in training, you won't need to remember. You can use those brain cells for more important things, like figuring out where you stashed your yearbook so you can look up the answers to those questions we asked you.

- **You need to know which training sessions have proven to be most helpful to your volunteers.**

If your most long-term nursery volunteers all credit Janice's training about how babies learn as their motivation for sticking with the program, that's something you want to know. And it's probably a reason you'll want every nursery volunteer exposed to Janice's training program.

"Training has an impact."

Training has an impact, and it's not only measurable by determining whether the objective was obtained. It's also measurable longitudinally, by seeing how it impacts long-term behavior and attitudes. If you have a tracking system in place you can see trends develop that will allow you to proactively place people in training sessions.

Create Tracking Systems

At minimum, create a folder for each volunteer to update which training sessions have been completed, and when. What you place in folders depends in part on where you'll keep them.

If you're planning to include the notes taken during volunteers' placement interviews and the results of background checks, you must treat folders as confidential, keep them in a locked cabinet, and monitor who has access to the keys. Your volunteers were assured of appropriate confidentiality when they were interviewed; you must maintain it.

If you're simply tracking sessions taken and ongoing notes about sessions that might be appropriate, you're probably safe having the information easily accessible. But check with legal counsel first; if all records you maintain are considered personnel files, take appropriate precautions.

And the same holds true if you use computer spreadsheets to track sessions.

How to track training your volunteers have completed

A sample Continuing Education Sheet is available for your adaptation and use on page 103. Create a sheet for each of your volunteers.

The title of the sheet is strategic; most educators are familiar with the term "continuing education," and it sets an expectation that volunteers will continue to grow in their knowledge and skills.

Plus, the term is broader than just the training sessions you offer at your church. As you'll see in the next section, continuing education can come from many sources—and it's good for you to note any that volunteers bring to your attention.

If you have a medical doctor who attends a neurology conference and spends two days learning about how children learn, do you think a distilled version of that information will be of value to your Sunday school teachers? Absolutely! Indicate the doctor's training event on her sheet; you may want to tap her expertise later to create a training session.

Of course, none of your volunteers are accustomed to reporting what happens at work when they go to church. Few of your staff will think to tell you that they were out of town for a convention that included significant training.

That's why you'll have to ask.

During the meeting when you introduce the Continuing

Education Sheet, suggest examples of how work training might apply to your church's programs and volunteers.

Some possibilities might be . . .

A police officer who receives training on child safety and can then provide insight into how your children's ministry department might be better equipped to protect children in its care,

An accountant whose continuing education class includes up-to-date information about what volunteers can and can't deduct as charitable donations when it comes to serving at the church,

A buyer for a craft store who is given a close-up look at new craft materials coming out in the next year, and can then suggest decorating items to the vacation Bible school director.

Ask your volunteers what they know and what they're learning that might be helpful to other volunteers. Add a quick comment at staff meetings that you'd like to hear about any training your volunteers have received—any training at all. You may choose to not follow up on some items (the hunter who passed his expert marksman course probably won't be able to turn it into a training session), but you'll know the expertise is available.

You can serve as the center of that information web, but only if you recall what you've been told . . . which brings you back to filling out your volunteers' continuing education sheets and updating them regularly.

How to track which training sessions are most useful

This is a three-step process:

1. Document what you've done.

You first need to document what training has been offered through your volunteer ministry and the content of each session. Without a record of that information, you'll never be able to determine which of those sessions was most valuable.

If you aren't already capturing notes from each training session, start at once. If possible, videotape or audiotape each session, too. This allows you to have a library of "instant" training sessions for volunteers who enter a ministry and need to get up to speed. It also allows you to know, in two years, what happened in that training session everyone says changed their lives.

Remember how you couldn't recall which training session every volunteer took? You won't remember the content of each training session, either—even the ones you led.

Capture the content and keep it on file.

2. Create a catalog.

Create a catalog of training sessions you offer, and keep it current. Include descriptions of the sessions and what each session's objectives are—why a volunteer would want to attend. Also indicate who leads the session.

If you feel there's a need to offer the session regularly (once per year, once per semester, or whatever), go ahead and schedule it on the church calendar now. Though orientation sessions are often "on demand" sessions, given when the volunteer first signs on, many training sessions can be taken after a volunteer is in place.

You'll need the catalog when you implement the third step in the evaluation process—asking current volunteers to indicate which training sessions were especially helpful to them.

3. Ask for feedback.

Give each volunteer a sheet listing the training sessions he or she has attended, a copy of the catalog, and a copy of the Best Ever Sheet. A sample copy of a Best Ever Sheet is on page 104, and you're welcome to use and adapt it.

"Look for trends by ministry area and by success of the volunteers."

The catalog will serve as a memory-jogger for volunteers. It's unlikely volunteers will remember the names of sessions they attended eight months earlier, but they'll probably recall the names of the trainers and the course objectives that were achieved.

Ask volunteers to complete the Best Ever Sheet and turn it in to you. As you collect a number of Best Ever Sheets, look for trends by ministry area and by success of the volunteers.

If your top-performing small group leaders all cite a few training sessions as beneficial, be sure that every small group leader goes through those sessions.

To be sure, there are variables when it comes to training sessions. The person presenting can play a huge role in making a session enjoyable and communicating the content effectively.

The relevance of the material may change depending on what's happening in the church or culture.

And the timing of the session can play a role, too. A session on "how to lead small groups of children" will be far more timely the week before vacation Bible school than during Christmas break. Volunteers who attend will be able to use the learning almost immediately in the summer, and in the winter they'll be distracted by the holiday.

But trends will emerge—and only by tracking them can the big picture of what you should put in place as standard training emerge. Your goal is in several years to determine a baseline of training sessions every volunteer should go through, and a second tier of training for each ministry group.

And may we encourage you to eventually add training sessions that are more for your volunteers than their roles? For instance, most volunteers are busy people. They might appreciate a training session on how to maintain life balance, or a session on time management—anything that helps reduce stress.

Adding a few "personal fulfillment" sessions as elective training will make your volunteer ministry a friendlier place to serve.

Sources for Training and Trainers

One way to add variety to training sessions is to make sure it's not always you leading them. Several sources of alternate training sources have been mentioned already, but for your convenience here's an expanded list. How many of these sources have you tapped?

Community experts

Contact the United Way, fraternal groups, or college instructors who teach courses in areas that are of interest. Not all will have a ready list of experts who are eager to come lead training, but some will. And for the cost of mileage and a warm handshake you can have real experts provide input.

Do a thorough job briefing outside speakers about your group and what to expect. Be clear about your values and the outcomes you want the training to provide. Work with the experts to reach a clear understanding of what they'll cover. And seek permission to record their presentation before the training event itself. Some experts may be uncomfortable granting permission.

> "You have some experts at your church."

Inside experts

You have some experts at your church, you know.

Be on the lookout for training that your volunteers experience in their professional lives that could easily translate to their volunteer roles—or someone else's volunteer roles. Your doctor who learned about brain research and learning might sing in the choir, but the expertise is relevant to your Christian education department. If the doctor is willing, ask her to work with you to create and lead a training session with your children's workers.

Seminars

Take advantage of training offered in your area by Christian publishers or Christian organizations.

One such seminar for children's ministry is the Children's Ministry Magazine Live Workshop (offered by Group Publishing annually). The inexpensive pricing on most half-day or one-day seminars makes it possible for you to take your entire staff.

Similar touring seminars are available for other groups of volunteers in your church.

Training with other churches

If your training session is skill-based rather than centered on knowledge specific to your church, invite other churches to attend. "How to relate to youth" is going to be valuable to youth workers of all denominations, and it will cost you very little more to present the training to a room of thirty people instead of a room of ten.

A bonus: Ask for the same courtesy in return, and take advantage of training provided by other churches.

Books and articles

It's very possible you'll never see the items again, so don't circulate anything you feel you can't live without. But publications that address relevant issues can be shared among those volunteers who could benefit from them. The secret is to attach an interactive routing slip and to make it easy for volunteers to pass along the publications.

If volunteers have a box or a mail slot in the church office, this is fairly simple. If not, as a team work together to create a system for exchanging items in a timely fashion.

If you discover that many of the helpful articles are from one or two magazines, contact the publisher and ask for a group discount subscription. Then you can distribute the entire magazine to appropriate volunteers.

An interactive routing slip is on page 106 for you to adapt for your use.

When these articles or books return to you (think positively!), add them to a permanent library of source material. If they were worth circulating, they're worth keeping.

On the other hand, if you wouldn't keep the information, don't interrupt your volunteers' lives with a request they read it.

Show and Tell

If you or a colleague in the volunteer ministry attends a convention or seminar that's paid for by the church, set it as policy that the person who attends must present what was learned when the person returns. This policy keeps your attendee sharp and on the lookout for usable ideas while at the convention, not lying on the beach instead of attending sessions.

An easy way to position this is to ask for a show and tell session that describes three ideas volunteers can put to use immediately and three that should be considered long-term.

Give convention-goers a large tote to fill with materials from the convention vendors, too. Often there are great give-aways that can be used at the church. If the bag gets too cumbersome, it can be shipped to the church instead of being dragged on the plane.

> "Ask for a show and tell session."

And finally, give your convention-eers 20 or 30 dollars to buy audio tapes of sessions that were especially useful. Listening to a tape as you drive isn't the same as being there, but it's an affordable way to experience the workshop. And the tapes can become part of your permanent library.

Orientation and Training As a Retention Tool

Does it seem odd to think of your orientation and training as tools that keep volunteers active in your church? It actually makes perfect sense.

The effort you invest in creating outstanding orientation and training opportunities communicates to volunteers. It sends a signal.

It signals that someone—you—notices them and is concerned about their comfort and effectiveness. They know you're willing to go the second mile to see they have the skills and information they need.

It signals that you value them, and that they're part of a team.

It signals that they serve in a church and a ministry program where they're encouraged to grow in their own faith, their own skills, and their own relationship with Jesus.

And who wouldn't want to hang around a place like that?

Your efforts are sending a signal, all right. It's a signal of loving concern.

Thanks for what you're doing for and with your volunteers. Together you're accomplishing amazing things.

And here's good news: There are more amazing things for you ahead in the next volume of this Volunteer Leadership Series. You'll focus on volunteer encouragement, evaluation, and accountability—with a close look at recognizing volunteers, too.

Onward and upward!

Training Forms for Volunteers

Sample Volunteer Handbook Acknowledgment Form

Please complete this form and return it to the Director of Volunteer Ministries. Before you can be placed in a volunteer role, this form must be on file in the Volunteer Ministries' office.

Please read this handbook carefully. It contains the policies, procedures, philosophy, and expectations relating to volunteering at First Christian Church. When you've completed reviewing this handbook please complete and sign the following statement. Return it to _____, the Director of Volunteer Ministries.

A copy of this acknowledgement form appears at the back of this handbook for your records.

I, _____, acknowledge that I've received and read a copy of First Christian Church's Volunteer Handbook. The Handbook contains the policies, procedures, philosophy, and expectations relating to volunteering at First Christian Church.

I've familiarized myself, at least generally, with the contents of this handbook. My signature below acknowledges that I understand the information contained in this handbook and agree to comply by it.

I understand this handbook isn't intended to cover each and every situation I may encounter as a volunteer, but is intended to be guide.

Signature _____

Date: _____

Program Evaluation Form

We're always looking for ways to improve our orientation program. Your filling out this evaluation helps us find ways to make the experience even better in the future.

Did the orientation program meet your expectations? Why or why not?

_____

_____

_____

Was the orientation program complete?

_____

_____

What information did you find most helpful?

_____

_____

What information did you feel was missing?

_____

_____

What questions do you have that weren't answered?

_____

_____

What would you add to improve the orientation program?

_____

_____

What would you remove to improve the orientation program?

_____

_____

Training Session Evaluation

Please help today's Trainer to improve future training sessions by answering the following questions about today's session.

Date: _____ Session Topic: _____

Name of Trainer: _____ Your name: _____

How long have you been a volunteer at [Name of your church]? _____

1. What was the main objective of this session?

_____
_____
_____
_____

2. What were other objectives you remember?

_____
_____
_____

3. How would you rate the pace of today's session?
Too slow   Slow   About right   Fast   Too fast

Why was that?

_____
_____
_____

4. How challenging did you find today's session?
Not at all   Not very   Neutral   Somewhat   Very

Why was that?

_____
_____
_____
_____

5. How relevant was the training to needs you're feeling now?

Not at all   Not very   Neutral   Somewhat   Very

How could the training have been more relevant to your needs?

_____

_____

_____

6. In your estimation, how well prepared was the Trainer?

Not at all   Not very   Neutral   Somewhat   Very

Why was that?

_____

_____

_____

7. Please write below about any part of the session about which you're still unclear, or have questions:

_____

_____

_____

8. Please offer any suggestions or further comments regarding this session:

_____

_____

_____

9. What other issues or items would you like to address on another day?

_____

_____

_____

Volunteer Continuing Education Sheet

Name of volunteer: _____

Volunteer positions held: Dates:

_____   _____

_____   _____

_____   _____

_____   _____

Church training sessions attended: Date: _____

_____   _____

_____   _____

_____   _____

_____   _____

External training attended (describe): Date:

_____   _____

_____   _____

_____   _____

_____   _____

Best Ever Evaluation Sheet

You're the best—and we want to know how you got that way!

In an effort to provide the best training sessions possible, we like to find out what training is most helpful and has had the greatest impact on your effectiveness.

Please take a few minutes and consider the list of training sessions you've attended. If you can't remember what was covered at each session, consult the Training Session Catalog. Then answer the following questions as honestly as you can.

Return this sheet to _____ as soon as possible.

Thank you.

1. Which training session was most memorable for you?

_____

Why?

_____
_____
_____
_____

2. Which training session was most relevant to you?

_____

Why?

_____
_____
_____
_____

3. Which training session provided information or skills you've used most often?

_____

What is that information, or those skills?

_____
_____
_____

4. Which training session would you recommend to someone else entering our area of ministry?

Why? _____

_____

_____

_____

5. Which training session seemed least helpful to you?

Why? _____

_____

_____

_____

Sample Interactive Routing Slip

Notice how there's accountability built in to this routing slip—and a chance to write a review.

Volunteer Ministry Routing Slip

The attached published piece is making the rounds . . . but not if you slow it down! Please read the attached and add your comments within one week. Then slip it into the Volunteer Office mail slot of the next person on the list.

Thank you!

Mary Jones
Volunteer Director
Date: _____

To:	Date received:	Date passed along:
Jackie Sampson	_____	_____
Aaron Loop	_____	_____
Jeff Knowles	_____	_____
Jim Wood	_____	_____
Jodi Forbes	_____	_____
Shanell Frahm	_____	_____
Brian Shiazi	_____	_____
Janelle Spencer	_____	_____

Share your comments below. Write your initials after your comments, please.

A WOW! Idea I found:

Sample
Volunteer Guidelines

Sample Volunteer Orientation Guidelines

First Christian Church Volunteer Orientation
Nursery Guidelines

What a blessing you'll be to parents as you provide a caring, nurturing, Christ-centered experience for their infants as parents worship. And you'll help babies associate feeling safe and secure with being at church.

Our first concern is safety. The following policies will help us make our nursery safe for babies and nursery workers alike.

- Nursery staff responsible for working an assigned shift must provide staffing or find a replacement from the list of approved substitutes. If a husband and wife are scheduled to work together and neither can come, then they must find two replacements. Notify the nursery director of any staffing changes.

- Three adults will work in the nursery on Sunday mornings (a nursery supervisor, an infant staffer, and a toddler staffer). On Wednesday night two adults will work in the nursery (a nursery supervisor and one infant staffer). This ratio must be maintained—no exceptions.

- Youth volunteers will be limited to one at any given time.

- Only the posted number of babies and toddlers can be in the nursery at any one time. If more children are presented, do not admit them until a certified nursery staff member has joined the existing staff to maintain the posted ratio of children/staff. Never exceed the posted ratio.

- Nursery staff must arrive 20 minutes before the Sunday service, Wednesday night program, or special service. On Sundays arrive at 9:10 A.M., and on Wednesdays arrive at 6:25 P.M.

- All nursery staff will wear nametags and greet each parent and child warmly.

- On a child's first visit to the nursery the parent must fill out a Nursery Information Sheet, which will then be kept on file in the nursery cabinet for future reference.

- Give parents a copy of the Nursery Handbook when they check their child in for the first time.

- Give parents a copy of the Nursery Handbook when they check their child in for the first time.

- No male volunteers are allowed to change babies' diapers.

- Parents will sign three adhesive tags when they check in children. Give one tag to the parent, affix one to the child's back, and put the third tag on the child's diaper bag.

- Parents of infants will complete the Infant Information Sheet when they check babies into the nursery.

- Use the digital pager system to notify parents to return to the nursery if necessary. Nursery supervisors have all been trained how to use it, and instructions are posted by the pager console. Nursery supervisors have the authority to decide when parents need to be notified.

- If a child is hurt but not seriously enough to page the parent, a parental notification form will be completed by the nursery supervisor on duty and given to the parent. A copy of the document will be kept in the church office.

- Diaper changing procedures are posted.

- The sickness policy is posted at the nursery door where both staff and parents can easily see it. Enforce the policy—no exceptions. If a child is turned away from the nursery, give the parent a copy of the policy.

- Fire and tornado procedures are posted, and two drills will be held annually.

- All nursery staff must complete the required safety background checks (which include a police check) and the three-hour First Christian Church Certification Program.

- Pictures of the nursery staff and their certification information will be posted to reassure parents of our preparation and professionalism.

- Children will remain inside the nursery until retrieved by an authorized person. Parents must have their retrieval tag, which must match the child's back tag. Parents must sign out their child.

- At the end of each nursery session, the nursery supervisor will complete a nursery supply summary and leave it in the church office. Nursery staff will also put clean bedding on any cribs that have been used. Deal with used bedding as instructed on the posted laundry instruction sheet.

- At the end of each nursery session, toys will be cleaned with a diluted bleach solution of 10-1 water/bleach ratio.

Volunteer Bill of Rights

I have the right to . . .

- Have my volunteer experience in the church encourage a healthy relationship with Jesus Christ.

- Use my God-given abilities, skills, and passions in significant ministry that gives something to the corporate body of Christ.

- Be respected as a full partner in ministry.

- Be young. Be old. Be any age and still valued in ministry.

- Be placed in a ministry role based on my gifts and abilities, not my church's need to find warm bodies to fill a slot in the organizational chart.

- Have a job description that provides me with the information I need to know whether I'm doing what's most important for me to be doing.

- Be provided with the resources and training I need to be successful.

- Receive regular evaluations so I can know how I'm doing and where I can improve.

- Serve in an environment where I'm well aware of the safety risks.

- Be respected if I say "no" to a request to serve in a specific volunteer role.

- Be valued—as a child of God and part of the body of Christ.

- Be expected to set boundaries that allow me a healthy work/life balance.

- Be retained as a volunteer not by guilt, but by the joy of serving others, serving God, and serving the church.

VOLUNTEER ENCOURAGEMENT, ACCOUNTABILITY, AND EVALUATION

Marlene Wilson, Author and General Editor

Group's Volunteer Leadership Series™
Volume 6
Group's Church Volunteer Central™

Loveland, Colorado

Group's Volunteer Leadership Series™, Volume 6

Volunteer Encouragement, Accountability, and Evaluation

Visit our Web site: **www.grouppublishing.com**

Credits
Author: Marlene Wilson
Editor: Mikal Keefer
General Editor: Marlene Wilson
Chief Creative Officer: Joani Schultz
Art Director: Nathan Hindman
Cover Designer: Jeff Storm
Production Manager: Peggy Naylor

Unless otherwise noted, Scripture taken from the HOLY BIBLE, NEW INTERNATIONAL VERSION®. Copyright © 1973, 1978, 1984 International Bible Society. Used by permission of Zondervan Publishing House. All rights reserved.

Produced with the assistance of The Livingstone Corporation (www.LivingstoneCorp.com). Project staff includes Chris Hudson, Ashley Taylor, Mary Horner Collins, Joel Bartlett, Cheryl Dunlop, Mary Larsen, and Rosalie Krusemark.

Library of Congress Cataloging-in-Publication Data

Wilson, Marlene.
Volunteer encouragement, accountability, and evaluation / Marlene Wilson.—
        1st American hardbound ed.
        p. cm. — (Group's volunteer leadership series ; v. 6)
        Includes bibliographical references.
        ISBN 0-7644-2750-4 (alk. paper)
        1. Voluntarism—Religious aspects—Christianity. 2. Christian leadership. 3.
Church work. 4. Voluntarism—Evaluation. I. Title. II. Series.
BR115.V64W555 2003
253'.7—dc22   2003022123

10 9 8 7 6 5 4 3 2 1   12 11 10 09 08 07 06 05 04

Printed in the United States of America.

Contents

Introduction

Because you are leading volunteers (or soon will be), I'm guessing that you have been a volunteer yourself. In fact, you may be volunteering right now as you create or revitalize your church's volunteer ministry.

We volunteers know the secret: When we have a volunteer job we're prepared to do, and we have all the materials and information we need to be successful in doing that job, it's *fun*.

Not only do we *enjoy* volunteering, we *delight* in it. It's fulfilling and satisfying.

Each of the volunteers serving in your church deserves to have a delightful experience. And here's the good news: You can make it happen!

In this last volume of the Volunteer Leadership Series, we'll focus on five more pieces of the volunteer leadership jigsaw puzzle. They're pieces you'll fit together to create delightful experiences for your volunteers . . .

Expectations often determine whether a person has a delightful, ho-hum, or poor volunteer experience. We'll look at how you can manage expectations in your volunteer ministry—your expectations and your volunteers' expectations, too.

Evaluation happens when volunteers find out how they're doing. This doesn't have to be a challenging time—if anything, it's a time of celebration! When it's handled correctly, an evaluation is something volunteers actually *enjoy*. I'll share with you how to set up the evaluation system so it's fun for you to give evaluations.

Accountability is expecting each person in the volunteer ministry to do what he or she agrees to do, and do it on time and with excellence. Here's practical help with building accountability into your ministry, and dealing with volunteers who are—and aren't—accountable.

Recognition of volunteers may become your favorite part of working with volunteers! Here are dozens of ideas for shining the spotlight on volunteers, honoring their service, and helping them feel good about their involvement.

Encouragement is like oxygen: Every volunteer needs it in abundance. We'll examine how you can create an atmosphere where encouragement is a natural part of your ministry culture.

Delight your volunteers and not only will you be serving them, you'll also go a long way toward keeping them on board as volunteers in the future, too.

Delight your volunteers. They'll delight you in return.

ONE
Expectations

**How to manage expectations in your volunteer ministry—
yours and those of your volunteers and leaders.**

Let me share a story with you . . .

My first year on staff at the Volunteer and Information Center in Boulder, Colorado, we did a pretty good job increasing the number of volunteers. But at the end of the year we realized there was a group we hadn't effectively involved: senior citizens.

We decided to form a task force, with the goal of getting more senior citizens on board as volunteers.

The first problem was that I didn't have a *clue* why seniors weren't volunteering. Were we doing something wrong? Was there something we weren't doing that we needed to do? I had no idea. I was totally in the dark.

The second problem was that I didn't have the slightest idea where to start building a task force.

I visited a senior center and told the director I was looking for someone to tell me what to do. I needed a person who was over 60 years old, was a good organizer, and who would give me free advice. The director said she'd see what she could do.

> "I didn't have the slightest idea where to start . . ."

Within a few days a woman by the name of Clara Clifford appeared in my office. She stood in front of my desk, crossed her arms, and said, "I hear you've got a problem."

I admitted she was right: I *did* have a problem. I needed to find someone who would tell me how to get seniors involved as community volunteers.

Clara pulled up a chair and sat down. She interviewed me for 90 minutes, probing to see what we'd done. She kept coming back to what my plans were for next steps.

"I don't *have* any next steps," I kept telling her. "I'm not sure *what* to do."

Finally Clara leaned back in her chair, sized me up, and said, "You're serious about this, aren't you?"

I confirmed I most certainly *was* serious. I'd just been subjected to an hour and a half of interrogation. How could I *not* be serious?

"Then I'll take it," Clara announced firmly.

> "She was told that her opinion mattered—but it didn't."

Here's the happy ending to that story: In one week Clara had 17 seniors on her task force.

Within a year she increased senior citizen involvement from 10 volunteers to 150 volunteers. The next year it rose to 250 volunteers. When it reached 350 seniors, I had to find more funding to keep the program from stalling out for lack of money.

Later, once Clara and I became friends, she explained what had happened in my office, why I'd been questioned with such intensity.

It seemed that Clara had served on a number of boards. She'd even reached state and national leadership in some of the organizations in which she served. But too often she'd been appointed to a position of authority only to discover that the current leaders didn't really want to hear what she had to say . . . or let her do significant work.

She was told that her opinion mattered—but it didn't.

She was told that she'd been heard—but nobody listened.

She was told that she would be given something important to do—but she wasn't.

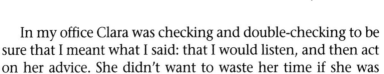

In my office Clara was checking and double-checking to be sure that I meant what I said: that I would listen, and then act on her advice. She didn't want to waste her time if she was just going to be a token senior on a board.

Clara wanted to make her expectations clear, . . . and to be sure I was clear about what I expected, too. In doing so, Clara showed tremendous wisdom.

Clear, expressed expectations are essential in volunteer ministry—and in life, too.

What Are Expectations?

Expectations are our assumptions about the future—how we anticipate things will go.

In a perfect world expectations are based on clear communication and agreements. But in the absence of those, people base their expectations on assumptions, implications, and wishful thinking. And that's a recipe for disappointment.

You see, what a person expects from a situation becomes that person's definition of what's reasonable and fair. And if others fail to meet those expectations, well, they're not being reasonable. Or fair. And they're certainly being a disappointment.

> "Expectations are our assumptions about the future—how we anticipate things will go."

This principle operates *even if people never actually articulate their expectations*—to themselves or others! Expectations have the power to shade and interpret situations without ever making themselves known.

Here's an example . . .

Suppose you receive a letter saying you've won the grand prize in a contest you don't even remember entering. Your name was drawn out of a hat and you're about to receive a check for a "substantial amount of money."

So you begin to plan what you'll do with the windfall. You'll give some to your church, some to your family, and with the rest maybe you can do some traveling. But where will you go? That depends on how large the check turns out to be. It's "substantial," but what does that mean?

Will you be able to book a vacation at Disneyland? Or better yet, Australia. And if you're in Australia, why not do it right with a two-week guided tour? And a stop-over in Hawaii to rest up, of course . . .

When the check finally arrives and you tear open the envelope, you find a thousand dollars and your heart sinks in disappointment. Substantial? They call *this* "substantial"?

Had the check arrived without your knowing it was coming, you'd have been delighted. You would have celebrated because it far exceeded your expectations. You thought you'd only find bills in the day's mail; instead there was a *thousand dollars*!

But because of your high expectations, now the check you received seems like pocket change. It won't finance your dream vacation. It doesn't feel fair. That's the power of expectations.

> **"That's the power of expectations."**

And make no mistake about it: Both volunteers and volunteer leaders have expectations about volunteer roles.

The Importance of Clear Expectations

Since we're expecting something from our volunteer experiences, let's take a tip from Clara and be clear about those expectations.

Here's where all your hard work will pay off. Because you have provided job descriptions and careful placement and you have helped set realistic expectations in the minds of your volunteers, they know exactly what they'll be doing. They know who they'll report to. They know how they'll be evaluated.

Of course, if you've not done those things, . . . well, it's not too late to do them. Without the clarity that comes with job descriptions, interviews, and careful placement, you'll struggle with unclear expectations regularly.

Clear expectations help both volunteers and volunteer leaders to have a realistic view of how the future will unfold, how tasks will be accomplished, and what the outcomes will be.

Before we move too far along, I'd like to share a quick word about expectations and volunteers. There are two general expectations that have proven to be true again and again in my decades of experience working with volunteers:

1. Volunteers want to do their best.

I've yet to meet a person who signed up to help in a classroom or at the food pantry with the intention of doing less than excellent work. Volunteers sign on the dotted line with every intention of meeting and exceeding your expectations. Many things can get in the way of their delivering an excellent effort (we'll discuss a few later), but it's safe to assume the best about your volunteers and interact with them accordingly. Volunteers are typically enthused, inspired, and happy to be on the team.

2. When volunteers fail to meet our expectations, it's not always the volunteer's fault.

As leaders, sometimes the problem is with us. *We* have failed to provide adequate information. *We* have assumed something that isn't true. *We* have not defined clearly what we expect.

If the problem lies with us, we can fix it. And if the problem lies with a volunteer, it's *also* our responsibility to proactively work to resolve it.

We may work directly with the volunteer or only with the person who supervises the volunteer, but we're likely to get involved. So let's talk about communicating clear expectations.

> "If the problem lies with us, we can fix it."

Clear Expectations Require Clear Communication

Again, if you've worked through all the steps described in this Volunteer Leadership Series, you've probably already established many clear expectations for volunteers.

But there are still things you will need to explain—and

have explained to you. Remember that volunteers are your *partners* in ministry; they have many valuable lessons to teach you, too. Communication is a two-way street.

Your ability to communicate clearly will help you in every aspect of handling expectations. Communicating clearly will help volunteers know what *you* expect. Your skills as a listener will help volunteers let you know what *they* expect. Clear communication helps everyone win.

> "Clear communi-cation helps everyone win."

I've spent my entire career as a leader in volunteer ministries and agencies learning to communicate clearly, and I *know* I still have things to learn.

But here are three things I *have* learned again and again. I want to share them with you because they're fundamental truths about communicating clearly with volunteers. Owning and integrating these three truths into your own approach with people will help you manage expectations.

1. Everything you do communicates.

You can't *not* communicate. Even silence communicates something.

Here's an example . . .

Let's say you have a disagreement with a friend. Later you call and leave a message saying you'd like a return call so you can discuss the issue further and reach an agreement.

If several days pass and you haven't heard anything, you may call and leave another message. Then if a few more days pass without a return call, you may become angry or worried.

Is your friend ignoring you? Is your friend so angry he can't tolerate the idea of speaking with you? Is your friendship over? Or is your friend unable to phone back because he's ill? Should you call hospitals, or phone a mutual friend who can confirm your friend is still alive?

Notice: *Your friend is communicating with you even though he hasn't said a thing.* His silence is speaking—but you don't know what it means and may very well assume the worst.

You're communicating all the time—like it or not.

Interpersonal communication includes both content and emotion. The
tone of your voice and your body language speak loudly about what's really
being said. If your emotion and content
are inconsistent, then the message is apt
to be scrambled.

> "You're com-
> municating
> all the time—
> like it or not."

And for some reason, scrambled messages *always* take on
the most sinister, negative meaning possible. It's a phenomenon that defies the law of averages, like dropping buttered
pieces of toast (they always somehow land butter side down!).

For example, suppose you congratulate a volunteer on a
job well done. You say "Great job!" as you hurry past the volunteer in the church hallway. You look preoccupied and distracted (you're rushing to a meeting, so your mind is partially
elsewhere), and you don't make eye contact. You don't give
the volunteer time to respond. You deliver a "hit and run"
affirmation that's sincere, but half-hearted. The result is a dual
message: "I'm pleased—but not really."

Because your body language wasn't consistent with your
words, the volunteer has to choose: Does she believe the
words, or the actions?

I'm willing to bet she'll believe the actions.

It's easy to forget that we communicate in so many ways . . .

- Through touch—a tap on the shoulder or hug, a pat
on the back or handshake. They all have strong
meaning to both sender and receiver. When you
touch, touch carefully and appropriately.

- Through visible movement—pointing a finger, wink-
ing, smiling, scowling, folding our arms. These communicate volumes without using a word, and often
speak "louder" than the words we use.

- Through words and other audible symbols—including speaking, crying, and laughing, or a combination
of these. Even a snort can imply that you don't agree
with what has just been said to you.

- Through written symbols—in words, graphs, or even pictures. It's easy to be misunderstood when you send letters or e-mails, so be cautious. A rule of thumb: If what you need to communicate is corrective or confrontational, don't write it. Meet face to face, or at least talk voice to voice. Words are so easy to misunderstand.

2. Speak the truth in love.

In Ephesians 4:15 we read:

> *Instead, speaking the truth in love, we will in all things grow up into him who is the Head, that is, Christ.*

That biblical admonition requires that we be both truthful and loving at the same time. It's a hard balance to maintain.

When we strike this balance we speak directly and clearly, and get to the point. We don't gloss over issues. We don't adopt the conflict resolution strategy too many volunteer managers embrace: They *ignore* a problematic volunteer, hoping he or she will simply go away.

Speaking the truth in love requires us to take into account the words, feelings, and body language of the other person in the conversation. We must be present and caring even if we're unhappy. There's no room for blasting a volunteer for a mistake or using sarcasm in any way, shape, or form.

> "Straight, clear communication is exceedingly rare in the world."

Speaking the truth in love demands that we be clear about what we want—our expectations—and that we hear the expectations of others.

This sort of straight, clear communication is exceedingly rare in the world, and, sadly, in the church. But it's healthy and helpful. It spares volunteers sleepless nights as they try to interpret what we want, hope for, or envision based on our subtle insinuations.

When you speak the truth in love, so much can happen that's positive. It's worth learning this language of love.

3. Listening is communication, too.

I don't know who first observed this fact, but it's true. The world is full of good talkers but good listeners are so rare they're practically an endangered species.

I've been told the average talker speaks at a rate of about 175 words per minute, but the average listener can receive about 1,000 words per minute. Because of this tremendous gap, most people develop some very bad listening habits.

They let their attention drift to other things.

They assume they know where the talker is heading.

They use the time they're not paying attention to figure out how they'll respond—as soon as the talker stays quiet long enough to allow for a response.

But listening is more than just not talking.

A friend told me about a little boy who was in a music appreciation class. When he was asked to distinguish between *listening* and *hearing,* he replied, "Listening is wanting to hear." What a great definition! *That's* what listening is—"wanting to hear"!

> "Listening is more than just not talking."

We all say we want to hear, but it's not uncommon for us to miss the vast majority of what people say to us. Don't believe me? Outline the sermon you heard when you were last in church. How much of what your pastor said have you retained?

The challenge for us as leaders in volunteer ministry is to train ourselves to listen deeply. To hear not only what's on the surface but also to hear what is *beneath* the surface.

Our goal is to listen for the heart of what's being communicated. This requires that we pay attention to the whole person. As Jim stands before us, we "hear" his life situation as he brings it to our relationship. We hear his actions, his body language, his subtle emotional cues, his voice quality, his voice volume, his eye contact patterns, his unconscious gestures. When they're all on our radar screen, then we're really listening.

> "Our goal is to listen for the heart of what's being communicated."

We can do it—listening is a set of skills, not a rare gift that God has given to only an anointed few. I don't deny that listening is a complex process that can break down at any number of points and, if that happens, our expectations can get lost in the muddle. But the need to communicate clearly remains, and not just because it's the only way to be sure our expectations are being understood. It's also how we know that we are understanding the expectations of others.

And it's where we do ministry. Listening—heart-to-heart listening when we connect deeply with volunteers—is a gift to us both. When we move past discussing the weather to discussing how we feel about our faith, or the illness of our parents, or the pain we're feeling—that's ministry. We become open and truthful. We share who we really are.

There's no shortcut when it comes to clear communication. And there's no set of skills you can use that will give you a better return for your effort!

How Do You Set Expectations about Quality?

Just as volunteers want to do well in their volunteer roles, you, too, want the entire volunteer ministry to function well. We all want quality to be our hallmark.

But how do you get quality work from everyone in your ministry?

Here are some suggestions . . .

Communicate not just what work is to be done, but how it's to be done.

For instance, it's not enough for a volunteer to just show up on time to deliver a children's message. The volunteer must show up on time and be *prepared*, too. But what specifically makes a children's message a *quality* message? Is preparation enough . . . or is there more?

If supervisors of volunteers are providing excellent orientation and training, your volunteers will have a clear understanding of what quality looks and sounds like. But that happens only if volunteers' supervisors are consistent and clear. Be sure volunteer supervisors do an excellent job with orientation and training!

Ask: "What do you need from me that you're not getting?"

Ask every volunteer this question every three to six months. It gets at whether the volunteer's supervisor has a leadership style that's connecting effectively.

For instance, if Jane is a relatively "hands-off" supervisor and Shawn needs more guidance than Jane is providing,

> "There's no shortcut when it comes to clear communication."

this question gives Shawn permission to ask for more help. This question also opens up discussions about training or materials that Shawn might feel he needs to be successful.

Ask: "What do you wish you knew about your volunteer job that you don't know now?"

Pose this question to each volunteer every three to six months, too. We want volunteers to feel comfortable in their jobs. If they answer this question by telling us they're unsure how to handle classroom discipline, or if they have a question about designing the church newsletter, we know we've got a problem.

Until volunteers feel adequately trained, they're likely to feel fearful or uncertain. This question gets at what your volunteers feel about their training.

If you regularly ask open-ended questions that are designed to solicit evaluations and probe areas where you can improve the volunteer ministry, then you'll find out if there's a problem with quality *before* the program begins to suffer.

Identify the problem that's interfering with quality and then set expectations for dealing with it.

Remember: Your volunteers want to see high quality, too. They're not out to deliberately disappoint you or the people they serve.

In my experience, the following three most common reasons for poor quality efforts from volunteers aren't all the fault of the volunteers at all. If anything, they can be traced back to us as leaders.

A lack of aptitude

At its core, this is usually the result of a volunteer being placed in the wrong position. Perhaps the placement interview didn't adequately reveal the volunteer's God-given abilities, skills, and passions. Maybe the volunteer didn't choose to reveal them in order to be placed in her current role—where she's failing.

This situation needn't end a volunteer's service to the church. Instead, simply place the volunteer in a new role that's more appropriate. There's no shame in failing to thrive in a position that's not in line with one's abilities, skills, and passion for ministry, but the volunteer may feel embarrassed anyway. Communicate your willingness to reassign the volunteer, and offer support in the transition.

Another alternative is to change the job so it fits the volunteer. Some positions are flexible enough to be easily adapted.

Communicate to the volunteer your expectation that things can't remain as they are; that change is needed. Then, with the cooperation of the volunteer, facilitate change.

A lack of skill

Picture a Sunday school teacher who loves children, loves teaching, and is ready and willing to lead a class every Sunday morning. Yet, this individual lacks the skill that comes with experience. Leave him alone with the fourth-grade boys more than 20 minutes and the room is reduced to charred rubble and chaos.

> **"Look to redirect the volunteer to another role."**

If there's aptitude but a lack of training, provide training. Use audio tapes, video tapes, provide books to read, identify workshops to attend. Even better, provide a mentor to come alongside the volunteer and help him grow in his skills.

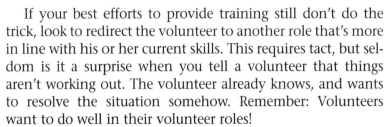

If your best efforts to provide training still don't do the trick, look to redirect the volunteer to another role that's more in line with his or her current skills. This requires tact, but seldom is it a surprise when you tell a volunteer that things aren't working out. The volunteer already knows, and wants to resolve the situation somehow. Remember: Volunteers want to do well in their volunteer roles!

It's unfair to a volunteer to suggest that he or she is failing and yet be vague about the standards of excellence you require. "You're not good enough" is a message none of us like to hear. It's damaging, de-motivating, and seldom true. What *is* true is that the Sunday school teacher in question isn't able to maintain classroom discipline and create a learning environment.

Outline again what a well-disciplined classroom looks like, and help the volunteer see where there's room for growth. Jointly determine what will happen so the teacher can get the skills he needs. Then work the plan you've jointly agreed will do the job.

You've set fair expectations about quality because you've described what "quality" means in this context, and you've shown that it's possible to get there.

A lack of motivation

Sometimes it seems that a volunteer just doesn't care. A teacher no longer prepares adequately, a committee member skips meetings without explanation, a church treasurer lets checks and bills stack up.

> "Find out what the problem is and deal with it."

Don't assume that a change in behavior necessarily signals a character flaw, or a total lack of concern. Rather than become offended, find out what the problem is and deal with it. If the volunteer reports directly to you, find out if the issue is your leadership style. If that's the problem, you can work to change how you relate to the volunteer.

A volunteer may seem less reliable if there's a problem in the ministry area in which the volunteer serves. The group may be experiencing conflict, which often de-motivates volunteers. If that's the situation, deal with it.

A personal or professional problem may be consuming the volunteer's attention, leaving little time or energy to fulfill the volunteer role. Find out if it's a temporary or long-term issue; if it's the former, offer a short-term leave of absence and find out how you can support the volunteer through the crisis. If it's a longer-term concern, let the volunteer resign with your blessings rather than fade away.

> "Quality, like beauty, is in the eye of the beholder—until you define it."

And perhaps the volunteer just needs a reminder that what she does is important—and others are counting on her.

Quality, like beauty, is in the eye of the beholder—until you define it. If an expectation of quality is church attendance a minimum of three times per month, then say so. If the expectation is that they create lesson outlines a week in advance, be specific. You can't hold volunteers accountable to unexpressed expectations. Until you clearly communicate what you want, you're unlikely to see it.

When you see a lack of quality that isn't responding to your proactive involvement as the volunteer supervisor, be prepared to act.

Your people matter, but so do the ministry roles they're in. If the quality of a ministry program is suffering because of a particular person who can't or won't make the necessary changes to improve, prayerfully consider how to remove the volunteer.

But first focus on what *you* may be contributing to the situation.

In his book *The Five-Star Church,* Alan Nelson puts it this way, "Assume that you are part of the blame whenever quality does not take place. Perhaps it was poor communication or training."

Good advice. He goes on to share the risk of stopping there

without taking corrective action, "If you do nothing, . . . team members who are responding well can resent the lack of equity."[1]

> "Focus on what *you* may be contributing to the situation."

Don't get caught in the blame game, trying to determine exactly whose fault it is that a volunteer is failing to deliver quality after you've set clear expectations. Act—so the problem doesn't continue as you sort out who's responsible for what.

It's *essential* to confront problem situations. The first time a deadline is missed or a volunteer fails to show up for a scheduled event, deal with it. Make sure the unmet expectation is understood by everyone involved. There may be valid reasons why a commitment wasn't honored. But as a volunteer leader, you won't know until you raise the question.

And a word of caution: Don't try to "rescue" a failing volunteer by getting the staff (or other volunteers) to jump in and save the day. That action on your part sets an expectation, too, and may become standard procedure. You don't want to create that world, because you'll live in it.

Expectations aren't reality, but unless you are intentional about creating a culture where open, clear communication is what's normal, expectations may be as close to reality as anyone gets.

Attitudinal Blocks: When Your Expectations Aren't Met

Are you familiar with "attitudinal blocks?" Unfortunately, you probably are—and they can drain the fun out of running a volunteer ministry.

Think of attitudinal blocks as roadblocks on the way toward effective volunteer leadership. You're moving right along, expecting clear sailing, when suddenly you round a corner and smack straight into one. It can take your breath away and put you on the sidelines awhile.

You may never encounter the four attitudinal blocks I outline below, but many leaders of volunteer ministries do. I bring them to your attention for two reasons:

1. You'll know you're not alone if you encounter them, and

2. I don't want them to derail you as you move ahead in your ministry. Unmet expectations can do that to you.

> "It's *essential* to confront problem situations."

Don't think these problems are imaginary or far-fetched. The dramatic scenarios I describe below are based on actual situations. I present them as dramas so you can use them as role-play exercises in a small group or in a workshop for volunteer leaders.[2]

Attitudinal Block 1: You expect as the volunteer ministry leader to be considered a full member of the team—but you aren't.

Actors: Volunteer ministry leader, senior pastor, assistant pastor, and secretary

Setting: Church office

Volunteer leader: I'd find it helpful if we could set up a weekly meeting to get together and exchange information and concerns.

Assistant pastor: That's hard to do, since we're all operating on different schedules.

Senior pastor: Our schedules are constantly shifting. There isn't a time during the week we're even all here at the same time.

Secretary: I feel a need for an information-exchange meeting, too. I get telephone calls and sometimes don't know information people want. Maybe if we all got together, it would help me to get more lead time on information and be able to "plug in" better.

Assistant pastor: But you already do a great job keeping ahead of things, and we both update you at least once a day.

Senior pastor: The church doesn't work like other organizations. We're always on call. We can't just set up a weekly meeting and always make it work. We've tried before, but it's impossible to maintain.

Volunteer leader: I understand it'll be a challenge, but I still want to set a time for a weekly staff meeting, if only to help me. I feel responsible for the information being shared with me regarding needs and how church members want to help. At our meeting we could discuss how to best meet the needs of all our programs and people, and decide who would be best at dealing with them. I'd feel better if I knew we were following up effectively when someone wants to get involved in one of our ministries. I think we're letting lots of possible volunteers fall through the cracks.

Secretary: And I'd feel better if I knew everyone was being contacted. I feel bad whenever I type up the church directory and see names of people I haven't seen at church for a long time. Maybe they're being contacted, but if so, I don't hear about it.

Senior pastor: Well, I suppose we could *try* scheduling a standing meeting again and see how it works out. When do you suppose we could all meet?

They set a date, but the senior pastor then cancels because he later discovers he'd already booked that time for another meeting.

Attitudinal Block 2: You expect to be welcomed by the pastor, but instead you're perceived as a threat.

Actors: Pastor, lay leader
Setting: Pastor's office

Lay leader: I've been meaning to ask you, Pastor, how is our new volunteer coordinator doing? She's been on board here six months and I'm curious as to how it's working out.

Pastor: (hesitantly) Well . . . by and large, it's going very well. I mean she's very enthusiastic and a real achiever. She's getting things organized around here right and left! (Pause) But sometimes I'm afraid she goes a little bit overboard.

Lay leader: How so?

Pastor: Well, sometimes she strays into my domain. I mean our roles are still pretty fuzzy about who's supposed to do what.

Lay leader: That could get frustrating for both of you, I'm sure. Give me a "for instance" and maybe I can help.

Pastor: Well . . . several times she's actually gotten into doing *ministry* . . . and that's what I'm here for!

Lay leader: What kind of ministry are you talking about? Can you give me an example?

Pastor: Last week when Mrs. Peterson died so suddenly, the family called her to go talk to the Petersons' teenage daughter—and that was while I was still helping get things straightened out at the hospital. Why didn't they let me know the girl needed help—instead of calling her? After all, *I'm* the pastor here!

Lay leader: It sounds like you're angry about that.

Pastor: Of course I'm not! I'm just . . . well, I guess I *am* angry. *I've* been called to be the pastor. What do you expect me to do—just sit here and let her take charge? Her job description says *she's* responsible to *me*.

Lay leader: You mean she's not communicating with you?

Pastor: Oh, she does that fine. It's just that she's supposed to find volunteers, plug them into programs, and run that show. *I'm* supposed to do ministry. That's my job.

Lay leader: So, it's when she starts caring for people that you get upset.

Pastor: I just don't want the congregation to get confused. Pretty soon they won't know where to turn—to her or me.

Attitudinal Block 3: You expect current church leaders to enthusiastically embrace the volunteer ministry—and they don't.

Actors: Volunteer leader, secretary
Setting: Church office

Volunteer leader: Mary, do you have a minute? I've just got to talk to someone!

Secretary: Sure, come on in. The pastors are gone and it's quiet for the moment. What's on your mind?

Volunteer leader: It's last night's council meeting. I'm so frustrated, I'm ready to quit!

Secretary: What happened?

Volunteer leader: It's not what happened—it's what didn't happen . . . again! I asked for time on the agenda to report on the results of the one-to-one interviews we've been conducting with church members the last two months. I wanted to remind the committee chairpersons to call the people I've referred to them.

Secretary: Sounds great. What happened at the meeting that upset you?

Volunteer leader: First of all, I ended up last on the agenda again—even after the purchase of a new garden hose! It was 10:30 and I could tell everyone just wanted to get out of there and go home, but I plunged ahead anyhow.

I asked four committee chairpersons about how their follow-up calls were going and not *one* of them had contacted one referral. Not one! Matt said he's been too busy. Amy says she hates hearing "no." Dave said it's easier to do things himself. And Roxie said she always feels like she's begging when she calls people.

Mary, these people *want* to help. They *want* to be called! Here are these "pewsitters" everyone gripes about finally volunteering for committees, and no one calls them. It's ridiculous!

Secretary: I can see why you're upset!

Attitudinal Block 4: You expect that you've got things under control, but you discover there's room for improvement.

Actors: Pastor, volunteer leader (who's been in that role for three years), and three members of the volunteer ministry task force (who've just returned from a "Volunteerism in the Church" workshop they attended with the pastor and volunteer leader.)

Setting: Church office

Pastor: This is our first meeting since the workshop on volunteer ministries. I hope everyone is still as enthused as I am about the planning we did at the workshop.

Task force member 1: I sure am!

Task force member 2: Can't wait to try out some of those new ideas!

Task force member 3: It was terrific to rethink where we're going with our ministry and what's really possible.

Volunteer leader: You know, when I got back, I realized we're already doing most of it—they just had fancier terms for stuff I've been doing for a long time.

Pastor: You've got some great things in place, but it's always a good idea to take a look now and then to see if we can improve on a good thing.

Task force member 1: For instance, we've never done personal interviews with our people—we've relied on time and talent sheets and casual conversations. My hunch is we really don't know a lot of our people.

Volunteer leader: When you've worked with them as long as I have, you know them. I just haven't written it all down. But just ask me who is good at almost anything that needs doing and I can tell you in a minute. No sense making things more complicated than they have to be.

How Do You Solve These Attitudinal Blocks?

> "You can't mandate that attitudes change; you can only seek to understand."

I wish I knew.

The fact is there's no simple solution for becoming a fully accepted member on a team that's closed. Or for changing the attitude of a threatened pastor. Or for convincing church leaders that the volunteer ministry is valuable. Or, for that matter, overcoming resistance to change—our resistance, or other people's resistance.

What all these situations have in common is that they are, at heart, "people problems," and they have to do with expectations. They defy a quick, simple formula answer that fits all situations. Each attitude is personal, and flows out of someone's beliefs, experiences, and values.

You can't mandate that attitudes change; you can only seek to understand the people who hold those attitudes . . . and then work to change the attitudes by providing information and proven results.

When you're staring across a conference table at a row of disbelieving faces, it's hard to think the church board members will ever change their minds and will fund the volunteer ministry.

But they will.

When you see your pastor shake his head and tell you—yet again—that there's no way he'll approve your interviewing each church member about their abilities, skills, and passions, it's hard to believe that his heart can change.

> "You are on a mission that requires faithfulness and tenacity."

But it can.

You may be facing an uphill climb as you create an excellent, sustainable, thriving volunteer ministry. Maybe that's something you should have expected. To think something so valuable and precious could be birthed or taken to the next level without some childbirth pain isn't very realistic.

So set your expectations accordingly. Determine you'll be in the process for the long haul. Called by God and given a vision of your church that means being doers of God's Word as well as hearers of God's Word, you are on a mission that requires two things:

1. *Faithfulness*—to hear God and do what he tells you to do.

2. *Tenacity*—the decision not to give up.

Robert Greenleaf recounts a childhood story about a dogsled race in his hometown in his book, *Servant Leadership.*[3] Most of the boys in the race had big sleds and several dogs.

Greenleaf (only five years old) had a small sled and one little dog. The course was one mile staked out on the lake.

As the race started, the more powerful contenders quickly left Greenleaf behind. In fact, he hardly looked like he was in the race at all.

All went well until, about halfway around, the team that was second started to pass the team then in the lead. They came too close and the dogs got in a fight.

Pretty soon the other dog teams joined in, and little Greenleaf could see one big seething mass of kids, sleds, and dogs about half a mile away. So he gave them all wide berth, and was the only one who finished the race . . . which made him the winner.

> "If you are reasonably sure of your course— just keep going!"

As Geenleaf reflects on the gargantuan problems we sometimes face, he refers to that scene from long ago. He concludes:

"I draw the obvious moral. No matter how difficult the challenge or how impossible or hopeless the task may seem, if you are reasonably sure of your course—just keep going!"

And *that's* an expectation you can meet: never giving up.

---

1. Stan Toler and Alan Nelson, *The Five Star Church* (Ventura, Calif.: Regal Books, 1999), p. 93, quoted in Marlene Wilson, *The Effective Management of Volunteer Programs* (Boulder, Colo.: Volunteer Management Associates, 1976), p. 161.

2. This section about "attitudinal blocks" quotes heavily from Marlene Wilson's *How to Mobilize Church Volunteers* (Minneapolis, Minn.: Augsburg, 1983), pp. 77-83.

3. Robert K. Greenleaf, *Servant Leadership: A Journey into the Nature of Legitimate Power and Greatness* (New York/Ramsey/Toronto: Paulist Press, 1977), p. 14.

Evaluating Your Ministry

Make sure your volunteer ministry stays on target and is effective by using these evaluation tips and techniques.

Some things just naturally go together—apple pie and ice cream, fish and water. I'd like to suggest another natural pair—planning and evaluation.

In the context of your volunteer ministry, there are two general sorts of evaluations that you will do:

1. Evaluating the ministry itself.

2. Evaluating volunteers who serve in the program.

We'll get into evaluating volunteers themselves later in this volume, but for now let's walk through evaluating your volunteer ministry. It's essential to do this, and it's something that many volunteer ministry leaders never take time to do at all, let alone do consistently every six months or year.

Evaluating Your Volunteer Ministry

You really can't evaluate your volunteer ministry unless you've done thorough planning. As we begin a discussion on evaluation, I am assuming that you have become familiar with the process of planning and creating job descriptions we've shared in this Volunteer Leadership Series (see volume 3), and also that you are on your way to achieving both.

"Planning and evaluation are tightly linked."

Planning and evaluation are tightly linked. You can't do a good job evaluating your ministry or your volunteers unless you've developed a mission statement and planned how to implement it, and you've created job descriptions for volunteers. Have you done all of those things? Great, because *the better you plan, the easier it will be to do evaluations.* After all, evaluation is simply deciding if where you've gone is, in fact, where you intended to go—how well you have followed your plans and implemented your goals.

You'll recall that in order for a *goal* to become an *objective,* it has to be specific, measurable, achievable, delegated, and move you toward fulfilling your mission statement. You probably struggled to create goals that fit all these criteria.

> "Did you do what you said you'd do?"

Well, it was worth the effort! Not only will those objectives you created help you do great ministry, but they will make it easy to do evaluation. Because they're measurable, you can tell if you succeeded in doing what you set out to do.

Did you do what you said you'd do? Did you do it on time? Within budget? And if not, did you . . .

- fail to delegate responsibility to someone to achieve the objective?

- not allow enough time or money for it?

- let other, newer priorities change your overall goals for the year, but forget to change your objectives and plans?

Remember, plans can change at any time. God may send you and your volunteer ministry off in a different direction, accomplishing your mission in a new way. That's God's privilege—but did you all agree that's what was happening? And did you change your action plans in writing?

Why Evaluation Matters

I'm a person most would probably describe as a "people person," and I'll bet you're one, too. That's why you're involved in a volunteer ministry—you enjoy people and love to help them grow.

So the idea of chaining yourself to a desk so you can crunch numbers and evaluate your ministry might seem like a waste of time. You'd rather be out helping volunteers be successful.

I understand—but it's still vitally important that you thoroughly evaluate your program on a regular basis. How else can you know if you're being effective, and demonstrate to your church leadership that the ministry is worthy of ongoing support?

Embrace the idea of evaluating your ministry. It may not be the favorite part of your job now, but it will help you know how to better serve and support your volunteers.

Maybe you think you're already doing a thorough job of evaluating your ministry. Let's briefly test that theory. Take the following test and see what you learn . . .

Are You Already Effectively Evaluating Your Ministry?

Use these sample questions to help you determine if there's room for more effective evaluation in your volunteer ministry.

Rate each of the eight areas based on this scale:
5 = Always; 4 = Regularly; 3 = Sometimes; 2 = Rarely; 1 = Never

___ We formally evaluate our volunteer program, analyzing our progress on the goals and objectives we have set for ourselves at least once per year.

___ We formally evaluate each volunteer to see whether he or she is accomplishing assigned tasks.

___ We talk with volunteers about their "job satisfaction," while listening carefully to their dreams, desires, wants, and needs regarding their work.

___ We provide an effective way for volunteers to give feedback to those people who are in charge.

___ We encourage volunteers to give feedback about how they perceive the quality of our ministry and the quality of their supervision.

___ When a new volunteer begins service, we hold orientation sessions.

___ When a volunteer leaves, we schedule and conduct an exit interview.

___ We contact a broad range of folks, within and outside of our program, to ask them to evaluate our effectiveness.

You have a possible score of 40 points. If you scored less than 35, you're missing significant opportunities to evaluate your program and volunteers, and to benefit from the feedback.

Myths about Evaluation

Evaluation is a tool you use to determine if your program—and the people in it—is doing what it's supposed to be doing. The evaluation process is as essential to the health of any volunteer ministry as is the planning process

Yet, evaluation is the tool most often neglected by church groups. Why? Probably because many of us have mistaken notions about what evaluation is and does. Let's examine and put to rest some of those myths.

Myth 1: We're not perfect, so evaluations are only going to hurt us by displaying all our flaws.

Fact: Evaluations, to be valid, must highlight both "well-dones" and "opportunities for improvement."

Example: At First Church, the people wanted to do a thorough evaluation of their volunteer-led food pantry. They braced themselves for lots of bad news about their budgeting, programming, personnel, and leadership, because the program had seemed to languish during the past winter.

Instead, they were pleasantly surprised by two facts that surfaced in the analysis: (a) A large new homeless shelter had been set up in a neighboring town, so that most of the hungry people in the area were now heading there for food and temporary lodging; (b) in spite of the new shelter, the church members discovered they'd been consistently feeding more people each year during the previous five years.

Their perceptions about the program had been flawed until the facts were uncovered.

Myth 2: Evaluations are purely statistical and boring.

Fact: Evaluations can be set up to record feelings, dreams, desires, visions, suggestions, and comments about what has happened—or what *should* happen. These can be more insightful and instructive than any statistics generated.

Example: After the vacation Bible school program at Second Church, informal survey forms were distributed to the teachers, parents, and children. The forms asked a few simple questions about what people liked, didn't like, and what they would suggest for improvement for the coming year.

The statements were printed up (anonymously) and distributed for everyone to read under two categories: strengths and weaknesses. Surprisingly, this was a very powerful and poignant experience for everyone. The "strengths" comments were heartwarming and encouraging. The "weaknessess" suggestions, for the most part, were right on target. And plans were made for realistic change. Later, most participants said: "What a positive experience!"

Myth 3: Evaluation is something done by specialists.

Fact: Rarely do churches hire professional consultants. In fact, most churches aren't "mega-sized" and therefore consultancy is ruled out. Instead, all participants involved in a project or program are invited into the evaluation process by the current leadership.

Example: After Joe had spent six months leading the Men's Retreat Planning Committee at Third Church, he was exhausted. Yet, because the retreat was such a success, he had a warm glow every time he thought about how his efforts contributed. Joe figured that glow was enough of a reward, so he was surprised when Pastor Smith set up an appointment with him and the rest of the committee members to evaluate how the process had gone for everybody. They all talked together, informally. They also filled out a Retreat Planning Feedback Questionnaire to analyze during a second meeting.

Joe and his committee members knew they had the skills to plan and produce the retreat. Clearly, Pastor Smith thought they had the skills to evaluate it as well.

Myth 4: Evaluation is an end in itself, a final report to wrap up a project.

Fact: Evaluations should help you decide what to add, drop, change, or keep. Program adjustment is the goal and chief benefit.

> "It's important to do both objective and subjective evaluations."

Example: At Fourth Church, the children's pastor did a complete organizational development process, surveying all aspects of children's programming. He helped the participants develop a mission statement, set goals and objectives, analyze and gather resources, and put plans into action.

A year later, when the evaluation process was completed, the leaders, volunteers, and parents decided to drop the high school "coffee shop" while adding a softball league for sixth through ninth graders. The evaluation process, in itself, was a tool for producing that change. Everyone knew there would be ongoing change and continual adjustment, because the new ministry configuration(s) would be evaluated annually.

Don't let believing these myths stop you from evaluating your ministry. They're myths—not accurate representations of evaluation or what it can offer you and your ministry.

Of all these myths, perhaps the one likeliest to stop volunteer ministry leaders from evaluating their programs (and volunteers) is the second myth: Evaluation is nothing more than stale, boring statistics.

Listen, it's important to do both objective *and* subjective evaluations to get an accurate picture of your ministry.

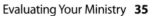

Consider the difference between the two . . .

Objective Evaluation

This type is simple if you've planned well. Just review all of your objectives for the year and determine whether your volunteer ministry accomplished what it set out to do—on time and within budget. If not, try to determine why. Then feed what you learn into next year's planning process.

The evaluation may reveal that you wrote a worthwhile objective but didn't allow enough time or didn't have the right person in charge. Or maybe you'll find that the need for a certain program no longer exists. Now you can drop or change that objective next year.

Subjective Evaluation

This type of evaluation is more difficult and rarely done in churches. Too bad, because a subjective evaluation is essential if you're going to be responsible for your people as well as your program.

You see, you've got to know whether your volunteers grew spiritually and as persons as a result of their involvement as volunteers. You need to know how they felt about the experience, whether their ideas were sought or ignored, and whether or not they received the support, training, and recognition they needed.

And did they feel they were truly in ministry?

These aren't small questions, and they reveal important information.

Dietrich Bonhoeffer was a mid-twentieth-century theologian and a martyr to the Nazis. In his book, *Life Together*, he suggested several questions any Christian community needs to ask to determine if the work it's doing is on target:

> Has the fellowship served to make the individual free, strong, and mature, or has it made him weak and dependent? Has it taken him by the hand for awhile in order that he may learn to walk by himself, or has it made him uneasy and unsure?[1]

As a leader in your church's volunteer ministry, you need to know how participating in the ministry impacts people. Does it cause them to grow in their relationship with Jesus, or become a distraction to their spiritual growth?

You are involving Christians in ministry. You are helping your church do the work God has called it to do. You are cooperating with the purposes and plans God has for his people. It stands to reason, then, that the fruit of your efforts will be positive and good. But until you check through a thorough evaluation, you'll never know for certain.

The Three Big Questions

In my experience, there are three questions that must be part of your ministry evaluation:

1. What should we evaluate?

2. Who should do the evaluations?

3. What do we do with the evaluation results?

Let's examine these three questions in order . . .

Question #1: *What* Should We Evaluate?

It seems obvious to say, but you need to decide what elements of your ministry you want to evaluate. That decision will determine what tools (such as surveys and individual interviews) you'll need to gather relevant information, and to do a helpful analysis.

Again—if you've got solid goals and objectives in place, that's the place to start. They are designed to be specific, measurable standards that can be evaluated easily.

For instance:

- Did you recruit and place 25 teenage mentors in nine months?

- Did you set up three new food distribution centers, with four volunteers regularly scheduled to oversee each one?

- Did you implement a teacher-training program and graduate five new Sunday school teachers in the past quarter?

If you accomplished your objectives, then you can go on to ask: *How well is it working?* If you were able to accomplish an objective but it burned out half your volunteer staff to meet the deadline, there's a hidden problem. What looks like a success actually wasn't one—the cost was too high.

And if you *didn't* accomplish your objectives, you can ask: *What will we do about it—if anything?* Perhaps you could get those 25 teenage mentors if you recruit in two more high schools. Or maybe you want to abandon the mentoring program because you've discovered the liability insurance premiums for the program have doubled in price and you can no longer afford it.

It's challenging to evaluate a ministry. The elements of the program you choose to measure, the specific people you choose to interview—they all have a unique view of the program.

It's important that you move past general impressions and get down to hard numbers and real statistics. It's not that "soft" questions—the ones that call for judgment from the people being interviewed—are worthless. They're valuable! In fact, you must ask some questions that get at the reputation of your volunteer ministry. Here are some "soft" questions you might want to ask . . .

> "It's challenging to evaluate a ministry."

- Are volunteers enriching and extending paid staff efforts in achieving the purpose of the church, or are volunteers simply window dressing?

- Is the money expended on the volunteer ministry reasonable and justifiable when cost per volunteer is computed?

- Is the ministry accepted and supported by staff and administration? Do recipients of the ministry's efforts regard the ministry as valuable to them?

You can gain a world of insight by listening to the answers to these questions.

But you're also looking to discover quantifiable information. What can you measure and use as a yardstick from year to year to see if you're improving, static, or sliding backward in your effectiveness?

I'd suggest you find ways to measure the following items:

Time is a resource given by your volunteers, both individually and in groups. Find out how many hours have been given per week or month, or whatever time period you're evaluating. Use simple record sheets such as sign-in and sign-out sheets, or have volunteers report monthly how many hours they've given to the ministry.

Look for trends: Do you have more volunteers, but they're each giving fewer hours? Do you have some volunteers who give a great deal of time, and some that you seldom see? Are there more volunteers in the winter than in the summer, and how might you use that information in planning?

Turnover rate is a critical marker to track, too. How long does the typical volunteer stick with the ministry? Are there different turnover rates in different sorts of volunteer positions? If so, what does that tell you? What could you do to impact the average length of service among your volunteers? When volunteers consistently leave before the completion of their assignments or commitments, you've got a problem! Or when the average length of service remains only a few months, something needs changing.

Budget is a major concern. Are you under budget? Over? Right on the money? Is there a predictable time of year when the budget is tight or loose? What factors impact that? Which parts of your program seem to be marginal when you consider the "bang for the buck" factor? What might that information imply?

Achieving goals is perhaps the most obvious objective standard to check. Did you get things done you set out to do?

Question #2: *Who* Should Do Evaluations?

In the same way it was important to have key "affected individuals" represented in the planning process, it's important to have them in the evaluation process, too. These people should have a say in how the evaluation is conducted, and what is actually evaluated.

Affected people who should be represented in this process might include the volunteer manager, the volunteers, church staff, administration, and church members. All need to have the opportunity to evaluate the ministry from their perspective.

There are many tools that could be used to conduct the evaluation. However, because every volunteer ministry is unique, I strongly suggest that your task force drafts its own evaluation tool.

Don't worry—you don't have to start from scratch! There are denominations and other church groups that have created evaluation tools. If you have a denominational affiliation, check with your office. But one downside of using a denominational tool is that they're generally very specific to a single denomination; those tools don't translate well for use in every church.

> "You don't have to start from scratch!"

Let me outline the major issues you should include in your evaluation. Ask your task force to draft specific questions to fit under each heading.

1. Mission statement

Ask questions about whether the church's mission statement is effective, reviewed regularly, or needs to be adjusted. Ask the same questions about your volunteer ministry.

2. Volunteer ministry job descriptions

Ask questions about expectations, and the clarity and awareness of written job descriptions.

3. Identifying and interviewing volunteers

Ask questions about how volunteers are identified and interviewed in terms of their abilities, skills, passion, personality, and desire to serve.

4. Matching volunteers and ministry positions

Ask questions about how volunteer's abilities, skills, and passions are connected to church ministry needs.

5. Recruiting volunteers

Ask questions about interviewing, describing positions, offering choices; the entire volunteer recruitment process. And include questions about marketing the volunteer program, too.

6. Training volunteers

Ask questions about how effectively you're providing orientation, education, retreats, and training courses.

7. Supporting volunteers

Ask questions about how your ministry is encouraging, recognizing, and offering support to all your constituencies.

8. Completing a volunteer ministry assignment

Ask questions about what happens when a volunteer ends a project or term of office.

9. Evaluating the volunteer ministry as a program in the church

Ask questions about how the entire volunteer ministry is functioning as a ministry area of the church. What's your reputation? How effectively are you involved? Are you thriving and energized by the power sources discussed in volume 2 of this Volunteer Leadership Series?

The person directing the ministry should constantly conduct an ongoing, informal assessment. Feedback from staff and volunteers, observations, comments at meetings, volunteer reports, statistics and records—these all provide a picture of the ministry's ongoing health.

"Don't neglect periodic formal assessments!"

But even if you are doing the job with such informal evaluations, please don't neglect periodic formal assessments! You'll find them useful as you prepare budgets and goals for the coming year. Use questionnaires and/or interviews with representatives from each of the groups affected by your volunteer ministry.

The person who directs the volunteer ministry needs to become a real fan of doing ongoing evaluations. Why? Because in the course of those evaluations the volunteer leader is able to discover and correct problems before they become unmanageable. This assumes, of course, that leaders intend to act on the data and insights they gain from the evaluation process.

Question #3: *What* Do You Do with Evaluation Results?

Ivan Scheier answered this question well:

• Disseminate

• Discuss

• Do Something

• Don't File [2]

In other words, *act on results.*

May I suggest you carve that one in stone? Hang it on your office door where you'll see it often—as well as those who work with you in the volunteer ministry.

"You must act!"

You must act! Bring together representatives of all the groups involved in an evaluation and talk about what you've discovered. *But don't stop there.* Keep bringing your group together for the consequent re-planning and adjustment process.

This group will . . .

• Objectively examine the results.

• Explore alternative courses of action.

• Develop recommendations for improvement.

• Draw up a plan.

• Act on the plan.

A note: Don't forget all the good that's getting done! Be sure that in the course of discussion and planning the strengths of the program are recognized, reinforced, and celebrated.

Evaluation not only enables, but forces, us to examine the quality and value of our programs. Yes, we certainly want to know how to do the thing we do more effectively. But that's not enough. Let's also ask the hard questions about *why* we do them, and what happens as a result.

Exit Interviews

When you interview individuals who are leaving your program for some reason, it's not technically an evaluation of the volunteer ministry itself. But if you'll sift through exit interviews with an eye for trends, you'll get wonderful feedback about how your volunteer ministry is functioning. Exit interviews are used in many businesses because:

- The feedback about the company is often direct and clear; the employee is leaving and therefore more likely to be candid with comments.

- Who is better able to provide accurate feedback than someone who is familiar with the company, its policies and procedures, and its management?

Your church isn't a company, but the benefits of exit interviews are transferable. Don't miss this opportunity to find out how your ministry is doing, where you can improve, and where you're doing wonderful work already.

Set up the exit interview for *every* volunteer who leaves a position; don't reserve these interviews only for volunteers who leave while happy . . . or who are released from their positions. If you "cherry-pick" just people who are happy, you'll think everything is wonderful. If you consider only what disgruntled people say, you'll quickly become discouraged. Talk with everyone.

You might consider having someone other than yourself or the volunteer's supervisor conduct the interview. If there's a personality conflict, the volunteer might be more likely to reveal that information to someone else. You're looking for honest answers, so remove obstacles that might interfere with honesty.

> "Set up the exit interview for *every* volunteer who leaves."

My friend Betty Stallings has developed an exit interview for volunteer organizations you can easily adapt and use for your ministry.

Sample Volunteer Exit Survey Form

1. To what extent did you feel you reached the expectations listed in your job description? Share your reasons for any "gap" you perceive.

2. Was the time allowed to accomplish your volunteer work realistic? Explain your answer.

3. Did the church provide adequate orientation, training, supervision, and resources for you to accomplish your job? Comment, and offer suggestions for improvement.

4. What's been your greatest satisfaction on the job?

5. What's been your greatest disappointment on the job?

6. Were other volunteers and staff receptive and appreciative of your volunteer work? Explain your answer.

7. What were areas of growth in your volunteer job?

8. Overall, would you rank your performance as:
❑ Superior, exceeding expectations
❑ Excellent, you met expectations
❑ Needing improvement, you didn't meet expectations.
Explain why you chose the answer you chose . . .

9. What type of work and time commitment do you desire for next year? (Note: Only ask this if you would offer another position to the volunteer.)

10. Please share any other comments or suggestions.[3]

Courtesy of Betty Stallings

1. Dietrich Bonhoeffer, *Life Together* (New York: Harper and Row, 1954, 2003), p. 49, quoted in Marlene Wilson, *How to Mobilize Church Volunteers* (Minneapolis, Minn.: Augsburg, 1983), p. 66.

2. Ivan Scheier, quoted in Marlene Wilson, *The Effective Management of Volunteer Programs* (Boulder, Colo.: Volunteer Management Associates, 1976), p. 91.

3. Betty Stallings, "The Church and Its Volunteers" in the series *The Ministry of Volunteers* © 1979, Office of Church Life and Leadership, United Church of Christ. This was reprinted in its entirety, by permission, in Marlene Wilson, *The Effective Management of Volunteer Programs,* pp. 136-142.

THREE
Accountability: Your Part in Preventing Problems

Help for solving most volunteer-related problems before they happen, and four questions to ask when a problem does appear.

As you evaluate your ministry and your volunteers, you'll find opportunities to improve, to define problems, and then to do something to improve. That's the essence of accountability.

Nobody likes focusing solely on problems, but part of accountability is objectively examining problem areas and seeking to fix them. In these two chapters on accountability you'll see how that's done.

In this chapter we'll ask several important questions:

- Could the problem be the system?

- Could the problem be you?

- Could the problem be unresolved conflict?

- Could the problem be a difficult volunteer?

This final question is an important one, but I will deal with it fully in chapter 4.

Could the Problem Be the System?

Let me say again that working with volunteers is almost always a happy, fun, and rewarding experience. If you've been involved for any length of time, you already know this! And to keep your volunteer leadership experience on this high level of fulfillment and success, one particular attitude is crucial: When a problem arises, it's best not to immediately assume that an individual is at fault.

> **"Working with volunteers is almost always a happy, fun, and rewarding experience."**

That's right. Don't look to the individual volunteer first. Rather, look to the *system*—your policies and procedures, both official and unofficial.

I'm hoping you're already assuming the best of your volunteers and nurturing respectful, positive relationships on your team. With those attitudes in place you'll know that volunteers don't attempt to deliberately create difficulties; if anything, they go out of their way to *not* cause problems. When problems do arise, it's often the case that a change in the system or in the environment will bring everything back in line. You don't need a change in personnel.

But what, exactly, is a "system problem?" A little story here might help you visualize the phenomenon.

Imagine a company that produces widgets. It has two manufacturing plants, Plant A and Plant B, and at each location there's a hierarchy of managers. Plant A produces the widget and Plant B produces the packaging within which the widget will be shipped and displayed on store shelves.

All has been going well for years, until yesterday. Suddenly the packages are too small for the widgets! The vice president at Plant A picks up the phone and calls the vice president at Plant B. "What's going on with you guys over there?" he hollers. "The packages are too small! Here are the specifications we need . . . "

The conversation is brief; the crucial information is relayed. The packaging vice president then immediately calls his plant manager into the office. "What's wrong with you, Fred? The packages are too small. Check out these specifications!"

Fred hurries back to the plant and calls his foreman into the office. "Jake, are you nuts? You're really messing up here, and

I'm not going to stand for it. Look, these packages are too small."

Jake runs from the office and hustles over to Phil's package-sizing machine and yells: "Phil, look at your calibrations! They're off by a country mile!"

Phil says: "But I thought Geraldo, the widget-sizing guy over in Plant A, was now making a new, smaller widget! Boy, I guess I was wrong about that—and sorry about the loss of millions of dollars."

At this point, Jake realizes he has several choices. He can assume there's a personnel problem and fire Phil for incompetence. Or, he can go back and talk to his plant manager, who will talk to the vice president, who will call the other vice president over at Plant A. Then that vice president will talk to his plant manager, who will call his foremen, who will speak to Geraldo. And perhaps Geraldo will need to be fired, which should take care of the widget-sizing problem.

> "Adjust the system; solve the problem."

But Jake chooses a third alternative, a quick "system fix." He decides to install a phone next to Phil's machine so that Phil can talk to Geraldo about the widget sizes he's been instructed to produce. In fact, now the two workers can talk about specs and calibrations any time they want.

And guess what? For as long as Phil has access to that phone, there is never again a packaging problem!

That's just one example of how a system solution can be just what the doctor ordered when a program problem arises. Adjust the system; solve the problem.

There are countless possibilities for system problems, of course. So how could this type of thing occur in a church or other volunteer situation? Think about it . . . and test your creative problem-solving skills in a couple of possible scenarios—

Suppose . . .

Your Sunday school superintendent keeps forgetting to give you the attendance report after classes on Sunday mornings. Sometimes he lets you know as he passes you in the hall. At other times he calls later in the week and gives you a number. You, in turn, are either late or inaccurate in your reporting to the Christian education board. And you're getting pretty angry about that superintendent.

Your recommendations for a system change that could help . . .

_____

_____

_____

_____

(*A possible suggestion:* What if you both agreed to install a clipboard with attached pencil on the superintendent's wall? It could hold an attendance form ready for filling in, along with displaying your fax number, e-mail address, and phone number at the bottom of each page.)

Suppose . . .

Each day, after the kindergartners have their vacation Bible school snack time in the gym, there's at least one banana peel left on the floor. The custodian wants you to reprimand the teacher for being so incompetent.

Your recommendations for a system change that could help . . .

_____

_____

_____

_____

(*A possible suggestion:* Could you ask the teacher to stop serving bananas for snacks? Could the kids have their snacks outside? Or could a trash can be placed in the gym?)

Bottom line: Sometimes system problems are a quick fix, with few people involved. A few conversations, an update in your procedure manual, and it's over.

But sometimes they're at the heart of a large, far-reaching problem, and changing the system will require a significant amount of time and energy. Do it anyway—it's worth it.

When you sense that the system itself is your main problem, take these three actions—

1. Check the program evaluations you've done and see whether there are any holes. (Look for steps you may be skipping in the volunteer leadership system outlined in this series, or steps you aren't doing well.)

2. Set priorities, along with actions steps, for changing and improving the system. Make sure those priorities are communicated; you may not be the only one skipping steps!

3. Give yourself one to two years to do the fix or "plug the holes." Quick fixes are quick—but not always a fix. Take the time to do it right.

Could the Problem Be You?

Maybe you don't need to focus your concerns on the system at all. Maybe it's just a matter of looking in the mirror.

When the problem is you, it's usually because you aren't taking care of you. That is, maybe you aren't adequately

> "Quick fixes are quick—but not always a fix."

managing your own stress so you can more effectively manage the stresses among and within your volunteers. When leaders are stressed-out and maxed-out, ministries tend to experience more problems, and small wonder. The leaders don't have spiritual, emotional, and physical reserves deep enough to deal with issues that arise.

So consider your own life right now. Is it one of joy—or stress? Is it one that you'd like to maintain for a long period, or would you change it if you only knew how?

How's your stress level?

Most of us who are involved in church leadership can relate to hectic situations like these:

- The alarm didn't go off and you missed your 8:30 volunteer staff meeting.

- The senior pastor turned down that proposal you submitted three weeks ago.

- The church secretary was out sick, so you answered phones all day.

- You got stuck in a one-hour traffic jam on the way home from work.

As the pressure mounts, so does your blood pressure, and soon your head aches or your stomach hurts, you begin snapping at everyone (including strangers), your heart pounds, and you find yourself either becoming more aggressive or withdrawing into yourself.

> **"Is your life one of joy— or stress?"**

You're experiencing stress, and it's part of daily life for most of us. To be sure, a little stress isn't a problem. But when there's too much, or we are overwhelmed by it, stress can take a hefty toll. Stress has been linked with most major health problems, including heart disease, hypertension, ulcers, and cancer.

And like it or not, stress is no stranger in the church. As the leader of a volunteer ministry, you're responsible for the quality of work performed by people you don't pay and whom you may not directly supervise. That's stress!

You've got to learn to handle stress well for several reasons, not the least of which is that without mastering stress you'll never last long in a ministry position. You'll feel the joy and fun drain from your ministry; it will become drudgery you'd rather avoid.

Plus, when you handle stress well, problem situations tend

to gradually diminish—for reasons that have nothing to do with your volunteers or pastor.

Handling stress well can mean:

- **You don't overreact.** If you're overly stressed, you'll overreact to people and situations that appear to be problems. You'll treat small interruptions as major issues—because in truth the problem is you. You've got to understand and recognize when inner stress is fogging your vision and warping your assessment of others and the work they are doing.

> "Like it or not, stress is no stranger in the church."

- **You model stress-free volunteerism.** If you've learned how to recognize and manage your own stress levels, you can then model and teach those skills to your volunteers. It's amazing how many "problem people" can become ideal volunteers if their stresses are cared for. If they're nurtured and given hope, they can set about their tasks with renewed energy and positive spirits. It doesn't *always* work that way, of course. But isn't it worth trying to salvage those who, because of stress, are unhappy—and are making others unhappy?

Let's revisit those stressful scenarios I listed on page 50. There are three stressful components in each of them:

1. **The stressor**—the event or incident in the environment that arouses stress.

2. **Your perception of that stressor**—which determines how it affects you.

3. **Your reaction or physical and emotional response to the stressor, based on that perception**—it's not the same for everybody.

This information explains why some people view a seemingly

stressful incident calmly while other people are running in circles, panicked and screaming.

Let's take the traffic jam, for instance. One person impatiently views it as an intrusion on his freedom of movement and a maddening inconvenience, while the person in the next car may regard it as a chance to listen to a favorite CD or unwind before reentering his or her life with the family. It's the same traffic jam—but the perceptions and reactions are very different. The traffic jam is stress-*inducing* to one driver and stress-*reducing* to another driver.

> "Most people handle the vast majority of potentially stressful situations successfully."

That un-stressed driver is undoubtedly employing one of the three stress-management strategies listed below. They're the same options we all have when we feel the tension of stress building:

- Remove yourself from the situation or stressor,

- Reengineer the situation so it's no longer stressful, or

- Teach yourself to react differently regarding things you find stressful that you can't change or leave.

Prolonged, unrelieved stress is the most debilitating kind of stress, so work on taming those stressors first. Although you can list dozens of sources of stress in your life, probably very few of them are actually creating problems for you.

Most people handle the vast majority of potentially stressful situations successfully. Appropriate stress is often what provides excitement and zest in our lives, and many days would be boring if all traces of stress disappeared.

But there are those long-term stressors that can do us damage. Equally damaging is responding to a small stressor as if it were a life-threatening, fire-breathing dragon attacking you.

Here are four questions that will help you determine if a stressor deserves a five-alarm response, or can just be identified and shrugged off:

1. Is there really a legitimate threat in this situation?
2. Is your interpretation of the event more of a threat than its actuality?
3. Is the event really worth a fight?
4. If you do decide to fight, will it make any difference?

> "The only direction for getting off a pedestal is down."

Your goal is to learn to expend an appropriate amount of energy on problems or stressors based on their long-term importance to you. If you overreact to small things (like traffic jams and lost socks), you'll use up your ability to handle stress on the small stuff. There will be no energy left to tackle the big stuff.

In your volunteer ministry you will undoubtedly be challenged—that comes with the territory. At times you'll be overworked. And you'll probably feel unappreciated now and then (we all do).

But you can be attentive to your own stress, health, and happiness—and make sure that when problems arise, your presence helps resolve them, not create them.

You Aren't the Messiah

A seductive temptation for volunteer leaders is to try to be all things to all people (often referred to, appropriately enough for church volunteer ministry leaders, as the "Messiah Complex"). It leads to longer and longer hours, more and more projects, weekend and evening commitments, and eventual burnout.

It often appears easier, quicker, and more effective to do things yourself rather than invest the time and effort to recruit, train, and supervise a team for effective ministry. Besides, it's kind of nice to feel you have climbed on that pedestal called "indispensable," right? But remember: The only direction for getting off a pedestal is down, and it behooves you to climb down before you fall off.

You are *not* the Messiah! You are simply a person who works with and through others to accomplish ministry goals. And how those other people feel about working with you has . . .

tremendous impact on both the quality and quantity of work they'll do,

which has a great impact on your own perceptions of your effectiveness as a manager,

which has an awesome impact on both your own stress level and that of your subordinates,

which has a mind-boggling impact on your health and peace of mind,

which has a gargantuan impact on how many "problem volunteers" you are encountering (or creating?)—*and* how you deal with them.

If you're trying to do too much for too long, I can tell you this: When problems pop up in the ministry, one of the culprits will probably be you.

In my book, *Survival Skills for Managers*, I list several suggestions to help manage the stress in your life:

1. Clarify your value system so you're expending the greatest amount of time and energy on those things of greatest value to you.

2. Take good care of yourself physically through exercise and good nutrition.

3. Create and use personal support systems.

4. Learn to let go of past resentments, toxic relationships, and bad health habits.

5. Seek variety, and develop a well-rounded personality—avoid being a one-dimensional workaholic.

6. Maintain optimism and keep some optimists around you.

7. Try to make the workplace and work itself more enjoyable.

> 8. Don't let small things become a hassle.
> 9. Take responsibility to change what needs to be changed.
> 10. Value and develop creativity and flexibility.
> 11. Have faith that things can be different.[1]

Have I overstated my case about the importance of your personal stress management and honoring your limitations? I don't think so.

You see, most of the effective volunteer managers and leaders I've known have been, first of all, effective as *persons*. By that I mean they are well-rounded, involved, enthusiastic life-long learners who always see themselves on a "journey of becoming." As such, they're fully qualified to deal with people who are living out less than their potential, and those who are "problems" because they're stressed, in the wrong job, or have determined to handle life's problems in ways that—sadly—irritate others!

We can only approach those folks with love and kindness when we have the emotional and spiritual energy to do so. Will we seek to redeem every problem situation and its participants for the good? Yes, but we'll also approach these persons with firmness and decisiveness.

Why? Because our volunteer ministry is at stake. Kingdom work must move forward.

Could the Problem Be Unresolved Conflict?

Any time we get serious about accountability, we'll run into conflict. That can be uncomfortable for Christians because we figure that if we truly love one another—like the Bible says!—then interpersonal discord won't happen.

"We become chronic avoiders and deniers."

The result is that we become chronic avoiders and deniers. We let conflicts fester instead of dealing with them openly and well.

One of the best resources I've seen on this subject is a video by Elaine Yarbrough titled *Managing Conflict.*[2] I'm sure that some of my thoughts about conflict resolution are hers, filtered through my experience. One of the most eye-opening discoveries I've made about conflict is that there's a positive, productive side to it—and a positive, productive way to deal with it.

Consider . . .

- When in conflict, seek a resolution that everyone involved can accept. It's not always a "win-lose" situation. With creativity and resolve we can usually find a "win-win" solution.

- Remember that conflict produces lots of energy. We get fired up and passionate. Let's remember to use that energy for good, especially directing it toward problem solving.

- As you seek resolution, be sure you're digging down to the real issues, not just the on-the-surface presenting problems. It's easy to solve the wrong problems just so we can say we solved something.

- Keep in mind that conflict is neither good nor bad. It simply is.

- Make problem-solving your goal rather than trying to make everyone happy and friendly. Not everyone may emerge happy, but they can emerge heard and valued.

> **"Conflict is neither good nor bad."**

The first thing for us to accept is something that probably feels completely wrong: *Conflict is not bad.* It's not good, either. Conflict simply exists. It's the by-product of having so many of us crowded onto this planet, each of us with our own agendas, interests, goals, and values. We come into conflict because we're all here. About the only place you can pack people close together without conflict erupting is in a cemetery.

What's required is that we choose to not let conflict poison our relationships. Instead, we can let it be a powerful catalyst for significant change—perhaps change for the better.

Conflict itself isn't fun or painless. But it's not always bad, either, as demonstrated by how tough times, challenges, obstacles, and even affliction can prompt our spiritual growth. Consider this passage from the book of James:

> *Consider it pure joy, my brothers, whenever you face trials of many kinds, because you know that the testing of your faith develops perseverance. Perseverance must finish its work so that you may be mature and complete, not lacking anything. (James 1:2-4)*

When you encounter conflict—and you will—keep in mind that, if we choose:

Our trials can produce patience.

Our sufferings can produce mercy.

Our sicknesses can produce antibodies.

Our loneliness can produce compassion.

Our sadness can produce pity.

Our anger can produce righteous action for change.

I'd like to suggest that when conflict arises, you choose to make your first response (after the initial shock or pain): "I wonder what new—and potentially wonderful—results this situation could produce?"

Conflict always generates great energy; your job is to direct and focus that energy toward problem-solving activity rather than toward people-destroying activity. Learning to make conflict constructive makes working with volunteers even more fun and rewarding.

It takes some effort to make conflict into something positive, of course. I think two essential skills are needed:

1. To know when you're "stuck"—and how to get unstuck with certain conflict-diffusing techniques, and

2. To master four steps to reaching agreements.

The rest of this chapter will help equip you in both areas. While having conflict is neither good nor bad, letting conflict simmer and stew is most definitely *not* good.

When You Get Stuck

When conflicts arise, you need to seek a win-win solution—one where everyone involved is heard, understood, and emerges with something he or she needs.

The following techniques can help you get "unstuck" and move toward a win-win solution. These techniques will help defuse a conflict situation. Keep in mind they're just tools and temporary fixes, though—you don't want to slap an adhesive bandage on a broken bone and assume everything will heal up fine.

When you find yourself in conflict, invest the time to resolve it thoroughly.

Use "I" statements.

When you express feelings in a conflict situation, it's wise to use "I" statements rather than "you" statements. It's easier to avoid making accusations—or appearing to make accusations—when you're talking about your own feelings rather than the other person's feelings

Confronting, even with the best of intentions and with heartfelt love and concern for the other person, is a volatile process. It's better to share what you know to be true (your feelings and motivations) rather than what you only assume to be true (the other person's feelings and motivations).

"Confronting is a volatile process."

Here's an example of the difference in these approaches. You'll note that both comments refer to the same event. At the church board meeting there was a comment made about Frank. Now Frank is talking with the person who made the comment.

Using an "I" statement: *"I feel bad about something I heard in the meeting last night. I'd like to talk it over."* Notice that this sounds like a report, not an attack. Frank is owning his feelings.

Using a "you" statement: *"You said something hurtful last night. You need to deal with it."* This sounds like an accusation—an attack. The person Frank is confronting will likely grow defensive very quickly.

See the difference? Who would you rather talk with about a problem or conflict: someone using "I" statements or someone who is on the offensive?

Try turning these examples of confrontation into "I" statements:

"You never send out the agenda far enough in advance. You're not giving me time to prepare for our meetings."

_____

_____

_____

_____

(Here's one possible revision of the statement above: *"I've noticed that I'm receiving the agenda pretty close to our meeting times. But I'd like more time to prepare."*)

"Clearly, you don't care how I might be hurt by this."

_____

_____

_____

_____

"Some of us in this program think you're being insensitive about causing embarrassment."

_____

_____

_____

_____

> "Let go of the belief that for you to personally be successful in resolving conflict, everyone must come out liking you. . . . Keep in mind that people around you need you to be effective more than they need you to be nice."—Sue Vineyard [3]

Use a "when-feel-please" formula when confronting others.
This is an excellent way to frame your statements when you have a (usually minor) grievance about someone's behavior that you need to raise—without starting a fight. It's direct, incorporates an "I" statement, and is specific about what can be done to remedy the situation. Your comment to the person with whom you have conflict combines these three elements. Here's how the three-part statement works:

1. Identify when the issue arose: "When you open the windows early in the morning . . ."

2. Identify a feeling: "I begin to feel cold . . ."

3. Use the word *please*: "So, could you please wait until later in the day to do that?"

Here are some other examples:

"When you come home late without warning, I feel neglected and unimportant. Honey, please give me a phone call when you know you're going to be late."

"When you tell the guys at the club about an upcoming church meeting, I feel left out of the loop. Could you please call or send me an email, since I'm not a club member?"

Avoid rhetorical questions.
Need I say more here? We all do it, so see if you recognize yourself in any of these questioning statements—whether they've been uttered at home, school, work, or church:

"Why can't I depend on you?"

"Why can't you see that you're putting people off?"

"Wouldn't it be better if you just _____?"

"Why can't you be more like your brother?"

"Why do you say such things?"

"Is this casserole too salty or what?"

"Why can't you ever learn?"

"Who said you could do that?"

Most rhetorical attacks start with the question "Why," which is usually a clue that what follows will be worthless for increasing understanding and cooperation. "Why" is one of the least effective approaches to resolving conflict; questioning is a great way to fan flames of anger.

Instead, state your feelings, needs, and ideas directly.

Leave all sarcasm behind—forever.

Humor in relationships is dangerous. A well-placed joke can work wonders in a tense situation, but joking can also backfire. It's often not worth the risk to make light of something that's potentially a sore subject between you and another person.

> "Here's Marlene's Rule about Sarcasm: Banish it."

My advice is that you should avoid joking with volunteers. If you do choose to joke with a volunteer, be wise. Know who you're dealing with. Be sure what you're saying cannot be construed as offensive—and that's tough to do!

And here's Marlene's Rule about Sarcasm: Banish it. It's *never* worth the risk. It offers a multitude of opportunities for misinterpretation and hurt feelings. What you say may sound cute at the time, but it will come back to haunt you later.

Four Steps for Getting to an Agreement

There's no right or wrong way to reach agreements when people are in conflict. Whatever works . . . works! However, I'd like to summarize four basic steps that often produce an excellent chance of reaching good agreements.

Step 1: Discover and emphasize what the participants hold in common.

You discover common ground by bringing people together and getting them sharing about "where they are." Ask everyone to respectfully take a turn speaking, and ask that everyone else respectfully listen without comment.

Your job is to note the areas, no matter how small, where people already agree. These are the places to begin building an even broader "island" of agreement. After sharing, highlight areas of agreement. Everyone may be surprised at the common ground already held!

Step 2: Attempt to "un-freeze" stalemates.

During the sharing you'll uncover specific places where conflicting parties are in an apparent deadlock. For instance, some volunteers want your instructional program to be held during morning hours. They are quite adamant about this because it fits with their home and school schedules.

Other participants demand an evening program that won't cut into their day jobs. In order to work at bringing the sides to some kind of resolution, you might try one or more of these approaches:

- **String it out.** Not every conflict can be solved in one sitting. Your first goal may be to get agreement that you'll meet several times to deal with the conflict.

- **Reduce the personal pain.** Explore what it is about a solution that causes the most pain for persons on either side of the issue. How can you eliminate or reduce some of that pain? For example, could you arrange for morning childcare for those who need to be home until noon?

- **Suggest pay-offs.** What will it take to get people to accept a less than ideal solution? Can you compensate or reward them in ways that make it worthwhile for them to re-arrange their work schedules?

- **Create compromises.** Get both sides to agree to give in so that they can meet in the middle. For example, meet in the evening during the first month, and in the morning during the second month.

- **Find a new alternative.** One side wants a morning program, and the other side wants an evening program. But what if instead of meeting as a group for instruction, you set up a system of one-on-one mentoring? Then pairs of individuals could meet together based on their own personal schedules.

The key: Creatively brainstorm solutions without setting limits. In the initial stages everyone should know that no possible solution will be considered foolish or out of bounds. Let the possibilities be raised and "placed in the hopper" for future consideration. Creative thinking is the key.

> "Creatively brainstorm solutions without setting limits."

Step 3: Produce a written contract that outlines all specific agreements between the parties.

Make this summary as clear and as simple as possible. This can be as simple as e-mailing meeting minutes with a clear statement about how the conflict was resolved and how people agreed to proceed. Or it can be a more formal document that's filed in the church office, perhaps after everyone has signed it. Use your common sense about how elaborate you need to be, based on the gravity of the issues.

Don't generalize; be specific. And consider building in consequences everyone is aware of, should one or more persons break the agreement.

Step 4: Schedule a follow-up meeting.

This meeting creates an opportunity for your evaluation process, and guarantees that you won't come to agreements and then forget about them. It's human nature to slip back into old patterns of conflict unless we're diligent about monitoring our progress.

1. Marlene Wilson, *Survival Skills for Managers* (Boulder, Colo.: Volunteer Management Associates, 1981), pp. 189-221.

2. The video *Managing Conflict* (1997) by Elaine Yarbrough is from the Yarbrough Group, 1113 Spruce Street, Boulder, Colorado 80302. Phone: (303) 449-7107.

3. Sue Vineyard, *Stop Managing Volunteers* (Downers Grove, Ill.: Heritage Arts Publishing, 1996), p. 88.

FOUR
Accountability: Evaluating Volunteers

Discover how to make evaluations friendly, not frightening. Doing evaluations in a way that's helpful. Plus, how to handle difficult volunteers.

Uh oh . . . a problem has arisen. You look at the system for solutions. You look to your own stress levels and check for burnout. Then you work toward constructive conflict resolution if there's a disagreement.

But suppose the root of the problem turns out to be a particular volunteer? And no matter how much you try to find a solution, every finger keeps pointing back to that one specific person?

"Problem volunteers" are rare but they do happen. When it comes to evaluating a volunteer who's a problem, let me urge you to embrace these two accountability principles that need to be applied to *all* volunteers:

1. **Never lower standards for volunteers.** It's the ultimate put-down for volunteers to feel that what they do is so unimportant that it doesn't matter if they do it well—or even at all.

2. **View volunteers as unpaid staff and always hold them accountable for their commitments and actions.** If it would matter if your paid pastor did it, it matters if a volunteer does it—or doesn't do it. Treat paid and unpaid staff the same.

> "Problem volunteers" are rare but they do happen."

What Exactly Is a "Problem Volunteer"?

If a volunteer is unable to function in his or her role, that's a problem . . . but he or she may *not* be a problem volunteer.

If you see that the problems generated by a volunteer far outweigh the good coming from his or her efforts, or if that volunteer is intentionally making things difficult for everyone and therefore damaging your team or volunteer ministry, *that's* a problem volunteer.

So how do you handle that sort of person?

Let's approach this issue in two ways: by being *proactive* and *reactive*.

We'll focus on proactively preventing problem-volunteer situations in the first place—by making sure we're conducting ongoing performance reviews. Being proactive is one way you can make certain you very seldom, if ever, see a problem volunteer.

Then we'll talk about being reactive—how to react when it's obvious that no solution other than separating a volunteer from your program will work to keep your ministry healthy.

Being Proactive

The great news is that you can prevent lots of problems in your volunteer ministry simply by being proactive with evaluations (also called performance reviews). After all, performance reviews have the potential to be overwhelmingly positive—and most are!

> "Think of performance evaluations as an *affirming* event."

I want to encourage you to think of performance evaluations as an *affirming* event, not one to be feared, ignored, or (as in some church settings) avoided. They're times we can celebrate what volunteers have accomplished and what a difference they're making in the church.

If you're focusing on the "well-dones" as well as the areas that could use improvement, you'll find your conversation well-seasoned with words like *success, growth, affirm, new opportunity*, and *mentor*. When volunteers walk away from their evaluations, they should feel ten feet high, even if you've identified some things to work on.

Why?

Because volunteers *want* to get better at what they do. They *appreciate* your taking the time to carefully observe them and suggest ways they can make an even bigger impact. Volunteers are *grateful* you notice and take them seriously.

See why evaluations can be a fun time?

Betty Stallings helps us look at the review process in a nutshell, using four key concepts:[1]

Key Concept 1: Schedule reviews with regularity.

Successful performance reviews connect the person who assigns the work with the person who does it, so the two can talk. It may seem obvious that this is a good idea, but it's amazing how many churches fail to schedule such periodic reviews, although the church can only benefit from such a move (see concept 2).

In the review meetings, volunteer and leader discuss what they expect from themselves and each other and how well those expectations are being met. Performance reviews should be nonthreatening, constructive, supportive, flexible, and empowering. The aim: to encourage volunteers to stretch for high standards and determine how the church can help the volunteer achieve his or her goals.

Performance reviews can be effective and renewing. But that won't happen automatically. Here are the essential elements for success:

1. As they enter the organization, volunteers should be told of the feedback system, including the system of performance reviews.

2. Be sure both the volunteer and supervisor share how things are going.

3. Base performance reviews on previously agreed-upon standards, job descriptions, tasks, deadlines, available resources, and intervening circumstances.

4. Avoid surprises. If ongoing supervision and conflict resolution have taken place there will be no new issues raised at the review.

5. Depending on the size and culture of your church, the process can be formal or informal. Do what makes sense.

6. It's best to gradually include current volunteers who have not previously been reviewed. Self-assessment may work best as the system is initiated.

7. Schedule reviews for a specific time or they'll be put off.

Key Concept 2: Benefit from the reviews.

You'll discover all kinds of benefits—to the volunteers and to your entire organization—when you start using volunteer performance reviews. Here's a short list of benefits:

1. The process is a strong statement that volunteers are important and that both volunteers and organizations are held accountable to their agreements.

2. Reviews are encouraging, since volunteers want to be successful and typically respond well to feedback.

3. Reviews are a good time to express appreciation for volunteer efforts and acknowledge accomplishments.

4. Reviews enable volunteers and volunteer ministries to re-negotiate their working agreement for the next time period.

5. Reviews provide an opportunity for planning to improve volunteer performance in the future (for example, training or new placement).

6. Reviews allow volunteers to express concerns and "escape" an unfavorable situation.

7. Reviews allow staff to share concerns and "dismiss" a volunteer if the situation requires that action.

Key Concept 3: Define it, with agreed-upon standards.

At the heart of a good volunteer review is a clear description of volunteer job responsibilities and success indicators. Plus, you and your volunteer should have a shared view of

Barriers to Effective Performance Reviews

Betty Stallings often asks her workshop participants: "What are potential barriers your organization will need to overcome to do performance reviews successfully?" Here are some of the typical responses and strategies for overcoming the barriers:

"Even our staff isn't reviewed."
Initiate reviews with staff before initiating volunteer reviews.

"We don't have any policies on reviewing volunteers."
Work together to institute policies on performance reviews and dismissal.

"Current volunteers are resisting the idea."
Involve current volunteers in developing the forms and processes.

Here's an outline for a performance-review process that incorporates concept 3.

Before the Session

1. Have the volunteer fill out a self-assessment form.

2. Review the volunteer's job description, goals, and standards, and evaluate "job performance" (how volunteers did their jobs) versus "job expectation" (how volunteers were expected to do their jobs).

3. Do a performance review based on the job expectation versus job performance.

During the Session

1. Together, review the agreed-upon job expectations.

2. Share positive feedback and give appreciation for service.

3. Volunteer: share self-assessment and assessment of church support.

4. Supervisor: share assessment of volunteer's performance.

5. Discuss any barriers that volunteer experienced in carrying out the position.

6. Discuss future plans for the volunteer in the organization (such as position or goals).

After the Session

1. Write a report for the volunteer's file.

2. Follow-up on action plans or agreements made.

hoped-for outcomes and agree on what factors will contribute to those outcomes.

Key Concept 4: Decide it, and take action.

Outcomes from volunteer performance reviews can range from "applause" to dismissal—by the supervisor or by the volunteer.

One way to keep volunteers continually involved in your ministry is to use reviews as a time to discuss a volunteer's readiness for a new challenge, the need for a change, or the desire to take a break for awhile. These are all legitimate reasons that a volunteer may leave your ministry, at least temporarily.

> "Use reviews as a time to discuss a volunteer's readiness for a new challenge."

As a side note, when your reviews frequently point to significant problems meeting expectations, you might look into productivity and morale. If there's been low productivity or morale on the part of the volunteer, it's important to discuss remedies. Here are some of the possible reasons you'll want to explore:

- Is the volunteer bored with the routine?

- Are there personality differences between the volunteer and his or her supervisor, or on the team?

- Is there idleness because of a fluctuating workload or insufficient staff?

- Is there a lack of interest in the work?

- Are the assignments poorly defined?

- Is there inadequate supervision and/or training?

- Are policies misunderstood?

- Is there resentment because of too much work or unrealistic deadlines?

- Is there poor communication within the work team (staff/volunteers)?

- Is the volunteer experiencing emotional stress and personal difficulties?

- Is participation erratic?

- Does the volunteer feel appreciated?

- Have staff or organizational changes impacted the volunteer?

- Is there staff resistance to utilizing volunteers?

The flip side of evaluating a volunteer's performance is to first know whether you're meeting *their* legitimate, ongoing needs. Something I ask potential volunteers who have a history of volunteerism is why they left the last place they volunteered.

I've been astounded at how frequently I heard things such as:

"I never knew what they wanted me to do."

"I didn't even have a job description."

"I didn't know who I was responsible to, so I never knew who to go to with questions, ideas, or problems."

"They never provided any training to help me do what I was asked to do."

"Nobody ever told me if what I was doing was helpful or not."

"I was asked to do more and more, and I finally just burned out!"

Here's what volunteers repeatedly have said they want and need:

- To be carefully interviewed and appropriately assigned to a meaningful task

- To receive training and supervision to enable them to do that task well

- To be involved in planning and evaluating the program in which they participate

- To receive recognition in a way that is meaningful to them

- To be regarded as unique persons

- To be accepted as a valued member of the team

Are you currently providing those things to your volunteers? Don't assume you are: *Ask*. See what volunteers tell you.

To a great extent, how a volunteer performs reflects directly on the volunteer's supervisor. It's the supervisor who provides training, equipping, encouragement, and supervision.

If you provide what volunteers legitimately need, you'll hang on to your people longer, they'll be more fulfilled and effective, and you'll see better performance. All of which translates to far happier volunteers—and fewer "problem volunteers."

Advice for Those Just Starting to Do Performance Reviews

Like most things, you get better at doing reviews the more you do them. If you're new at this, perhaps this short list of suggestions will help.

Do be clear about a volunteer's interests and needs.

When you meet with a volunteer to do an evaluation, it's not about you. It's about the volunteer. So before you present a list of things you think the volunteer could do better, show a genuine concern for the volunteer's needs.

Keep in mind that back when you or a colleague first interviewed the volunteer, you gathered information about the volunteer's interests. The review is a wonderful time to explore if the volunteer's experience has matched initial expectations.

You can get at how reality is matching expectations by exploring . . .

- Does the volunteer's position connect with his or her interests?

- Is the volunteer still interested in the position?

- Does the volunteer enjoy serving in the position?

- Have relationships formed that make serving in the position fun for the volunteer?

- Is the volunteer satisfied with his or her level of involvement in planning, implementing, and evaluating in the ministry area?

Do clarify a volunteer's current interests by asking the right questions.

Here are some questions you'll find helpful to ask . . .

- What if?

- What will it take?

- Why not?

- What would be the perfect situation?

- How do you like to be treated?

- What problem(s) are we trying to solve?

- What is your goal?

- What concerns you the most?

- When are you most irritated? most satisfied?

- What's a situation when things went well?

- What do you want? What would it mean if you got it?

Do be professional about the review process.

Do performance reviews one-on-one and respect confidentiality. Make the process feel safe for volunteers. You can hold a review in a coffee shop, on the subway, or sitting on a park bench as long as you're both comfortable and feel confident you won't be overheard. The location of the discussion isn't what makes it "professional." Your attitude does that.

Do provide an opportunity for volunteers to evaluate their own performance.

When you ask, "How do you think you did?" you learn a *lot*. And while volunteers are speaking, listen attentively so you can ask follow-up questions.

Do be positive and focus on achievements at least as much as the areas that need improvement.

Again—make evaluations positive experiences.

Do make the discussion a dialogue, not a monologue.

If you're doing all the talking, you're missing much of the benefit of the review process. Be sure you ask questions and then give volunteers the encouragement and time to answer. Expect give and take, and be prepared to answer questions as well as ask them.

Do bring the job description and any other written materials related to the volunteer's position.

You'll want to review them and may, if the situation calls for it, make changes. Keep the option open for making changes to accommodate the volunteer and strengthen the volunteer ministry.

Do summarize what was discussed and decided.

It's helpful for you to get together briefly later so both you and the volunteer can sign the summary. As you read through it and make sure it's accurate, you have yet another chance to clarify the information.

Do be open to change.

Things change. People change. Goals change. Use the performance review to check out whether the volunteer wants to change directions or the terms of his or her service. Maybe with a new baby in the house it's time to take off six months or a year. Perhaps the fact the volunteer recently retired means she's open to taking on more responsibility. Not all change is bad!

And here's something you *don't* want to do . . .

Don't neglect your mentoring responsibility.

Mentoring and coaching can be the most rewarding parts of your job. Catch your volunteers doing good things and applaud them. If you see something positive, reinforce the behavior and celebrate it together.

The flip side of this is to watch for the other kinds of routine activities they may be doing—things that are just making everything harder for them.

I once watched a brand new carpenter's apprentice trying to nail two 2-by-4 boards together at the ends, to form a right angle. He put the boards on the ground and began nailing. But as he hit the nail, both the boards would move a foot or two away from him. He kept at it for an agonizing several minutes. Eventually, the foreman came over and, with an irritated look, said: "Watch." The experienced carpenter stepped on the ends of both pieces and quickly pounded in the nails.

> "If you see something positive, reinforce the behavior."

Are there times like that in the volunteer program? You'd better believe it. Keep your eyes wide open, and you'll see people doing all sorts of unproductive things because they're inexperienced.

They need someone to gently suggest a better approach. That's the way good coaches and mentors do it. And when important learning takes place, a warm feeling of "mission accomplished" begins to spread throughout the ministry.

Being Reactive

I once had a troublesome volunteer working for me when I was executive director of a volunteer agency. Jill (not her real name) was creating a problem for other volunteers and, as the director, it was my place to deal with the situation.

I became aware of the problem when three different volunteers separately told me they didn't want to work in the Volunteer Center on Tuesdays. When I inquired what was happening on Tuesdays, they reluctantly told me they didn't like working with Jill. They said she was extremely bossy and always telling them what to do, though she wasn't a supervisor.

Note that the problem was already in place. Jill was one of those rare "problem volunteers" that I said appear very infrequently. But there she was . . . and she was creating a problem that was costing me volunteers.

Let me tell you how I handled it so you can benefit from my experience.

The first thing I did was check out the information personally rather than take someone else's word for it. In this case, I stayed in the office the next Tuesday and saw that Jill was indeed bossing everyone around. What the volunteers had reported to me was accurate.

It's my policy—and I'd suggest it be yours—to never confront in public. I asked Jill to stay after work so we could talk privately. She agreed, and once the rest of the staff left, the two of us sat down in comfortable chairs.

> "As the director, it was my place to deal with the situation."

I stated honestly what the problem was, being as specific as possible in describing the behavior I'd seen with my own eyes. I asked Jill if she was aware of the effect her behavior was having on the other volunteers. Jill said she wasn't aware of any impact, so I told her that three volunteers had asked not to work with her because she bossed them around. Jill shrugged and said, "Oh, I've always been like that."

Jill's response wasn't unexpected. The world is full of people who aren't aware of the speed with which they roar through life or the volume at which they operate. In Jill's case, she simply didn't see any problem in having a take-charge attitude that had probably served her well other places in her life.

Except that attitude wasn't helping in the Center. I told Jill I wanted us to come up with a mutually agreeable solution to the problem. I explained to Jill that her behavior wasn't acceptable and that we needed to arrive at some solution before she left.

I invited Jill to offer her suggestions first, and she just sat there, staring at the floor, the wall, at anything but me. So I then suggested the solutions I had jotted down beforehand as I considered how to resolve the solution—without losing Jill.

It's important for you to understand that the goal of our talk wasn't to rewire Jill so she was meek and mild. That wasn't going to happen, and I certainly didn't have any right to demand it.

And I didn't necessarily want to lose Jill as a volunteer. I was willing to do so, but that was by no means my first choice! I wanted her to understand that.

So I suggested Jill could work alone in the back office, or perhaps she could consider volunteering somewhere else. She rejected both these options because she was lonely, and we at the Center were her "family."

Finally, Jill reluctantly said, "Well, I guess I could stop doing it."

I enthusiastically supported that suggestion!

"But," I said, "you told me you've been bossy all your life, so this is going to be a hard behavior to change." I insisted that we set a date to meet once a week to chat for a few minutes about how she was progressing. I also told her I would be getting feedback from her fellow volunteers to hear about how she was doing.

I followed up. We met weekly for over two months. The first few weeks the reports were that "Jill was genuinely trying," and eventually I heard, "She's improving!" Finally the volunteers were reporting that they found they really liked Jill, and enjoyed working with her.

> "Never confront in public."

The day came when Jill and I met for our weekly meeting and I said, "Congratulations! Behavior change isn't easy, but you did it. We don't need to meet any more."

Jill stood up and said to me, "This wasn't easy for you, was it? You must have cared about me quite a bit."

I replied that no, it wasn't easy, but I *did* care for her a great deal. She added, "People have disliked me all my life, and nobody ever bothered to tell me why. Thank you."

This was a significant growth experience for us both. I'm also happy to say that Jill stayed on as a volunteer at the Center for five more years.

In all my decades of experience in volunteer management, I've had to encourage just one volunteer to leave—and that was because of a breach in confidentiality. I truly believe that as you put into practice the sound principles we're encouraging in this series, such situations will be extremely rare.

Nevertheless, we do have to face the possibility: Suppose a volunteer goofs up consistently and over the long-haul? Can we ever "fire" them? I hear this question in every volunteer leadership training session I lead.

My basic response is that if you're serious about holding volunteers accountable and they fail to do the job, or they have inappropriate attitudes, boss others around, or procrastinate repeatedly, then you must react accordingly. Ask yourself, "What would I do if I were paying this person to do this job?" . . . and then do it!

First, review the job description with the individual to see if he or she is clear about what originally was agreed upon. It's amazing how often this first step clears up the problem.

Second, clarify the problem and be explicit about your expectations.

Third, examine the alternatives together. What would it take to fix the problem? Is it a change of behavior or attitude, meeting deadlines, changing ministry jobs, fixing the system, or providing training? What are the options?

"This was a significant growth experience for us both."

Finally, agree on an alternative, and set a time line to implement it. Monitor the progress, giving support and affirmation along the way.

If the volunteer either doesn't follow through—even after two to three chances—or is nasty about being held accountable, I'd "fire" the person. If you keep rescuing the individual, you both lose. This is a hard truth, but tough love may be your only option.

Here are seven guiding principles to keep in mind if you decide to let someone go . . .

- **Use direct dialogue.** You have a tough task when termination becomes necessary. It won't get any easier if you avoid the hard truths, or try to candy-coat the problems this person is creating. Meet the issues head on, and avoid talking with third parties—even if the volunteer has already done this.

- **Document the process.** There's a great deal of emotion in play; use a process and documentation (a sample termination form is provided below) to help you stay on track. You need to be able to clearly state the events and actions that brought you to the place of asking someone to leave the volunteer ministry.

> "What would it take to fix the problem?"

- **Handle the dismissal privately.** Jesus put it like this in Matthew 18:15: "If your brother sins against you, go and show him his fault, just between the two of you. If he listens to you, you have won your brother over."

- **Search together for a better fit.** Maybe this particular person just needs to find the right place. For example, if this person is having trouble getting along with others, there may be a volunteer position she can handle without lots of daily interpersonal interactions. Can this person do a great job of creating a web site, organizing e-mails, writing the bulletin each week, or overseeing computer maintenance? Be creative in this exploration together! The so-called "problem volunteer" may become an ideal kingdom worker once his or her true abilities, skills, and passions are uncovered and put to use in the church.

- **Keep your focus on the program goals.** The conflict-solving process, even if it involves termination, isn't the end of the story. Getting the volunteer ministry back on track and the terminated volunteer placed elsewhere in God-glorifying, kingdom-building, fulfilling service are what you want. This conflict shouldn't be a permanent barrier to Christian unity.

- **Agree on a follow-up schedule.** You're not trying to remove this person from the church! But when volunteers feel hurt or believe an injustice has been done, they'll sometimes cut themselves off from fellowship.

Sample Termination Interview

Volunteer Name: _____

Date of Interview:_____

Summary of reasons for termination:
(*Document the events, problems, and tasks.*)

Interview Checklist:
Be sure you cover each of these items:

___ Discuss and complete this evaluation.

___ Explore alternative jobs.
    If jobs were proposed, list what they were and
    whether they were accepted or rejected.

___ Agree on specific follow-up plans.

___ Schedule follow-up meeting.

    Date of meeting: _____ Location: _____

___ Extend continued church fellowship.

___ Pray together.
    Mutually recognize God's leading and grace in
    this matter.

___ Other:

To Be Used at Follow-up Meeting:

___ Determine if the individual is active in ministry.
If so, where? Is the new ministry role satisfactory
to the volunteer? Why or why not?

___ Determine if the individual is involved in the fellowship of the church.
Why or why not?

Be available for spiritual counsel and mentoring, and communicate clearly that the transaction wasn't personal but instead a systemic and organizational necessity.

> "Conflict shouldn't be a permanent barrier to Christian unity."

• **Notify others who will be affected.** You'll need to tell certain members, staff, and others that the volunteer will no longer be with the ministry. Do this in an objective manner and make sure your notification method leaves no subtle insinuations or innuendoes. Be sure you communicate *exactly* what you want to say. In most cases, you won't have to explain reasons or causes.

Finally, at the risk of overstating my case, I want to emphasize how rare it will be that anyone will ever be asked to leave your ministry. In fact, if you're putting into practice the principles outlined in this series, *you will never have to face that unpleasant task.* You see, the authors of this series firmly believe that volunteer motivation and retention are the result of doing other things right—most of which you're probably already doing in an excellent way.

Among these practices are . . .

- Valuing relationships and celebrating them.

- Valuing experiential, applicable, and learner-centered training for volunteers.

- Respecting volunteers as full partners in ministry.

- Monitoring volunteers for signs of burnout.

- Conducting regular performance reviews.

- Fostering an environment where there's no put-down humor or victims.

- Creating a culture that volunteers can count on to be fair, forgiving, and fun.

Read that last word again . . . *fun!*

I use the word generously when I talk about working with volunteers because it's really the story of my life with them. I can't imagine how it could be different for you. After all, I figure you're already doing many of these things listed above—and many other good things too. If so, then I know you're enjoying working with your volunteers. Just keep loving them and treasuring their fellowship.

1. The information in the "Key Concepts" section draws heavily upon Betty Stalling's workshop on "Evaluation," pp. I-6 thru I-12.

FIVE
Encouragement through Recognition

You're already encouraging volunteers through interviews, careful placement, and positive evaluations. Now add recognition to the mix and delight your volunteers even more!

Betty Stallings is a recognition expert. One thing she emphasizes is that we tend to think of recognition as the last thing we do for a volunteer after they've finished a project, and just before he or she heads off into the sunset.

Not true! In this chapter I'm going to let Betty describe how recognition—and the encouragement it provides—can be infused throughout your ministries . . . and throughout a volunteer's experience.[1]

Betty herself caught the "disease of volunteering," as she puts it, from her father. Here is her story—and her valuable insights about recognition in volunteer ministry.

A Treasure

At the time, Betty's father was 86 years old and had lived in a multi-care institution for nearly five years. The one thing that made him feel important was serving on different committees.

About a year earlier he'd gone to visit Betty in California, intending to stay for a week. He got off the plane in his wheelchair, a little bag tucked onto his lap. When Betty and her father reached her house, he went right to his room to unpack, then called Betty in to see what he'd carried so carefully in the little bag on his lap.

He pulled out an undershirt and carefully unfolded it. Nestled inside was a coffee cup bearing this inscription: "You are a treasure."

"Daddy, who else knows this about you?" Betty asked.

He sat up straight and said, "I'm the treasurer of the Recycling Club at the home."

Betty's first thought was that letting her dad be the treasurer of *anything* was a frightening thought.

"But then I stopped to feel gratitude," Betty says. "Some caring person had taken time to see my 86-year-old father and notice that he was, indeed, a treasure. And my father cherished the gesture enough to carry a coffee cup from Boston to California to show his daughter."

> "Daddy, who else knows this about you?"

That kind of encouragement and recognition is what keeps us alive. We make an incredible impact when we remind each other what treasures we are in each others' lives, even with something as simple as a coffee cup. Those little reminders keep us going through the tough times, because we know we're not alone. Somebody noticed.

Recognizing and encouraging volunteers is a huge part of your calling as the leader of a volunteer ministry. So let's dive into how you can be effective.

We'll start by thinking about a time you were—or weren't—recognized in a volunteer role.

Then we'll explore what Betty calls the "Four P's of Recognition"—making it Personal, Plentiful, Powerful, and Practical.

Next, we'll find that not all people like to be recognized in the same way, and you'll discover techniques for delivering the perfect touch at just the right time to keep your volunteers encouraged and recognized.

Finally, we'll wrap up with a list of recognition ideas you can use right away in your own volunteer ministry.

How Have You Been Recognized?

Think about your own recognition experiences . . .

Describe a volunteer job you've held at some time in your life. Why did you hold that job?

What motivated you to do—and keep doing—this job?

In what ways did that organization recognize you? What was meaningful, and what wasn't meaningful?

What did this experience teach you about recognition of volunteers?

What is your current philosophy about recognition? What shaped it?

For your recognition efforts to be encouraging to your volunteers rather than a nuisance, I'd suggest your efforts include four characteristics:

Recognition Must Be PERSONAL

One person who filled in a chart like the one shown here concluded: "Recognition is a very personal thing. You have to know the persons you're recognizing. If you don't know them, it can be a really horrible experience. But if you know them and recognize them, it'll be an experience that will be with them forever."

Personalizing recognition efforts means you'll never again find yourself sitting through a discussion like this one:

"So, how are we going to recognize volunteers this year?"

"Let's give them plaques. I think plaques are great! People love plaques."

"Plaques? I *hate* plaques! Why don't we give them a flower pot to put on their desks?"

"That's hokey! Who wants flowers? They just die and you have to throw them away."

Notice that every comment about what might be a great recognition reflects a personal bias about what the speaker enjoys or doesn't enjoy. It's not about the volunteers at all.

The best recognition offers personal validation. You place a person in the right job. Then you notice what this particular individual wants and needs, and you fulfill those wants and needs. That's 95 percent of recognition.

If we've put people in the wrong jobs, then our creative recognition ideas won't help much. And if we don't understand what's motivating a volunteer, we can't recognize the volunteer appropriately.

But if we know the person and what motivates him or her, we can zero in on a recognition that will be meaningful. Following are four suggestions Betty shares about how to narrow down your thinking until you've got the perfect idea.

1. Make it special for just little ol' her. An organization for which I worked sent me a card on October 13th. It wasn't a national holiday but it *was* my anniversary as a staff member. That date was special only to me; someone had kept track of my time at that company and noticed the passing of exactly one year. I felt truly and deeply honored, though I can't remember a single word written on that card.

2. Make it a visual feast of the feat. I once helped out behind the scenes with a local theater organization. I was in the background the whole time, while the actors did their thing in the spotlight. In recognition of my service, however, the cast put a picture of the production on a plaque and wrote on it: "Betty, Thank you for helping make this play possible!" That plaque reminds me about the feats we accomplished as a team.

> "If we know the person, . . . we can zero in on a recognition that will be meaningful."

3. Make it fit the personality profile. The real challenge is to make everyone in the group feel special. But people are so different in what communicates encouragement and appreciation. How do you make sure you connect with everyone?

Although it's possible to put together an event that contains enough diverse elements to speak to each volunteer, it only works if ahead of time you ask, "How can everyone feel special when they leave this event?"

4. Make it timely—ASAP. The timeliness of recognition is important. The closer to the accomplishment or project, the better. That's why it's not necessarily the best way to wait until the end of the year or the close of the event to recognize people.

And here's a bonus idea: To recognize someone who showed up just once—invite the person back! If it was a good one-day experience, chances are the volunteer might come back again, and you've gained a new, highly motivated volunteer.

The bottom line: Recognition doesn't take that much time, but it *does* take planning, sincerity, and action on a very personal level.

Recognition Must Be PLENTIFUL

Like the old story about voting in Chicago: Do recognition early and do it often. For recognition to be encouraging, it needs to be an ongoing aspect of our overall leadership style.

Betty works with a City Council that always starts meetings with recognition of a volunteer who's doing good work in the community. They begin by patting somebody (really, themselves!) on the back for making good progress. Then they proceed on an upbeat note to tackle the problems waiting for them.

Encouraging recognition has to permeate your volunteer ministry and hopefully your church. Everyone on staff needs to be convinced of its importance, not just you. You can't be the only person recognizing others, the designated cheerleader. That won't feel right.

This means that spontaneity is just fine. Recognition will often be informal and spontaneous. And it will be more powerful for that spontaneity.

When to Recognize Volunteers

Effective recognition doesn't only happen when a project is completed. It needs to be plentiful and ongoing. Here are some quick ideas about when you can recognize people:.

- At the sign-up table

- On the first day

- Daily

- Monthly

- Annually

- At the end of a project

- On special days

- On sick days

- Upon departure

- Your ideas? Jot them below:

Recognition Must Be POWERFUL

Betty serves on a board that, at every meeting, recognizes one of its members for something they've done since the previous meeting. Sometimes it's funny, it's always spontaneous, and it's definitely effective.

Says Betty, "We all show up in case we're going to get this recognition. We know we need to be there, and because it's done at the beginning of the meeting, we know we need to arrive on time. A room full of very busy people who manage to make every meeting and on time—that's the power of even *potential* recognition!"

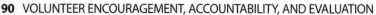

How Do You Say "Thanks"?

Just saying "Thank you" is powerful in itself. Here's a guide to helping you clarify what you think and feel about saying thanks.

To me, saying "Thank you" means the most when . . .

Saying "Thank you" means little if . . .

The most creative way anyone has ever thanked me was to . . .

The way we usually say "Thanks" around here is . . .

Some of the people I/we need to say "Thank You" to this week are . . .

Some creative ways to do this might be . . . (just brainstorm a little).

What did you learn about yourself here? Discuss your ideas with other leaders. What suggestions do they have?

Betty attended an event years ago in which she helped the organizer. After the event the organizer was thanking Betty for helping. As they spoke, the organizer absent-mindedly put her hand into her jacket pocket. She didn't realize there was anything in it, and Betty could tell that she was somewhat surprised to find a partial roll of Lifesavers. She smiled and handed the roll to Betty, saying, "You've been a real Lifesaver today!"

Later, speaking at a conference, I told this Lifesaver story and went on with my workshop. At the end of the day, when I returned to my desk, there on top of my papers sat a red Lifesaver. I don't know who put it there, but it was a special moment for me.

It was so small, but it was so very powerful.

Recognition Must Be PRACTICAL

You may hear objections to the practice of recognizing volunteers, which can keep you from having a truly encouraging ministry. Here's Betty's advice for addressing those excuses—most of which fall into the "it's not practical for us" category.

"There's no money in the budget for this sort of thing." Recognition doesn't have to cost a lot of money. Explain that you don't need a catered banquet—just some rolls of Lifesavers!

"Volunteers say they don't want or need recognition." Except—they do. Maybe they're saying they don't need another plaque, but be assured: They'll welcome appropriate recognition.

"The paid staff aren't even recognized!" In a church where paid staff are not recognized, there may not be enthusiasm for recognizing volunteers. Give it a try anyway. Even better: Recognize the paid staff, too! One woman told me that in her organization, the volunteers nominate staff people for recognition. I thought that was powerful and effective.

"One of our sacred cows is standing in the way of personal recognition." Nobody *says* this, of course, but it's the problem. And you can't shoot a sacred cow unless you're prepared for lots of beef(s).

Maybe someone thinks it's undignified. Or that it diminishes the value of service if someone says "thanks." Or maybe it's as simple as the fact the church has never before recognized volunteers, and therefore it isn't something that needs to be done now. With tact and wisdom see if you can at least herd the sacred cow to one side of the aisle so you can slip past it.

> **"You can't shoot a sacred cow unless you're prepared for lots of beef(s)."**

When recognition is personal, plentiful, powerful, and practical, it encourages and edifies your volunteers. That's probably no surprise. What might be surprising, though, is how many people give of themselves as volunteers when they receive little or no encouragement or recognition at all.

Consider this story from Betty's life as a trainer and consultant . . .

> In one of my training sessions an elderly woman told her story of being her church's "coffee lady." She said she served coffee between services for 13 years without fail.
>
> "What did they do to recognize you over the years?" I asked.
>
> Her response was heartbreaking: "One gentleman did come up to me once at the break and said, 'Your coffee is always too cold.'"

The man at least noticed this woman's ministry. And his criticism was apparently the only form of recognition that came to a faithful servant for more than a decade.

How sad. May it never happen this way at your church. But wait . . . is it happening that way right now?

Recognizing Teams As Well As Individuals

It's great to recognize individual volunteers. But don't forget that most of our volunteer efforts are, at heart, team efforts. So it's smart to find ways to regularly celebrate, affirm, and recognize the volunteer ministry team as a whole.

A common approach is to plan an annual banquet at the end of each church year. You could make it like an "awards banquet" for a sports team, or you could make it part of a larger service of worship and praise to God.

In any case, when it comes time to recognize and affirm team members, be sure you've developed categories of excellence. Provide recognition for various achievements and outstanding work (make these honors real and deserved). If it's a celebration strictly for the leadership team, then invite all team members and celebrate the completion of one or more particular projects. Highlight every aspect of the success, and recognize the contributions of each person involved.

If your leadership group is small and you want to be less formal, then simply plan a dinner (or breakfast) out together. Make plans to highlight and celebrate team successes. You might also hand out mementos or small gifts, such as logo coffee mugs or gift certificates to appropriate stores.

Here are a few other ideas from Betty for encouraging and recognizing a team . . .

Start a Team Project scrapbook. Include memorabilia and photographs from special projects, events, and achievements.

Create a Recognition Sheet. Make it available for people to complete at any time. Leave space for the team member's name, the date, and a brief explanation of how that team member had a special impact on the ministry's success. Ask the person completing the sheet to sign it, and send it to the team leader. The team leader can then trumpet the accomplishments publicly.

Create an Affirmation Board. The same concept as above, but post the sheets of paper where everyone can see them. Ground rule: All comments must be positive and affirming!

Hand out a Team Rose. Start each leadership meeting with a time when members can recognize and affirm one another. Then together decide who will receive the single rose-in-a-vase for that week.

Schedule a team meeting as a "Surprise Celebration." You've heard of a surprise birthday party? How about a surprise

Affirmation Party? Fill the meeting room with balloons, and make refreshments available. Then celebrate all the good that's been accomplished in the past month, quarter, or year. Be specific about what has happened, and who did what. Consider blending in a time of praise and worship to the Lord, who guided and strengthened everyone involved.

Hold a staff appreciation luncheon. Use the time to say thanks and to recognize the volunteers' efforts. Don't conduct business.

Connect Recognition to Motivational Preference

I mentioned in volume 4 of this series that I have learned to recognize several kinds of people when it comes to motivational preference: Affiliators, Power People, and Achievers. I promised to suggest ways that you could provide encouragement and recognition that was tailor-made for each of these motivational preferences. I'm going to defer to the expertise of Betty Stallings once again, and share what she's learned about providing recognition for motivational preference.

Recognition Based on Motivational Type

Affiliators

Awards and Acknowledgements
1. Name and photo appearing in newsletter
2. Recognition in presence of family, peers
3. Personal notes and verbal greetings from supervisor
4. Cards for special anniversary or birthday
5. Gifts and notes from clients
6. Banquets, potlucks, picnics
7. Attending a social event with other people

Job Benefits That Encourage Ongoing Commitment
1. Opportunities for socialization and meeting new friends
2. Personalized on-the-job training

Power People

Awards and Acknowledgements

1. Public recognition (in front of peers, in media)
2. Awards named for them
3. Letters of commendation noting their influential achievements or impact
4. Notes from influential people, community leaders, and other notables commenting on their effect on humankind

Job Benefits That Encourage Ongoing Commitment

1. Assignments providing opportunities for influence, teaching, and interaction with high officials
2. Assignments with impressive titles
3. Work with a good deal of authority involved
4. Board of Directors position

Achievers

Awards and Acknowledgements

1. Plaques, badges, pins (tangible awards)
2. Letters of special commendation on their achievement(s) to boss, newspaper, or school
3. An award named in their honor
4. Nomination for local, state, national awards
5. Résumé documentation
6. Promotion to a more responsible job

Job Benefits That Encourage Ongoing Commitment

1. Entire responsibility delegated to them and latitude given to them on the way it is done
2. Opportunities to set goals, create innovative ideas
3. Work to succeed or exceed a specific goal[2]

Encouragement is like a breath of fresh air in the lives of volunteers. Most people simply don't hear much encouragement or receive much recognition in daily life. It's rare—and therefore precious.

Encouragement and recognition will help you hang onto the volunteers who are already involved, and also create the sort of culture that attracts new volunteers. You've already built a wonderful culture as you have instituted job descriptions, interviews, placement, and evaluation. Excellent, encouraging recognition practices are the icing on the cake.

> "Encouragement is rare—and therefore precious."

In the church, all the members are part of the body of Christ. We're all working toward the same mission. We all play a crucial role.

I truly believe there are plenty of believers out there, willing and able to help us do anything that needs doing in the church. We just need to love and care for them as Christ cares for us.

Winning Encouragement and Recognition Ideas for Your Volunteer Ministry

I urge you to develop recognition methods in three categories: ideas to use regularly to provide ongoing support, ideas you will use informally, and those you will use formally for special occasions.

Some of the ideas presented below are my own; some I've gathered from others. We offer them as a way to "prime the pump" of your own creativity. Add your own ideas and then plan to implement as many as possible in the future:

To Offer Ongoing Support

- Set up a Suggestion Box for suggestions from volunteers only.

- Give a personalized coffee mug to each volunteer.

- Implement a "Release Time" each week or month. This

would be a chance for volunteers to pursue volunteer enrichment activities, or just have some time off for rest and relaxation. One Colorado church cancels all children's programming in August to give children's ministry volunteers a month off.

- Throughout the year, pay attention to the environment in which your volunteers labor and have meetings. Make surroundings pleasant, comfortable, and stocked with all the practical items and tools they need (if possible, include some "luxuries"). What a morale booster this is!

- Set up support groups for your volunteers. When these groups meet, they can share their experiences, concerns, solutions, and ideas. They can pray for one another and develop their own creative ideas for mutual self-support.

"Encourage volunteers to create new ministries."

- Encourage volunteers to create new ministries that will match their skills and desires to serve (rather than always slotting people into current ministries).

- Be sure your church pays the costs and expenses of any training seminars or workshops you recommend. Schedule such events regularly for increasing volunteer competency and self-confidence.

- Invite volunteers to form a worship committee that meets with the pastor and other worship leaders. Together, plan a creative worship service that focuses around the theme of volunteer ministry—and don't recruit at the service!

To Informally Recognize Volunteers
- Send a birthday, anniversary, or Christmas card.
- Offer impromptu verbal affirmation: What's important is who gives it and what accomplishments are mentioned.

- Involve volunteers in the long-range planning of your church.
- Invite volunteers to church staff, planning, and other significant meetings.
- Regularly send out press releases to local media outlets. Tell all about the marvelous work of your volunteers in the various programs. Name names, and be specific about what is being accomplished. (As appropriate, also include information about how particular volunteers serve in other groups in the community. We're in this together!)

> "Constantly send out thank-you notes about a job well done."

- Constantly send out thank-you notes about a job well done, no matter how small the job may have been. It deserves praise, for it was done for the kingdom.
- Praise your volunteers to their family and friends. (How could this hurt?)
- In the church bulletin regularly or occasionally list the persons who volunteer in your church and/or the community. Regularly do this on bulletin boards and within the church newsletter, as well.
- Give small gifts occasionally, but tie them to an affirmation. Use the following examples to come up with your own individualized ideas.

What a bright idea!
(Note stuck to a light bulb.)

No one holds a candle to you!
(Scented candle or pack of birthday candles.)

You are a LIFESAVER!
(Candy with a note.)

Thanks for raisin' the tough questions!
(Mini boxes of raisins.)

To Formally Recognize Volunteers

• Have a birthday lunch once a month to celebrate all volunteer and paid staff birthdays that occurred during that month.

• Give the volunteer a promotion to a higher-level volunteer position, a more responsible job. Make it public.

• Make notes in the personnel records, and let the volunteer know it. Include a letter from the director and others that will stay on file. Document community involvement this way, too.

• Nominate a volunteer for community recognition.

• Give a gift of appreciation. For example: a certificate of recognition, a book, or other memento appropriate to the volunteer ministry. Other ideas for gifts include: pens, paperweights, coffee mugs, photographs, videos, gift baskets, concert/sports tickets (get them donated), a laminated copy of an article about them in the newspaper. Or consider giving coupons good for one day off without an excuse or lunch with the director.

• Provide opportunities for your volunteers to speak! Perhaps have a regular column in your church newsletter for the "Volunteer Viewpoint."

• Consider having a Volunteer of the Week (or month or year). Give special privileges or "perks" to this person—such as providing a special parking slot right next to the church entrance! Place their pictures in a prominent place.

Keep in mind the volunteer's job when you're giving encouragement.

There is a tremendous difference in volunteer jobs, and few differences are as significant as this one: Does the volunteer supervise others, or not?

Every volunteer position is important. Every position has its challenges. But as a ministry leader you know what stresses can come with supervising others. And that means if you're going to support and encourage your volunteers who supervise others, you've got to *supersize* that support and encouragement!

When you're considering how to encourage a volunteer, keep in mind the environment in which the volunteer serves. Some positions have more responsibility (and perhaps more stress) associated with them than other positions might have.

Here are the three general levels of responsibility we identified earlier, and some ideas for encouraging people in each:

High Responsibility Volunteer Jobs

These people are often responsible for assigning tasks to others, and actually shape areas of ministry. They have the stress of *doing* reviews as well as receiving them, so you have much in common. Make these volunteers one of your top priorities.

Ways to encourage people in this sort of position include . . .

- *Personally invest in these volunteers.* If you have an organizational chart, it's likely these volunteers report directly to you. So it makes sense for you to be providing extra mentoring opportunities, and chances to grow in their abilities. See if these volunteers wish to be discipled by you or another church leader, then make that happen.

- *Deliberately include them in information loops.* Few things are as demotivating as working in an information vacuum. You want your ministry to be a place where the right hand *does* know what the left hand is doing. The first time your volunteer assigns people to do a task that turns out to be irrelevant, motivation sinks through the floor.

- *Provide stress release activities.* A movie ticket (or two, with an offer to have someone provide babysitting so the volunteer can take a spouse out on a date). Or if your budget is thin, a bag of microwave popcorn and gift certificate for a video rental. You'll have to find out what each volunteer enjoys (A pass to the zoo? A prepaid game of bowling? A magazine gift subscription?) to make a personal gift, but that's the point: You took the time to find out. And you appreciate that the volunteer is making a significant contribution.

Medium Responsibility Volunteer Jobs

These people are often implementing fairly defined tasks. They don't supervise other volunteers but may supervise a function—this is the volunteer who keeps the lawn mowed all summer, or who keeps the kitchen organized. That function is their responsibility.

Ways to encourage people in this sort of position include . . .

- *Help the volunteer hone his or her skills.* You honor the volunteer and the importance of what the volunteer is doing when you say, "Great job keeping the grounds looking sharp. Here's a subscription to a magazine that's all about lawn care, or a ticket to a lawn care show at the civic center."

- *Join the volunteer and ask for a demonstration.* Especially if the volunteer works alone, having some company will be welcome. Plus, showing up and asking questions is affirming.

Low Responsibility Volunteer Jobs

The duties performed by these volunteers are clearly defined and specific. Often, these positions are the "bite-sized" commitments that last either for a short time, or that are seemingly unimportant.

Ways to encourage people in this sort of position include . . .

- *Make sure they know they're important!* If at all possible, have the pastor or another recognizable church leader sign letters of thanks to these volunteers. Even better: Ask the pastor to walk through the church some Sunday thanking the nursery workers, greeters, and parking lot attendants who are often overlooked.

- *Give the worker a gift that connects his or her volunteer job to the larger church mission.* Making the connection is critical. If the volunteer is a parking lot attendant, give him or her a keychain. If the person is a greeter, give her a welcome mat for her home and thank her for making the church a welcoming place.

Constantly Improve Your Encouragement-Giving Skills

That was a good start on creative, practical recognition ideas, but more important than your doing lots of encouraging things is your becoming a consistently encouraging person. Hone your encouragement-giving skills until encouragement flows out of you naturally.

> "Encouragement is infectious; it spreads quickly."

Encouragement is infectious; it spreads quickly. But somebody has to get it started. Let it be you!

If you're not convinced that an encouraging spirit (accompanied by encouraging actions) is a crucial piece of volunteer-managing character equipment, then just open your Bible. You'll find countless examples of encouragement coming not only from Jesus and other leaders, but from other believers. Consider these passages . . .

> *I long to see you so that I may impart to you some spiritual gift to make you strong—that is, that you and I may be mutually encouraged by each other's faith. (Romans 1:11-12)*

> *Therefore encourage each other with these words. . . . Therefore encourage one another and build each other up, just as in fact you are doing. (1 Thessalonians 4:18; 5:11)*

> *Encourage one another daily, as long as it is called Today, so that none of you may be hardened by sin's deceitfulness. (Hebrews 3:13)*

> *Let us consider how we may spur one another on toward love and good deeds. Let us not give up meeting together, as some are in the habit of doing, but let us encourage one another —and all the more as you see the Day approaching. (Hebrews 10:24-25)*

Fill your ministry with encouragement and recognition and you'll create a culture that's fair . . . forgiving . . . and fun! That's how it's been for me, and I know it will be the same for you.

Volunteers are wonderful people. They're choosing to give of themselves and their time to serve others. But that alone doesn't take away the very real, very legitimate needs they have in their own lives. With your guidance, the volunteer ministry can help meet many of your volunteers' needs even as they're serving others. And there's nothing more encouraging than having your needs met!

Volunteers are people, and as people they have a desire to belong someplace where they are appreciated and valued. You can provide that.

They want to know their opinions matter. As you listen deeply, you'll provide that.

They want to give themselves to something bigger than themselves. As you connect them with appropriate volunteer positions in the church, you'll help them serve in the kingdom of God.

They want to be challenged, to grow, to become excellent in doing things that matter. The volunteer positions you'll help them find and the training you'll help them receive will let that happen.

The encouragement that comes from participating in the volunteer ministry is more than a passing "feel-good" experience. You're more than a cheerleader who rallies the troops. What happens in a volunteer's heart can be a life-changing experience. It can build new skills, rekindle old passions for service, and encourage lasting relationships—including a relationship with Jesus Christ and his church.

1. The content of this chapter draws heavily from Betty Stallings' Volunteer Management Program video presentation, *Recognition: Letting People Know You Noticed.* Betty B. Stallings is a premier trainer, consultant, and author specializing in volunteerism, nonprofit fundraising, board development, and leadership. She can be reached at 1717 Courtney Avenue, Pleasanton, CA 94588.

2. The chart "Recognition Based on Motivational Type" is from Betty B. Stallings.

What I Still Believe

Wise words and encouragement—for you.

I was asked to close this series on Volunteer Leadership with some "wisdom, insights, and inspiration." This challenge got me thinking about the concept of wisdom, and led me to revisit one of my favorite quotes from T. S. Eliot:

> "Where is the life we have lost in living?
> "Where is the wisdom we have lost in knowledge?
> "Where is the knowledge we have lost in information?"

–T.S. Eliot, *The Complete Poems and Plays 1909-1950*, Copyright 1971 by Esme Valerie Eliot (New York: Harcourt, Brace & World, Inc.), p.96.

Pondering the idea of wisdom, and reflecting on this quote, I decided these are the things I believe about wisdom:

- Wisdom deals with the "why" questions; knowledge and information deal with the "what and how."

- Wisdom deals with future implications; knowledge and information tend to concentrate on the present.

- Wisdom deals with principles and values (paradigms); knowledge and information deal with practices.

- Wisdom seeks to understand the questions; knowledge and information look for the answers.

- Wisdom is going deeper; knowledge and information tend to just keep getting broader.

Wisdom deals with the "whys" of what we do, with the future implications of our decisions, and with the principles and values underlying our decisions and practices. Wisdom calls us to be willing to ask hard questions that move us deeper into the meaning of what we do.

It's not that knowledge and information aren't important! They're essential in helping us reshape, re-form, and innovate our practices in the field of volunteer leadership. Knowledge and information keep us viable and appropriate. That's why this series is devoted to the practical, day-to-day "how-to's."

But I find an intriguing tension between knowledge/information and wisdom. As I pondered this, it became clear to me; it is often the challenge of what to let go of—and what to hold fast to—in the midst of all the changes. As T. S. Eliot also said:

> "We shall not cease from exploration, and the end of all exploring will be to arrive where we started—and know the place for the first time."

–T.S. Eliot, *The Complete Poems and Plays 1909-1950*, p.145.

I want to share with you some powerful principles that have stood the test of time through more than 35 years of my writing, teaching, and doing volunteer leadership in churches and nonprofit settings. They're what I still believe after all this time about leadership, management, volunteerism, and groups.

Thankfully, I know these principles in a new way (for the first time!) from the vantage point of age and experience. The years have certainly brought about change in what I know—the "how-to's"—but the principles stand.

I share these principles with you, knowing that the real value isn't what I'm writing here. Rather, I hope it will encourage you to make your own list!

My Powerful Principles

1. Volunteers are priceless.

I have a strong, foundational belief about volunteers that undergirds and fuels all the work I've done through the years. I can sum up this belief in a simple line I heard more than 30 years ago:

"Volunteers are not paid—not because they're worthless, but because they're priceless!"

Contrast that attitude toward volunteers with others you may have witnessed:

"Volunteers are nice, but not necessary."

"Volunteers are more work than they're worth."

"They're okay, as long as they don't cost us anything."

"We'll use them to save money, but they should be seen and not heard."

The attitudes of your church leadership toward volunteers permeates your church and has a dramatic effect on how volunteers feel about serving there. I believe in volunteers. I urge you to do the same.

2. People must be as important as programs, products, or profits.

The truth is that leaders either grow or diminish those who work with them. So if we meet our goals at the expense of the health, well-being, and growth of our people, we've ultimately failed. Everything we do in a volunteer ministries program must be grounded in these basics of theology:

• The priesthood of all believers

• The whole body of Christ

• The giftedness of each child of God

Revisit volume 1 of this Volunteer Leadership Series regularly to let these theological truths sink deep into your thinking and values. We haven't always embraced these theologies. For example, in the 1950s many churches focused on creating excellent programs. We decided to only let those who were excellent singers sing . . . only the excellent musicians could play during worship services . . . and we lost people who weren't professional performers.

In the 1990s corporations focused so much on products

and profits that they sometimes worked people literally to death—at least the death of their marriages.

People are important, too. They're designed for eternity.

3. People become committed to plans they help make. So plan *with*, not *for*, people.

This idea has gone through several fads and phases over the years, such as: "participative management" and "quality circles." Organizations spent millions bringing in gurus to teach them how to do planning . . . but many organizations never caught *why* planning with people makes sense.

It makes sense because the real wisdom is in the group itself. That's where the corporate genius resides, as well as the motivation to see plans succeed.

Far too often it became a gimmick to manipulate groups, and that always failed. People are too smart for this!

Stephen Covey observed, "It simply makes no difference how good the rhetoric is, or even how good the intentions are. If there is little or no trust, there is no foundation for permanent success. Only basic goodness gives life to techniques."[1]

4. Mission motivates; maintenance does not.

That's why one of your primary tasks is casting the vision, then keeping it alive.

Vision must be tied to tasks—that provides action.

Action must be tied to vision—that provides purpose and meaning.

Vision alone isn't enough. Action alone isn't enough.

Make sure everyone who works with you—volunteers and staff—knows your mission and how their work makes it happen.

5. Integrity and trust are the leader's most powerful assets; they have to be carefully and patiently earned.

If this is true, then the foundation for all team building is three-pronged: truth, trust, and clear expectations.

6. You must care for and tend your teams.

As go your teams, so goes your ministry. Watch carefully, so you know how a team is developing. You may see . . .

A *Parasitic* Team (competitive) where 1 + 1 = less than two.
A *Symbiotic* Team (cooperative) where 1 + 1 = 2.
A *Synergistic* Team (collaborative) where 1 + 1 = 3.

Grow healthy teams that move toward synergy. It's so simple—but so often overlooked because of expediency.

7. Avoid the trap of becoming either a specialist or a generalist.

A specialist is someone who knows more and more about less and less, until they know practically everything about almost nothing. A generalist is someone who knows less and less about more and more until they know almost nothing about everything.

8. Be yourself—no one else is better qualified.

In other words, be true to your principles and not swayed by fad or fashion. There is no substitute for being congruent in what you say and what you do—it builds trust in others and gives you peace of mind. For example, be sure to use volunteers yourself. It's what gives you credibility and makes you an effective advocate for volunteerism.

9. The key to wise leadership is effective delegation, and the key to delegation (and motivation) is getting the right people in the right jobs.

May I share a tip with you that has served me well for many years? Do not only accept—but actually seek out someone who knows more than you do where you need help. Then let them do the job—and be glad they succeed!

How do you get the right people in the right jobs? Know them by talking to them (interviewing) and observing them in action. Watch when their eyes light up. McClelland's Theory of Motivation of achievers, affiliators, and power people has been incredibly helpful to me here.

10. Motivating others is critical to your success.

I believe what John Gardner said about motivation: "Leaders do not create motivation . . . they unlock or channel existing motives."[2]

Let your own enthusiasm, excitement, and dedication to your mission shine through your work—it's contagious! My late husband, Harvey, used to say to me, "You love what you do so much—you don't even know it's work." How blessed I've been.

12. To become advocates and innovators, develop these three C's in your life: curiosity, creativity, and courage.

With those qualities in your life, be alert to identify problems and challenges that "have your name on them" (because of your past experience and skill), and take ownership of them.

Don't worry about knowing how to solve the problems; figuring it out is the fun part. And you don't need to know how it will all turn out. Just step up to the plate and take on issues when it's time to engage; let go when it's time to let go.

13. I can't help others if I don't stay well myself. So take care of me!

In this world it's often a great challenge to survive. But plants survive. Dogs and cats survive. I want to live embracing life with empathy and a zeal borne out of passion. That's living . . . and that's my goal.

I've heard it said that each of us is a house with four rooms—physical, mental, emotional, and spiritual. Most of us tend to live in one room most of the time. But unless we go into every room every day, even if only to keep it aired out, we're not complete people. What a vivid metaphor for health and wholeness! If you're serious about staying well, you will find time to:

Do the necessary housecleaning to rid your rooms of clutter and toxic waste. This means "letting go" of lots of stuff! (You can't stumble on things that are behind you.)

Know your own needs. If you can't name your own needs, then you don't deserve to have them met.

Be sure to not only visit each of your rooms every day, but slowly and lovingly furnish those rooms with things that nourish you, replenish you, and

give you joy. No one can do that for you. We need to be the caretakers of our own lives.

14. It's important to keep the soul in our work.

Wayne Muller tells the story of a South American tribe that would go on long marches, day after day. All of a sudden they would stop walking, sit down, rest, and then make camp for a couple of days. They explained that they needed the time to rest so that their souls could catch up with them.[3] A concept I love.

My hope for you is that you'll rise to the challenges in volunteer ministry with clear vision, a list of your own powerful principles, new and creative "how to's," and all the energy, enthusiasm, dedication, joy . . . and yes, *soul*, you have! That you have the wisdom to determine what to keep, what to change, what to drop—and what to create.

To do this you'll need the courage of pioneers, the ingenuity of entrepreneurs, the enthusiasm and fearlessness of five-year-olds, the dedication and compassion of volunteers, and the wisdom of Solomon.

One final thing: You'll need the firm faith that nothing worthwhile is ever impossible with God's help.

1: Stephen Covey, *7 Habits of Highly Effective People* (New York: Simon and Schuster, 1989), p. 21.

2. John Gardner, *On Leadership* (New York: The Free Press, A Division of Macmillan, Inc., 1990).

3. Wayne Muller, *Sabbath: Restoring the Sacred Rhythm of Rest* (New York: Bantam Book, 1999), p. 70.